Henry Wager Halleck, Antoine Henri Jomini

Life of Napoleon

Vol. 3

Henry Wager Halleck, Antoine Henri Jomini

Life of Napoleon
Vol. 3

ISBN/EAN: 9783337350222

Printed in Europe, USA, Canada, Australia, Japan

Cover: Foto ©ninafisch / pixelio.de

More available books at **www.hansebooks.com**

LIFE

OF

NAPOLEON.

By BARON JOMINI,
GENERAL-IN-CHIEF AND AID-DE-CAMP TO THE EMPEROR OF RUSSIA.

> "Je fus ambitieux; tout homme l'est, sans doute;
> Mais jamais roi, pontife, ou chef, ou citoyen,
> Ne conçut un projet aussi grand que le mien."
> VOLTAIRE. *Mahomet.*

TRANSLATED FROM THE FRENCH.

WITH NOTES,

By H. W. HALLECK, LL.D.,
MAJOR-GENERAL UNITED STATES ARMY;
AUTHOR OF "ELEMENTS OF MILITARY ART AND SCIENCE;" "INTERNATIONAL LAW,
AND THE LAWS OF WAR," &C., &C.

IN FOUR VOLUMES.—WITH AN ATLAS.

VOL. III.

NEW YORK:
D. VAN NOSTRAND, 192 BROADWAY.
LONDON: TRÜBNER & CO.
1864.

Entered, according to Act of Congress, in the year 1864, by
D. VAN NOSTRAND,
In the Clerk's Office of the District Court of the United States for the Southern District of New York.

Electrotyped by SMITH & McDOUGAL, 82 & 84 Beekman-street
Printed by C. A. ALVORD, 15 Vandewater-street.

CONTENTS.

VOL. III.

CHAPTER XIV.

CAMPAIGN OF 1809 IN AUSTRIA.

FROM THE DECLARATION OF WAR BY AUSTRIA TO THE TREATY OF VIENNA.

PAGE

Austrian Policy—Character of the Times—Military Preparations of Austria—She excites Insurrection in Germany—Secret Societies—The State of Westphalia—Situation of Prussia, and of the other European Powers —Insurrectionary States of the Tyrol—Austria takes the Initiative in the War—Her Plan of Operations—Position and Number of her Forces —The French Army—Relative Numbers of the opposing Forces—Berthier sent to rally the French Army—Advance of the Austrians—Faults of Berthier—Napoleon arrives at Ingolstadt—Difficulty of forming a Junction with Davoust—Advance of the Austrian Right toward Ratisbon—New Movements of Davoust—Battle of Thann—Junction with Davoust effected—Dispositions against the Austrian Centre—Affair of Abensberg—Movement of Davoust—Hiller defeated at Landshut—Davoust attacks the Austrian Centre—Advance of Napoleon—Battle of Eckmuhl—Retreat of the Archduke—Remarks—Napoleon marches on Vienna—Operations in Italy—Continuation of Napoleon's March—Tardy Projects of Prince Charles to save his Capital—Napoleon's second Entrance into Vienna—Dispositions for the Passage of the Danube—Motives of this Undertaking—Difficulties of its Execution—Preparations for effecting the Passage—Kolowrath's Attack on Lintz—Massena crosses to the left Bank of the Danube—The Archduke attacks the French—Battle of Essling—Council of War, and new Projects of Napoleon—Death of Lannes—Remarks on the new Position of the French—Reply to Rogniat's Criticisms on the Battle of Essling—General Remarks on the Tactics of Battles—Military Operations in Italy—Battle of the Piave—Eu-

gene pursues the Austrians—Retreat of the Archduke John on Gratz—
Junction of the Armies of Napoleon and Eugene—Insurrection of Westphalia and Prussia—Affairs of the Tyrol—Operations in Poland—Situation of Affairs in Germany—Affairs of Rome—The Pope transferred to
Savona—Measures of Napoleon for repairing the Check received at Essling—Eugene marches against the Archduke John—Battle of Raab—
Results of this Battle, and Siege of Raab—The Archduke John disobeys
the Orders of the Generalissimo—Bombardment of Presburg—Marmont's March—Operations of Guilay—Combat of Gratz—General Situation of Military Affairs—New Passage of the Danube—Operations on
the Morning of the fifth (July)—Position of the opposing Forces—Preliminary Attack of the French—Battle of Wagram—Defeat of the Austrians—Remarks on the Battle—Retreat of the Archduke, and Pursuit
of the French—Battle of Znaim—Armistice—Its Conditions—Motives of
Austria in ratifying it—Situation of Affairs in the North of Europe—
Operations in Tyrol—Negotiations with Austria and renewed Hostilities
—Maritime Expedition of the English against Rochefort, Naples and
Antwerp—Change of the British Ministry—Stabs' attempt to assassinate
Napoleon—Austria finally decides to make Peace—Treaty of Vienna—
Positive Results of the Peace—Sensation it produces in Russia—The
French destroy the Fortifications of Vienna—Expedition for the Subju-
gation of the Tyrol—Remarks on the Campaign.................... 13

CHAPTER XV.

CAMPAIGN OF 1809 IN SPAIN.

FROM THE ASSAULT OF OPORTO TO THE SIEGE OF GERONA.

State of Affairs in the Peninsula—First Operations of Soult—Combats of
Chaves and Braga—Assault of Oporto—Soult takes the left Bank of the
Minho—Victories of Medellin and Ciudad-Real—Difficult Position of
Soult—Combat of Amarante—New Descent of Wellington into Portugal
—He attacks Soult at Oporto—Soult's Retreat—Ney's Operations in the
Asturias—Misunderstanding between Soult and Ney, and the consequent
Evacuation of Galicia—Wellington's Advance on Madrid—Joseph col-
lects his Forces for an Attack—His Dispositious for Battle—Wellington's
System of Battles—Battle of Talavera—Operations of Soult, Ney, and
Mortier—Retreat of the Allies—Battle of Almonacid—Ney defeats Wilson
—Remarks on these Operations—Soult succeeds Jourdan as Joseph's
Chief of Staff—Combats of Tamames and Alba do Tormes—Arrizaga
beaten at Ocana—Inaction of Wellington—Intrenched Camp of Torres
Vedras—Romana quarrels with the Junta of Seville—Blake's Efforts to
deliver Aragon—Operations of Suchet—Combat of Santa Maria—Combat
of Belchite—St Cyr's Operations in Catalonia—Siege of Gerona—General
Remarks on the Operations of this Campaign—Operations of the Russians against Sweden—War between Russia and Turkey............. 142

CHAPTER XVI.

CAMPAIGN OF 1810 IN SPAIN.

FROM THE SIEGE OF GERONA TO THE LINES OF TORRES VEDRAS.

PAGE

Napoleon's Marriage with an Austrian Princess—He again offers Peace to England—Preparations for a new Campaign in Spain—Napoleon's Plan of Operations—Soult's Plan—Division of the Army—Invasion of Andalusia—Joseph's fatal Delay—Capture of Seville—Sebastiani takes Grenada and Malaga—Remarks on Joseph's Operations—His Return to Madrid—Internal Dissensions in Spain—The English Faction triumphs—Military Organization of the Provinces of the North—Soult neglects to take Badajos—Inaction of Wellington—Soult invests Cadiz—His Occupation of Andalusia—Operations in the North—Chances of Napoleon's Success—Massena's Expedition against Portugal—Sieges of Ciudad-Rodrigo and Almeida—Position of Wellington—Third Invasion of Portugal—Battle of Busaco—Massena turns the Position—Devastating System of the English General—Lines of Torres-Vedras—Massena's Position—Sufferings of his Army—Junction with Drouet—Remarks—Suchet's Success in Catalonia—Combat of Margalef—Sieges of Lerida and Mequinenza—Operations of Augereau—Siege of Tortosa—General Remarks on the War—Bernadotte elected Prince-Royal of Sweden—Reunion of Holland — Consequent Negotiations with England — Annexation of the Mouths of the Ems, the Elbe, and the Weser—Napoleon's Tour in Holland—Senatus-consultum on the Reunion of Rome—Council of Paris—Religious Fanaticism—Continuation of the War between Russia and Turkey.. 199

CHAPTER XVII.

CAMPAIGN OF 1811 IN SPAIN.

FROM SOULT'S CAPTURE OF BADAJOZ TO ITS RECAPTURE BY WELLINGTON.

General Review of the Foreign Relations of France—Faulty Relations with Prussia—Proposed Alliance—New Difficulties with Russia—Prospects of closing the War in Spain—Dissensions between Joseph and my Generals—New Cortes to be assembled at Madrid—Critical Situation of Massena—Soult marches on Badajoz and Olivenza—Siege of Badajoz—Remarks on the Operations of Soult—Attempt to raise the Siege of

Cadiz—Affair of Chiclana—Retreat of the Allies—Soult marches to the Support of Victor—Massena evacuates Portugal—Battle of Fuente di Honore—Massena retires to Salamauca—Remarks on Massena's Retreat—Beresford threatens Badajoz—He captures Olivenza and lays Siege to Badajoz—Soult marches to its Succor—Battle of Albuera—Napoleon directs the Junction of Soult and Marmont—Wellington renews the Siege of Badajoz—He is again forced to retire into Portugal—Operations of the Spaniards in Andalusia—They are defeated by Soult—Wellington and Marmont near Ciudad-Rodrigo—Hill surprises Girard—Suchet on the Ebro—Figueras surprised by the Catalans—Suchet prepares to attack Tarragona—Memorable Siege of that City—Further Operations of Suchet—He prepares to attack Valencia—Siege of Saguntum—Battle of Saguntum—Investment of Valencia—Siege of that Place—Reduction of Peniscola and Gandia—Remarks on Soult's Operations in the South—Winter Campaign of Wellington in Estremadura—He captures Ciudad-Rodrigo and Badajos—Remarks on these Operations—Insurrection in Spanish America—General State of Affairs in Spain—Continuation of the War between Russia and Turkey.............. 257

CHAPTER XVIII.

CAMPAIGN OF 1812 IN RUSSIA.

PART I.—ADVANCE TO MOSCOW.

Causes of the War with Russia—Opinions of Napoleon's Counselors—Military Chances of Success—Negotiations with Russia—Fruits of the Continental System—Occupation of Swedish Pomerania—Alliance with Prussia—Pacific Proposals to the Emperor Alexander—Offensive and Defensive Alliance with Austria—Result of the Negotiations with Russia—Proposals of Peace to England—Ultimatum of Russia—Napoleon repairs to Dresden—Return of Narbonne—Pradt's Mission to Warsaw—Ligneul's Mission to Sweden—Preparations for opening the Campaign—Diversion of the Turks—Dispositions of the Russian Army—Its Organization—French and Allied Army—Plans of Napoleon—Passage of the Niemen—The Russians retreat on Drissa—Napoleon's Delay at Wilna—Mission of Balaschof—Reply of Napoleon—Poland—War between England and the United States—Operations against Bagration—Napoleon advances on Polotsk—Camp of Drissa—Alexander retires to St. Petersburg—Operations of Barclay—Combats of Ostrowno—Operations of Bagration—Affair of Mohilew—Halt at Witepsk—Operations of Napoleon's Wings—Tormassof defeats the Saxons—Operations of Oudinot—Turkey, Sweden and England—Council of War—Barclay takes the Offensive—Napoleon's March on Smolensko—Battles of Smolensko—Retreat of Barclay—Results of the Campaign—Ney passes the

Dnieper—Hazardous March of Barclay—Pursuit of Ney and Murat—
Battle of Valoutina—Retreat of the Russians—Position of Napoleon—
Battle of Gorodeczna—Affairs of Polotsk—Napoleon resolves to advance
—Character of the Country—New Generalissimo of the Russian Armies
—Preparations for Battle—Position of the Enemy—Plan of Attack—
Battle of Borodino or the Moscowa—Remarks on this Battle—Napoleon
enters Moscow—The Russians burn the City—New Projects of Napoleon—The Russians march on Taroutina—Embarrassing Position of the
French.. 314

LIST OF MAPS

TO ILLUSTRATE

JOMINI'S LIFE OF NAPOLEON

VOL. III.

23. MAP OF THE VALLEY OF THE DANUBE, FROM RATISBON TO PRESBURG, to illustrate the Campaigns of 1808 and 1809.
24. BATTLE OF ABENSBERG, 20th April, 1809.
25. BATTLE OF ECKMUHL, 22d April, 1809.
26. BATTLE OF ESSLING, 21st and 22d May, 1809. (Sheet 1.)
27. BATTLE OF ESSLING, 21st and 22d May, 1809. (Sheet 2.)
28. BATTLE OF WAGRAM, 5th and 6th July, 1809. (Sheet 1, 5th July.)
29. BATTLE OF WAGRAM, 5th and 6th July, 1809. (Sheet 2, 6th July.)
30. MAP OF PART OF PORTUGAL, to illustrate the Defense of Lisbon, by the lines of Torres Vedras, October and November, 1810.
31. MAP OF PART OF RUSSIA, to illustrate the Campaigns of 1812.
32. BATTLES OF SMOLENSKO AND VALTELINA, 17th, 18th and 19th August, 1812.
33. BATTLE OF BORODINO, 7th September, 1812.

CHAPTER XIV.

WAR OF 1809 IN GERMANY, OR THE CAMPAIGN OF WAGRAM.

Austrian Policy—Character of the Times—Military Preparations of Austria—She excites Insurrection in Germany—Secret Societies—The State of Westphalia—Situation of Prussia, and of the other European Powers—Insurrectionary State of the Tyrol—Austria takes the Initiative in the War—Her Plan of Operations—Position and Number of her Forces—The French Army—Relative Numbers of the opposing Fo. ces—Berthier sent to rally the French Army—Advance of the Austrians—Faults of Berthier—Napoleon arrives at Ingolstadt—Difficulty of forming a Junction with Davoust—Advance of the Austrian Right toward Ratisbon—New Movements of Davoust—Battle of Thaun—Junction with Davoust effected—Dispositions against the Austrian Centre—Affair of Abensberg—Movement of Davoust—Hiller defeated at Landshut—Davoust attacks the Austrian Centre—Advance of Napoleon—Battle of Eckmuhl—Retreat of the Archduke—Remarks—Napoleon marches on Vienna—Operations in Italy—Continuation of Napoleon's March—Tardy Projects of Prince Charles to save his Capital—Napoleon's second Entrance into Vienna—Dispositions for the Passage of the Danube—Motives of this Undertaking—Difficulties of its Execution—Preparations for effecting the Passage—Kolowrath's attack on Lintz—Massena crosses the left Bank of the Danube—The Archduke attacks the French—Battle of Essling—Council of War, and new Projects of Napoleon—Death of Lannes—Remarks on the new Position of the French—Reply to Rogniat's Criticisms on the Battle of Essling—General Remarks on the Tactics of Battles—Military Operations in Italy—Battle of the Piave—Eugene pursues the Austrians—Retreat of the Archduke John on Gratz—Junction of the Armies of Napoleon and Eugene—Insurrection of Westphalia and Prussia—Affairs of the Tyrol—Operations in Poland—Situation of Affairs in Germany—Affairs of Rome—The Pope transferred to Savona—Measures of Napoleon for repairing the Check received at Essling—Eugene marches against the Archduke John—Battle of Raab—Results of this Battle, and Siege of Raab—The Archduke John disobeys the Orders of the Generalissimo—Bombardment of Presbourg—Marmont's March—Operations of Giulay—Combat of Gratz—General Situation of Military Affairs—New Passage of the Danube—Operations on the morning of the fifth (July)—Position of the opposing Forces—Preliminary Attack of the French—Battle of Wagram—Defeat of the Austrians—Remarks on the Battle—Retreat of the Archduke, and Pursuit of the French—Battle of Znaim—Armistice—Its Conditions—Motives of Austria in ratifying it—

Situation of Affairs in the North of Europe—Operations in Tyrol—Negotiations with Austria and renewed Hostilities—Maritime Expedition of the English against Rochefort, Naples and Antwerp—Change of the British Ministry—Stabs' attempt to assassinate Napoleon—Austria finally decides to make Peace—Treaty of Vienna—Positive Results of the Peace—Sensation it produces in Russia—The French destroy the Fortifications of Vienna—Expedition for the Subjugation of the Tyrol—Remarks on the Campaign.

Austrian Policy.—I had hoped that the conference of Erfurth and our success in Spain, would induce Austria to give up her idea of engaging alone in a contest against France; but in this I was mistaken. The court of Vienna pursues a tenacious policy, yielding only when necessary to gather strength to renew its old purposes. Some have absurdly attributed this perseverance to the oligarchic form of its government; in reality, nothing is less oligarchic than the cabinet of Vienna; the prime ministers, who are changed with the external policy of the government, are very frequently plebeians by birth, or nobles from parts of the empire other than the hereditary states. Some of the emperors have left the government to be carried on by their councillors; but such was not the case with Maria Theresa, or with Joseph II. The government of Austria, instead of being an oligarchy is a mixed monarchy; in Austria and Bohemia it is absolute, but limited in Hungary, and almost republican in the Tyrol.

The decisions of a government are, undoubtedly, very much influenced by the large landed proprietors and the principal nobility of the state; but a government which, in this nineteenth century, acts only for the interest of a few families, will soon be overthrown. In a republic of demagogues, where the rulers are changed every year, there can be no permanent state policy; but all other forms of government are susceptible of pursuing a permanent course, for there are always precedents in the diplomatic archives of the state, which serve as guides to the chief of that department, both in peace and war. There are always permanent as well as temporary views of state policy. It is always an object for a state to have more real strength than its neighbors, as this is the best means of preventing an attack. The strength of a state may be either positive or federative; it may be strong in its own positive power, or by its alliances. Where a single state becomes so great, in its own positive strength, as to endanger the safety of others, its neighbors resort to these federative means, either for self-protection, or for aggression against the single positive power. At one time France was near overthrowing the federative power of the European sovereigns; at another, the latter triumphed over all my efforts. *My age would never understand the necessity of uniting with me to establish an equilibrium against England. The slavery of the Continent results from the want of such an equilibrium.* Political preponderance is gained either by conquest or by family alliance. The results are not absolutely the same, but the real difference is not important. From Henry IV. to Louis XV., the Bourbons, who are not an oligarchy, have pursued a permanent course of policy; the means have necessarily varied with the change of events.

The policy of Austria differs, therefore, in no way from that of other states. If the monarchy of Francis II. has been able to resist violent shocks, it is because it has a warlike people, and a good system of recruiting its forces; because its geographical position is singularly favorable for defense, and lastly, because, in great danger, it is rescued from shipwreck by Russia or England.

The position of Austria towards us was a false one; this was made so, first, by the revolution, which produced the first coalition; second, by the invasion of Switzerland, which produced the second coalition; and third, by the annexations of Italy to France, which caused the third coalition.

After the second coalition, Austria was constantly in fear of our preponderance; she seized every occasion to oppose this preponderance; in 1809 she did well in seeking to profit by this opposition. There certainly was nothing of an oligarchic character in this opposition. Nor is it necessary in this place to attempt to reconcile the abstractions of writers who have exhibited talents, but very little knowledge of national affairs. We will now return to our narrative.

Character of the Times.—The cabinet of Vienna thought that however successful we might be in Spain, it would require two hundred thousand men to occupy a country whose entire subjugation I had projected. The Austrian government, therefore, resolved to profit by this occasion to regain the sceptre of Italy and Germany; her armaments were doubled. England had, this time, no difficulty in concocting a new coalition; the imperial cabinet even anticipated the wishes of the court of London; and it must be confessed, that war, at this crisis, seemed in accordance with the wishes and interest of the nation. The Austrian army burned to repair the defeat of Ulm, and the people to regain their former rank among nations. Moreover, Austria received a subsidy of at least one hundred millions from the cabinet of London.

They were not ignorant at Vienna that Prussia was exasperated; that Westphalia was complaining of grievances; that Hanover and the Hanseatic towns, deprived of their commerce, detested a Continental system which was not likely to be for their immediate benefit; that Tyrol, displeased with the Bavarian rule, was ready to rise. They thought that the north of Germany would declare against us the moment the Austrian troops, falling in considerable numbers on Bavaria, should compel the French army to concentrate its forces. The Austrian envoy at Koenigsberg announced that Prussia desired war, and would very soon increase her forces to one hundred thousand men; the honor and interest of Prussia were too much involved to doubt the sincerity of her promises. Dalmatia, Italy, the Tyrol, the Valteline, Piedmont, Naples, and even Sicily, became the theatre of Austrian intrigues. Never did a storm seem more threatening.

My armies at this time were scattered from Naples to Madrid, from Hamburg to the gates of Lisbon; I, myself, was in Spain. Under these circumstances it was probable that the Austrians would, in the beginning, be successful, and that these early victories would insure others; they might rouse Germany, tempt Russia, revive the sinking courage of the Spaniards, and restore to the English ministry a popularity lost by the defeat of Moore, thus stimulating, through British resources, the Peninsula to further resistance.

Military Preparation of Austria.—Austria made every effort to raise a formidable military force. Her active army was to be increased to three hundred and fifty thousand men; one hundred and fifty battalions of militia (*landwehr*) were prepared for reënforcing it in case of need, and suitable resources were intended to keep up the regular army to its complement. They imitated our organization by dividing their forces into *corps-d'armée*. Six corps of about twenty-five thousand each, besides the reserve, were assembled in Bohemia to inundate Bavaria. Fifty thousand regulars, and twenty-five thousand militia, forming the eighth and ninth corps, were destined for the army of Italy, under the Archduke John. Finally, an army of forty thousand men, under the Archduke Ferdinand, was to invade the Duchy of Warsaw. This division of forces has been deemed objectionable; it is said that Poland and Italy were to be conquered in Germany, for any success on these two points would be useless, should I become victorious on the Danube. But it cannot be concealed that Austria had to apprehend an insurrection in Galicia, in case Poniatowski appeared there with forces superior to theirs; and this motive alone, without any other political considerations, might have justified a considerable secondary detachment in that direction.

This Power incites Insurrection in Germany.—The cabinet of Vienna, not trusting alone to this great development of its forces, thought to add the revolutionary measures which had already been so effective in Spain. Forgetting the just complaints which it had made against the system of propagandism of the French Directory, it scattered through all Germany, an appeal to the people to rise against their existing governments, that is, against us; a measure useful, perhaps, for the success of the Austrian projects, but contrary to its own rules of political morality—rules, on which, only a few years before, this same power had based its complaints against the French Republic. Bavaria, Saxony, Westphalia, and the Tyrol, were inundated with these appeals which were posted up in every place where the Austrian column passed. The Archduke John did the same thing in Italy; thus seeking to make the war national and universal. They sought to again incite the people to war, instead of subjecting the points of difficulty to the results of military and political combinations; they sought to transform Europe into one vast field of battle, where they could assail us on all sides, because we had, as conquerors, required temporary sacrifices in order to counteract the preponderating force of English influence. A government has a right to arm all its own citizens for national defense; but I leave it to professors of public law, to decide whether such appeals can properly be made to the people of another government, and whether *insurrection* can be made the basis of a political system. It appeared simple and natural for the king of Prussia to appeal to the Prussians, and the king of Saxony to the Saxons;

but, I repeat, the frontier of the state is the line of demarcation of such right. If, in 1805, I had wished to incite the Hungarians, I had only to give the word; but I have never sought to produce insurrection, not even in Poland.

Secret Societies in Germany.—Independent of these measures of Austria, a vast conspiracy was extending itself through all Germany. Secret and mystical societies, under the title of *fåderés-de-la-vertu* were first established in every part of Prussia and afterwards throughout all Germany, in order to rally all my enemies on one common centre of action. Many different passions combined to increase these societies, in which were collected, through the common sentiment of hatred to us, men of the most antagonistic principles. The equestrian nobility of Germany, deprived of their privileges; the learned metaphysicians of the university, who discoursed about the principles of liberty and equality which fill the glowing pages of Demosthenes and Cicero; the soldier, humiliated by the reverses of the national arms; the bourgeois, vexed by the expense of the military cantonments and the stagnation of trade and manufactures—all were impatient of our occupation. In a word, the German aristocrats, demagogues, idealogists, soldiers, patriots, all united in desiring, not the return of the old Roman Empire, but the emancipation of Germany, its absolute independence, the reëstablishment of its maritime relations. It would be unjust to attribute crime to sentiments so natural. But it may be said that these brave men understood neither my position nor my intentions; they precipitated themselves into an opposition of which they did not appreciate all the consequences. They were made the blind instruments of my fall, from which they derived no advantage whatever.

Notwithstanding their immense ramifications, these societies were a long time enveloped in the most profound mystery; a fortuitous circumstance revealed to me at the same time their existence and their danger. The two chiefs of this political association were then in Austria; one at Vienna, and the other (the duke of Brunswick-Oels), was raising a corps in Bohemia.

State of Westphalia.—Westphalia was to be the focus of the explosion. Here England had preserved most of her adherents, and here my own partisans were the least numerous. Hanover suffered from the loss of her maritime communications; moreover, this country had formerly enjoyed a kind of paternal administration; her princes, devoted to the throne of opulent Albion, were relieved from the necessity of taxing their own people in order to sustain the luxury of their palaces, and to support a military force so disproportionate to the resources of the country; moreover, much English money was distributed in Hanover by way of subsidies and pensions. Under our administration, on the contrary, it was subject to the heavy imposts incident to conquest.

Hesse was still more unfortunate. Since the accession of the house of Hanover to the throne of England had placed this power in more intimate relations with the petty princes who surrounded this electorate, the Hessians had always furnished numerous contingents under English pay; in the wars of Spanish succession, in that of the Seven Years, in the American revolution, in the coalition of 1793, they were seen fighting under the banners of Great Britain. By this order of things the Prince gained guineas; the officers and soldiers pensions; and the country, which had no foreign relations or honor at stake, thus acquired a more abundant circulation of money. This country, little given to *industrial* pursuits, was poor; its administration was neglected, but not oppressive.

Since I had transformed this country into the kingdom of Westphalia, it had contributed to the support of a numerous army, a more sumptuous court, and a more complicated administration; what was still worse, the sum of twenty millions of dotations, annually assigned to my generals, was imposed on these unfortunate provinces—a wound the more incurable, as most of this money was expended in France. It was evident that if this system continued twenty-five years, Westphalia would be taxed to the amount of five hundred millions of francs, a sum equal to the intrinsic value of the soil. On the other hand, in the same length of time, the English subsidies would amount to between fifty and sixty millions. If to this there be added the enormous expenses occasioned by the passage through the country of three large armies, it must be confessed that there were motives for the spirit of insurrection which was manifesting itself. I was not ignorant of the enormous impositions laid on Westphalia. They were made in conformity to system, but not intended to be permanent. In case these provinces were restored to England on a maritime peace, they would be exhausted and incapable of injuring me, while France would be enriched at their expense. If retained by France, it was for my interest to offer them an incorporation into my empire as a recompense for the evils they had suffered during this state of transition.

Situation of Prussia.—Prussia, from very different motives, was in much the same situation as Westphalia; she was neither my ally, nor a province of my empire, but my sworn enemy. Three years of military occupation, of extraordinary contributions and humiliations, the loss of her most wealthy provinces, were more than sufficient to exasperate her.

Kings, called by Providence to the office of governing a people, should do all in their power to promote the national glory and prosperity; their duties towards other nations are of a more limited and different character. If I was right in doing all in my power to promote the glory and prosperity of France, it was no less the duty of Frederick-William to do the same in order to restore Prussia to the ranks from which she had fallen. Unskilful panegyrists have represented me as the most *debonnaire* of princes, my projects as the most philanthropic, and all those who opposed me as blind men and as traitors. This is absurd; history should not be written thus. It is natural that a Frenchman should regret the failure of projects calculated to secure the supremacy of the French empire; but he ought not to take it ill that the Prussian exerted all his energies for the restoration of his humiliated country; such conduct would indicate the want of impartiality, justice, and good faith. Interest and honor are the general motives which influence the conduct of men; interest and honor called to arms the Prussians, Westphalians, and the inhabitants of the Hanseatic cities.

Of the other European Powers.—But with the other inhabitants of Germany and Italy under my influence the question was very different; they had not the same grievances of which to complain. If Rome, Florence, Venice, and Genoa could complain of the temporary decline of their prosperity, they had at least the expectation of a future, rich in glory and hope, which was not the case with the north of Germany.

Posterity, which will judge better than my cotemporaries, the importance of my contest with England, and the future results of her overwhelming maritime power, will find that I employed the only honorable means for reducing it, and that I was obliged to sacrifice some evident but partial interests to secure the accomplishment of my immense undertaking. These interests, in being armed against me, obeyed only the law of nature. For this they can hardly be blamed. But those are most blameable for whose advantage and interest I sought a continental supremacy and the humiliation of England, and who, nevertheless, have been my calumniators. If Hannibal, ruining for half a century the prosperity of Sicily and Spain, in order more effectually to oppose Rome, had at last given the empire of the world to Carthage, would they have dared to accuse him of being a despot and a barbarian, trampling under foot the interests of the people? Had he succeeded, the Carthaginians would have paid the highest honor to his name.

It was on Prussia and Westphalia, that Austria and the great German conspiracy based their hopes. The duke of Brunswick-Oels, having been deprived of his hereditary rank and power, and being, therefore, more interested than others in the success of the project, was to give the signal by debouching from Bohemia, with a legion of Prussian deserters which he had there organized. In Westphalia, Colonel Dornberg, of Jerome's guard, deeming himself, like Marlborough, authorized to leave the service of a master imposed by conquest and rejected by public opinion of the Westphalians, was to secure the person of this prince as a hostage, and establish a regency. Major Schill, who had distinguished himself as a partisan about Colberg, was to leave Berlin with his regiment of hussars and all insurrectionary Prussians, surprise Wittenberg and Magdebourg, then act in concert with the duke of Brunswick in Saxony. That the Prussian army established in Silesia would follow this movement, was so much the more probable, as the Prussian court of Königsberg, would not have time to prevent it; it is even said that Scharnhorst, the minister of war, was privy to the plan and secretly favored it. The court of Vienna left no means untried to obtain the formal accession of Prussia; not only were negotiations carried on by the Baron of Wessenberg at Königsberg, but General Steigentesch was sent there as a commissioner to arrange a plan of operations on the probable hypothesis of concluding an alliance.

Insurrectionary State of the Tyrol.—But if Austria counted much on a powerful support in the north of Germany, she had no less to hope from the insurrectionary spirit of the inhabitants of the Tyrol. New Guebres, these mountaineers joined to their natural spirit of independence a decided aversion to the Bavarians, and a kind of attachment to the house of Austria, whose government, paternal toward them, had avoided interfering with their customs and immunities. Greatly resembling the smaller Swiss cantons in many respects, they were not inferior to the sons of William Tell, in bravery and skill of arms; and, like them were organized in companies of *franc-tireurs* or *carabiniers*, or in battalions of militia. The hatred of the Tyrolese toward the Bavarians extended back for ages, and resulted as much from old quarrels of the fuedal *seigneurs*, as from more recent local disputes, or clashing commercial interests. The king did all in his power to change this state of things; but the expenses incurred by Bavaria in 1800 and 1805, and for the support of her military establishment, rendered it necessary for the ministers of Maximilian Joseph, to treat the Tyrol the same as the older Bavarian provinces, and to curtail some of the immunities which had been enjoyed under the Austrian rule. Feelings were exasperated at these innovations; Austria perfectly understood the state of things here, and still retained in this country a multitude of agents who were making every preparation for a general insurrection, when the proper time should arrive. The marquis of Chasteler, who had commanded in that country in 1800, was at the head of the corps which bordered on the frontiers of the Tyrol, and, in concert with Councillor Hormeyer, held all the threads of the conspiracy.

Chasteler was a French subject, of Belgian origin; which circumstance irritated me against him. He, on his side, exhibited a bitter animosity against me, which caused me to make severe reprisals; if he had treated me more justly, I should have taken pride in being generous to him, for I always regarded him as a man of talent. Being chief of staff to Kray and Suwarrow in 1799, he contributed no less to the success of the allies in Italy, than he had, at Mayence in 1795, to the success of Clairfayt against Pichegru. The proper position of a man of his stamp was not at the head of an insurrection of peasants.

The priests and *aubergistes* (inn-keepers), exercise great influence in these countries; the former address themselves to the religious feelings of the people, while the latter direct their temporal interests. A rich *aubergiste* in the Swiss cantons and in the Tyrol has numerous dependents; he influences those of his own class by the superiority of his education; he usually traffics in all the products of the country, and thus becomes the principal medium of trade; this constitutes him a man of authority. One of these tavern-keepers, named Hofer, was distinguished by his great stature, his wild and uncultivated character, and the superiority which he derived from his physical advantages and his business capacity. Stimulated by the priests and Austrian agents, and placed afterward at the head of the popular risings, Hofer became a party leader, whom some have praised to the skies, and others decried to the lowest degree; he was a man of heart, but without decision of character; he was the mere scape-goat of the ignorant flock, an instrument in the hands of men more adroit than himself. He had personal bravery, but, in such a case, this is one of the least essential of the several qualifications of a party-leader. The Capuchin Haspinger, also had great influence with the people.

Austria takes the Initiative.—But Austria could hope nothing from these elements of discord, till she herself took the initiative. The signal, so long expected, was finally given about the first of April. Certain of being immediately sustained by Austria, the Tyrolese determined to set the example. In an instant, a thousand beacon fires, lighted on the tops of the highest mountains, gave the signal in every direction for the general rising. Each valley formed its insurgent forces into a battalion, veteran soldiers forming its skeleton, or at least acting as its principal officers. Masses of peasants, thus armed and organized, overspread the country in every direction, surprised and massacred or took prisoners the three or four thousand Bavarians, who were posted in different parts of the country; a column of two thousand French, coming from the depôts, under the orders of General Bisson, met the same fate. This insurrection gradually spread even into the Voralberg, and large parties extended themselves to the vicinity of Kempsen, threatening Wurtemberg.

Her Plan of Operations.—Simultaneously with this the Archduke Charles passed the Inn, on the tenth of April, directing his march on Munich and Ratisbon, where he was to assemble an army of one hundred and eighty thousand combatants. To this tardy commencement of operations they added another fault no less grave. The imperial army, at first assembled in Bohemia toward Pilsen, had only five or six days' march to make, in order to fall on Ratisbon, or upon Wurtzbourg, in the very centre of my scattered corps. An order from superior authority directed this army on the Inn, to debouch by the Iser and Munich in Bavaria; this line of march was triple the length of the other. But instead of making this *détour* for the purpose of gaining the decisive point, it was intended to move directly away from it. This blunder secured the safety of my army. The fault has by some been attributed to General Grune, and by others to General Meyer, but the Archduke Charles was made to suffer by it, and in the popular estimation, the responsibility was thrown on him, though in reality he disapproved the project.

Position and Numbers of the Austrian Forces.—Had it not been for this strange march, the army, of which the Archduke Charles was made generalissimo, might have begun operations in March. But in consequence of these new dispositions, it could not begin till April, and even then was divided into two masses, separated from each other by the Danube. The two corps remaining in Bohemia, were to debouch by the left bank on Ratisbon; the centre and reserve, forming three corps, advanced by Schaerding; the left, composed of the corps of the Archduke Louis and General Hiller, marched by Munich and Landshut. In addition to this force of one hundred and seventy thousand combatants, there were the extraordinary levies, which would soon be disposable; Amende's division which was to debouch in Saxony; Jellachich's division, flanking the left at Salsbourg; General Chasteler's forces, acting in the Tyrol; the army of the Archduke John on the Tarvis; a detachment at Grachatz, to cover Croatia against Marmont; and a large body of *landwehrs* (militia) organizing in the Carinthia, as a reënforcement.

The French Army.—Not yet knowing what direction the enemy would give to his forces, I was not without anxiety respecting the course which he might pursue. My position was not dangerous, provided I could concentrate my forces before the Austrians should undertake operations sufficiently serious to prevent this junction. I had still at my disposal a force sufficiently respectable to cause the cabinet of Vienna to fear they would not gain so easy a victory as they had represented to the emperor. Their only chance was to fight us before I could collect my scattered troops. Davoust's army of occupation had just been dissolved. This marshal, after leaving good garrisons in the fortifications of the north, marched from Erfurth with about forty-five thousand men, and directed himself by Bamberg on Ratisbon. Oudinot, who commanded the reserve at Frankfort, marched toward Augsbourg with his corps of grenadiers. Massena, who, at the head of thirty thousand men, was marching by Lyons toward Spain, returned in all haste from Strasbourg on Ulm. Bernadotte, whose corps had been dissolved after the flight of the troops of Romana, received orders to take command of the Saxons. A part of his forces were to guard the Hanseatic cities, while the division of Dupas reënforced Oudinot.

The reserve of cavalry, which had dispersed on numerous points, marched in different directions toward the Danube; thirty thousand Bavarians, under Marshal Lefebvre, cantoned on the Iser, with their light troops on the Inn. The troops of Wurtemberg, assembled at Heidenheim. All the other contingents of the Confederation, were organizing to reënforce the different *corps-d'armée* and to cover our communications. I had also eighteen thousand Poles, and about the same number of Saxons, Westphalians, and Dutch. But these allies had sufficient to occupy them at home, to hold Prussia in check, and guard Hanover and the north of Germany, against the great naval expedition threatened by the English. To impose on the cabinets of London and Berlin, I announced the formation of an army of the north under Bernadotte, numbering eighty thousand men; whereas, I had in reality, directed him to march with two Saxon divisions along the frontiers of Bohemia on the Danube, leaving all the other contingents to guard their own countries. My army in Italy, which numbered less than forty-five thousand men, under the Viceroy, I hastened to reënforce with all my disposable troops in the Peninsula.

Organization and relative Numbers of the Opposing Forces.
—The Austrian forces numbered over three hundred thou-

Cн. XIV.] THE WAR OF 1809 IN GERMANY. 29

sand men, and one hundred thousand *landwehrs* (militia), and seven hundred pieces of cannon, as follows :

1st. Under the Archduke Ferdinand, in Poland..................	40,000
2d. General Amende's division in Saxony.......................	13,000
3d and 4th. The two corps in Bohemia (50,000), and the centre and left under the Archduke Charles (125,000)...........................	175,000
5th. The Austrian divisions of the Tyrol (10,000), and Chasteler's Tyrolese (20,000).........	30,000
6th. The army of Italy, under the Archduke John..................	55,000
Total................	313,000

7th. Of the Landwehr or Militia, 25,000 were organized at the beginning of the campaign, but they were afterward increased to 100,000, making a grand total of over 400,000 men.

The French and allied forces, numbered only a little more than 300,000 in all, with 560 pieces of cannon, as follows:

1st. Poles (18,000), and the Russian army which did not arrive till afterward (35,000).................................	53,000
2d. Saxons, under Bernadotte, Dutch, under Gratien (20,000), and the Westphalians, under Jerome (15,000). These remained in the north	35,000
3d. Main army, 2d corps, under Lannes and Oudinot (25,000), 3d corps, under Davoust (45,000), 4th corps, under Massena (30,000), 7th Bavarians (30,000), and 8th Wurtembergers (12,000), in all *	142,000
4th. Badois, Hessians, of Nassau, troops of the Confederation, etc....	12,000
5th. Army of the Viceroy and Macdonald (45,000), division of the interior, (15,000)..	60,000
6th. Corps of Dalmatia, under Marmont.......................	15,000
Total.............	317,000

---

* At the beginning of this campaign, the king of Bavaria wished to place the Bavarian troops under the command of his own son, a young man of character, but entirely without military experience. Napoleon would not give his consent. "Your army," he wrote to the king, "must fight in earnest in this campaign. It concerns the conservation and extension of the aggrandizements which Bavaria has received. Your son may be able to command, when he shall have made six or seven campaigns with us. Meanwhile, let him come to my head-quarters. He will be received there with all the consideration due to him, and he will *learn our trade*." The king of Wurtemberg, also wished to appoint a general to command the Wurtemberg contingent, and objected to the appointment of Vandamme. Napoleon also refused this request, and placed Vandamme in the command.

It was by this firm resistance of all outside pressure in the selection of officers for particular commands, that Napoleon succeeded in almost always having the right man in the right place. No amount of political influence or personal

Berthier is sent to rally the French Army.—I dispatched Berthier to collect my forces in Germany, at Ratisbon, if hostilities had not commenced, and between Donawerth and Augsbourg, if the Austrians had taken the initiative. He had been at his head-quarters but a few days, when, thanks to the wise precaution which I had taken, to establish a telegraph in Germany, I learned at Paris, on the twelfth of April, in less than forty hours, the passage of the Inn, which had taken place on the tenth. Every thing being prepared beforehand, I instantly set out for the theatre of war, and after an interview, on the fifteenth, with the king of Wurtemberg at Louisbourg, and with the king of Bavaria at Dillingen, I reached my head-quarters at Donawerth, on the seventeenth. Those who love comparisons will search in vain, in ancient and modern history, for an example of celerity and admirable precision equal to that which characterized the beginning of this campaign.

Advance of the Austrians.—I was much disquieted about the state in which I found affairs. Berthier had brought my army to the very brink of ruin. But, fortunately, the Austrians were six days in marching fifty miles, from Brannau to Landshut on the Iser. This gave us time to look about us.

On the sixteenth, they attacked the bridge of Landshut, which was defended by the Bavarian division under Deroi, who fought in retreat, to save himself from being cut off by the enemy's columns that passed the Iser above and below

---

solicitation could induce him to risk the lives of his men and the success of his campaigns, by placing inferior men in command. In this case, he resisted the solicitations of two crowned heads, his allies, on whose good will much depended. But he knew that much more depended upon his military success, and he was not weak enough to endanger that success in order to gratify the wishes even of kings. Had he yielded, the results of this war might have been very different. Happy the country, whose ruler has the firmness to do what he believes to be right, regardless of the political and personal influences by which he may be surrounded.

that city. Although Wrede was at Straubing, and the Prince Royal at Munich, the Bavarians succeeded in effecting a junction at Neustadt, which would have been impossible if the enemy had pushed them lively. The Archduke could have been at Ratisbon on the fifteenth, and united all his corps at that place to successfully destroy our divided forces. It was not till the seventeenth that one-half of my forces had advanced as far as the Little Laber, by the three roads which lead from Landshut to Ratisbon, Keilheim, and Neustadt. Hiller marched on Mosbourg ; Jellachich had entered Munich ; the two corps of Bohemia had penetrated into the upper Palatinate, and were leisurely moving on Ratisbon. These last turned toward Amberg on the division of Friant of Davoust's corps, which flanked its march in coming from the Thuringia. It will thus be seen that if the enemy had arrived there two or three days sooner, he would have rendered the concentration of my army very difficult.

Faults of Berthier.—My arrival at the theatre of war was exceedingly fortunate. Berthier was committing fault after fault. My instructions to him were precise : he was directed, as I have already said, to rally the army at Ratisbon, if hostilities were not already begun, but, if the enemy had taken the initiative, to concentrate it at Augsbourg and at Donawerth. Even had I directed him to concentrate at Ratisbon, unconditionally, he ought to have seen that what had been admissible when he left Paris, was no longer possible under the existing circumstances. But in his whole twenty campaigns he had not been able to learn the first idea of strategy ; he not only acted contrary to my instructions, but he did what I had most to fear. Davoust, appreciating the danger of a march on Ratisbon, moved by Hemau on Ingolstadt; this was wise ; Berthier, on the contrary, directed him to return by the left bank to Ratisbon. He even ventured to order Lefebvre to retake Landshut. This was exposing both to destruction, by an eccentric movement which nothing could justify.

Napoleon arrives at Ingolstadt.—I arrived at Ingolstadt on the eighteenth. My first care was to send two officers to Davoust to direct him to leave Ratisbon in all haste, in order to meet us on the Abens. Savary was one of those charged with this dangerous mission, penetrating, with a hundred Bavarian horse, between the Austrians and the Danube.

Difficulty of forming a Junction with Davoust.—It was indispensable to maintain our position in front of Neustadt, for if the enemy should be able to reach that point, Davoust would be inevitably cut off. I united in the position of the Abens all the forces I had at my disposal. These were the Bavarians, Wurtembergers, and a division of cuirassiers, forming, in all, about forty thousand men. The enemy was marching on the Abens with one hundred thousand : if he had pushed forward with resolution, it would have been all over with us ; we should have been driven into the Danube before the return of Davoust, and before the arrival of Oudinot and Massena, to whom I had sent orders to join me immediately. These last two would, in that case, have considered themselves exceedingly fortunate in falling back behind the Lech, leaving Davoust to his unfortunate fate. My only hope of safety was in the dilatory movements of the Austrians, or in their misconception of my position and my projects.

The Archduke moves to the right, toward Ratisbon.—The Austrian army had already, on the eighteenth, begun their movements on the Abens. The Archduke suddenly suspended this march. He had just learned that Davoust was moving toward Ratisbon ; this was an additional reason why the Austrians should have established themselves at Abensberg without delay, on his line of retreat ; but Prince Charles drew a different conclusion. He left General Hiller, with two corps of about fifty thousand men, to observe us on the Abens, while he himself, with the three other corps of about sixty-five thousand combatants, established himself on Rohr with the intention of moving against Davoust the next day. Hiller's forces consisted of his own corps, which was at this time at Mainbourg, the corps of the Archduke Louis, near Siegenbourg, and a reserve of some seven or eight thousand men.

New Movements of Davoust.—At break of day, on the nineteenth, Marshal Davoust left Ratisbon for Abensberg. The great road runs along the Danube in a *coupe-gorge* formed by the woody heights between Abbach and Post-Saal. The artillery and the cuirassiers were to slip along into this mouse-trap, while the four divisions of infantry flanked this march by moving along the heights where two small roads had been discovered; the one on Peising, and the other on Saalhaupt and Tengen. The divisions of Gudin and Morand took the first of these roads to the right; St. Hilaire and Friant followed the one at the left. Montbrun, with the light cavalry, flanked the march, and formed the rear guard by occupying Abbach. One regiment only was left at Ratisbon to retard the march of fifty thousand Austrians coming from Bohemia by the left of the Danube. In order to second the arrival of Davoust, I directed Lefebvre to debouch from Abensberg on Arnhofen with the left of the Bavarians.

The Archduke Charles at the same time fell back from Rohr on Ratisbon. This prince acted on the supposition that Davoust had not yet left that city, but had remained there impassible. It was well to move toward Ratisbon, but this movement should have been made by Post-Saal, that is, along the only road by which Davoust could effect a junction with me. The Austrians advanced in three columns; the right, consisting of twenty-three thousand men, on Eglofsheim; the centre, of about twenty-five thousand men, on Dintsling; and the left, of fifteen thousand men, on Tengen. A corps of about six thousand men, under the orders of General Thierry, was left in the direction of Abensberg to maintain the communication between General Hiller's corps and the *corps-de-bataille*.

These dispositions were evidently faulty. The Gordian knot was to be cut at Abensberg or at Post-Saal, by throwing there the corps of Hohenzollern, of Rosenberg, and of the Archduke Louis. Abensberg being the nearest to the Austrian corps at Rohr, and most distant from the headquarters of Davoust's column, it was probable they would arrive there in time. Post-Saal, on the other hand, closed the door of the *Caudine forks*, through which the French corps would be obliged to defile. These two points might easily have been occupied by throwing on Abensberg the Archduke Louis, reënforced by the two corps of reserve, and by pushing forward the corps of Hohenzollern and Rosenberg on Post-Saal, *en potence* upon the heights of Hausen. A hundred thousand combatants massed in this way on important points would have decided the campaign and the fate of Davoust.

Battle of Thann.—Notwithstanding the faults committed by our adversaries, and the precision of my manœuvres, which formed in this respect so strong a contrast with theirs, we barely escaped from our great peril. No sooner had St. Hilaire and Friant arrived on the heights between Saalhaupt and Tengen, to protect the march of Davoust in the bottom of the defile, than they were assailed by Hohenzollern. But as the latter was isolated, the forces at this point were equal; and while the right of the archduke was moving in such a direction as to meet none of our forces, the French repelled the attack of his lieutenant. The combat was severe; twenty thousand of my veterans were not disposed to yield to an equal number of Austrians. The prince of Hohenzollern was unable to maintain his position; near six o'clock, P.M., he was driven behind Hausen, with a loss of four thousand men.

Davoust effects his Junction with Napoleon.—Taking advantage of this success, the right of Davoust had tranquilly continued its march on Abensberg, where it formed a junction with the Bavarians On reaching Arnhofen, it encountered the little Austrian column of Thierry, charged with covering the interval between the Archduke Charles and his brother. For the better accomplishment of this object, it had advanced toward Arnhofen with the intention of checking the march of the Bavarians, whom Marshal Lefebvre was moving from Abensberg on the road to Ratisbon, in order to connect himself with Davoust. The detachment of the enemy, attacked in front by the division of Morand, and in rear by the Bavarians, was driven with loss on Offenstetten, fortunate in not being all taken prisoners.

Napoleon's Dispositions against the Austrian Centre.—The events of the nineteenth had entirely changed the face of affairs. The junction of Davoust with my army not only relieved all my anxiety, but placed me in a position threatening to the enemy. By his untimely extension of his right, the archduke had not preserved a connection sufficiently intimate with the corps which he had left on the Abens. We were established opposite the interval which separated the two parts of the Austrian army, so that we could throw ourselves, in mass, between these parts, prevent their junction, and beat them in detail. The only way for the enemy to avoid this misfortune was to execute, in all haste, a concentric retreat on Landshut. To prevent him from undertaking this movement, I resolved to take the offensive instantly, directing the attack upon the enemy's left. I directed the first blows here, because I expected that the operations against this wing would be powerfully assisted by the grenadiers of Oudinot, or the corps of Massena. The former had arrived on the nineteenth at Pfeffenhausen, and the latter was to reach there the next day. They were also to menace the left of Hiller and his line of retreat on Landshut.

Affair of Abensberg. — I immediately made my dispositions. Davoust was left with twenty-five thousand men near Thann and Hausen, to keep in check the enemy's right. With the remaining sixty thousand men I advanced against the Archduke Louis. As it was important for me to prevent the Archduke Charles from sustaining his brother, Lannes was to throw himself with the other two divisions of Davoust and the cuirassiers of Nansouty on Rohr, in order to get possession of the road from Keilheim to Landshut, and to intercept all communication between the two wings.

After having harangued the Bavarians and Wurtembergers, I left the division of Wrede at the bridge of Siegenbourg to hold in check the Archduke Louis, and to attack him afterwards when the proper moment should arrive. I threw myself on the right of the prince with the Wurtembergers and the two Bavarian divisions of Lefebvre; the first by Offenstetten on Rhor, and the second by Kirchdorf. Lannes was to assist and cover this movement; on arriving at Rohr, he was to reconnoitre Adelshausen and the valley of the Laber, in order to drive back any forces which the Archduke Charles might send in this direction, and thus effectually sever the enemy's centre.

Fortunately for us, the Austrian left was much scattered. Hiller, with twenty-two thousand men, was on the march from Mainbourg to Pfeffenhausen; the Archduke Louis, with ten thousand, was in position at Siegenbourg; the Prince of Reuss, with fifteen thousand, at Kirchdorf, and General Thierry, with five thousand, at Offenstetten. The latter, too feeble to resist the superior forces which were advancing on all sides, fell back on Rohr, and came in contact with the columns of Lannes. He was overthrown and driven back as far as Rottenbourg, where he was reënforced with fourteen thousand men, whom Hiller had marched in haste from Pfeffenhausen. But these reënforcements did not arrive in time to secure the passage of the Laber; Lannes impetuously crossed the bridge, pell-mell with the baggage and fugitives of the enemy.

In the mean time, the prince of Reuss and Bianchi, attacked in front by Lefebvre, and in flank by the Wurtembergers, were obliged to fall back on Pfeffenhausen. The Archduke Louis, pressed in front by Wrede, and threatened to be turned on his right by the other columns, also put himself in retreat on the same point. My allies, who under the French colors, had learned to rival us in vigor and courage, pursued the enemy lively, as far as that place. The Austrians this day lost more than seven thousand men.

Davoust observes the Archduke.—Davoust found no difficulty in executing the order which I had given him, to hold the Archduke Charles in check. This prince, who with any other adversary would have been the first general of his age, permitted himself to be overawed by the ascendency which I had gained over him. Instead of operating against Davoust, he put himself on the defensive. For this purpose he refused his left, ordering Count Hohenzollern, to recross to the right of the Gross-Laber at Neider-Leuerndorf. The column of the right, on the contrary, received orders to extend itself still further from Eglofsheim on Ratisbon. The regiment of infantry, which Davoust had left in this city, was now invested on the right of the Danube by this column, and on the left, by one of the corps from Bohemia, which had marched on Stadt-am-Hof. This regiment surrendered. For twenty-four hours it had occupied fifty thousand Austrians; it had accomplished its task. The other corps from Bohemia was engaged, we know not why, in the direction from Amberg to Ingolstadt.

This battle affords a striking example of different combinations for the employment of masses. One hundred thousand Austrians of the first, second, third, and fourth corps, found themselves occupied by twenty thousand men under Davoust; while twenty-five thousand Austrians of the fifth corps were crushed by sixty-five thousand French and their allies. Notwithstanding the derangement of his first calculations, the Archduke Charles thought he ought still to maintain himself between the Danube and the Gross-Laber, in order to give Hiller the means of rallying on his left. But how could he suspect me of being so foolish as to allow his lieutenant to tranquilly make a lateral movement which it was so easy for us to intercept?

Defeat of Hiller at Landshut.—On the twenty-first, Hiller, wishing to avoid the fate of Prince Louis, fell back on Landshut. I followed him with the division of Wrede, the Wurtembergers, and the corps of Lannes; that of Oudinot had orders to descend on the same point after passing the Iser at Mosbourg; the same operation was prescribed to the fourth corps (Massena). I directed Lefebvre to descend the Laber with the two remaining Bavarian divisions, General Demont's division, and a brigade of cuirassiers, in order to form a connection with Davoust, and to lighten his duties. The roads were obstructed with the immense baggage-trains of the Austrians, which fell into our hands. Hiller attempted to defend the passage of the Iser at Landshut; but this was near costing him dearly. Warmly attacked by the division of Morand, in front of the city and in the faubourgs, he might have been cut off by the division of Claparede, which was approaching from Mosbourg on the right bank of the Iser; but this general imprudently halted his troops to await the arrival of Massena, who had remained at Mosbourg in order to hasten the march of his corps. It was important for me to disable Hiller, so that he could not renew the attack while I turned my efforts against the Archduke Charles. I ordered an immediate attack; General Mouton, whose courage knew no obstacles, forced the bridge by one of the most vigorous attacks in that war. The routed enemy fled in the direction of Oeting, where he passed the Inn the next day, leaving twenty-five cannon, and near ten thousand men *hors-de-combat*.

Davoust attacks the Austrian Centre.—I had reïnforced Davoust because I feared that the archduke might attack him while I was occupied with Hiller. But the archduke resolved to wait until he received some news of Hiller, and to draw in the corps of Kolowrath from the left of the Danube. Bellegarde's corps, being more distant, could not arrive in time to take part in the battle; it was, therefore, merely drawn in from Stadt-am-Hof.

Davoust correctly judged that the best means of occupying the enemy in his perplexity, and of deceiving him respecting the strength of the opposing corps, was to attack him at once. After effecting a junction at Leuernsdorf with Lefebvre, he advanced along the left bank of the Gross-Laber. Near Unter-Leuchling he encountered the centre of the enemy's forces, which the archduke had moved to that place from Duitzling. The engagement was warm and continued from eleven o'clock in the morning till night. Count Hohenzollern, who had moved along the left bank of the Gross-Laber, passed the river at Eckmuhl and reïnforced the prince of Rosenberg, who was fighting at Unter-Leuchling. The enemy maintained his position; but Davoust accomplished the object he had proposed. Profiting with address by the broken character of the ground, he extended his troops in such a way as to make them appear double their real numbers, and so well imposed on the archduke that he gave up all idea of acting on the offensive. The loss on both sides in this contest was about three thousand men *hors-de-combat*.

Napoleon advances to the Centre.—Having completed the defeat of Hiller, I sent in pursuit Marshal Bessières, with the divisions of Wrede and Molitor, of the corps of Massena, and three regiments of cavalry. Oudinot was left in reserve at Landshut. I directed myself against the Archduke Charles with Nansouty's division of cuirassiers, the corps of Lannes, the Wurtembergers, and the mass of Massena's troops. The archduke, leaving the corps of Bellegarde at Stadt-am-Hof on the left of the Danube, had withdrawn Kolowrath's corps, which had passed the river on the night of the twenty-first. Being thus reënforced to seventy-five thousand combatants, it was to be supposed that this prince would not suffer himself to be any longer held in check by Davoust.

Battle of Eckmuhl.—I left Landshut on the morning of the twenty-second, directing myself on Eckmuhl. The enemy had the same day combined an offensive movement. But the manner of its execution merely favored my projects. Instead of falling on Davoust in the morning, with all his forces, he directed his principal efforts toward Abbach, where we had only some light troops, and suspended the attack until afternoon to await the corps of Kolowrath, which could not sooner reach Abbach. The corps of Rosenberg, which had fought the previous day, received direction to maintain its position in order to serve as a pivot for the contemplated movement of the Austrian army. It followed, therefore, that we were opposed only by this single corps, which was reënforced with a reserve of eight thousand men.

Toward two o'clock in the afternoon I debouched from Eckmuhl against the centre of Rosenberg with the Wurtembergers. Lannes, who now commanded the divisions of St. Hilaire and Gudin, attacked and turned the enemy's left

with the latter division. The right was at the same time
assailed by Davoust, with the divisions of Morand and
Friant, and one of Lefebvre's Bavarian divisions. For three
hours the Austrians sustained this unequal contest. Rosenberg, though surrounded by our eight divisions, still hoped
to be sustained, and fought with the most heroic courage.
There are few instances where Austrian troops have fought
so well.

The archduke, disconcerted by this attack on his left,
stopped the advance of his right, and sought only to cover
his retreat. This retreat was effected about six o'clock in
the afternoon, before Massena, who formed the rear of my
column, could advance far enough to take part in the fight.
I threw all my cavalry in pursuit of the flying forces. The
enemy's cavalry, which sought to protect the retreat on
Ratisbon by defending Eglofsheim, was overthrown in the
evening; our troops drove them back, fighting, as far as
Koffering; it drew on the infantry in the rout. The cuirassiers of Nansouty and Saint-Sulpice, charge and sabre the
broken battalions;—all fly in disorder toward Ratisbon.
The Archduke Charles rallies with the reserve of John of
Lichtenstein, and succeeds in arresting the pursuit, which
had been favored by a bright moonlight.

A part of my troops came from Landshut, and were greatly
fatigued. I also feared the disorder of a night pursuit. If
I had pursued, as the Prussians did at Waterloo, the enemy's
army shut in by the Danube would have been greatly cut to
pieces; but our success was already sufficiently brilliant, and
I was unwilling to expose it unnecessarily. Fifteen stand
of colors, a great number of prisoners, and numerous cannon,
remained with us as trophies of the battle of Eckmuhl, in
which the enemy lost at least ten thousand men.

The Archduke returns into Bohemia.—The Austrian
army, in the vicinity of Ratisbon, still numbered more than

eighty thousand combatants, including the corps of Bellegarde. My forces were not as numerous; nevertheless, Prince Charles did not venture to risk a new battle, with the Danube in his rear; and instead of calling in the corps of Bellegarde, he determined to join it. Not daring to concentrate all his forces on the single bridge of Ratisbon, he constructed one of pontons below, and the passage was effected on the morning of the twenty-third, under the fire of our batteries. Several charges, which were made to cut off the retreating columns, were not attended with all the success desired. A rear guard had remained in Ratisbon to cover the retreat; I directed it to be attacked. A wall and ditch could not arrest the impetuosity of our troops; finding an opening, they penetrated the city with the bayonet, and captured a part of the six battalions which still remained. The enemy burnt the wooden bridges in his rear, and barricaded the great stone bridge of Ratisbon.

The emperor of Austria, who had repaired, with his court, to Schaerding in the hope of participating in the triumph of his armies, and also to be ready for negotiations with the German princes, was informed, on the night of the twenty-third, of the defeat of his troops, and immediately departed for his capital.

Remarks.—Never had my success been more brilliant or decisive, and never was it better deserved. The combat of Thann against the Archduke's centre; the battle of Abensberg, which isolated his left; the affair of Landshut, which completed his defeat; the battle of Eckmuhl, a second time against the centre; and finally, the combat of Ratisbon, completing the overthrow of his army, form a series of events without a parallel in history. On the twelfth of April, I was in Paris; ten days after, I had gained two great battles and decided the campaign in the heart of Germany.

I might have said, with still greater reason than Cæsar, *veni, vidi, vici.*

Napoleon marches to Vienna.—As soon as the Archduke had put the Danube between his army and mine, he fell back on Cham, where he arrived on the twenty-fifth, after having been joined by the second corps of Bohemia. I did not care to follow him on the left bank of the river; leaving Davoust at Ratisbon with orders to observe him, and to follow me as soon as he ascertained positively that the enemy's army had departed for Bohemia, I directed the main body of my forces to Vienna by the right bank, with the resolution to crush the corps of Hiller, if he should have the temerity to dispute my entrance into the capital.

Some have blamed me for not having, on the contrary, pursued the then scattered army of the Archduke Charles. I was deterred from doing this by several reasons; first, the woody chain of the Bohmervald mountains offered to the enemy defensive positions of great advantage; secondly, the Archduke Charles had written me a letter showing a desire on his part to treat. By pursuing Hiller, I might complete his ruin, and dictate a more advantageous peace in Vienna. On the other hand, by attacking the enemy in the mountains of Bohemia, Hiller, with the Archduke John and Chasteler, coming from Italy and Tyrol, might collect eighty thousand fresh troops on the Danube, at the instant when the Archduke Charles, reënforced by the *landwehrs* of Bohemia, would charge me in front.

But let us return to the operations of Hiller whom we left in full retreat on the Inn. This general, seeing that he was not pursued across this river, concluded that I had turned my efforts against the principal army, and determined to effect a diversion. On the twenty-seventh of April, he repassed the Inn with the thirty-five thousand men which he had left, and attacked Wrede's division at Neumark. The

Bavarian general was in some degree surprised, and found himself engaged in an unequal combat ; he would have been lost had it not been for the devotion of Molitor, who disengaged him and covered his retreat on Wilsbibourg. This affair, which cost us fifteen hundred men, led to no result. In the night of the twenty-fourth and twenty-fifth, Hiller received information of our victories over the principal army, and made all haste to recross the Inn.

Operations in Italy.—At the moment when the Archduke Charles appeared in the plains of Ratisbon, his brother, the Archduke John, descended the mountains of Carniola on the Frioul, at the head of fifty thousand men. Eugene covered Italy with a combined army, whose force did not exceed forty-five thousand combatants. He had to assist him, Generals Grenier and Macdonald. Still young and inexperienced, Eugene soon exhibited all the *aplomb* of an old warrior. Brave, calm, and capable of understanding military operations, he always knew how to profit by the counsels of able men—a talent often more successful than the inspirations of superior genius.

He, nevertheless, committed an error at the outset. He had just concentrated the mass of his forces in front of Sacila, but was still waiting for a division of infantry and the reserve of cavalry from Verona. The irruption of the enemy was sudden ; the brigade of Sahuc, established as an advanced guard at Pordenona, was surprised, and the 35th regiment, was, in part, captured. Eugene, fearing the moral effect which a retreat might produce on the vacillating spirits of the Italians, deemed it best to assume the offensive, thinking that he had to contend only with the eighth corps of the enemy. He marched on the sixteenth of April, and attacked the enemy between Sacila and Pordenona, making his effort on the right, which was not the true strategic direction. The enemy, supported by the reserve, warmly disputed the village of Porcia. But soon the ninth Austrian corps arrives on the ground and the Archduke John, throwing it on our left, turns that wing and forces Eugene to retreat, notwithstanding the resistance opposed by Broussier against forces double his own. The defile of the Livenza, whose waters were swollen, caused disorder in our centre and right; all crowded to the passage of the Brugnera; fortunately, the enemy did not push his success, and Eugene, reënforced on the Piave, by the arrival of troops which he was expecting from Verona, succeeded in rallying his broken battalions, and brought back the army in good order to the Adige, after having thrown two brigades into Venice and Palmanova. Chasteler who had swept the Tyrol, and was now to act in concert with the Archduke John on the Adige, was about to triumph at Innspruck, and lost the opportunity to anticipate us at Rivoli.

The archduke, satisfied with his present success, and obliged to detach three divisions for observing Venice, Palmanova, and the operations of Marmont in Dalmatia, occupied the well-known position of Caldiero, with the intention of waiting to hear the results of movements to be made in the south of Italy, or the success of his brother in Germany; but, in respect to this last hope he was soon undeceived, and the news of the events of Ratisbon reached Italy very opportunely, to restore confidence to my partisans and to the camp of Eugene, at the same time that it destroyed the hopes of my enemies.

Napoleon continues his March on Vienna.—The retreat of our army in Italy, instead of checking my march, was only an additional motive for my advance on Vienna.* On the

---

* On passing the mouldering towers of the castle of Diernstein, in which Richard, the Lion-hearted of England, was so long and cruelly imprisoned, Napoleon reined in his horse, and said to Berthier and Lannes:

" Richard, also, was a warrior in Syria and Palestine. He was more fortunate than we were at St. Jean d'Acre. But the Lion-hearted was not more

twenty-seventh, I moved my headquarters to Muhldorf. Lefebvre, with the Bavarians, was directed on the Tyrol, where the insurrection, more serious than we anticipated, was threatening to extend into Bavaria and cut off our communications. Massena, Lannes, and Bessières marched on Vienna; Davoust and Vandamme followed them in echelons; Bernadotte, with his Saxons, moved on Ratisbon by turning Bohemia. Hiller had abandoned the Inn without resistance; but he resolved to defend the passage of the Traun, in the formidable position of Ebersberg. A wooden bridge, a hundred toises in length, presented an obstacle still more formidable than that of Lodi, since it terminated in a fortified town, commanded by a castle, and crowned by heights very difficult of access. To effect a passage here against thirty thousand men and eighty pieces of cannon, was not very easy. Massena was not ignorant that I expected to turn this impregnable post by Lambach; but the impetuous valor of General Cohorn drew him on to a bloody fight. Three Austrian battalions, left imprudently in advance of the bridge, were overthrown, and driven at the point of the sword to the gates, which were closed. Cohorn forced the

valiant than you, my brave Lannes. He beat the great Saladin. Yet hardly had he returned to Europe than he fell into the hands of persons who were certainly of very different calibre. He was sold by a duke of Austria to an emperor of Germany, who, by that act only, has been rescued from oblivion.

"These were barbarous times, which they have the folly to represent to us as heroic, when the father sacrificed his children, the wife her husband, the subject his sovereign, the soldier his general, and all without shame or disguise! How much are times changed now! You have seen emperors and kings in my power, as well as the capitals of their states, and I exacted from them neither ransom nor sacrifice of honor. The world has seen how I treated the emperor of Austria, whom I might have imprisoned; and that successor of Leopold (the duke), and Henry (the emperor), who is already more than half in our power, will not be worse treated on this occasion than before, notwithstanding he has attacked us with so much perfidy."

When making these remarks, little did Napoleon imagine his own fate in St. Helena! If the English had good cause to complain of the captivity of King Richard in Diernstein, how much greater their own disgrace for their long and cruel confinement of Napoleon on a solitary rock in the ocean!

gates, and penetrated into the great street. Massena deemed it best to sustain him—first, by the remainder of Claparede's division, and afterward, by that of Legrand. The fight was fiercely waged from street to street, and from house to house.

Claparede had just gained possession of the castle, when Hiller threw on the city four new columns, which penetrated at the point of the bayonet. It was a horrible butchery : the houses, filled with the combatants and the wounded, were set on fire ; the encumbered state of the streets prevented any egress ; never did war present a more awful scene. At length the Austrians, wearied with the carnage, yielded Ebersberg, and our troops advanced against the heights, where a combat still more unequal was waged. The arrival of Durosnel's division of cavalry by the right bank, and the certainty that he would be turned and surrounded by Lannes, at length decided him to retire, in all haste, on Enns.

Lannes having debouched the same day from Lambach on Steyer, all this butchery was utterly useless. I expressed to Massena great dissatisfaction at his useless sacrifice of his men ; but I afterward excused him, for I learned that Hiller's obstinate defense of his position in front of the bridge across the Danube at Mauthausen, had induced Messena to believe that the Archduke Charles, coming from Budweis, had the intention of crossing to the right bank of the Danube at that point, so as to unite with Hiller and cover Vienna. The bold and obstinate attack of Massena rendered this movement impossible, and the success was the more honorable to our troops, as a part of them fought here for the first time. It cost Hiller six or seven thousand, and we lost four or five thousand brave men, a part of whom were destroyed in the flames.

Tardy Projects of Prince Charles to save Vienna.—The Archduke Charles, reaching Horasdiowitz, the first of May, thought himself pursued by my whole army ; while in reality, even Davoust, after having made a simple demonstration, fell back on Straubing so as to follow me in echelons in the valley of the Danube, and Bernadotte, who had relieved him in the direction of Ratisbon, also followed the same route. Supposing us caught in a *cul-de-sac* between Straubing and the mountains of Bohemia, the archduke thought that Hiller would be able to defend the Inn long enough to allow him to march by Budweis. The Aulic council flattered themselves with the same project, and directed the Archduke John not to renounce rashly the political advantages which his success promised in Italy, but if forced to retire, to fall back on the interior of Austria. The Archduke Charles, cruelly undeceived by the news of the passage of the Inn, the capture of Lintz and of the combat of Ebersberg, remained at Budweis from the fourth to the seventh of May. This delay will always appear an enigma in the military life of this prince, as also the still longer delay at Schaffausen and Zurich in 1799. Nothing can justify such delays but the necessity of giving repose to the troops, and of reëstablishing order, discipline and confidence, by a slow and deliberate march. But such considerations should have been made subordinate to the necessity of covering Vienna, either by preceding me to Krems, or anticipating my arrival in the capital. From Budweis to Vienna is six days' march; and the archduke might have arrived there on the tenth, and Hiller on the ninth. The former at last put himself in motion toward Zwetel with the intention, undoubtedly, of reaching Krems; but hearing that we had already passed Molck, he felt that all hopes of covering Vienna were useless, and that he must now devise means for defending that capital. Hiller received orders to cross the Danube at Stein, destroy the bridge, and by forced marches, descend the left bank of the river so as to reach Vienna and occupy the Islands. If it had been merely to rescue the troops of Hiller, nearly surrounded by Lannes and Massena, the resolution would have been a very proper one; but if, for the salvation of the Austrian monarchy, it was necessary to save the capital, it would have been preferable, to direct Hiller to gain, by a forced march, the defile of Siegartskirch; to defend there for twenty-four hours the access to Vienna, then to encamp under the walls of that place, and await the archduke, who might have reached there about the eleventh of May.

At any rate, the first care of the archduke should have been, if he could not cover Vienna, at least to effect its rescue by debouching from that city, as I did from Dresden in 1813, and by making strong demonstrations on our communications. General Kolowrath, directed on Lintz with twenty-five thousand men, would take possession of the bridges and the city. The Archduke John, forming a junction with the corps of the Tyrol and Jellachich's division, which still remained at the sources of the Enns in the valley of Rotenmann, would then advance on Lintz at the head of fifty or sixty thousand men to join Kolowrath. They vainly flattered themselves that the presence of seventy thousand men on my direct communication, would change the face of affairs; but we shall soon see that this plan was not carried into execution.

Napoleon's second Entry into Vienna.—The disappearance of Hiller's corps, permitted us to advance with redoubled celerity, and, on the tenth of May, we reached the walls of the capital. This was just one month after the Austrians had invaded Bavaria, and twenty-seven days' after the news of that invasion had reached me at Paris.

In order to secure our position, it was important for us to seize upon Vienna; but this did not seem so easy a matter as in 1805. Instead of sending out to invite us into the city, the government directed the Archduke Maximilian to prepare means for defense. This prince was to have a corps of fifteen thousand men, composed of veterans and militia; the right division of Nordman was also to reënforce him; moreover, a part of the citizens took up arms, so that, if reports be true, the prince had at his disposal at least twenty thousand men.

In order to incite the troops and citizens, they were reminded of the resistance which Vienna had opposed to the Visir Kiuperli, and of the defense of Saragossa by the Spaniards; but we were not Turks, and the good people of Vienna are not Aragonese. The lines of defense surrounding the city were not in a condition to resist us; the Archduke Maximilian abandoned the rich faubourgs, in order to concentrate his forces in the old enciente, which was regularly bastioned, but imperfectly armed. The Aulic Council had made better preparations for besieging Mayence than for defending their own capital. Nevertheless, the archduke, with so considerable a body of men, was capable of greatly embarrassing my operations. I understood the value of time much better than my adversaries, and I was not disposed to lose a second. I tried the effect of some shells thrown into the city, and they replied by a heavy fire from the ramparts, without sparing the faubourgs. I took pity on these poor inhabitants, and renounced my plan of bombarding the city, and resorted to other and still more effectual means. I caused the communications of the archduke with the great bridge of the Danube, to be attacked on both flanks, directing Massena toward Simering, so that he could penetrate into the island of the Prater. A similar attack was directed from Dobling, on the island of Jagerhans, further up the river. If we were now to anticipate the enemy in our arrival at the great bridge of Tabor, which they had neglected to connect with the place by fortifications, the archduke would be made prisoner, with his fifteen thousand men. The fear of this

CH. XIV.]   THE WAR OF 1809 IN GERMANY.   51

induced the prince to evacuate the city and destroy the bridge of Tabor, leaving General Oreilly, with six hundred men, to perform the ungrateful task of signing the capitulation, which was done the next day, the thirteenth of May. At the moment when the Archduke Maximilian was evacuating Vienna, General Hiller arrived at his destination, and united with the retreating troops near Spitz. He caused the islands to be occupied, but it was too late to save the capital: the bridge of Tabor was destroyed.*

Dispositions for the Passage of the Danube. — I now directed all my attention to the means of passing the Danube. While separated from the enemy by so large a river, it would be difficult to understand his operations. Moreover, we had been fifteen days separated from the army of the archduke by the mountains of Bohemia, and had lost track of it.

* While at Vienna, an incident occurred characteristic of Napoleon and of his manner of enforcing discipline. One of the chief surgeons of his army was quartered in the house of an aged canoness. While under the influence of wine, the surgeon wrote her an insulting letter. She appealed to General Andreossy for protection, and the general took the letter to the emperor, who ordered the surgeon to appear on parade the next morning. Napoleon attended the parade, and, advancing in front of the ranks, called for the surgeon to step forward. Presenting the letter, he asked him if he had written it.

"Pardon, sire," said the surgeon, "I was intoxicated at the time, and did not know what I was doing."

"Miserable man," exclaimed Napoleon, "to outrage a canoness worthy of respect, and bowed down by the calamities of war. I do not admit your excuse. I degrade you from the Legion of Honor. You are unworthy to wear that venerated symbol. General Dersonne, see that this order is executed. Insult an aged woman! I respect an aged woman as if she were my mother."

Another characteristic incident is related of Napoleon while occupying the island of Lobau, after the battle of Essling. Passing a company of grenadiers, seated at their dinner, he remarked to them, "Well, my friends, I hope you find the wine good." "It will not make us drunk," replied one of their number, "there is our wine-cellar," pointing to the Danube. Napoleon was surprised at this answer, as he had ordered the distribution of a bottle of wine to each man. On investigation, it was found that forty thousand bottles, which he had sent to the army a few days before, had been purloined and sold by the commissaries. They were immediately brought to trial, and condemned to be shot.

We had every reason, however, to believe that if it had not already arrived, it would do so very soon. My army was not yet united; but we had no time to lose. Vandamme and the Wurtembergers had been left at Lintz to cover the great central debouche of Bohemia, and to secure the bridge, with the fortifications which had been laid out for its defense. Bernadotte, coming from Passau, with the Saxons, was to relieve him. Davoust was marching from San-Polten on Vienna. I had about this city the corps of Massena, and that of Lannes, the guard, and the cavalry of Bessières.

The Motives for this Undertaking.—I was uncertain of the position and plans of the archduke; but I deemed it best, at any rate, to go forth and meet him. Natural as was this resolution, it has nevertheless been censured by those who judge by the result, rather than by the motives which influenced my determination. They say, that, master of the capital and of one half of the Austrian monarchy, I might have waited in security the arrival of the army of Italy, without seeking to render my position more extended, more complicated, and, at the same time, more hazardous. Those who made these criticisms forgot the relative situation of the two armies after the memorable victories of Ratisbon. Counting on the ascendency which these victories were calculated to procure me over the enemy, it was desirable to have a debouche beyond the Danube, in order to continue offensive operations. If I should leave the archduke quiet possession of Bohemia, Moravia, and Hungary, he might be able to concentrate his troops, and reënforce them by the whole militia which they had begun to organize; the contest would then have been doubtful. If I should attack him in the condition of despondency, caused by the defeat of Ratisbon, I might expect to beat him, and end the war. In case I were reduced to the defensive, it would be of still greater advantage to me to possess both banks of the river, were it only to enable me operate on the left side in case the enemy collected large forces on the right. Without this advantage, I would possess only a hazardous line of operations, extending from Straubing to a narrow gorge parallel with Bohemia, where the enemy seemed to have established the theatre of his resistance. The archduke, based on Prague, had only to effect the concentration of the Austrian forces at Lintz to place me in a difficult situation. But, with a bridge across the Danube, I might accept battle on either side, being certain, in case of reverse, of finding the means of retreat to the opposite bank, for the archduke could not operate with forces sufficient to give battle on both sides of the river.

When I determined upon the passage, the enemy had not yet shown himself in the environs of Vienna, and could not then oppose the passage. But it was possible for him in a few days to occupy and fortify such positions as would render it very difficult. I made haste to profit by an occasion which might not again occur, and, notwithstanding the reverse which followed, I in a measure succeeded, for I crossed three-quarters of the river, and gained an advantageous place of arms, which enabled me afterward to cross the remaining arm of the Danube. My resolution and the motives of it, have not been appreciated by my censors, but that is not astonishing, for they attempt to measure me by themselves.

Difficulties of the Passage.—Of all the operations of war, there is none more hazardous and difficult, than the passage of a large river in the presence of an enemy. Every one has heard of the celebrated passage of the Rhine, at Tolhuis and at Kehl; but at Tolhuis, Louis XIV. was opposed by only seven or eight thousand Dutch, and at Kehl, Moreau encountered only a single brigade of the Circles. The two passages of the Danube which we effected at Lobau, will probably remain the most celebrated in the military history of an age prolific in great events. If we take into consideration the great care and precautions that are requisite, the immense amount of materials employed in such an operation, the concurrence of circumstances necessary to secure success, and the difficulties which may be occasioned by the slightest derangement on the part of the enemy, it is really surprising that an operation of this kind ever succeeds. Nevertheless, wonderful as it may seem, the most difficult military enterprises are commonly the most successful, from the simple fact, that greater care and precautions are employed in their execution.

From Schaerding to within two leagues of Vienna, the Danube flows through a narrow gorge between the mountains of Bohemia and Bavaria, but after passing the village of Nussdorf, its waters, as if in revenge for their former constraint, spread out over a wide surface forming a multitude of islands, that of Lobau being one of the largest. There are many points of passage in the vicinity of Vienna, but a practised eye will perceive, by a single glance at the map, that the point higher up the stream near the village of Nussdorf, is, of all others, the most advantageous for an army on the right bank, inasmuch as it here commands the left bank; the great Thalweg* being here only about one hundred and eighty toises in width, sweeps past a considerable island, capable of serving as a *tête-du-pont* for the first bridge, and a *point-d'appui* for the troops charged with opening or protecting the passage. An arm of about fifty toises in width, and a very gentle current, separates this island from the opposite shore; its passage would require no very extraordinary operation. The celebrated island of Lobau is situated about two leagues below Vienna; this island is about a league in length and three-quarters of a league in width; it is separated from the right bank, first, by another island of

* The term Thalweg is here used for the main channel.

about three thousand toises in circumference, and then by the main stream in which are five or six other small islands. This division of the waters of the Danube rendered them less deep and less rapid. The first arm, which separates Ebersdorf from the first island, is not less than two hundred and forty toises in width; the second, opposite Lobau, about one hundred and sixty; finally, a third arm separates this great island from the Marschfeld shore, and forms, as it were, a kind of ditch to the great central citadel; it is about seventy toises in width, but is divided in different places by islands. At Nussdorf, the main body of the Danube is only one hundred and eighty toises wide, and the small arm sixty; a passage at this place would, therefore, have the double advantage of being commanded by the high ground on the right bank, and requiring only one half the number of boats; moreover, it was directly opposite the Bisemberg, a mountain of difficult access, situated in a commanding position between the roads to Moravia and Bohemia. The possession of this mountain by us before the arrival of the archduke, would have been a matter of great interest, but after he had effected a junction with Hiller, the occupation of the Bisemberg not only became more difficult, but would actually facilitate the operations of the enemy against us. Under this point of view, the passage at the island of Lobau was the most advantageous; moreover, we would be able to float down to this point all the boats above Vienna, and in the small arm of the Prater. And lastly, the great extent of the island would afford shelter to the troops effecting the passage, in case the enemy appeared in superior force on the opposite side.

Preparations for its Execution.—No sooner had I reached Vienna than I directed my attention to the means of crossing the Danube. Lannes, who was stationed further up the river, was directed to make preparations for throwing a bridge across at Nussdorf, and St. Hilaire was directed to gain possession of the great island of Schwarze-Lake. Massena, who was encamped between Simering and Ebersdorf, was, on the contrary, directed to prepare to pass to the island of Lobau. These double preparations, at points some four leagues apart, divided the attention of the enemy, and enabled us to select the least difficult point for the construction of the bridge. St. Hilaire sent two battalions of voltigeurs in boats to make a lodgement on the island of Schwarze-Lake; but, receiving no timely support, these detachments were surrounded by General Nordmann, and, after a brave defense, forced to surrender. The zeal and skill of our pontoniers enabled them to overcome obstacles which any other troops would have regarded as insuperable. On the nineteenth of May they succeeded in throwing a bridge of fifty-four great boats across the two arms opposite Ebersdorf, under the protection of battalions of tirailleurs, who drove the enemy's troops from Lobau. This operation was now the more difficult, as the melting of the snow in the Germanic and Tyrolese Alps had so much swollen the waters of the Danube as to render the current frightfully rapid, at the very moment that we were attempting the passage. Notwithstanding all our care, we did not find a sufficient number of anchors to moor so many boats; but the pontoniers and artillery supplied the deficiency by large boxes of balls. Not having pontons enough for the bridge, we were obliged to resort, in part, to trestles. On the night of the twentieth the bridge was thrown from Lobau to the left bank, and the corps of Massena commenced the passage. That of Lannes, which came from Vienna, was immediately to follow; but it was directed not to leave the capital till the last moment, lest the enemy should take the alarm.

The waters of the Danube were rising rapidly; every moment, we were obliged to interrupt the passage of the troops, in order to adjust the bridges, which, being constructed of boats of different sizes, instead of regular pontons, were continually thrown out of place.

Kolowrath's Attack on Lintz. — While we were thus engaged on the bridge from Lobau, I learned that the Austrians had made a serious attack on the *tête-du-pont* of Lintz on the 17th of May. This attack was made by the entire corps of Kolowrath, twenty-five thousand strong. The Wurtembergers were nearly forced to yield to this vast superiority of numbers, when Bernadotte arrived with the Saxons and restored the equilibrium; the enemy was forced to renounce a work so well defended. This circumstance, instead of arresting our operations at Lobau, only induced me to redouble our ardor, for the archduke had evidently either divided his forces or had remained with the mass of his army at Lintz. Reassured by the arrival of Bernadotte, I directed Vandamme to approach as far as Mautern; Davoust, disposed in echelons between Molk and Vienna, was to assemble his forces, in all haste, under the walls of the capital.

Massena crosses to the left Bank of the Danube. — On the morning of the twenty-first, I pressed forward the passage with ardor, and disposed the troops of Massena in such a manner as to be prepared for any event. Opposite the island of Lobau is Marchfeld, an immense plain, cut only by the little stream which is formed near Wagram by the embanking of the Russback; the north side of the island is formed into a strong reëntering curve by the small arm of the river, but the east side is quite straight; on the bank of this branch of the Danube are the villages of Aspern and Essling, about half a league apart; being built of stone, and composed of a single street, these villages served as a kind of natural rampart. The cemetery of Aspern formed a real redoubt; at Essling, a large grain magazine played the same part ; to the south-east is the town of Enzersdorf, a post also susceptible of a good defense.

Our bridges had naturally been thrown to the north opposite the reëntering point between Aspern and Essling ; I placed the division of Molitor (of Massena's corps), in the first of these villages, and Boudet's division in the second. The other two divisions, as they arrived, were to form the reserve ; the cavalry of Bessieres was placed at the centre between these two bastions. The passage was interrupted almost every moment. The reports of the advanced guard greatly differed ; some said that only the advanced guard of the enemy was before us, while others thought his whole army was present. A large body of cavalry formed a mask which we could not penetrate. But this uncertainty did not continue long.

The Archduke attacks the French.—The archduke heard, between Horn and Meissau, of the fall of Vienna, and reached Bisemberg on the fifteenth. His army reposed there till the nineteenth. From the top of this mountain the enemy had observed all our movements, and by the nineteenth, had learned the construction of the bridge of Lobau. Previous to the fourteenth, the archduke had hoped to debouch from Vienna, as I did from Dresden in 1813 ; but he then saw that he had only to remain in observation where he was, and embrace the first opportunity to give battle when I should attempt to cross the Danube. Perhaps his waiting was in part induced by a desire to learn the issue of Kolowrath's attempt on Lintz. But he learned on the nineteenth, not only Kolowrath's defeat, but also that the Archduke John had not operated in that direction. On the twentieth, the Austrian generalissimo came at the head of Klénau's advanced guard, to examine the state of affairs opposite the island, and gave orders to his army to be ready to march the following day.

At nine o'clock on the morning of the twenty-first, the archduke, discovering from the top of the Bisemberg, the corps of Davoust on the march by the right bank of the Danube, thought that by falling on these troops which had already crossed the river, he would have to fight only one half of my forces. His army began their march about noon; the three corps of Hiller, Bellegarde, and Hohenzollern, were directed concentrically on Aspern, followed in reserve by the corps of grenadiers; Rosenberg's corps was to extend to the right and left of Enzersdorf, and then direct themselves on Essling. The reserve of cavalry was to march between these two principal masses. The prince of Reuss was to remain at the Bisemberg, to cover that point and threaten Davoust in the direction of Korneubourg. Eighty thousand men with three hundred pieces of cannon, were thus to fall upon the single corps of Massena, sustained only by the cavalry of Bessières. Nothing ever equaled the valor displayed by our troops in this critical situation. Molitor, posted alone in Aspern, receives the assault of the masses of Hiller and Bellegarde; Massena seeks to sustain that point, and the village is alternately in the hands of the opposing forces. The cemetery forms a kind of fort where the hero of Genoa and Zurich fights like a lion. Lannes, whose *corps-d'armée* is detained by the rupture of the bridge, takes command of Boudet's division, and defends Essling from the attacks of Rosenberg.

The enemy had crowded the greater part of his infantry around Aspern, where they had not room to move. The cavalry held the centre and protected the numerous batteries arranged to fire obliquely on the villages which cost so many brave men. This artillery fire even reached to our thin reserves. I ordered Bessieres to charge it; the light cavalry failed in the attempt; but our cuirassiers, led by D'Espagne, charged in turn, and forced the enemy to withdraw their pieces. At this moment the infantry of Hohenzollern, prolonged toward the centre, and our intrepid squadrons, led by Bessières, D'Espagne and Lassalle, dashed against it without the least hesitation; but all the Austrian battalions, formed by a recent order of the archduke, in columns of attack by battalions, presented small masses which nothing could break. The cavalry of Lichtenstein went to their assistance; ours, in its turn, fell back, and, after a triple charge, yielding to superior numbers and a murderous artillery, proudly resumed its place in the line. In this unequal contest the brave D'Espagne met a glorious death.

Dispirited by the repeated assaults on Aspern, the Archduke Charles hoped to meet with less resistance at Essling, where he had gone in person. Rosenberg, after a long circuit, had finally united his two columns, and made, in vain, two attacks on Lannes and Boudet. These assaults were repeated till evening, and the village burned, but Lannes, surrounded by flames and buried in projectiles, opposed them with intrepidity. Night here suspends the ardor of the combatants, but at Aspern their fury is redoubled; the archduke directs Hiller and Bellegarde to carry the place at all hazards. Massena, at the head of four regiments considerably weakened by the successive losses of the combat, opposes a barrier of iron against these two *corps-d'armée* of the enemy. In the midst of a storm of projectiles which burned a part of the village, he defends every house, alley and garden, with the most brilliant courage; the division of Molitor, having lost one-half of its number, is finally forced to give way, about nine o'clock in the evening. Massena flies to the division of Legrand, dashes at its head, into the village, and recaptures part of it; but the enemy remains master of the cemetery which has cost so much blood. Never was a day more glorious for the French troops than this; less than thirty thousand troops had bravely fought against eighty thousand under the concentric fire of an immense artillery. It was a miraculous defense.

The bridges, which had been many times carried away, and as often restored, at last were made sufficiently secure to enable the troops of Lannes and Oudinot to cross over during the night, and the guard and cuirassiers of Nansouty, at the break of day.

Battle of Essling.—On the morning of the twenty-second, our army being about fifty-five thousand strong, required a little more development. If Davoust had been present, I should have pivoted on the left, supporting that flank on the Danube, and making the principal attack by the right, but that operation required the presence of a third corps, and the necessary space for forming the troops and effecting a change of front without unmasking the bridges. The enemy intended to anticipate us. At two o'clock in the morning the attack was renewed on Aspern; and a little afterward it extended as far as Essling; this was directed by the archduke in person. Lannes was forced to abandon the place, except the granary, which formed a kind of redoubt; but being soon afterward reënforced by St. Hilaire, who had just arrived, he, in turn, routed the enemy. In Aspern, the combat was waged with the same obstinacy, and with the same results. Legrand's division, reënforced by that of Cara St.-Cyr, at first disputed the place with the Austrians, then captured General Weber and some hundreds of prisoners, and again established themselves in the cemetery.

It was time to think of extricating ourselves from this *coupe-gorge*. Davoust informed me that his corps had begun to pass, and, in fact, the division of Demont debouched from the bridges. I then determined to act offensively. The direction of the concave line of the enemy naturally indicated the point where we must begin our attack. Davoust was to debouch by Essling; Massena was to maintain his position in Aspern ; Oudinot and Lannes, forming the centre with the cavalry, were to pierce the enemy's centre, and, seconded by Davoust's left, crush the archduke's *corps-de-bataille*, and throw it back on the upper Danube. Oudinot, with his grenadiers, advances with impetuosity ; Lannes has drawn up his corps in echelons ; he throws forward the division of St. Hilaire, while the remainder of his forces sustains it and forms a second line. Our troops advance with audacity, and overthrow everything before them ; soon the first line of the enemy is penetrated. The Austrian artillery causes great ravages in the troops of Oudinot and Lannes, who are drawn up in a rather deep order of attack ; I, therefore, advise Lannes to deploy his forces as he gains ground. Marbot carries this order to St. Hilaire, who begins its execution. Claparède forms in this way Oudinot's corps of grenadiers, deploying his brigade, by the right, *en potence*, in order to oppose Rosenberg.

The archduke has too practiced an eye not to perceive the importance of the movement of my centre, and of the retreat of his first line ; he prolongs his corps on Breitenlée, where his headquarters are, and debouches with all his reserves on the same point. Lannes and Bessières sustain Oudinot ; the combat becomes fierce, both parties displaying the most admirable valor. Bessières passes through the intervals of our infantry, and, at the head of his squadrons, dashes upon those of the enemy, and then charges his infantry ; the boldest penetrate even to the Austrian headquarters at Breitenlée. The archduke seizes the colors in his own hands, and rallies the battalions which have yielded to the audacity of our troops. The battle is becoming hand-to-hand with our soldiers, whose advance nothing can now arrest. One effort more, and victory cannot escape us. . . . . . But this effort is now impossible ; for, at this moment, the most disastrous news destroys all our hopes. The great bridge of the Danube is broken by fire-ships, rafts, and heavy floating bodies directed against it by the enemy, and brought in contact with the bridge with fatal violence by the swift current of the stream ; the bridge, broken and scattered, floats far down the Danube ; the aid-de-camp, who brought me this alarming news, could give no definite information respecting the present position of the wreck, and I still had some hope of reëstablishing it ; but this hope was soon dissipated.

I could no longer reckon on the four divisions of Davoust, or the reserve of artillery, for offensive operations. But it was necessary to maintain our position till night, and return into our citadel of Lobau. The situation of a part of an army which first crosses a river in the face of a hostile army drawn up to receive it, is always critical ; but how much more is the position of this fraction when deprived not only of all assistance from its own army but also of all hope of retreat. In a forcible passage, whatever may be the advantage of the opposing army, the troops are animated by the certainty of being constantly reënforced, and of having the chances of success turned in their favor by the new battalions which are gradually brought into action. But in the affair of the twenty-first, we had not even this advantage, for the frequent rupture of the bridges, and the swelling of the Danube, whose waters overflowed the islands and avenues to the bridges, required all the heroic devotion of Massena, Lannes, and their soldiers, to maintain the advantage already gained. Notwithstanding the reënforcements received during the night, the situation of the troops was still lamentable, when the order for retreat, and the news of the rupture of the bridges which caused this order, made all feel that they had now to conquer or die.

My attitude, both calm and severe at the moment when I received this news, contributed to maintain the confidence of our brave soldiers ; no one knew that any thing had happened, till I had had time to ascertain whether there were any means of reëstablishing the bridges. Lannes was to maintain his position till this was fully ascertained; but this hope being soon destroyed, the marshal was ordered to return to Essling, and the fatal news, flying from mouth to mouth, informed our soldiers of the threatening danger. Instantly a sad silence succeeded to the shouts which usually precede victory; but even this silence, accompanied by perfect calmness, showed that every one was determined to do his duty. At the moment when Lannes was checking his advance by my orders, the archduke, who, better advised than the day before, had either carried the mass of his forces on the centre, or had been drawn there by the manœuvre with which I had threatened him, commenced a general attack with all the forces at his disposal, and under the terrible fire of his batteries. His troops, astonished to see ours halt, acquired new audacity, and believed themselves already victorious; when Lannes commenced retreating, the enemy's ranks were filled with enthusiasm, and they fell with vigor upon St. Hilaire, who formed the first echelon. This veteran of the army of Italy, pierced with a bullet, carried to his grave the regrets and admiration of all. His troops, for a moment alarmed at his death, nevertheless, continued their movement in good order. Lannes hearing of the death of his companion in arms, flew to the head of his command, and marched it boldly towards Essling; Oudinot followed him on the left.

The enemy, emboldened by his unusual success, at first pressed hard on Lannes' rear. Aspern and Essling again became the centre of all their efforts. Surrounding these two villages with a concave line, they pour in upon the French a most murderous fire. The battle continues without further manœuvres; it is a horrible butchery, but indispensable to save the honor of the army and the lives of those who remained exposed, for, to attempt to retire, in open day, by a single bridge, in presence of an enemy double our numbers and artillery, is to expose at least one half of these troops to inevitable destruction. The scene of the night before is renewed in these two villages, which are taken and retaken five or six times by the opposing combatants. Toward noon, the enemy attempts to turn Aspern by penetrating by a small woody island in the direction of Stadelau; he has already gained ground and is about to take the village in reverse and threaten the little bridges thrown across this branch of the stream. Molitor marches there with his division now reduced to three thousand combatants, and gathers new laurels, which Massena also shares. " Sometimes on foot and sometimes mounted, he is seen in the woods, on the island, in the village, sword in hand, directing the attack and defense." The intrepid Legrand, of whom I might say with even greater reason than of Gardanne, "he was a grenadier in stature as well as courage," displayed no less coolness and firmness in Aspern. In the mean time, the prince of Rosenberg also attacks Essling, and is sustained by the archduke, with a brigade of grenadiers. Five times he penetrates into the village, and five times Boudet, immovable in his redoubt, forces him to retire. Finally, at two o'clock, the archduke, having failed in twenty assaults against the two bastions of our line, decides, though late, to make a decisive attack on the centre. If this should succeed, the troops, thrown back on the little bridges which remain, can not prevent the enemy from destroying them, and the divisions compromised in the villages will be destroyed. The corps of Hohenzollern, sustained by twelve battalions of grenadiers, advances for this purpose. Lannes opposes a vigorous resistance; Hohenzollern is overthrown, and yields the honor of the attack to the grenadiers, who, led by the archduke in person, attack our artillery with the bayonet.

The cavalry at the same time attempt to penetrate between Essling and the Danube. But these efforts are useless. The archduke, astonished at our firmness and his own losses, renounces the attempt there, and directs his attack on Essling, which he finally carries. If he is left master of this place, nothing can prevent him from debouching on the Danube, and destroying the remnants of those brave troops who sacrifice themselves with so much devotion. I throw against him the cool and intrepid Mouton, (Count Lobau), at the head of the brigade of the fusiliers of the guard. The enemy's grenadiers are every where defeated; one battalion is captured in the granary and another in the cemetery. The fury of this attack, which surpasses every thing, proves to the archduke that he can obtain no more trophies against men who have resolved to conquer or die. It is near four o'clock; for thirty hours his troops have fought almost incessantly; even his reserves have been destroyed; he is satisfied with his successes, and this long and cruel tragedy degenerates into a cannonade, still well kept up by the enemy, but very inferior on our side for want of munitions. This cannonade, though less dangerous, was still somewhat destructive; a spent ball, thrown from Enzersdorf, struck Marshal Lannes, the most intimate of my companions in Italy, breaking both his legs. Capricious fortune wished to expend all her shafts on me. This news dismayed me. It was time to end this deplorable contest, for our artillery horses were all slain, and a great part of the pieces dismounted; as the parks of reserve had not been able to cross over, the ammunition was exhausted; it was necessary to keep up a supply by successive passages in boats.

Council of War and New Projects of Napoleon.—We had now to extricate ourselves from this difficult position, and to secure our retreat. I had just examined plans of the island of Lobau, to ascertain its capability to afford us a shelter for two or three days. I also assembled some of my generals in council. Some advised the repassing the Danube, but to do this required a bridge ; and even had there been a bridge, I should not have followed such advice, for I had no idea of a general retreat. Davoust, who was present, assured me that he could defend the right bank of the river against all the enterprises of the enemy, and give us time to reconstruct the bridges. Massena said, that in case of need, if the enemy should place himself on our line of retreat, he could cut his way out sword in hand.

I then addressed them in a few words, reviewing the chances of our position.

"A retreat can be effected only by boats, which is almost impossible ; it would be necessary to abandon the wounded, the artillery, and all the horses, and to disorganize the army ; the enemy may then cross at Krems or at Presburg, to fall on the rear of our scattered forces, and drive us from Germany, by raising against us the inhabitants of the country. We still possess great resources ; it will require only two or three days to reëstablish our bridges, and secure the means of either resuming the offensive or of effecting our retreat voluntarily and in good order. In a few days, Eugene must descend from the Styrian Alps ; Lefebvre will be called from the Tyrol, with a half of the Bavarians, and, even should the enemy by crossing the river at Lintz threaten our present line of retreat, Eugene will open a new and safe line on Italy, and we shall then be able to renew our operations with the eight *corps-d'armée* of Eugene, Marmont, Macdonald, Lefebvre, Bernadotte, Davoust, Oudinot, and Massena, besides the imperial guard and the reserves. We must, therefore, remain on the island of Lobau. Massena, you will complete what you have already so gloriously begun ; you can remain here alone, and impose upon the archduke, sufficiently to retain him before you for the few days which will be required. The ground of Lobau, which I have just examined, will be favorable for this object."

At these words, the eyes of my generals flashed with new fire; each one saw the extent of my resources, and the rapidity of my conception; it was agreed that a retreat should be begun at night, and that the last troops should fall back by two o'clock in the morning, preserving, if possible, the ponton bridge with a *tête-de-pont*, destroying only the small bridges of communication across the branch that masked the reëntering side of the island.

Death of Lannes.—At the moment when I was arranging these dispositions they brought before me the body of Marshal Lannes; he lay stretched out on a litter, just ready to expire. I threw myself upon him, and clasped him in my arms, addressing him by epithets the most dear. Those who witnessed this affecting scene would hardly accuse me of having a cold heart, inaccessible to sentiments of affection, as has so unjustly been alleged against me. In my cabinet, and at the head of military and political affairs, I have generally been able to overcome my natural inclinations, which were far from cruelty and cold insensibility; those capable of judging me would rather accuse me of yielding to bias of friendship.*

---

* For a more full account of this interesting scene between Napoleon and the dying Lannes, the reader is referred to the work of General Pelet on the campaign of 1809. While Napoleon often blamed the faults of his officers, and sometimes removed them from commands, he never treated them as the English did Admiral Byng. This is shown in his treatment of Baraguay d'Hilliers at Ulm, of Bisson at Friedland, and Berthier at Ratisbon.

Thiers says, that Napoleon "perceiving a litter made of some branches of trees, on which Lannes lay, with his legs amputated, ran to him, pressed him in his arms, spoke hopefully of his recovery, and found him, though heroic as ever, yet keenly affected at seeing himself so soon stopped in that career of glory. 'You are going to lose,' said Lannes, 'him who was your best friend, and your faithful companion-in-arms. May you live and save the army.'"

Napoleon, in his dictations to Montholon, at St. Helena, pays a merited tribute to Lannes and St. Hilaire.

Remarks on the new Position of the French. — But to return to my army. The retreat was effected in the manner fixed upon, without any obstacle on the part of the enemy, who had fallen back with the mass of his forces, leaving only his advanced guards in our presence. I established my headquarters at Ebersdorf. The boats were employed the following days in carrying over our provisions and military munitions, and in bringing away the guards and the wounded. Massena took the general command of all the forces on the island.

Our forces were now withdrawn to the island of Lobau; but our embarrassment was far from ended. Our communication with the right bank of the river was not yet restored; and my army was forty-eight hours on the island without provisions or ammunition. Fortunately, the Austrians did not trouble us. If they had attacked us the next day, the general opinion is, that we would have been unable to resist the fire of their three hundred pieces of artillery, and must have been destroyed. I, however, thought differently. The island of Lobau formed a real intrenched camp, surrounded by a ditch of running water, seventy toises wide, which could not easily have been crossed by the enemy in the presence of an army which had no other alternative than to conquer or die. The Austrian batteries were at a great distance, and they were ignorant of the destitute condition of our caissons. Moreover, these were partially supplied before night by the reception of several boat-loads of military munitions. Undoubtedly the enemy might have greatly annoyed us by his projectiles; but, then, we were partially covered by the woods on the middle of the island, and my soldiers, who had fought so bravely on the twenty-second without protection, were not likely to jump into the Danube at the approach of a few cannon balls. If the enemy's infantry had penetrated into the island, we should have been on equal terms; they would then have the river behind them as well as we, and I could have thrown myself upon them without hesitation, and have driven them into the Danube. It must be confessed, however, that an attack at this time would have augmented our embarrassment. It would not have cost the Austrians much, for we could not have attacked them, in turn, on the left bank. It is conceded that the archduke did not attempt every thing in his power to annoy us, but it by no means follows, as some of my enemies have endeavored to show, that such an attack would have effected our ruin.

The French army had surpassed itself;—in the first day's battle, thirty thousand men had fought heroically against forces triple in numbers and materials; and, in the second day, fifty thousand French had resisted ninety thousand men. Nevertheless, the Austrians, and the Archduke Charles, had done wonders; the most exacting could scarcely have desired more bravery than they exhibited in their grand attack. We did not recognise them as the same soldiers who had fought at Ratisbon.

The twenty-fifth of May, the bridges having been repaired, every thing was restored to order; and, the next day, the light cavalry put us in communication with the army of Italy.

Reply to Rogniat's Criticism on the Battle of Essling.— Such was the bloody battle of Essling, which is to be classed, like that of Eylau, among the battles in which fortune opposed me, but in which I, nevertheless, succeeded by my obstinate perseverance, and my superior combinations. This battle has not been wanting in critics, and, among others, General Rogniat has not spared me. He reproaches me with having made the attack on the twenty-second carelessly and without consideration. It may be sufficient to remark, in reply, that eight divisions, resting on the river, and to be immediately followed by four others, may very well begin a battle, in order to gain ground sufficient to manœuvre larger forces. If the bridge had not been broken, Davoust would have debouched on the right of Lannes, and then, if this marshal, beaten in the centre, as were the Romans at the battle of Cannæ, by the concave line of Hannibal, had been obliged to fall back, Davoust might soon have restored affairs by a change of front on the left of the enemy, like that which had been executed at Eylau, and which he repeated a few weeks after at Wagram.

Rogniat, moreover, imputes to me the fault of having formed the troops of Lannes in too deep masses on the centre of the concave line of the enemy, whose superior artillery poured in upon us a concentric and decisive fire. The justice of these reproaches may, at least, be contested. I never was foolish enough to renew here the too famous English column of Fontenoy, by throwing a single deep mass against the middle of a line of concentric fires. The position between Essling and Aspern was calculated to favor an attack on the centre, since our flanks were secured from attack by those two bastions. Moreover, it should not be forgotten that an army crossing a river in the face of a superior enemy has but few manœuvres from which to choose. Always, in debouching, it is necessary to rest the two wings on the river; otherwise, you risk losing your bridges; you must also have room in rear of your centre to form your debouching troops; this forces you to form either a semicircle or a salient angle on the centre. There is one exception to this rule, *i.e.*, when the passage is made while the enemy is at a distance, or is so situated as to be unable to approach your flanks. In that case, by a change of front, you may take up your position parallel to the course of the river, as Turenne and Moreau did on the Rhine—the former against Montecuculli, and the latter against Starray. But such was not our position at Essling. On the first day, it was necessary to retain the position between the two villages ; after getting our forces ready, we ought to have debouched under the protection of these two bastions, by an oblique movement, pushing forward the right wing, and refusing the left ; which was exactly what Lannes and Massena were intending to execute, if Davoust had been able to reach them. The only thing that can be said of this operation is, that, possibly, it might have been better to delay the offensive attack until the complete arrival of Davoust's forces, and then to direct it from Essling on Raasdorf. It was in this way that we afterward operated at the battle of Wagram. With respect to the *deep formation of troops*, which, it is alleged, Lannes employed against the enemy, I no more advised it than I do some of the other ideas of my critic. But had the troops of Lannes been drawn up according to the thin formation, there would not have been space for Davoust to form on his right ; this would have delayed Davoust's coming into action, and have exposed my centre, too thin for resistance, to the attacks of the enemy, while the third *corps-d'armée* was still moving into line. But, in fact, my centre was not entirely of the deep formation ; the troops were drawn up according to the mixed system. Claparède had his three brigades deployed, two facing to the north, and the third, formed crotchetwise, to cover themselves against Rosenberg ; St. Hilaire was also deployed. In fine, Rogniat's criticisms on this battle partake more of the spirit of general denunciation than of a just and searching analytical examination.

General Remarks on the Tactics of Battles.—Strategy has been almost a fixed science ; it is subject to rigid and almost invariable rules. But not so with tactics of battles, *i.e.*, the manner of drawing up troops on the field, and of bringing them into action. On this subject there is not the same unanimity of opinion among military writers. Indeed, there has been renewed, in our time, the old controversies on the respective advantages of thin and deep formations, subjects long since supposed to be exhausted.

There are various modes of drawing up troops on the field of battle; but none of them can be subjected to any thing like invariable rules. The ground, the character of the troops, and various other circumstances, govern each individual case. The thin formation of troops deployed has been constantly followed by Wellington, and some have concluded that, since he triumphed over our columns, this must be the best. In the rugged positions of Spain and Portugal, a defensive line ought to be deployed, and to rely on its fire. If Wellington resisted our columns at Waterloo until the arrival of the Prussians, it was because the deep mud destroyed the impulsion of these columns, and prevented our artillery from following them; under the circumstances they were too deep. The principal merit of a column is its impulsion; if the nature of the ground, or its too great mass, prevents it from moving with facility, we experience all the inconveniences of the formation without its advantages. The formation proposed by General Jomini has much merit. It is simply a line of battalions, in columns of attack, ployed on the central division of each battalion. This formation has less depth and more mobility than the column of Folard, and has greater stability than the thin or deployed formation. We frequently employed it in our earlier campaigns; but afterwards, as our armies increased in numbers, the desire of having our troops more concentrated and disposable induced us sometimes to form them in too deep and heavy masses. Instead of forming columns of battalions by divisions, we formed heavy columns of grand divisions by battalion, each grand division composed of twelve battalions. This formation was a fault at Albuera, Moskwa, and Waterloo, but not at Essling.

It should be observed that when a deep column is formed, or a line of small columns of attack by battalions, it is indispensable that the flanks should be protected with troops marching by file. The greatest difficulty with a column is in being compelled to stop and repel an attack on its flank. But if each flank is protected by troops marching by file, these troops will cover it from the enemy's charges, while the column continues its offensive impulsion.

The system of small squares by battalion, followed by the English, is not without advantages. A battalion of eight companies may be formed into oblong squares, three in front and rear, and one on each flank, these last marching by file. This mode of formation presents a front greater by one company than the column of attack of battalions by divisions. It has, however, much less impulsion than the column, but it is more advantageous when it becomes necessary to employ the fire, inasmuch as it has one-half more fire and one-half less mass exposed to the enemy's artillery. It is preferable to the thin formation of deployed battalions, because it has more strength, and may be moved over ground of almost any character.

The general rules for the tactics of battle, may be summed up as follows:

1st. In a defensive battle, the mixed formation of the first line deployed, and the second line in columns of attack of battalions by divisions, is deemed the most perfect.

2d. In an offensive battle, I prefer the formation in two lines of columns of attack of battalions by divisions on the central division, placing the columns of the second line opposite to the intervals of the first, so as to present less mass to the enemy's artillery, and to give greater facility for the movement of the columns in advancing and in retreat. The intervals between the battalions may be filled with sharpshooters or artillery.

3d. Where the troops are habitually formed in two ranks, each of these columns of attack will be composed of four divisions and, therefore, eight files in depth ; the column in this case has less depth in proportion to its front, and is less exposed to disorder, than when the troops are formed in three ranks, or the battalion is composed of more than four divisions.

4th. In order to give every possible advantage to the impulsive action, the command should be divided in depth, *i. e.*, each brigade should have its front and second line, so that every general officer will have the means at his disposal for forming a reserve without being obliged to seek it elsewhere.

5th. The formation of squares by battalions, may be employed with advantage on very level ground. It has less solidity and impulsion than columns of battalions ; but it possesses some advantages against cavalry and musketry. The parallelogram has the inconvenience of being more narrow and cramped on the flanks, but it has more mobility, more fire and greater front than the perfect square.

6th. The deep formation of heavy columns of grand-divisions with battalions formed in rear of each other, should only be used when the space is too narrow for a more extended formation. And even then the flanks should be protected by troops marching by file and also by sharp-shooters.

7th. These variations in *formations*, should not be allowed to influence the general principles of grand tactics as applied to the several *orders of battle*.

Military Operations in Italy.—But enough on this subject. Let us now return from our digression, and review the operations of the army of Italy, whose timely arrival at the appointed position effected so happy a diversion in our favor. In our previous relation we left it behind the Adige, after its ill-success at the battle of Sacile ; it was there reënforced by a division from the south of Italy. The Archduke John, forced to leave a corps to carry on the siege of Palmanova and observe Venice, advanced to Caldiero ; but on hearing of the battles of Abensberg and Eckmuhl, and of our march on Vienna, he feared that he might be cut off, and commenced a retreat. The Aulic Council, far from expecting this, had flattered itself that he would continue his successes in Italy, and thus effect a powerful diversion to the affairs in Germany.

The archduke, however, thought differently. Disquieted by the situation of Venice and the corps of Marmont who was guarding Dalmatia, and by the attitude of the viceroy who was receiving reënforcements, he thought he might expose himself to probable ruin, and that it would be better to rally on the Archduke Charles and save the monarchy. Allowing that the circumstances of the case justified this retreat, it may, at least, be said, that it might have been better conducted.

Battle of the Piave.—Having fallen back behind the Piave, the archduke thought that he would be able to defend the passage of this torrent which, like the Tagliamento, runs in a deep ravine, fordable except in time of the great rains or the melting of the snow. He therefore, halted behind this river, which Eugene passed with his army on the eighth of May; the operation was not simultaneous; his two advanced guards forded the stream a league apart. Desaix commanded the one on the left ; it debouched with boldness and was vigorously charged by the imperial cavalry under the orders of Wolfskehl. Eugene had not his infantry in position to be disposable ; the water was every moment rising from the melting of the snows ; it had become necessary to employ rafts for the passage of the troops. Wolfskehl at the head of three thousand horse, bravely charges the six battalions of Desaix formed in squares ; the Archduke John advances with the infantry to sustain him; his columns move slowly, and Desaix opposes an immovable barrier against the cavalry. Eugene, seeing the danger, flies to the menaced point, harangues the dragoons of Sahuc and Pully, and hurls them against the enemy. A bloody combat ensues; Wolfskehl is slain and his artillery captured. Our brave dragoons, notwithstanding their inferiority in numbers, drive the enemy's squadrons back upon the infantry of Colloredo, which has advanced into the plain, and throw it into disorder. This exploit gains time, and enables Macdonald to debouch with the division of Lamarque; Grenier follows with the divisions of Abbé. The archduke, who has lost the favorable opportunity, prepares for the main attack, at the moment when Eugene has united thirty-eight battalions of infantry, and four thousand horse. Eugene directs his attack by the right; Grenier executes it with the assistance of Macdonald; the enemy is every where vigorously pushed; but the country being cut up with dikes and canals, we are not able to profit by our success. The archduke attempts to pass the night behind a canal; the dragoons of Grouchy and Pully close, at eight o'clock, by a brilliant charge, the operations of the day. The archduke falls back on Conegliano, after having uselessly sacrificed seven or eight thousand men, in a battle which he should never have fought, or which, if fought at all, should have been conducted offensively at the moment when the French were acting under the disadvantage of a difficult passage of the river, conducted by successive embarkations. The result of this contest caused him to relinquish the idea of making a stand behind the Tagliamento, and he, in all haste, regained the Noric Alps, by the valley of Fella.

Eugene pursues the Austrians.—The viceroy, in imitation of my march in 1797, detached Macdonald with two divisions by the road to Laybach, in order to connect with Marmont; Serras took the central route to Predel; Eugene and

Grenier marched to the left on Malborghetto and Tarvis. The Archduke John hoped to effect his retreat without molestation, under protection of the intrenchments or forts with which he crowned the defiles of Malborghetto, Tarvis and Predel, on the two roads that lead to Villach, and of Prevald on the road to Laybach. He left small detachments in each of these places and retired twenty leagues to near Villach.

Eugene, who circumspectly followed in pursuit, on the seventeenth of May, captured the fort of Malborghetto, after a vigorous assault, not less honorable to the assailants than to the little Austrian garrison, most of whom died fighting.

Flitsch and Tarvis are carried in the same way, and Serras is equally successful at Predel, against a no less vigorous resistance. The troops of Macdonald easily gain possession of the intrenched camp of Laybach and the fort of Prevald. The commandants and militia-garrisons of these posts, surrendered after little or no opposition. We here took five thousand prisoners. Schilt made a sortie with the garrison of Palmanova, captured Trieste without opposition, and made several rich prizes there. These operations had the double advantage of isolating the Austrians from the English, by closing to the latter the ports of the Adriatic, and of facilitating the junction of Marmont. The previous retreat of Eugene behind the Mincio, had left this corps in Dalmatia in a dangerous position. General Stoischwitz had at first observed Marmont with eight thousand men; Knesewich, at the head of the Croat militia which had been assembled at Agram, was to assist Stoischwitz; and Zach, governor of Istria and Trieste, gaining possession of Capo-d'Istria in concert with the English cruisers, was to completely cut off his communications. Marmont, after the battle of Sacile, was summoned to surrender, and as he could do no better he refused to answer, and retired to the mountains to await the result. Numerous unimportant contests took place between this and the middle of May, when hearing of the retreat of the Austrians, he marched toward Carniole to effect a junction.

Retreat of the Archduke John on Gratz.—The Archduke John who had allowed his advanced guards to be crushed twenty leagues distant from himself, received at Villach, on the nineteenth of May, the letter of the Archduke Charles, directing him to march on Lintz. Although this movement was tardy, still it was possible of execution ; the prince, however, deemed it dangerous to throw himself in the midst of my army, with the viceroy in hot pursuit, and directed his march on Gratz. The division of Jellachich, which had operated in the Alps of Salsbourg, in order to connect Hiller with the Archduke John, being hemmed in on the right and left by our columns, received orders to march likewise from Rottenmann on Gratz, by the valley of the Muhr. It is overtaken at St. Michel, on the twenty-fifth of May, by the divisions of Serras and Durutte. Jellachich received battle between the Muhr and the rocks which inclose the valley. He was turned by the heights and pierced in front by the cavalry, and, out of seven thousand men, escaped to Leoben with scarcely three thousand.

The Archduke John, instead of being reënforced at Gratz by the troops of Jellachich as he had expected, found merely the wrecks of this division ; and fearing lest he might be hemmed in between my army and that of Eugene, he took the road to Kormond, on the twenty-sixth, still ignorant, it is said, of the result of the battle of Essling, of which he heard the news on the twenty-seventh. This prince has been reproved for not executing the orders of his brother ; some have even gone so far as to calculate the favorable results for the Austrian monarchy, which would have been produced by a march on Lintz. Without pretending to deny the momentary embarrassment which sixty thousand men well conducted might have caused us, it must, nevertheless, be remembered that I had in part provided for this danger by the position, in echelons, of my troops. Bernadotte had just arrived at Lintz; the Bavarians had just entered Iunspruck victorious, and they still retained Salsbourg; forty thousand Saxons and Bavarians would be found on the line of the Inn or the Traun, after they had destroyed the bridge at Lintz, in order to prevent the junction of Kolowrath and the Archduke John. The viceroy would have followed on the heels of the latter, and put himself in communication with the Bavarians on the one side and with me on the other. It is not difficult to imagine which, under these circumstances, would have been most embarrassed, myself or the Archduke John. After effecting my junction with Eugene, I would have turned upon the Archduke and made him experience the fate of Lusignan, of Provera, and of the other corps with which the Austrians have often attempted to surround me.

Junction of the Armies of Napoleon and Eugene.— Eugene, finding no obstacle on the road to Vienna, after the departure of his adversary for Kormond, pushed forward his van-guard to the mountain of Sommering, where they formed a junction with the light troops which Davoust had sent from Neustadt. This junction caused the greatest joy on both sides—a joy which was still further increased by the report that the bridges were restored; this completed the restoration of confidence. Eugene hastened to collect all his disposable forces to cross the chain of the Sommering, while the little division of Rusca guarded the Carinthia, and observed the Tyrol, and the division of Broussier besieged the castle of Gratz, guarded Styria, and observed the valley of the Linn.

Insurrection in Westphalia and Prussia.—The rapidity of my march on Vienna, and the importance of the operations that ensued, have forced me to omit all account of what was passing at this moment in Poland and the north of Germany, where a general insurrection was about to break out from the conspiracies of which I have already spoken. The plans of the duke of Brunswick-Oels, of Dornberg, and Schill, failed for want of concert in the execution.

According to the best accounts that can be obtained, the early part of May was fixed upon for this insurrection. Many accidents tended to derange a plan so complicated. Incited by the early successes of the Austrians in Bavaria, certain insurgents had assembled at Wolfshagen by the twenty-third of April. Jerome, informed of this event, directed Dornberg to march against the insurgents. Thinking his project discovered, and himself an outlaw, he fled and joined the rebels. Jerome was at first amazed at this news; then, presenting himself to his guards, he declared to them that he intrusted his person to their henor and loyalty. This generous appeal was addressed to brave men who knew how to appreciate it; and even those who were little disposed in his favor, swore that they would not abandon him.

Jerome's minister-of-war was a man well known for his cool judgment and decision of character. So well had he made his dispositions that his troops, from Wesel and Mayence to Cassel, all moved at once; and Dornberg, pursued, beaten, and dispersed by Rewbell, escaped with a mere handful of officers to join the duke of Brunswick in Saxony.

Schill, exposed by the seizure of Dornberg's papers, determined not to await his arrest. Leaving Berlin on the twenty-ninth of April, at the head of his regiment of hussars, he found the Saxon troops at Wittenberg not disposed to join his projects. He marched to Magdebourg on the seventh of May, where the Westphalian battalions were prevented from joining him by the firmness of General Michaud and Colonel Wouthier. He now threw himself on the lower Elbe, expecting aid from the English, who had announced a considerable armament for the Baltic, and who had, in fact, made demonstrations with several vessels toward Stade. General Gratien, who commanded a Dutch brigade at Erfurth, started in pursuit, while General Eblé caused him to be followed on the other side by the Westphalians.

The Prussian cabinet at Königsberg hearing, at the same time, the illegal operations of Schill and our victories, hastened with great zeal to disavow what it had probably never authorized. Schill was condemned; if we had been beaten at Ratisbon, he would have been declared a hero! Nevertheless, it would be absurd to suppose that his operation was directed by the cabinet itself, with the intention of declaring either for or against him according to the turn of affairs. Such a project would have been unworthy of the character of Frederick William.

Having collected only about twelve or fifteen hundred men, and being hotly pursued by the Westphalians, Dutch, and a brigade of Danes, he took refuge in the dismantled fortress of Stralsund. He was attacked here on the thirty-first of May, and completely defeated; being reduced to despair, he determined to sell his life as dearly as possible; but at last, covered with wounds, he fell lifeless upon the dead bodies of his enemies, which he had formed into a kind of rampart around him.*

The duke of Brunswick, left Bohemia, the fourteenth of May, with his legion of Death ;† but not finding in Saxony the support which he expected, he returned again to Bohemia. In fine, the victories of Abensberg, Eckmuhl, and

---

* Some say that he fell by the hands of his own conspirators.

† So called from their uniform which was all of black, with a death's head embroidered on their shakos, emblem of the eternal hatred which this prince and his soldiers had declared against the French.

Ratisbon, had spread terror throughout Germany, and held in check all who were disposed to join the conspirators.

Affairs of the Tyrol.—In the mean time the Tyrol had become the theatre of important events. Chasteler, hearing of my victories in Bavaria, left Roveredo to return to the north. Marshal Lefebvre, after having driven Jellachich from Salzburg toward Rastadt, ascended the valley of the Inn on Kufstein; he defeated the advanced guard of Chasteler and the insurgents, in the defiles of Lomer, St. Johann, Feursinger, and finally at Grattenberg. The Bavarians, still full of enthusiasm from their successes at Abensberg, and indignant at the excesses committed by their comrades, precipitated themselves like mad-men into the narrow defiles, and overthrew every thing before them. The main body of Chasteler's forces, completely defeated at Worgel and at Schwatz, fell back on the Brenner, where he received orders from the Archduke John to retire to the Carinthia. Chasteler now proposed a treaty of evacuation and an armistice; Wrede replied by sending him a decree offering a reward for his head! This insurrection had exasperated me against him; I stood on the brink of a volcano; his native country being now united to France, if he was resolved to still fight against me, he ought to have done so in legitimate warfare, and not in stirring up insurrection against me; I treated him as a bandit; his brain was affected by it.

The Tyrolese now gave up all idea of defense; and Lefebvre entered Innspruck on the nineteenth of May. The insurrectionary committee resolved to send to the king of Bavaria promises of submission; nevertheless, a part of the country still remained in arms, and the presence of the Bavarians was scarcely sufficient to restrain the exasperated inhabitants of the valleys.

Operations in Poland.—In Poland our arms experienced some reverses. The Archduke Ferdinand, at the head of thirty-six thousand men, had marched on Warsaw. Poniatowski, after having bravely fought against forces double his own at Razyn, concluded a treaty of evacuation and fell back on the Narew, under the support of Modlin. The government took refuge at Tykoczin. After this fine beginning, Ferdinand extended his forces along the Vistula, threw a bridge across the river at Gohra, and ordered it to be intrenched; he then carried his van-guard, under Mohr, before Praga, whose *tête-de-pont* was defended by the Poles. Poniatowski profited by this fault, fell on Mohr and defeated him at Grochow; he afterward sent Pelletier and Sokolnicki to seize upon the *tête-de-pont* which had just been begun at Gohra, and the two battalions charged with its construction. Ferdinand flew to their aid, but was too late; he then decided to descend the Vistula and seize upon the *tête-de-pont* of Thorn.

In a military point of view, this eccentric expedition into Poland is entirely inexcusable; for even supposing that the Archduke Ferdinand had carried his successes to the gates of Dantzic, still Austria, defeated on the Danube, must have fallen. But in a political point of view, this incursion was not so blamable; for if they had succeeded in dissolving the little Polish army and gaining possession of the Duchy and Thorn, they would flatter themselves that Prussia might be induced to join them by offering her the restitution of the provinces which were dismembered from her states by the treaty of Tilsit; but things turned out very differently.

Far from despairing because of the inferiority of his forces, Prince Poniatowski took, in conformity with my orders, the bold resolution to leave the enemy master of the left bank of the Vistula, to ascend the right and fall on Galicia. Encouraged by his successes at Grochow and Gohra, he threw himself on Lublin and Sandomir, and captured the former; General Sokolnicki took forcible possession of Sandomir, and

General Pelletier carried Zomosc by escalade, while Dombrowski threw himself with a single squadron into Posen, and incited the inhabitants of Great Poland, where he had exercised great influence since 1794. The Archduke Ferdinand turned back on his own steps the more rapidly as a corps of thirty thousand Russians under Prince Gallitsen, were advancing toward Lemberg, at the same time that Poniatowski consolidated his conquests in Galicia, and threatened the Austrian line of retreat. The militia levied by Zayonschech entered Warsaw the second of June. The archduke harassed in his retreat by Zayonschech, drove him back on the Pilica. Reaching Sandomir on the fifteenth, with his artillery of reserve, and hearing that this place was occupied only by the feeble brigade of Sokolnicki, Prince Ferdinand resolved to seize it in the night; the outworks are carried, and an Austrian column penetrates even into the body of the place; nevertheless, after ten hours of most noble defense, the Poles routed them with a loss of five hundred prisoners, and a thousand men *hors-de-combat;* but, as the garrison is destitute of almost every thing, Sokolnicki prefers to evacuate the place rather than compromise his brave soldiers in a new attack, and therefore rejoined the army. The archduke, now master of Sandomir, marches on the Pilica toward Petrikau; Zayonschech occupies Gohra; Poniatowski is at Pulawy and Radom. A few days after, the archduke again falls back on Sandomir; and finally, at the beginning of July, Poniatowski, reënforced by Zayonschech, compelled him to march toward Cracovia, which he occupied on the ninth. The Russians extend along the San and also approach Cracovia. But they do not desire to make conquests which might tend to strengthen the grand-duchy to whose very existence they are opposed. This fact accounts for the operations of the Russians at this time in Poland—operations of which historians have been so much troubled to ascertain the motives.

Situation of Affairs in Germany.—It is time to return to my army on the Danube. Although the immediate consequences of the battle of Essling might induce my enemies to think that they had gained a victory, still, as they allowed us time to reëstablish the great bridge, I was entirely satisfied respecting the ultimate consequences in a military point of view. But not so in its political results. All Germany might be shaken by it; they everywhere published the news of my defeat and subsequent retreat, giving all the details, and predicting my speedy and total overthrow. The Tyrolese, ready to make their submission, were again full of insurrection. General Amende got possession of Dresden, and, uniting with the duke of Brunswick-Oels, marched on Leipsic, forcing the court of Saxony to seek refuge in Frankfort. Another column, under General Radiwojewich, leaving Egra, penetrated to Bareith and Nuremberg, and overran the country, to incite the people to insurrection. Minds, which our victories at Ratisbon had cooled not a little, again became excited, and the chiefs of the secret association did not lose the occasion to stir up insurrection. Nor did the court of Vienna, on its side, fail to magnify their success at Essling, in order to induce Prussia to declare against me. The emperor, himself, wrote to the king; M. de Stadion, through the prince of Orange, urged this monarch to declare himself; the ambassador, Wessemberg, continued to negotiate. General Steigentesch, who had been to Königsberg, with the hope of concerting plans of operation, returned to Berlin, where he sought to incite not only the Westphalians, but also the people of Prussia. The fear of becoming compromised with Russia restrained Frederick William; nevertheless, his ministers, opposed to the solicitations of Austria merely the fear of a separate peace, which antecedents gave them good reasons to apprehend. This was good proof that but little further success, on the part of Austria, would be necessary to induce Prussia to declare against me. The advices which I received from England informed me of the near departure of a gigantic maritime expedition,—a true *armada*, greatly superior to that with which Philip II. formerly menaced Great Britain. Between forty and fifty thousand men, with one hundred field pieces, and an immense siege equipage, were prepared for embarkation ; including the maritime forces, more than one hundred thousand men were engaged in this armament. These troops would probably act either in the north of Germany or in Holland. A few successes in either of these directions would undoubtedly decide Prussia, whose faith was already shaken by the demi-victory of Essling. An army of one hundred thousand Anglo-Prussians, which, by insurgents, Prussian militia, and Westphalians, would, in a few months, be increased to two hundred thousand combatants, might shake my power, and entirely change the face of affairs. The delays and egotism of the English cabinet, however, saved me at this crisis.

Affairs in Rome.—But my affairs were still more complicated by what was at this time passing in the south of Italy. The English and Sicilians threatened Naples with a great expedition fitted out at Palermo. The Pope, encouraged by the chances which the war in Spain offered to my enemies, had hurled many anathemas against me in his consistorial allocutions. After his refusal to adhere to the Italian league, and the loss of Ancona and Urbin, which resulted from it, the Holy See was naturally hostile to us ;—it entered the coalition against me. The English, in order to incite Italy, and favor their expedition, became more than ever the auxiliaries of Rome. The time to execute my grand project seemed to me to have arrived, and I determined to make an end of it. On my entry into Vienna, four days before the battle of Essling, I issued a decree uniting Rome and the States of the

Church to the French empire. The Pope, as the spiritual chief of the Church, was to retain his palaces, and enjoy an annual revenue of two millions of francs, which was to be made up to him from the imperial treasury. This decree, which was communicated to Rome on the tenth of June, was followed the next day by a bull of excommunication — a measure, which would have been merely ridiculous were it not for the war with Spain, but which, under the circumstances, might render that war the more obstinate. In this strange philippic, Pius VII. did not hesitate to exhibit the principles of the disciples of Loyola, and all the surly pride of a Gregory VII., or a Boniface VIII. His bull contained, among others, the following sentence: "*Let sovereigns learn once more that they are subjected by the law of Jesus Christ to our throne and to our command ; for we, also, exercise a sovereignty, but a sovereignty much more noble, unless it be said that the soul is inferior to the flesh, and heavenly things to those of the earth.*"

The Pope transferred to Savona.—Just at this time the news of the battle of Essling reached Rome, the success of the Austrians being magnified by the usual Italian exaggerations; every thing combined to excite the populace. I had withdrawn from this capital all the disposable troops to reënforce the viceroy; and Murat had enough to do to defend his own capital from the expedition that was cruising against it. The governor of Rome, Miollis, had only a handful of soldiers. His reports of the state of things at Rome, and the indications of insurrection there, alarmed Murat. He charged Miollis to send away the Pope, so as to be more free to act in case of an actual outbreak in the city. This general transferred the holy father to Tuscany, within the domains of my sister Eliza; but the latter, fearing the responsibility of such a deposit, caused him to be conducted to Turin. On hearing of these events, I had the Pope transferred to Savona, where he would be treated with the respect due to his rank, until the favorable moment should arrive for executing my project of removing the chair of St. Peter, and establishing it in France. The firmness of Miollis, and the resolution of Murat, saved the south of Italy ; but the responsibility of the removal of the Pope I am willing to take, if need be ; for, although I did not direct this removal, I had projected it two years before.

Measures of Napoleon for repairing the Check received at Essling.—The storm which threatened the north, still more serious than that which troubled Italy, was tardy in its approach, and my adversaries thus gave me time to repair all my losses. In the accomplishment of this task I exerted all the vigor and rapidity of which I was capable. I had already given the prelude to these measures, by directing the construction of solid bridges, and the concentration of my forces about Vienna. The viceroy descended the mountains of Styria on Neustadt. Leaving to the Tyrolese a momentary success, Lefebvre and Wrede, at the head of the Bavarian troops, received orders to fall back from Innspruck on Lintz ; Bernadotte was to echelon on the Danube in such a manner as to join me in forty-eight hours.

As soon as our communications were reëstablished, I directed Davoust to place his divisions in echelons on Presburg, to oppose the preparations which the enemy was making to establish a passage there. The Archduke Charles, instead of marching there with his entire army, had merely detached the division of Bianchi, with orders to prepare a bridge, and to secure it by intrenchments, on an island separated from the right bank by a very small arm of the river. Davoust found the enemy occupied in throwing up these works, and caused him to be attacked. But as Davoust had no means of crossing this arm, of twenty toises, which separated him from the Austrians, he was unable to dislodge them, but he paralyzed all the advantages of their position by strongly occupying the village of Engereau, which almost entirely barred the reëntering angle formed by the Danube, opposite to the position occupied by the enemy's bridge.

On the Main, Junot assembled a *corps-d'armée* of contingents and provisional regiments, formed of French conscripts, in order to cover Saxony and Westphalia in concert with my brother Jerome. Augsbourg, now the centre of our depôts, was placed in a state of defense, and secured by a strong division organized by General Lagrange. I urged forward the reparation and increase of the defenses of Passau. Our parks soon repaired the losses of the campaign.

In order not to awaken the attention of the enemy, I left my camp at Ebersdorf to return to the palace of Schönbrunn, where they imagined I was dosing beneath its gilded canopies. All the month of June was employed in arranging the means and measures for restoring victory. Fortunately for us, England and Prussia interfered with these measures only by hatching new plots and stupid conspiracies, or by the partial organization of legions of adventurers.

Eugene marches against the Archduke John.—This forced silence was, nevertheless, broken by a few military operations; the most important were those of the viceroy against the army of the Archduke John. This prince in retiring on Hungary had added still more to his eccentric direction, by carrying the corps of Giulay into the Illyrian provinces, either because he feared that Marmont might invade these provinces, or because he wished to cover every thing in his retreat after the manner of Bulow.* On the other hand he expected to be reënforced in the direction of Kormond by the troops of the Hungarian insurrection. Situated as he

---

* Bulow recommends an army in retreat to follow eccentric lines—the surest possible mode of securing its own total destruction!

was, with both my army and the Danube between him and the Archduke Charles, I could detach against him as many troops as I might deem proper.

It was now important for us to enlarge our theatre of action about Vienna, and to get rid of this troublesome neighbor. I directed Eugene to march against him, and to get possession of Raab, a place strengthened by an old bastioned enciente with some counter-guards and demilunes; in fine, to push the archduke away so far as to enable the army of Italy to return to me when I should wish to begin operations. Eugene perfectly accomplished his task.

Battle of Raab.—The Austrian generalissimo had, in the mean time, dispatched orders to the Archduke John to march toward Presburg, and had detached ten thousand men in that direction to secure the junction, construct a bridge, and intrench the large island which would give to the Austrians the same advantages as were secured to us by Lobau. But nothing of this was done in time. Eugene marched on Kormond; on his approach the Archduke John fell back on Raab, where his brother, the Archduke Rainier, had organized the Hungarian insurrection; he took a very strong position, connected by his right to the place and to an intrenched camp. He numbered about twenty-two thousand old soldiers and eighteen thousand militia. Eugene reached the enemy on the thirteenth, and determined to attack him the next day. It was a day of happy presage—*the anniversary of Marengo, and the deliverance of Italy!* His troops, animated by the recollection of these great events and of their recent successes, crossed the Pancha, and attacked the enemy with impetuosity. Eugene manœuvred to form his line of attack by echelons on the right, but this soon degenerated into a parallel order of battle. Grenier charged the left of the enemy at the farm of Kismegger with the division of Serras, while the cavalry under Grouchy and Montbrun sought to turn that wing. Durutte sustained them on the centre ; on our left, Baraguay-d'Hilliers, with the Italians, attacked the village of Schabadegki, which was several times taken and retaken. Pacthod formed the reserve until the arrival of Macdonald, who was expected during the day. The enemy's reserves are now brought into action, which for a time renders the contest doubtful. The intrenched farm prevents our right from gaining any decided success. The Italians and Durutte are driven back. Eugene hastens to place himself at their head ; he recalls to their minds the victories they have already won, and exhorts them to new efforts, and, better still, advances the division of Pacthod to their support. The impulse is given, the right of the archduke is forced and separated from Raab. Durutte and Serras regain their lost ascendency, and push the centre. The enemy is routed and retreats toward Comorn, leaving four thousand prisoners, and three thousand men *hors-de-combat*. The Archduke John covers his retreat with his grenadiers and the *landwehrs* of Styria. These last on the day of the battle rival the conduct of the best regiment ; one of their battalions defend the farm of Kismegger to the death, the few that remain being sacrificed by our irritated soldiery. This victory of Raab, the more glorious for being gained over vastly superior forces, completed the consolidation of our position. The archduke rallied his forces under Comorn.

Results of the Battle and Siege of Raab.—This success, though important in itself, derived an additional interest from the character of the epoch in which it was gained. The Tyrol was then, more than ever, on fire. No sooner had the Tyrolese heard of the result at Essling, related by the Austrians with the greatest exaggeration, than they retraced the steps taken by the committee for giving in their submission, and assumed an attitude more threatening than ever. The departure of Lefebvre for Lintz with two divisions, left

General Deroi alone in the centre of the insurgent country; surrounded in the narrow valley of the Inn by forces quintuple his own, he deemed himself exceedingly fortunate in regaining Bavaria, by Rosenhaim, on the twenty-eighth of May.

The insurgents, now masters of the field, under the direction of Hormeyer, became intoxicated with their success, and made numerous incursions into the adjacent parts of the country. At the north, they annoyed Bavaria; in the south, they drove Rusca from the confines of the Carinthia; in the west, they made incursions into Swabia in concert with the insurgents of the Voralberg, and spread terror even to the Rhine. Chasteler, who had evacuated this country, leaving behind him only a single brigade of Austrians, under General Buol, crossed our posts of Carinthia and Styria to connect himself with the Archduke John; by connecting himself with the detachments of Zach and the corps of Giulay, he might give us trouble by debouching on our communications in concert with the Hungarian insurrection. The operations of Eugene, and the victory of Raab, dissipated these fears. It was important, however, for us to profit by the present success to gain possession of Raab itself. This place, situated near the confluence of the river Raab and the Danube, was fortified by an old enciente, of seven bastions, constructed against the Turks; between this place and the Danube was an intrenched camp of some three miles in circumference; but none of these works were either in good order or well armed. The possession of Raub was of great importance to the enemy, as it gave him a debouche on the right of the Danube. I, therefore, resolved to take this place cost what it might. The Archduke John had garrisoned it by only two thousand four hundred men, and half of these were militia. Eugene sent Lauriston to make the attack, with a park sent from Vienna. The place fell on the twenty-fourth of June, at the very moment when the Archduke Charles was directing measures for its succor; but they were too late.

The Archduke John's Disobedience of his Brother's Orders.—The Archduke Charles had much cause to complain of his brother's conduct; he had neglected to execute the march on Lintz, which had been directed, in order to act in concert on my communications; nor had he so manœuvred as to connect himself with the grand army by leaving Kormond in time to reach Raab and Presburg, and avoid giving battle with his isolated corps. In fine, he had posted himself at Raab contrary to instructions; had allowed himself to be forced into an eccentric retreat on Comorn, and had made no efforts to raise the siege of Raab. In truth, Prince John thought less of ranging himself under the colors of his brother, with a portion of his army, than of uniting in Styria and Carniola the several corps in the Illyrian provinces, under Zach, Chasteler, and Giulay. He hoped to form, 'n this way, an army of fifty thousand men, exclusive of the Hungarian levy, and to acquire glory on his own account, by acting against my extreme right and my communications. This, considered as an isolated plan, was not so very objectionable; but, by acting in this way on his own account, instead of obeying orders, he deranged the calculations of his generalissimo.

Bombardment of Presbourg.—After having deferred for a long time, he, at last, repaired to Presbourg, at the moment when I was directing its bombardment. It was important for me to remove all fears of a passage of the Danube, by destroying all the materials collected by the enemy for this object, and all the works that were in any way calculated to facilitate such an operation. It was also essential to draw the enemy's attention from the more important to some secondary point. Davoust summoned the Austrians to suspend the works on the bridge, or, otherwise, he would bombard the city. The emperor, Francis, was passing there at the time, to visit the remains of the army of Italy; Bianchi returned a sharp and provoking answer to Davoust's summons, and the firing immediately began. Our shells burned one-sixtieth part of the buildings. The Archduke Charles protested against it, and I promised him to stop the bombardment, which had no other object than to fix the enemy's attention in that direction. Davoust, at the same time, received confidential notice of the passage which I meditated, and orders to get possession of the *tête-du-pont* of Presbourg, or the island of Stadtaue, which flanked it. The latter place was carried on the thirtieth, with great valor, by the brave Colonel Decouz.

Marmont's March.—The grand epoch of the campaign was approaching. I was now only waiting for a considerable convoy of artillery and munitions, an augmentation of our bridge equipage, and the arrival of Marmont's corps, which we had left on the frontiers of Bosnia, and which was coming, rather slowly, it is true, to take part in the decisive battle. Being informed about the middle of May of our victories in Germany, and of the Archduke John's retreat before Eugene, Marmont assembled his forces at Zara, and advanced on the Save, in order to form a junction with the right wing of the army of Italy. After several pretty warm affairs on the banks of the Lika, on the twenty-first of May, and at Ottochatz, on the twenty-fifth, he marched by Fiume on Laybach, which place he did not reach till the third of June. At this moment Chasteler was evacuating the Tyrol, and endeavoring to effect a passage in rear of the viceroy; he threatened Villach and Klagenfurth, which places Rusca guarded with very weak detachments. He would have been lost if Marmont had only accelerated the march of his corps; as it was, he effected his escape by

Volkermarck and Stein behind the Drave. Although Marmont had great obstacles to surmount, in order to reach the Carniola, marching in the midst of three hostile corps, still, it was not impossible for him to have accelerated his march a few days. His greatest fault, however, was remaining at Laybach, from the third to the sixteenth of June, and allowing the bands of Giulay to march on Marbourg, and again prevent him from effecting his junction.

Operations of Giulay.—The Archduke John on leaving the Frioul had detached Giulay to Croatia, of which he was the military chief or *ban*. This general collected at Agram a division of seven or eight thousand men with a body of militia. He afterward received orders to march toward Marbourg, in order to connect himself with the archduke in the direction of Gratz. He was so tardy, however, in the accomplishment of this, that he did not reach that city till the fifteenth of June, after the defeat of the archduke at Raab, which was distant about fifty leagues. He then collected the several detachments which were scattered through these provinces in consequence of the operations, and, finding himself at the head of twenty thousand men, he hoped to prevent at least the junction of Marmont. For this purpose he advanced, the twentieth of June, on Windischfriestritz, with the corps of Zach and Knesewich; but Marmont, hearing at Gonowitz of his approach, and now moving with as much activity as he had formerly been slow and circumspect, he passed the Drave, by a forced march, at Volkermarck the twenty-second, and reached the Kaynach near Gratz, on the twenty-fourth. He expected here to unite with Broussier's division, which had remained at the siege of the citadel of Gratz.

Combat of Gratz.—As Giulay had allowed Marmont to escape, he now determined to prevent his junction with Broussier, by preceding him at Gratz; he reached Kalsdorf on the twenty-fourth, and pushed forward his cavalry to the gates of the city. Broussier had at first raised the siege of the castle in order to fall back two leagues on the road to Vienna; but on hearing that Marmont was about to debouch from Liboch on Gratz, he first drove the enemy from Kalsdorf and then resumed his position, with the understanding that he would reöccupy Gratz with a detachment, and effect a junction the following day at Kalsdorf. But the enemy was prepared to prevent the execution of this project, having eighteen thousand men encamped at the gates of the capital of Styria.

When the two battalions of the eighty-fourth, presented themselves on the twenty-fifth, Giulay attacked them with considerable forces. They threw themselves into a cemetery of the faubourgs, where they were surrounded and assailed on all sides; an active and bloody fight ensued. Broussier, on hearing the violence of the fire, detached three battalions to their assistance. These brave men cut their way through numerous enemies to join the eighty-fourth in the cemetery. The dead bodies with which the ground was covered proved the fierceness of the attack, and the heroism of the resistance. At last the enemy yielded, and our brave men embraced each other; but not satisfied with being delivered themselves, they carried the faubourg of Graben, took four hundred prisoners, and put twelve hundred men *hors-de-combat*.

This noble feat of arms, superior in some respects to any other in this campaign, commanded the admiration even of our enemies, and secured the junction of Marmont and Broussier.*

Giulay being unsuccessful against two battalions, deemed

---

* For this noble feat of arms, the eighty-fourth were presented with a flag with the inscription, *un contre dix*—one against ten.

it useless to contend with three divisions, and fell back on Gnass.

Marmont continued his march on the road to Vienna, and received orders to depart on the first of July, for the island of Lobau, where important events would render his presence necessary.

General situation of Affairs.—Our repose of five weeks on the island of Lobau had been, in every sense, the sleep of the lion ; I looked with a cool and tranquil eye upon the operations of the enemy by which they flattered themselves they would envelope me in their net. The incursion of General Amende and of the duke of Brunswick on Leipsic, that of another Austrian division on Barieth and Neuremberg, exciting insurrection as far as Mergentheim ; the Tyrolese and the inhabitants of the Voralberg, who disturbed Bavaria and spread even to the frontiers of Switzerland— were all indisputably embarrassing, but of a character calculated to disappear at the first decisive blow which we should strike on the Danube. The firmness and activity of the king of Wurtemberg contributed not a little to restore order in Germany ; he marched in person against the insurgents of Mergentheim, and with the assistance of General Beaumont, who organized our reserves and depôts at Augsbourg, restrained the mountaineers of the Voralberg. On the other side a new corps, formed in Franconia by Junot, was to act in concert with the king of Westphalia, to drive from Saxony the enemies who had invaded it.

New Passage of the Danube.—It was, however, in the plains of the Moravia (Marschfeld) that the possession of Germany was to be decided. My army was now increased to one hundred and fifty thousand men ; my artillery numbered four hundred pieces ; my bridge-equipage had been prepared on Lobau and the smaller islands, and I now waited merely for a convoy of munitions before effecting the passage. This passage was begun on the thirtieth of June, at the same place where we had crossed the river on the twenty-first of May. A bridge of pontons was thrown across in an hour and a half, under the protection of the artillery; every thing was now ready for erecting a pile-bridge which would be secure from floating bodies sent down by the enemy; and this bridge of timbers was prepared in even a shorter time than that formerly required for constructing a bridge of boats. I caused a field work to be erected to cover this bridge, and a regiment was found sufficient for its defense.

The Austrians had strongly intrenched Aspern, Essling, and even Enzersdorf, believing that we would again debouch by these same points; but they had neglected to fortify the eastern island between Enzersdorf and the Danube. Some have pretended that this was left on purpose by the archduke, as a snare for us, and that he did not intend to oppose our passage a second time, but to let us begin it, and then attack us when it was half executed. This, at least, is certain;—in a treatise on tactics, written by the archduke some five years before, the plateau of Wagram, and of the Russbach, is presented as a model of positions for defending the passage of a river, and the circumstances of the present case were then foreseen and fully discussed. It would seem that the archduke and his council had admitted, as a principle, that they ought not to prevent the beginning of a passage, but to attack us in the middle of the operation. For this purpose the army remained encamped about Wagram, from the Bisemberg to Glinzendorf; a corps of twenty thousand men only, under General Klenau, was left about the island of Lobau to guard the intrenched posts.

However this may be, I was ignorant of this project, and adopted a plan deemed, under all circumstances, best to secure the success of the enterprise. My first care was to fix the attention of the Austrians on the point where I had passed on the twenty-first of May, and where the erection of field-works gave reason to suppose the enemy was waiting in force. On the second of July, Massena caused the island of the Mill to be taken by his aid-de-camp, Pelet. A second bridge of boats was immediately thrown across the arm of the Danube, not far from the first ; this bridge, of seventy toises in length, was completed in two hours, so great were the dexterity and perfection acquired by our pontoniers in their duties. The enemy increased his opposition ; but nothing could restrain the ardor of our brave men. While this diversion was being effected, Eugene, Davoust, Wrede, and Bernadotte received orders to march rapidly from Lobau.

Having made sure of the result of these preliminary measures, it became necessary to think of dispositions for the grand enterprise. I had drawn up directions for this in an imperial decree of thirty-one articles, arranging everything with the utmost precision, for the operation was of so delicate a character that the least accident might destroy everything. On the evening of the fourth of July, after several movements, calculated to deceive the enemy, our troops were assembled on the eastern side of Lobau, where some battalions were thrown across in boats to get possession of the island opposite Muhlleiten. In two hours a bridge was established, and Oudinot passed over it with celerity. More than a hundred pieces of cannon, in the field-batteries which had been thrown up on the side of Lobau, thundered at the same moment along the whole line, spreading fear in every direction, and facilitating the operation by distracting the attention of the enemy, and protecting the troops and works on the other side. The night was dark and stormy ; the wind blew with violence, and the rain fell in torrents. The burning of the city of Enzersdorf, which was set on fire by our batteries, added to the terror and majesty of the scene. As soon as Oudinot had passed over to the left bank, I ordered the principal bridges to be thrown across to the island of Alexander. One of these bridges was completely constructed in a secondary arm of the river, and so arranged, by being fastened to the shore at the lower extremity, that the current would bring it round into position. If this idea was not new, it was at least the first time, to my knowledge, that it was ever carried into execution. By three o'clock in the morning, six bridges were completed, and our troops crossed over with a precision which was only interrupted for a short time, by a mistake which Berthier made in distributing my orders. Davoust was to form the right wing, and Oudinot the centre; but, by Berthier's mistake, Oudinot passed over on the right, and Davoust on the bridge of rafts, at the centre. This fault, in the logistics of the major-general, rendered it necessary for the columns to cross each other on the other side to take their assigned positions in the line-of-battle. Notwithstanding the tempestuous weather, I watched the operation with the greatest interest, flying from bridge to bridge, and from battery to battery; everything was executed with such extraordinary precision that all the articles of my decree were as punctually executed as if it had been a simple manœuvre on the field of practice.*

* In the planning and constructing bridges across the Danube, in this campaign, Napoleon had the able assistance of General Bertrand, a distinguished officer of engineers, and, at that time, an aid-de-camp to the emperor, with the rank of brigadier-general.

Count Henry Gratien Bertrand was born at Chateauroux, and first entered the military service in 1793. He accompanied Napoleon to Egypt as an engineer officer, and served with him in nearly all his subsequent campaigns. After Duroc's death, he was appointed Grand Marshal of the Palace, and commanded an army corps in 1813. He served with Napoleon in the campaign of 1814, and accompanied him to Elba; and again, after the campaign of 1815, he became the companion of his long exile in St. Helena. Nothing could induce him to leave his beloved emperor till he had closed his eyes in death. In May, 1816, he was condemned to death for contumacy. On his return to France in 1821, the sentence was annulled, and Bertrand restored to his rank of lieutenant-general.

His long and devoted attachment to Napoleon, and his kind and amiable

Operations on the Morning of the Fifth.— The splendid day, which followed the frightful night, presented the superb spectacle of an army of one hundred and fifty thousand men, with four hundred pieces of cannon, deployed majestically on the rich plains of the Danube. The village of Muhlleiten, the chateau of Sachsengang, the village of Wittau, and the bourg of Enzersdorf, are quickly swept of the small Austrian detachments charged with their defense. General Klenau, who commands the enemy's advance guard, fixes all his attention on Aspern and Essling, where Legrand's division, and the detachment of General Reynier, threaten an attack. The light division of Nordmann is the only one which disputes with us the ground between Enzersdorf and the Danube; it is driven back on Rutzendorf, from which place he is routed by General Oudinot after a sharp contest. Klenau, his right being turned by the fall of Enzersdorf, disputes in vain with Massena, Eugene, and Bernadotte, for the possession of the intrenchments of Essling and Aspern: the enemy is everywhere driven back; Rosenberg, who has rallied on himself the vanguard of Nordmann, is afterward driven by Davoust and Oudinot on Glinzendorf.

The archduke had not expected that our masses would be deployed with so much impetuosity and rapidity. In fact, there is no parallel in history. The armies of the Rhine, of the Sambre-et-Meuse, and of the Danube, had made a passage by surprise, at break of day, and forcibly established their bridges during the day, not completing the establishment of their forces on the opposite side before the second day; here, however, a formidable army, with an immense material, coming from Lintz, Vienna, Presbourg, and San-

character, caused him to be greatly beloved everywhere. On his visit to the United States, in 1844, the people received him with great enthusiasm in all the large cities which he visited. He died a few days after his return to his home at Chateauroux, and his remains were placed near those of Napoleon, in the chapel of the Hotel des Invalides.

Polten, to the general rendezvous of Lobau, had established six bridges, and crossed the Danube in a single night, notwithstanding the most terrible weather, and numerous defiles and islands, and on the following morning was drawn up and, in every respect, ready to receive the enemy, if he should venture to make the attack. This was a most admirable operation, exceeding all the calculations founded on experience, and rendering our success doubly certain.

Position of the opposing Forces.—So rapid and skillful was this operation, that the archduke, instead of attacking us the next morning at the entrance to our bridges, was obliged to receive, in the evening, a defensive battle. His army numbered about the same as ours; but the Archduke John and the prince of Reuss were detached, so that forty thousand men were not yet on the field. On the morning of the fifth, the archduke had in hand only Klenau, Bellegarde, and Hohenzollern, with his reserves of grenadiers about Gerasdorf, Kolowrath being still in rear of the Bisemberg, and Rosenberg being to the left of the *corps-de-bataille*. He had sent orders to the Archduke John, on the evening of the fourth, directing him to approach the main body with his twenty thousand men, in order to be ready to give battle the next day with the whole eight corps; if, however, the Archduke John should be engaged in the operation which had been prescribed opposite Presbourg, he might not arrive before the morning of the sixth; but, at all events, it was presumable that he would be ready to enter into action before ten o'clock.

Notwithstanding the number of our bridges and the celerity of our passage, our right and centre did not reach Rasdorf before three o'clock in the afternoon. This delay was due to the error in logistics, already mentioned, making the corps of Davoust and Oudinot cross in their march. We thus lost the favorable opportunity of giving battle to the half of the archduke's army on the fifth. Nevertheless, by six o'clock in the evening, our line was formed and the reserves in position, Massena forming the left between Breitenlée and the Danube, Bernadotte opposite Aderklaa, Eugene between Wagram and Baumersdorf, Oudinot between this village and Groshoffen, and Davoust on the right toward Glinzendorf, flanked by Grouchy with his division of dragoons. The guard, Marmont's corps, Wrede with ten thousand Bavarians, and the heavy cavalry, formed the reserve near Raasdorf.

The Austrians had placed their left, composed of Rosenberg and Hohenzollern, on the plateau between Neuseidel and Wagram, and along the Russbach, a deep rivulet, very muddy and difficult to cross, except by bridges; the centre, formed of the corps of Bellegarde and the grenadiers, was around Wagram; and the right, composed of Klenau and Kolowrath, was near the Bisemberg. The left formed an obtuse and reëntering angle with the rest of the line, which extended from Wagram by Gerasdorf to the base of the Bisemberg.

Preliminary Attack of the French. — As no forces were left to oppose the approach of the Archduke John, it was natural to suppose that he would arrive the next morning in time to take part in the battle. I now had five *corps-d'armée* opposite the Russbach and the plateau which overlooked the surrounding country; it was, therefore, important to profit by the present occasion. Notwithstanding the advanced hour of the day, I ordered an attack on this decisive position. The time required for the transmission of the orders, and the greater or less skill of the chiefs in executing them, made the attack somewhat disconnected. Oudinot did not succeed in forcing the passage of Baumersdorf, which General Hardegg bravely defended. Eugene debouched near Wagram; but being in the midst of the enemy's reserves, and without the support of Bernadotte, who was neither sufficiently prompt nor decisive in coming into action, the viceroy was attacked in front and flank, and driven back upon my guard. Notwithstanding all the efforts of Eugene, Lamarque, and Dupas, Bernadotte was also unable to maintain his position toward Wagram, and retired on Aderklaa, which place he also abandoned afterward. Davoust had not had time to enter seriously into action toward Neusiedel. The involuntary delay of the archduke in meeting us, had thus turned against us in the operations of this day; and it now became necessary for us to begin again on the following morning, with chances less favorable, inasmuch as the enemy might then be reënforced by fifty thousand additional men.

Battle of Wagram, July 6th.—The dispositions of both parties were completed during the night. I gave orders to my forces to concentrate more in mass; Massena was to close up toward Aderklaa, and Davoust toward Groshoffen. By this means I would have them ready to strike in whatever direction it might be necessary.

The archduke, on his side, resolved to make an offensive movement. Bellegarde, at the centre, was to occupy Aderklaa; Rosenberg was to debouch on Glinzendorf, to facilitate the junction of the Archduke John by Leopoldsdorf; Kolowrath and the reserves, descending from the Bisemberg, were to unite with Klenau, and push our left so as to force it back on the bridges to Lobau. This order was given at midnight, and did not reach all the corps at the same time. Rosenberg began the combat by marching on Gliuzendorf; this movement astonished me; Davoust attacked this corps in front, while I moved to the right, with the guard and the division of cuirassiers of the Duke of Padua and Nansouty. Rosenberg was driven behind the Russbach with loss. In the mean time, Bellegarde has occupied Aderklaa in force.

I profit by the concentration of Massena's troops to throw them on this village, before the arrival of the Austrian right, which has to descend from the Bisemberg. The hero of Aspern, who had fallen from his horse the night before, is obliged to ride in a calash in this battle, where he is to gather new laurels. Massena follows his column, which he can no longer lead in person, in the attack on the village; Aderklaa is carried; but, instead of occupying it in force, the head of the column debouches in front. Bernadotte advances to its right to assist it with Dupas and the Saxons. At this moment the right of the Austrians is seen toward Sussenbrun, and draws half of Massena's forces in that direction; while the archduke himself advances with his grenadiers on Aderklaa, and drives out Cara St.-Cyr, who falls back on the immovable Molitor. The Saxons are also forced to retreat.

The right wing of the Austrians fifty thousand strong, under Kolowrath and Klenau, continues to advance on Breitenlée and Hirchtetten. Massena has not a moment to lose to form in its front and cut off its access to Lobau. He flies along the road to Aspern, and encounters the enemy near Neuwirtshaus; he continues his flank march, notwithstanding several charges of the enemy. The fourth division, under Boudet, which had arrived at Aspern in the morning, debouches from that place; it receives the shock of the entire corps of Klenau; its right which is without support, is forced, and its artillery captured; it is compelled to fall back within the *tête-du-pont*. The enemy push forward to Essling, and reöccupies his intrenchments.

The theatre of the principal scene is thus completely changed; my masses had prepared to carry the position of the Russbach, right in front; now the main body of the enemy's forces is established crotchetwise on my extreme left, perpendicularly to the Danube, and menacing our bridges. This attack on one extremity, which furnishes to General

Pelet the singular idea of comparing this battle with that of Lutzen, from which it differs in almost every respect, is a manœuvre in war always skillful when it is directed on that extremity which is most advantageous and certain for the assailant. But such was not the case here : if it can not be doubted that it was very advantageous for the Austrians to direct their principal effort on the extremity near which lay our line of retreat, it must, nevertheless, be confessed that it is always very dangerous to make such a movement by gliding between a river like the Danube, and an army of one hundred and forty thousand men, brave and warlike ; under such circumstances the thing is not even practicable. Leaving Massena to hold this wing in check, without, however, engaging himself too far against unequal forces, I hastened to the centre where the troops which had assisted Davoust had just returned.

I had now but one of two courses to pursue ; the first, to join Davoust with my reserves and the corps of Oudinot, and attack the extremity of the enemy opposite the Danube, in order to crush it, and take the place which the army of the archduke had occupied in the morning, leaving the enemy to try his fortune on the Danube, over which I would have destroyed the bridges ; the second, to throw myself on the centre with the forces of Eugene, Bernadotte, Marmont, and Oudinot. The first plan was entirely the best ; but it would require the delay of an hour, during which the success of the enemy might become too dangerous. I, therefore, determined to adopt the second.

Eugene, who had marched between Wagram and Baumersdorf, was to change direction to the left and take the place where Massena had fought ; Marmont and the Bavarians were to follow. To give time to execute these dispositions, I ordered a charge of the cavalry of Bessières ; it advanced bravely, and its first charge was most successful ; but Bessières being injured by the fall of his horse, which was killed under him, the movement of the column was indecisive; Walther succeeds to the command, but does not know the object of the charge. This incident cools the attack and prevents its success; but it has suspended for an instant the progress of Kolowrath, who, however, soon resumes his march. It now becomes a matter of the highest interest for me to gain time to complete the movement which I directed the centre to make, in order to defend the ground left by our left wing; this care is confined to the brave Drouot, who advances in rear of our cavalry with sixty pieces of reserve, and is soon left alone in front of the line, with his formidable battery. He unmasks his pieces and pours into the enemy a shower of grape and ball, thus giving a prelude to the great blow which my centre is preparing to strike.

In the mean time, Davoust has received orders to attack and drive back the enemy's left. For this purpose, Friant and Morand pass the Russbach above Glinzendorf, and debouch between Siebenbrun and Murgraf-Neusiedel. Davoust attacks this village with the other two divisions; Oudinot has orders to limit himself to checking Hohenzollern toward Baumersdorf. Rosenberg is turned and forced back forming an angle with the right in rear. Davoust, Friant, and Morand seek to carry, by a vigorous blow, the tower of Neusiedel at the summit of the salient formed by the enemy's left. Here the most terrible combat is waged; the Austrians make every effort to prevent the debouch of Davoust; their bravest men, the emigrant Nordmann and the Hungarian Veczay, fall pierced with our bayonets. Rosenberg sends for assistance to Hohenzollern, who dispatches a part of his own corps to his aid.

At the same moment, Oudinot, impelled by military ardor and wearied with inaction while surrounded by the deadly fire of the enemy, determined to carry the passes of the

Russbach and ascend the plateau. His first brigades are driven back; he puts himself at the head of the third and carries every thing before him. Rosenberg, warmly pressed by Davoust, turned by Montbrun and Morand, and threatened in reverse by Oudinot, retreats in disorder on the road to Bockflies, not being able to form a junction with Hohenzollern. The firing is now heard to extend beyond Neusiedel; this is to me the pledge of victory. I immediately direct Massena to resume the offensive, and make all my arrangements for striking the decisive blow.

By means of these several attacks and the devotion of our artillerists, Eugene has been able to complete his movement. I now immediately form a formidable mass, placing Macdonald at its head; eight battalions are deployed, and thirteen others formed in close column on their two wings; in rear of these march the troops of Wrede and Serras; the light cavalry and cuirassiers of Nansouty are to cover the flanks; Durutte is to assist them on the left, and Pacthod on the right between Aderklaa and Wagram; Marmont and the Saxons are to sustain the army of Italy, a little to the right toward Wagram.

This formidable mass, deeper than that of Lannes at Essling, overthrows every thing that opposes its passage; it leaves Aderklaa on the right, and precipitates itself on the point of junction between the corps of the grenadiers and that of Kolowrath, to the right of the steeple of Sussenbrunn. The archduke is here in person. Bravery, *coup-d'œil*, activity, nothing is wanting to parry the menacing blow; but his efforts are of no avail. Notwithstanding the loss he sustains, Macdonald drives every thing before him as far as Sussenbrunn; but, attacked in front and flank by the grenadiers and Kolowrath, and his forces reduced to two or three thousand men, he is compelled to halt. I foresee this difficulty and direct the cavalry of Nansouty, to charge in order to disengage the column ; at the same time Durutte's division advances to the left and Pacthod to the right to second it ; the Bavarians and Serras, also enter into the line in their turn, and I advance the young guard to replace them as a reserve. Marmont and the Saxons charge at the same time on the corps of Bellegarde. Every thing yields to this vigorous effort ; Macdonald and the corps that follow him resume the impulse of victory, and drive the enemy beyond Gerasdorf. In the meantime Davoust and Oudinot, have continued their offensive march beyond the Russbach ; the latter, master of Baumersdorf and the plateau, throws himself on Wagram, and thus, by threatening Bellegarde in reverse, favors the operation of Marmont and Bernadotte. The impulse is felt simultaneously along the entire line. Davoust, however, is drawn on by the diverging retreat of Rosenberg and Hohenzollern ; a part of his corps pursues the former northward, while the remainder sustains Oudinot's attack toward Wagram ; it had been better if the entire corps had been directed on Wolkersdorf.

Massena, on his side, has reached Essling, and now carries the works of this place, in order to effect his junction with Boudet. At the same time, learning, from the progress of Macdonald's cannon, our success at the centre, he deems the favorable moment to have arrived for taking the offensive in his turn ;—he makes a vigorous attack on Klenau, and drives him back as far as Leopoldau ; preceded by the cavalry of Lasalle, he pursues with ardor. The Austrians, formed in squares in the plain, face about for a moment ; Lasalle charges them with vigor, but falls by a ball which struck him in the forehead ; the enemy, however, is pierced and pursued even to the base of the Bisemberg.

Defeat of the Austrians.—For the last two hours the archduke had seen the necessity of a retreat, and had given orders accordingly. Instead of being reënforced on the left by the Archduke John, he saw that wing overthrown by Davoust and Oudinot, and his centre pressed down by an irresistible mass; success was no longer possible, and by persisting in maintaining his position, he might endanger the two *corps-d'armée* engaged between the Russbach and the Danube; he, therefore, preferred to fall back in good order, and preserve his army in a condition to exert an important influence in the subsequent negotiations for peace. He had no motives for desperate acts, risking everything on the result of a single contest. In fact, the Archduke John, at four o'clock in the afternoon, was not within less than three or four leagues of the field of battle, and could take no important part in it. The couriers of his van-guard appeared at this moment in the direction of Leopoldsdorf, and skirmished with the flankers of our cavalry; some of the latter were wounded, and fell back spreading the most singular panic through our ranks. We had just established our bivouacs, the guards and reserves being near Raasdorf, when a general cry was heard from the right that the enemy had turned our flank and threatened the bridges. In an instant the equipages, wounded, and scattered troops take the road to Lobau; the alarm spreads from rank to rank, till, for a moment, the conquerors doubt their own victory. The cause of the panic is soon discovered, giving rise to jokes on the military courtiers who had judged of our operations from the middle of the park of equipages!

The archduke effected his retreat during the night, leaving me no other trophies than his dismounted artillery and some thousands of wounded and prisoners. His loss amounted to about twenty-five thousand men, and twelve generals, *hors-de-combat*. Our loss was nearly as great. The necessity of sending a part of our cavalry to the right prevented me from pushing vigorously the enemy that night. The Archduke Charles retired on Bohemia on the road to Znaim.

Rosenberg, being separated from him, took the road to Moravia. The emperor of Austria, who had remained at Wolkersdorf during the battle, on learning the defeat of Rosenberg and the approach of Davoust in pursuit, first retired to Znaim, and then departed for Hungary.

The army of Italy had covered itself with glory; on visiting it, I embraced Macdonald, who had here crowned the fame he had already won at Hooglède and Trebia, and I saluted him with the title of Marshal. The same rank was also conferred on Marmont and Oudinot.*

Remarks on the Battle.—In selecting his field of battle on the Russbach, to the north of Vienna, the archduke had three lines of retreat from which to choose; the first, to his right on Bohemia; the second, at the centre on Olmutz; and the third, at the left on Hungary. The first had the advantage of maintaining the Austrians in communication

---

* Thiers says: "Marshal Bernadotte, who, through his own fault or that of his corps, had been unable to keep the post assigned to him between Wagram and Aderklaa, nevertheless published an order of the day, addressed to the Saxons, in which he thanked them for their conduct on the fifth and sixth of July, and attributed to them, as it were, the winning of the battle. This manner of distributing to himself and his soldiers praises which he ought to have waited to receive from Napoleon, greatly offended the latter, because it offended the army and its leaders. To punish it, Napoleon wrote a most severe order of the day, which was communicated to the marshals only, but which was a sufficient reprimand for such an extravagance of vanity; for, being addressed to rivals, it was not probable that it would remain secret."

The following is a copy of this order: "His imperial majesty expresses his disapprobation of marshal the prince of Ponte Corvo's order, which was inserted in the public journals of the seventh of July. As his majesty commands in person, to him belongs the exclusive right of assigning to all their respective degrees of glory. His majesty owes the success of his arms to *French* troops, and not to others. The prince of Ponte Corvo's order of the day, tending to give false pretensions to troops of secondary merit, is contrary to truth, to discipline, and to national honor. To Marshal Macdonald belongs the praise which the prince of Ponte Corvo arrogates to himself. His majesty desires that this testimony of his displeasure may operate as a caution to every marshal not to attribute to himself more glory than is due to him. That the Saxon army, however, may not be afflicted, his majesty desires that this order may be kept secret."

with the north of Germany, where they flattered themselves that the appearance of the English would finally induce Prussia and Westphalia to declare in their favor. In taking this route, they would base themselves on Prague, the city, next after Vienna, the most important in the empire for its military establishments and resources; but it would expose the army to be cut off from the heart of the monarchy by a simple movement against its left, and be thus thrown back between the Elbe and the Rhine, where it would experience the same fate as the Prussians after the battle of Jena. The line of Olmutz was no less dangerous, without, however, offering the same advantages; by eight days of retrograde march, the imperial army would be thrown beyond its limits on Silesia and the lower Oder. The retreat on Hungary led to their natural base at the centre of the resources of the monarchy; it would secure a more vast theatre of operations, and if the army, by a new campaign, should find itself forced within the confines of Podolia, it would not be impossible for it to rally, by a lateral movement, on Olmutz or Prague, as a last refuge. In the situation of affairs left by the battle of Essling, Austria still hoping to act on the offensive, it seemed that the base on Bohemia, though more hazardous, was conformable to the political and strategic interests of the movement; but, when the great battle had been fought and lost, then this base became dangerous for a defeated army, and the archduke should not have manœuvred in such a manner as to be exposed to be driven back upon it in spite of himself. The error which he committed in directing his efforts to the right on the Danube, and allowing his left to be forced, was calculated to throw him back on Bohemia, whether he wished or not. Undoubtedly, it would still have been possible for him to gain the road to Nicolsburg, and afterward that of Goding, so as to throw himself into Hungary; but this would have been acting on the circumference of a

VOL. I:I.—8

circle, of which we held the chord ; and, even admitting that it had succeeded, we should still have confined the army in the gorges of the Krapacs, cutting it off from the centre of the kingdom ; this would have rendered its destruction none the less probable. If the archduke had had superior forces, so as to guard the Russbach sufficiently, and still be able to turn our left by Breitenlée and Aspern, it would have been well to attempt it ; but, on the contrary hypothesis, it would have been trusting too much to chance, and have given us the strategic and tactical key of the field, which was at Nieusiedel. It was this circumstance which dictated all my combinations, as soon as I perceived the situation of the enemy's forces. Some have thought that I would have acted more in accordance with the principles of the art, if I had directed my efforts between Aderklaa and the Russbach, or on Baumersdorf, after Davoust had got a footing beyond the Russbach. This would, in fact, have been a repetition of the manœuvre of Frederick at Leuthen ;—it would have been directing the decisive effort on the most important extremity, supporting it successively and obliquely by the whole line, without troubling myself about the operations of Klenau and Kolowrath. I might have pursued this plan, if I had had the field free around me ; but having the Danube in my rear, and my bridges to preserve in case of defeat, I preferred a manœuvre less brilliant, but more certain.

Retreat of the Archduke and Pursuit of the French.— The archduke, having retired with his forces, at the end of the battle, between Wolkersdorf and the Bisemberg, could still take either the road to Moravia, or to Bohemia, as he might choose. The first, however, was somewhat menaced by the cannon of Davoust, Marmont, and Oudinot, who were encamped between Wagram and Bockflies ; and it would have been rather difficult for the troops to reach it from the Bisemberg by a lateral movement, without running the risk of being anticipated on Nicolsburg. The main body of the army took the road to Znaim; Rosenberg alone continued his retreat on the road to Brunn.

By daylight, on the morning of the seventh, the rearguard of the enemy was seen on these two roads. From the contradictory reports which I received, I was uncertain which had been taken by the main body; it was possible that the army had been divided in order to gain time, but I had reason to think that the archduke would seek to gain Hungary by Nicolsburg, rather than to throw himself eccentrically on Bohemia. Davoust received orders to march on Nicolsburg; Marmont, reënforced by the Bavarians, first took the same road, but afterward turned aside on Laas; Massena took the road to Bohemia by Hollabrunn. I marched to Wolkersdorf with my reserve and Oudinot. Eugene, whose army had suffered severely, was destined to observe the Archduke John and Hungary, covering Vienna, our bridges and our line of communication. I reënforced him with the Saxons, the Wurtembergers, and a Bavarian division. These precautions were the more necessary, as, on the very day of the battle, General Chasteler and Giulay, who had united their forces, after the evacuation of the Tyrol, reëntered Gratz and Leoben, driving out the little corps of Rusca on Rottenmann; while the Archduke John, hearing the result of the battle, had repassed the Morava and halted at Marschek.

Battle of Znaim.—Massena, continuing to drive before him the main body of the army of the archduke on the road to Znaim, sustained several important combats; especially at Hallobrunn and Schongraben, where the Austrian troops of the prince of Reuss, who had not previously been engaged, fought with great bravery. The march of Marmont on Laas, threatened to precede the archduke to Znaim, and hastened his retrograde movement to that position.

This city, situated in amphitheatre on the slope of a spur of the Bohemian chain which commands all the environs, while the hillocks in rear are covered with vineyards, may be compared in its position with Caldiero. I did not learn till the tenth, at Wolkersdorf, the direction taken by the main body of the enemy. I immediately descended on Znaim, directing Oudinot, the guard, and Davoust, to repair to the same place. Marmont had advanced as far as Thesswitz, almost in the middle of the Austrian army, with Massena, however, only a day's march behind, hotly pressing the enemy's rear-guard. The archduke, thinking that Marmont was better sustained, did not venture to attack him. Arriving here in person and having examined the state of affairs, I now directed an attack to be made by our vanguards, in order to gain time for the remainder of my forces to come up.

The impetuous Massena was already hotly engaged, and it was necessary to sustain him. I then directed Marmont to debouch from Thesswitz, ascend to the plateau, and relieve the fourth corps which was alone exposed to the enemy's attacks. Davoust, coming from Nicolsburg, and Oudinot and the reserve, from Wolkersdorf, could not arrive in time to enter into action before the next day, and it was, therefore, important for me to conceal from the enemy our present inferiority of numbers; it was, nevertheless, necessary to keep him in the vicinity of Znaim, so that, on the arrival of Davoust and the cavalry, I might cut him off by Brenditz from the road to Prague.

Armistice.—The emperor of Austria had sent to me the prince of Lichtenstein to propose an armistice. Under present circumstances nothing could be more agreeable to me than a cessation of hostilities; every moment gained was now a decided advantage to me, and if the suspension led to peace I should be delighted. It was with difficulty that the firing could be stopped, for so fiercely were the troops engaged on both sides that several officers were wounded in their endeavors to suspend the combat. The armistice was discussed during the night ; my officers thought I now ought to complete the overthrow of a power like Austria, which was incessantly interfering with all our enterprises, and which was too lacerated ever to forgive the quadruple humiliation to which we had subjected her arms. Taking into consideration the uncertain state of Germany, the unfavorable news from Spain, and the serious preparations of the English, I was influenced by great national and political interests, rather than by the military opinions of these brave generals, who could not, however, then fully comprehend the crisis of my affairs. I, therefore, broke off the discussion, saying, *there has been enough blood shed ; I accept the armistice.*

Its Conditions.—The negotiator was the same who had terminated the war of 1805 ; we soon came to an agreement on the conditions, the line of demarcation accorded to us the occupation of the Circles of Znaim and Brunn ; it followed the course of the Morava to the confluence of the Taya ; thence along the road to Presburg, including that city ; the great Danube as far as Raab, then the river of that name, and the frontiers of Styria and Carniola as far as Fiume. The citadels of Gratz and Brunn, the fort of Saxenbourg, the Tyrol and the Voralberg were surrendered to us. The armies of Poland were to retain their respective positions.

The limit on the north of Germany was the line of the Confederation of the Rhine. The surrender of Fiume completed the isolation of the Austrians from England, so that British subsidies, arms, and agents could no longer reach the former power, except clandestinely ; we occupied with our troops a third of the Austrian monarchy, being thus in position to support war by war, and to supply the wants caused by the campaign in the several branches of service, especially in transportation, clothing, and equipments.

Austrian Motives for ratifying the Armistice.—Nevertheless, this armistice was far from being a sure guarantee of peace. The Emperor Francis was hardly disposed to subscribe to all the sacrifices which I was in condition to impose; he therefore made some difficulties in ratifying the armistice. They proposed a new system of operations by reënforcing the Archduke John with the corps of Chasteler and Giulay, who, since the departure of Marmont had occupied Gratz and Leoben, and by taking advantage of my march on Moravia to act on my communications, and advance on Vienna. The news, however, of my return to Schonbrunn, the march of Macdonald on Gratz, and still more the description of the situation of my affairs in Moravia, presented to him by the Prince of Lichtenstein, finally induced him to ratify the armistice on the eighteenth. This, however, was done, less through pacific views, than for the purpose of gaining time for a general movement of his armies. The court and diplomatic head-quarters were at Comorn; the Archduke John was called there for consultation. He advised renouncing the idea of basing themselves on Prague, so as not to lose their communications with Hungary and expose themselves to be thrown between the Elbe and the Rhine, but restore the theatre of the war to its true base in Hungary, making the grand army march by Hradisch on Comorn; the Archduke John was to operate to the left, with fifty thousand men on Raab; while the corps of Croatia was to turn back so as to act more vigorously with the Austrian detachments, which had recently had some success in gaining possession of Laybach and Zara, and menacing Trieste. The Hungarian insurrection (militia levies) would form the connecting link between these two armies. The Archduke Charles, being forced to retire in disgrace, was to resign the command to the emperor himself. This little politico-military revolution, which was attributed to Stadion, and was the result of strategic views more prudent than a retreat on Prague, instead of an obstacle to the armistice, rendered its ratification the more necessary for the execution of the projected movement.

Operations in the North of Europe.—This armistice put an end to the operations in Poland, where Poniatowski had just seized on Cracovia, and was preparing to connect himself with my right in Moravia by continuing to manœuvre in that direction. The Archduke Ferdinand regained the frontier of Hungary. The Russians occupied Galicia, and extended themselves even to the sources of the Vistula.

The cessation of hostilities was the more timely for us in the north of Germany, where the Austrians had recently gained some success, and where the English had made a small debarcation. My brother Jerome had collected a corps of ten thousand men to drive the enemy from Dresden, by acting in concert with the few Saxons still remaining under the orders of General Thielmann. On the other side, Junot was coming for the same purpose from Franconia; they were to effect a junction in Voigtland. The archduke had sent General Keinmayer into Saxony to give form and object to the insurrectionary operations which were attempted in that country. This general, uniting with the duke of Brunswick and the division of Amende, and acting in concert with the corps of Radvojewich, sought to prevent the junction of Junot and the king of Westphalia. He encountered the former near Gefrées on the ninth of July, and drove him back on Barcith. Jerome fell back on Schleitz, and, on hearing the victory of Wagram, and the descent of the English, decided to rally his corps on Erfurth. The Austrians, having entered Dresden on the twenty-first, refused to evacuate the place, under the pretense that the armistice was applicable only to the grand army. It required hostile demonstrations to induce them to return to Bohemia.

These events left the duke of Brunswick-Oels in a false position on the frontiers of Bohemia, with his legion of adventurers in British pay ; but, worthy heir of his name, he took the resolution of joining the English, who finally effected a small debarcation on the North Sea. Expelled from these countries for the last three years, the English had still maintained a clandestine intercourse with the Hanseatic towns, whose whole existence depended on their maritime relations. Masters of the rock of Heligoland, they had transformed this arid island into a vast depôt of colonial wares and all kinds of arms. It was at the same time an arsenal and a vast bazaar. The whole coast, from Amsterdam to the Sound, was full of English agents, who spread in all directions the news of the expected arrival of a considerable army. The agitation became general.

After having thus promised the expedition, which was now to descend at Antwerp, they finally sent two or three thousand men to debark on the coast from Cuxhaven to Bremerlée. Osnabruck and Hanover, in conformity to their promises, formed a partial insurrection. If ten thousand men had been landed a month sooner, the results might have been of the greatest importance.

The duke of Brunswick now decided to leave Freyberg, in order to join the English on the coast. This plan, although favored by the insurrectionary state of the country, and the proximity of Prussia, where the prince could have found a refuge for his own person if reduced to the last extremity, was bold, and executed with energy. At the head of three thousand desperate adventurers, he passed Leipsic and took the road to Halberstadt. He here found only a regiment of Westphalians under the grand marshal of Jerome's court, an ex-officer of the navy, and more brave than experienced.

After an honorable resistance, Meyronet was wounded and taken prisoner, and the remains of his regiment were incorporated into the ranks of the enemy. The main body of the Westphalian and Dutch troops were, at this time, observing the coast of the north. General Rewbel, on hearing of the defeat of Meyronet, marched in all haste from Bremen to Brunswick, with five thousand men. The Dutch general, Gratien, and the same Thielmann who played so important a part against us three years afterward, pursued the duke on Holberstadt. This prince reached the ancient capital of his father, on the first of August, at the very moment when Rewbel was approaching on the other side. Having no time for hesitation, he attacked this general, whose infantry immediately took to flight, and would, perhaps, have joined the insurgents, had not the enemy been arrested by the brilliant valor of the Westphalian cuirassiers and the regiments of Berg. Being unable to force a passage against such unexpected resistance, and having already had two horses killed under him, the prince returned to Brunswick; hearing here that the English had just left Cuxhaven, he threw himself into the country of Oldenbourg, reached Esfleth, embarked on the seventh of August with his few brave followers, and established himself at Heligoland, where he continued till 1813, to form projects for disturbing the tranquillity of the north of Germany.

Operations in the Tyrol.—Affairs in the Tyrol had taken a more serious turn. General Buol, whom Chasteler had left there with three or four thousand men, on learning the condititions of the armistice, thought to comply with them by returning into Styria. This news enraged the Tyrolese to the utmost extent; they threaten to oppose by force the departure of the Austrians, and to massacre all the French prisoners, so as to render a treaty of peace impossible. The Austrians succeeded, however, by a little address, in retiring within the line of demarcation laid down in the armistice, having first surrendered Sachsenbourg to the troops of Rusca. I directed Lefebvre, with the Bavarians and some French troops, to return on Innspruck; Rusca ascended the Drave; and a Franco-Italian division advanced by the Adige. The Tyrolese, instead of yielding, seemed to acquire new energy by the departure of the Austrians.

Lefebvre, after a decisive combat on the eleventh of August, was forced to retire into Bavaria; Rusca succeeded with difficulty in regaining the Corinthia, but the Tyrolese ventured to follow him even there; and the Franco-Italian division was driven back to the gates of Verona. I could not, at this moment, detach a force sufficiently numerous for the reduction of this country, for, notwithstanding the armistice, peace was far from being certain, and, instead of weakening my army, it was more important than ever to keep it in force. I, therefore, directed Rusca to negotiate with the insurgents, and propose to them to send a deputation to me to decide upon some plan for the future government of their country. He proposed to them, if they disliked the Bavarian rule, to unite with the kingdom of Italy, and even gave them some hope of establishing their absolute independence. They, however, rejected all his propositions.

Negotiations with Austria, and Preparations for a Renewal of Hostilities.—Negotiations were opened at Altenbourg, on the seventh of August, between MM. Champagny, Metternich, and Nugent. But they made very little progress. The court of Austria, which had now retired to Buda, was in no haste to terminate them, for the descent of the English on Belgium, the march of Wellington on Madrid, the success of the Tyrolese, and the new plan of operations which had been adopted, contrary to the advice of the Archduke Charles —all combined to raise the hopes of the cabinet of Vienna, which now pretended to regard the overtures of Champagny as excessively severe. If the English had consolidated their operations in Castile, and had been successful in their descents on our coast, there is no doubt that Austria intended to renew hostilities. She continued to recruit her armies, to incite Prussia to declare against us, and to multiply her projects of future operations.

I employed these moments of respite in my usual way, of working with still greater ardor than during the war itself. It was at this time that, wholly influenced by my love for the brave men whom I commanded, I instituted the order of the Trois-Toisons (Three-Fleeces). I thought to eclipse the Golden-Fleeces of Spain and Austria, and all other orders of modern chivalry, by conferring this decoration on those only who had assisted at my three entries into Vienna, Berlin and Madrid. My object was to consecrate the recollection of these great events; but the project would have been attended with injustice, inasmuch as some of the most valiant of my generals would have been excluded from this order. The decree was, therefore, never carried into execution. I also at this time directed my attention particularly to administrative matters for supplying the wants of my armies and regulating the affairs of my empire. I imposed on Austria a contribution of one hundred millions of francs, to be collected into the public chests from the ordinary revenues of the countries which we occupied.

I prepared the fortifications of Vienna, the *tête-du-pont* of Spitz, Raab, and Gratz, so as to prolong the defenses of these places if necessary, or to demolish the works in case we had to evacuate them.

I very much increased my bridge equipage, so as to act on the lower Danube and in Hungary, and organized a considerable flotilla to facilitate our transports, and protect our operations on the banks of the river.

The reserves of conscripts, the provisional regiments, and

the contingents of the Confederation, were sent to the north to reënforce the eighth *corps-d'armée* under Junot, whose forces already numbered near thirty thousand men, exclusive of the Westphalians, who constituted the tenth *corps-d'armée*. My own army was also augmented at this time by some thirty thousand men, who were discharged from the hospitals, and more than six thousand from the depôts.

Austria, in the meantime, had not neglected her levies;— a large number of *landwehrs* (militia) had been organized and united with the troops of the line. Taking advantage of the present position of affairs, she now decided that the propositions of Champagny were inadmissible. The emperor, Francis I., wrote a letter to me, by Count Bubna, declaring that the proposed conditions of peace would dishonor his throne and destroy his monarchy. I directed the duke of Bassano to confer with his envoy, in hopes that they might come to a better understanding than the negotiators of Altenbourg.

I had proposed to the Emperor Alexander of Russia, to send a minister to take part in these negotiations. He declined the offer, but gave his assent to whatever I should do, recommending me, however, to not deal too harshly with his ancient ally. There was much tact and address in this refusal, for Russia did not wish to see Austria too much humbled, nor to assist in her dismemberment. This course was the result of good political policy; some writers, however, have mistaken its motives, and attributed it to a project on the part of Russia to ultimately abandon my alliance.

I now received the news of the failure of the English expedition against Antwerp and their consequent retreat. This was certainly no reason why I should abate my pretensions with Austria; I, therefore, replied to the emperor, on the fifteenth of September, demanding the cession of a million and a half of inhabitants on the Inn and in Illyria, to reënforce the kingdom of Italy and give a suitable frontier to Bavaria. I also required New Galicia for the Duchy of Warsaw.

Maritime Expeditions of the English.—The maritime expeditions of the English were so intimately connected with what was, at this time, passing in Austria, as to justify a brief account of them in this place.

England had done but little more, on this occasion, in favor of her continental allies, than she had done in 1807 for the war in Poland. In fact, the cabinet of London, seeing that this war would occupy us at the same time in Austria and Spain, and oblige us to scatter our forces from the Tagus to the Danube, made immense preparations to profit by the circumstance; but it directed its views especially to enterprises calculated to advance its own private interests. If this power had not attempted so many things at the same time, it might have produced more important results; but, seeking to act merely in a capacity of an auxiliary, carrying on its operations on the territory of its allies, it thought to embarrass us the more by multiplying the number of its expeditions. The danger with which she was threatened by the league of Tilsit, had induced England to put forth all her resources, and to augment her troops by every means in her power. She was able to send abroad one hundred thousand men; and a thousand millions of money were employed in preparing immense amounts of provisions, artillery, arms, and military munitions, for numerous projected maritime descents. She spared neither gold nor iron, and the progress of the mechanical arts, acting as an auxiliary to the manual power of her artisans, had transformed England into a vast workshop. Such forces, if well directed and assisted by the armed inhabitants of Spain, Portugal, Holland, and all the north of Germany, were well calculated to effect a powerful diversion in favor of Austria.

Our colonies, and those of our allies, were not at this time sufficiently valuable for England even to deign to covet them. She could no longer desire to possess either Cuba or Spanish America, for both were now her allies. Cayenne, Martinique, Senegal, and St. Domingo, had all fallen, and the Isle-of-France, being blockaded, would also, sooner or later, be compelled to surrender. The British East India Company were preparing an expedition against Amboyne and Batavia, places which the Dutch were no longer in condition to sustain, since they had lost Ceylon and the Cape of Good Hope. The garrisons of the Antilles were alone sufficient for the capture of the few ports which we still possessed there. These colonial interests, which, in 1783, had been matters of such high importance, were now so completely eclipsed by the mighty continental conflicts, that England employed in them only a few secondary detachments, and engaged in them merely as a pastime.

The increase which she had now given to her land forces enabled her to plan more extensive enterprises; to carry on war in the Spanish Peninsula, and, at the same time, to act offensively on the banks of the Scheldt. By the month of April, an immense armament was ready to act on the first favorable opportunity. Wellesley, who had returned from Portugal after the affair of Vimiera, was sent back to the Peninsula with a corps of twenty thousand men, to take the command of the English divisions and revenge the defeat of General Moore. Another expedition under Gambier and Lord Cochrane, about the middle of April, attempted to burn our Rochefort squadron, which, reënforced by a detachment from Brest, lay at the anchorage in the roads of the Isle-of-Aix. An infernal machine of fifteen hundred barrels of powder and four hundred shells, directed by Cochrane himself, exploded without producing the slightest effect. They then made an attack on the squadron, throwing Congreve rockets into it. This was the first time these projectiles were ever used against us. Four fine vessels were burnt while laying at anchor, but the others, having more skillful commanders, escaped into Charente. Gambier was subjected to a court of inquiry for not having destroyed our entire squadron, and the ship-yard of Rochefort ; and, with much more justice, I had our officers tried for having lost their vessels.

About the middle of June, twenty thousand Anglo-Sicilians, under General Stuart and Prince Leopold, appeared off the coast of Calabria near the rock of Scylla, whose castle was taken and again lost. A detachment of this army was sent to take possession of the little Ionian Islands, and to cruise before Corfu. Stuart hoped, as in 1805, to surprise some point of the coast, and land a body of men to form a nucleus for the insurgents. He took possession of the islands of Ischia and Procida, and showed himself with great ostentation before Naples, and other points of the coast. But the inhabitants every where manifested their attachment to a government which had destroyed the abuses of its predecessors, and driven out the brigands who had previously infested this beautiful country. Murat was well suited to the Neapolitans, who on this occasion proved their devotion to his throne. Stuart returned to Sicily without venturing to land his troops.

A more serious enterprise was fitted out against our superb establishment at Antwerp ; an immense fleet of thirty-nine ships of the line, and thirty-six frigates, with smaller vessels and gunboats, and transports carrying a land force of forty thousand men, was sent to take possession of this place, burn our fleet, destroy our ship-yards and docks, and then fill up the channel of the Scheldt so as to render it impassable. The importance which England attached to this expedition, is the best possible proof of the wisdom of my project of rendering this the first port in Europe. The English, however, before risking themselves on French soil, waited to learn the result of the first operations of the campaign on the Danube. Some, however, attribute this delay to a want of unanimity in the English ministry in the choice of a commandant, Wellington being then engaged in the Peninsular War. At last, on hearing the news of the battle of Wagram, they deemed it high time to act; and, on the first of August, the fleet of Admiral Strachan landed Lord Chatham's army on the island of Walcheren. The heir of this great name, the elder brother of Pitt, proved that generations succeed, without resembling each other. He committed innumerable faults in the execution of this enterprise, which, if well conducted, would infallibly have reached Antwerp. The most convenient route for reaching this place from the coast, is the road leading from Blakenberg by Bruges and Ghent; it is paved for the distance of twenty-four leagues. The coast at this time was so entirely stripped of all means of defense, that there was not the slightest obstacle to prevent the landing at this point of thirty thousand men, who could have reached Antwerp on the third day with the whole train of artillery with which they were most amply provided. The remainder of the army and fleet might have entered the Scheldt so as to fix our attention on Flushing and the island of Cassand. Our fleet, taken unawares, would have found retreat impossible. Antwerp was almost completely destitute of a garrison;* and the capture even of the fort, called the Tête-de-Flandre, on the opposite bank of the Scheldt, would have secured the success of the enterprise.

Chatham took the bull by the horns; fearing to compromise himself on the main shore, he manœuvred with his right before Breskens and the island of Cassand, which he

---

* The garrison of this place consisted, at first, of only about two hundred invalids and recruits.

did not venture to attack, and, on the thirtieth of July, landed his forces on the north side of the island of Walcheren, and laid siege to the city of Flushing. One of his divisions afterward captured Goes in the island of South Beveland, and, favored by the bad conduct of a Dutch general, succeeded in capturing Fort Batz,* which is situated on the point where the Scheldt is divided into two arms. This was a serious loss, but not sufficient to decide the result of the enterprise, so long as we retained possession of Forts Lillo, Frederick Henry, Leifenshoeck, and the Tête-de-Flandre, which are situated on the banks of the great Scheldt between Batz and Antwerp. General Rousseau, who had made such excellent dispositions at Cassand, now had time to throw, on the fourth of August, a reënforcement of two battalions into Flushing, which was commanded by General Monnet ; the English fleet had thought to cut off the communication between this place and Breskens.

The defenses of Flushing were ill constructed and in ill condition ; they consisted of a single enciente without any covered way. General Monnet, seeing the indefensible condition of the place, thought to retard the operations of the siege by strong sorties. But, notwithstanding the intrepidity of General Osten, these sorties against intrenched lines and well-armed batteries were vigorously repelled, and merely tended to discourage the garrison without producing any beneficial results. On the thirteenth of August the English opened a heavy bombardment, not only from their land batteries, but also from their flotilla of gunboats. There were no bomb-proof casemates for the protection of the troops, and the town was set on fire in numerous places. After three days of heavy bombardment, Monnet capitu-

---

* No defense whatever was made of this place, the commandant allowing himself to be surprised.

lated (the sixteenth), surrendering himself and four thousand men prisoners of war.

As no part of the body of the place had been breached in the slightest degree,* Monnet was afterward tried and condemned by a council of war.

If he could not remain exposed to such a fire he ought to have attempted to open a passage from the place, or to have insisted on a free sortie for his garrison. It is certain that he did not do all in his power to save his command, but still the sentence of the court was rigorous.†

In the meantime the condition of Antwerp had very much changed. The king of Holland, hearing of the approach of the enemy, had marched there in all haste with his guards and five thousand troops, who took post in the environs on the twelfth of August; and the commanding generals in Belgium and Picardy collected a force of seven or eight thousand men.

Our fleet had ascended the Scheldt, and taken refuge under the guns of the forts. These means were sufficient to defend the place for a considerable length of time, but not enough to protect it from danger. My ministers, seeing the full extent of the danger, not only sent to the Scheldt all

---

* Alison attributes the reduction of this place, in a considerable degree, to the fire of the shipping, and one or two recent writers of little authority, copying from him, have paraded this attack as a proof of the superiority of guns afloat over guns ashore. Nothing can be more absurd. An English officer, who was employed in the siege, says, he "went along the entire sea-line the very next day after the capitulation, and found no part of the parapet injured so as to be of the slightest consequence, and only one solitary gun dismounted, evidently by the bursting of a shell, and which could not, of course, have been thrown from the line-of-battle ships, but must have been thrown from the land batteries."—(Colonel Mitchel). This account of an eye-witness is fully confirmed by other historians; whereas, the statements of Alison are wholly without foundation.

† The surrender of this place was influenced by the sufferings of the inhabitants of the town, rather than to any want of efficiency in the garrison. Monnet acted from sympathy, rather than good judgment.

the men they could collect from the depôts of the north, but also ordered a levy of thirty thousand national guards from the neighboring departments ; this levy was extended even to Burgundy. France responded to this appeal with noble enthusiasm, the single Department du Nord alone sending ten thousand men ; and battalions were soon marshaling there from all direction. Marshal Moncey commanded a part of them ; and Bernadotte, who had left after the battle of Wagram, was appointed commander-in-chief, and reached his army on the sixteenth of August, the very day on which Flushing capitulated. Within six days he had under his command a force of thirty thousand men, and although these troops were not of a very military appearance, still they were full of zeal and ardor.

After having waited till the twenty-sixth of August, hesitating whether he should land on the right bank of the Scheldt and march on Antwerp, Chatham, seeing his blow parried, retook the road to England, leaving a third of his army at Flushing.

I had had cause to complain of the conduct of Bernadotte on the Danube, and was surprised at his nomination ; I, therefore, caused him to be replaced by Bessières. This officer repaired to the island of South Beveland, and surrounded Walcheren with batteries, so as to prevent any excursions of the enemy.

The damp climate and marshy grounds of Walcheren produced fevers, which, in the rains of autumn, became a real pestilence ; in a week's time, the sick list of the English numbered nearly ten thousand, exclusive of the sailors in the fleet, who were also subject to the contagion. The obstinacy of the English government in retaining a post so fatal to the lives of its soldiers, was due either to the intention of renewing the enterprise, if the war with Austria continued, or to a desire to draw that power into a rupture of the armistice, by holding out this proof of the determination of England to effect her long announced diversion in favor of her continental ally. But whatever was the object, it completely failed; for Austria decided to make peace, and England, after a useless sacrifice of her best troops in the hospitals of Flushing, finally ordered the evacuation of Walcheren. But before this evacuation took place, they destroyed all the works and naval basins at Flushing, with the establishments which had been made there for such heavy shipping as could not reach Antwerp, for want of sufficient depth of water in the port. The destruction of this arsenal was a misfortune, but we consoled ourselves with the preservation of the more important place of Antwerp.

Change in the British Ministry.—The results of this expedition, contrasting so strongly with its enormous preparations, the largest, indeed, that England had ever made, and the total loss of between eight and ten thousand men,* furnished abundant materials to the enemies of the ministry for opposition to their administration. This ministry had certainly exhibited sufficient hatred to me, sufficient activity in their attempts to injure me, and sufficient solicitude for extending the influence of England; but a great want of skill in the employment of its means. The very day on which this expedition landed at Flushing, and fifteen thousand English were exhibiting themselves on the coasts of Naples, the army of Wellington, previously victorious at Oporto and Talavera, was very near being enveloped on the Tagus, and forced to pass under the Caudine forks. The news of these several operations reached me during the nego-

---

* Toward the middle of September, one-half of the garrison of Flushing was in the hospitals, and the average number of deaths was from two to three hundred a week. The actual number of men lost in Belgium, was over seven thousand, and twelve thousand eight hundred and sixty-three of those who returned were reported sick, a large number of them afterward dying from the effects of the disease.

tiations with Austria. I did not in any respect change my dispositions; but I must confess that, for a moment, I feared the combined movements of Wellington on Madrid, and Chatham on Antwerp, might induce Austria to continue the war, and this circumstance, connected with the course pursued by the Emperor Alexander, contributed not a little to make me desire a peace. But I was soon relieved from this perplexity by the double retreat from Talavera and Flushing.

The ministry which had directed these enterprises, could not satisfy public opinion in England on the causes of their failure; Canning and Castlereagh imputed to each other the faults of these expeditions, and terminated their rivalry in a duel, which completed the dissolution of the cabinet. On the twenty-second of September, the marquis of Wellesley, brother of Wellington, succeeded Canning in the department of foreign affairs; Lord Liverpool replaced Castlereagh in the war office; Lord Chatham yielded the department of Ordnance to Lord Mulgrave, whose place in the Board of Admiralty was filled by the Duke of York; Percival took the post of first Lord of the Treasury and Chancelor of the Exchequer.

Stabs' attempt to assassinate Napoleon.—While my negotiators were disputing about the spoils of Austria, I remained at Schönbrunn, employed in my ordinary occupations of administration. Spain, Belgium, France, and our colonies, were all objects of my solicitude. I took relaxation from these occupations by daily parades in the court of the palace, and by *simulacra* of battles, executed by my guards in the plains of Penzing. But this kind of recreation was very near proving fatal to me. One of those fanatical Teutons, whom the scholastic exaltation of the universities had exasperated against me, entered the circle of my generals and presented himself before me. Unhabituated to the commission of crime, he hesitated, muttered some words, and retired; then returned a second time. Rapp, in repelling this German Brutus, perceived that he carried concealed arms, and caused him to be arrested. On his trial before a military commission, this visionary confessed his project, and paid with his life the penalty of his crime. He was a Saxon by birth, and his name was Stabs.

Austria concludes to make Peace.—The double negotiations between our plenipotentiaries at Altenbourg, and between Maret and Bubna, failed to reconcile Austria to the conditions which I prescribed. She continued to exaggerate her own resources and our embarrassments; but the news of the retreat of the English, and his failure to draw Prussia into the coalition, and, especially, the address with which the Duke of Bassano informed the Austrian envoy of the reënforcements which I had received, and which I still expected, finally decided the Emperor Francis, to yield to the force of necessity. Toward the end of September, Bubna took to the emperor Maret's *sine qua non*, and returned accompanied by the prince of Lichtenstein, who had signed the armistice of Austerlitz. This prince was one of the bravest officers of cavalry, and a good citizen, but a mediocre politician. He now, however, had but one course to pursue, for he was obliged to submit to my demands. Prince John signed, on the fourteenth of October, the treaty of Vienna, but not without complaining of the heavy sacrifices it imposed.

Treaty of Vienna.—This treaty, more harsh than any of the preceding, cost Austria more than three and a half millions of inhabitants. I gave to Bavaria Salzbourg, the Innviertal, with Braunau, and Hausruch, an important district of the sources of the Traun; this secured to that power a superb, and even offensive, frontier against Austria. I united, under the name of the Illyrian Provinces, a part of Carinthia, Carniola, Dalmatia, and Croatia, which formed a warlike population of a million and a half of inhabitants, and extended my frontiers to the Drave. These acquisitions, more important in their political and military influence than in the mere increase of population, changed the face of Europe; – they carried my eagles from the Noric Alps to within forty leagues of Vienna; the capital of Austria, dismantled by my orders, was now exposed to my phalanxes; in six days' march I could even take it in reverse, by debouching by Lake Platten and separating it from Hungary. The Austrian monarchy would be a mere satellite, revolving within the orbit of my empire; it lay entirely at my disposal. Nor was this the only advantage. I might eventually renew my plan of the partition of the Ottoman Empire; and, if so, the acquisition of these provinces, extending my limits to the confines of Greece and Bosnia, would be of immense advantage in the execution of that grand project. And, if circumstances should induce me to renounce the dismemberment of Turkey, I would nevertheless find, in the possession of Illyria, the means of building up our fine maritime establishments at Venice and Corfu. At any rate, by gaining possession of the coast countries, I would separate Austria from British influence, and force her to adopt the continental system. Thus had I, in four years, extended to the gates of Vienna and the shores of Greece the limits of France, to whom Pitt had contested the possession of Belgium. So far, all was well. But to these conditions I had added the cession of western Galicia to the duchy of Warsaw, contrary to the treaty of Tilsit. The secret articles of the treaty of Vienna stipulated for the reduction of the Austrian army to half its existing numbers; the discharge of all officers and soldiers belonging to the countries ceded to France and her allies; and, finally, the payment of eighty-five millions of francs.

Results of this Peace.—This peace, at first sight, secured far more advantages than that of Tilsit; but, if we consider the article of the treaty, which was calculated to offend Russia, and the family alliance which was afterward negotiated, it will not be doubted that it was less advantageous than it appeared. It was a question, however, which was decided in the negative at Moscow in 1812, and at Prague in 1813. It finally resulted in alienating both Austria and Russia, whereas, I ought to have attached to myself at least one of these powers. Already, as early as 1805, the famous Thugut, then in retirement at Presbourg, but still exercising a powerful influence over the mind of Francis I., had indirectly hinted on the reciprocal advantages to the two courts of renewing the relations of 1756, preceded by a family alliance. The treaty of Presbourg destroyed the effect of this vague proposal. But the Emperor Francis, in the letter which he wrote to me after the battle of Znaim, still spoke of the advantage of uniting the two powers. *Their happiest days*, said he, *were those when they were most intimately allied!* This was enough to convince me that it only depended on myself to renew this grand alliance; but to make it a durable one, I ought not to have begun by destroying and humiliating him whom I wished to make my friend. I ought rather to have acted the magnanimous, to have entered into the spirit of the overture of the Emperor Francis, proposing to him the alliance offensive and defensive of 1756, leaving to him his states, and, if I still determined to reënforce the duchy of Warsaw, and restore, some day, the kingdom of Poland, to secretly stipulate indemnities for Galicia. It will be said that this would have abruptly broken off the alliance of Tilsit, in order to form another less advantageous. Not so. A renewal of the alliance of 1756 with Austria would have been no violation of the treaty of Tilsit. To reconcile the two, I had only to renounce my project of restoring the kingdom of Poland. Moreover, if the cession of Galicia to the duchy of Warsaw had not already weakened the alliance of Tilsit, it would have been broken by my marriage, six months later.

Reception of the Treaty by Russia.—The secret articles of the treaty of Tilsit virtually forbid all aggrandizement of the duchy of Warsaw; and to give it, notwithstanding, near a million of inhabitants, was to announce to Russia that I purposed the restoration of Poland. I vainly flattered myself that I should be able to pacify Russia, by giving her the district of Tarnopol, and assuring her that I would not attempt the reëstablishment of Poland; but she distrusted my promises. The Emperor Alexander, therefore, on receiving the treaty of Vienna, sent for Caulaincourt, and said to him plainly, that he saw my intentions; that he would not become the aggressor, but would prepare himself for whatever might happen, and be ready in case he were attacked. I might very well have justified the course I had pursued by alleging the conduct of the Russians during the campaign. In reality, the Russians were individually dissatisfied with the peace of Tilsit, and especially with that article which created the duchy of Warsaw, for they dreaded the restoration of Poland as much as the loss of their own empire, and were ignorant of the secret article which forbade its reëstablishment. It was on this account that they were individually dissatisfied with the war, and ill-disposed to fight against the Austrians, and provoke the insurrection and emancipation of Galicia, seeing that this event might operate against themselves. The Russian government, however, knowing all the conditions of the treaty, was disposed to abide by its stipulations. I must, therefore, confess that in this matter I exhibited more independence and boldness than address and foresight. I desired the restoration of Poland, and I was not likely to exhibit, on this occasion, anything like a pusillanimous regard for the opinions of Russia.

Austria was conquered, and I held her fast in my talons.

I had seen the hostility which directed her councils, and I thought less of gaining her by reciprocal advantages, than of chaining her submissive to my car;—fear often makes, among nations, more friends than true interest. On the first outset of war, Austria would either be forced to declare for us, or I would begin the war by marching to her capital in eight days and effecting the dismemberment of her monarchy. The second campaign would be against those who should attempt to interfere between me and Austria, without being able to afford the latter any assistance in time. If the campaign of 1812 had not taken an unfavorable turn, my project would have been declared superb, and no one would ever have thought of discovering its errors. I must confess, however, when I reflect upon the situation of affairs of 1809, that the project was bold and audacious, rather than wise. It was in the end unfortunate, perhaps, for Russia as well as for France and myself, that the Emperor Alexander declined my proposition to appoint some one to assist in the negotiations of Schönbrunn. In that case, the difficulties of the cession of Galicia would have been avoided ; for, on the objection of the Russian minister, I should either have abandoned the project, or have made some other arrangements satisfactory to that power. Moreover, we might have so modified the conditions imposed on Austria, as to have made us an ally of the house of Hapsburg.

But enough of these hypotheses ;—let us now return to a relation of facts.

The treaty of Vienna was so ill calculated to favor any ulterior alliance, that, until the last moment, I had doubts of its ratification, and made preparations for a renewal of hostilities. But, notwithstanding the opposition of both Metternich and Stadion, it was finally ratified on the twenty-second of October.

Destruction of the Fortifications of Vienna.—As soon as

I learned that Austria had ratified the treaty I set out from Munich for Paris, having first directed the demolition of the fortifications of Brunn, Raab, Gratz, Vienna, and Spitz. I had twice been made to appreciate the embarrassment which Vienna might have caused us had it been well defended, and the great advantages which we derived from its possession. Under our new relations, which resulted from the treaty, this capital would hardly decide for me *con amore*, although it might through fear. I had caused all the bastions to be mined during the armistice, and I now directed their explosion. These bastions, which had formerly been the safeguard of the monarchy, now formed the most delightful promenades of the Viennese, who were both grieved and humiliated by their destruction. This measure affected the pride of the inhabitants more sensibly than the loss of two of their best provinces, and made me more enemies in Austria than two disastrous wars. On the supposition of a probable alliance, this measure was impolitic; but, at the time when I ordered it, there seemed no possibility of such an event, for my neglect to notice their two indirect appeals would seem to cut off all probability of a renewal of the subject, and the present sentiments of the emperor and his cabinet were too decided to hope for any immediate change.

Expedition for the Subjugation of the Tyrol. — I now directed against the Tyrol forces sufficient for the subjugation of the country. General Drouet (Count d'Erlon), with the Bavarians and a French division, advanced by the north and the valley of the Inn, while Eugene directed some columns of the army of Italy by the valleys of the Drave and the Adige. The three divisions, under the orders of Baraguey d'Hilliers, were destined for the same object, and General Vial marched by Roveredo, in order to assist them. But the approach of these seven divisions did not intimidate these fierce mountaineers;—our columns were concentrated after several combats; Wrede reached the Brenner, and Baraguey d'Hilliers, the town of Brixen. But the columns which attempted to penetrate the lateral valleys, were assailed by a fanatical multitude; two battalions were taken at St. Leonard, and our posts were assailed at Silian, at Prunecken, and at Brixen, so that Baraguey d'Hilliers had difficulty in saving them. It was found necessary to call the division of Durutte from Carinthia. Yielding, at last, to the evidence of their senses, these brave but erring men sent in their partial submission;—the chiefs of those who provoked the massacre of the Bavarians, were tried and shot. Hofer still fought for a time with a few hundred men, and at last took refuge among the rocks; but, betrayed and discovered, he was arrested and conducted to the prison of Mantua, where he, also, was tried and condemned to death. If courage could be any safeguard against such a fate, certainly Hofer had been entitled to a pardon; but he perished, a victim to imperious necessity and the stern laws of war.

Remarks on the Campaign.—This expedition, which terminated in January, closed the campaign of 1809, so new, so extraordinary, and so rich in great lessons. This campaign in Austria had unveiled to me new dangers, and shown how precarious was my position amidst the adventurous passions, and interests, and ambitions of all Europe. The focus of resistance was not merely in Spain, Portugal, England, Prussia, Germany, Holland, or at Rome; it had also numerous ramifications even in France. The information which I received proved to me the dissatisfaction and ambition of Talleyrand and Fouché; the latter had betrayed himself in the council during my apparent embarrassment in the island of Lobau. He had taken upon himself to raise companies of the *élite* of the national guards in several departments, without the authorization of the Council of the Empire, (which was composed of the ministers and grand dignitaries under the presidency of Cambacérès), saying, that if I gave lustre to France, France should show that my presence was not necessary to repel the enemy,—a patriotic truth, without doubt, but an ill-timed and useless expression, accompanied by an illegal and factious measure. But it is time to return to the operations of Wellington in Spain, where the war was scarcely less fertile in important events than on the Danube.

CHAPTER XV.

CAMPAIGN OF 1809 IN THE SPANISH PENINSULA.

State of Affairs in the Peninsula—First Operations of Soult—Combats of Chaves and Braga—Assault of Oporto—Soult takes the left Bank of the Minho—Victories of Medellin and Ciudad-Real—Difficult Position of Soult—Combat of Amarante—New Descent of Wellington into Portugal—He attacks Soult at Oporto—Soult's Retreat—Ney's Operations in the Asturias—Misunderstanding between Soult and Ney, and the consequent Evacuation of Galicia—Wellington's Advance on Madrid—Joseph collects his Forces for an Attack—His Dispositions for Battle—Wellington's System of Battles—Battle of Talavera—Operations of Soult, Ney, and Mortier—Retreat of the Allies—Battle of Almonacid—Ney defeats Wilson—Remarks on these Operations—Soult succeeds Jourdan as Joseph's Chief of Staff—Combats of Tamames and Alba de Tormes—Arrizaga beaten at Ocana—Inaction of Wellington—Intrenched Camp of Torres Vedras—Romana quarrels with the Junta of Seville—Blake's Efforts to deliver Aragon—Operations of Suchet—Combat of Santa Maria—Combat of Belchite—St.-Cyr's Operations in Catalonia—Siege of Gerona—General Remarks on the Operations of this Campaign—Operations of the Russians against Sweden—War between Russia and Turkey.

State of Affairs in the Peninsula.—In turning from the ensanguined banks of the Ebro to observe what was passing on the Danube, we left St.-Cyr at Tarragona, nearly surrounded by the armed population of Catalonia; Junot, amidst the ruins of Saragossa, seeking to calm angry Aragon; Joseph, with the reserve, at Madrid; Mortier's corps, *en route* from Saragossa to join the king; Victor and Sebastiani, guarding the line of the Tagus; Ney, occupying Galicia; Soult, marching on Portugal; the division of Lapisse, at Salamanca; Kellerman at Valladolid; and the other detached divisions, occupying and organizing Biscay, Navarre, Castile, and Leon. I have already explained the motives which induced me to send Soult into Portugal after the defeat of the English army under Moore; the chances of his success in subjugating this kingdom, and in avenging the defeat of Vimiero; the strong measures taken by the Prince Regent and his executive council to oppose us; and, finally, the dispositions of the English, who remained under the orders of General Craddock.

First Operations of Soult.—After having resigned Galicia to the troops of Marshal Ney, Soult marched on Tuy, in order to pass the Minho at that place. The heavy rains which fall in Galicia during half the year had swollen this river, and the overflowing of the marsh opposite this city greatly increased its width; the want of boats, (all those in the vicinity having been removed by the enemy), and the proximity of Valencia, added so much to the difficulty of the enterprise, that Soult was forced to renounce his project, and, leaving the mass of his materials at Tuy, to ascend the river toward Orense.

Combats of Chaves and Braga.—Romana had incited these provinces to insurrection, and his corps seemed disposed to defend them. After having defeated him at Ribadavia and Monterey, Soult advanced on Chaves and captured it, taking two thousand prisoners. The Anglo-Portuguese generals, not less alarmed at the march of Victor on the Tagus than at the approach of Soult, had concentrated between Leyria and Abrantes to complete the organization of the troops of the line in English pay, and of the regular militia levied by Portugal. The defense of the mountains of Tras-los-Montes was left to the insurgent masses under General Friere and the division of Silveira. Among these insurgents there figured a battalion of students formed by the bishop of Braga. Frightful anarchy reigned in these assembled masses; all accused the chiefs who had allowed the French to enter and take Chaves; a crowd of peasants attacked General Friere and massacred him, and also his aides-de-camp, the commanding officer of engineers, and even the corregidor of Braga, whom they accused of lukewarmness, or of connivance with us. The command of this insurgent multitude was given to a Hanoverian colonel who was himself utterly astonished at the popular effervescence around him; but his only course was to submit to the demands of these fanatics who cried aloud for battle. He received the attack of Soult, on the twentieth of March, on the heights of Lanhozo and Carvalho-d'Este in front of Braga, where he was defeated and put to flight. Our troops had the generosity to treat the enemy as prisoners of war, notwithstanding they had mutilated many of our men with the most revolting barbarity. The inhabitants of the beautiful city of Braga, to the number of twenty-five thousand were all put to flight.

Assault of Oporto.—On the twenty-sixth, Soult's army advanced to Oporto, where fifty thousand insurgents had assembled in arms under the orders of the bishop, who had two generals as his lieutenants. The environs of this city are composed of a multitude of small hills, which give it a most agreeable aspect. These heights had been covered with redoubts, erected under the direction of the English and Portuguese engineers, and their ramparts were armed with two hundred pieces of artillery. To leave a city like this in his rear, would have been feasible and proper only in case he were to effect a junction with Victor on a fixed day, to act in concert against the regular Anglo-Portuguese army in the valley of the Tagus. But as nothing of this kind had been concerted between the generals, Soult thought the only proper course for him to pursue was to assault Oporto and and make himself master of the place. So exasperated were the militia and insurgents, that they tore in pieces one of their own chiefs, and the Portuguese generals were obliged

to resort to subterfuge in order to receive a flag of truce.
Soult begged them to save the city from the horrors inseparable from an assault; but while they were parleying, they captured by an unworthy stratagem, General Foy, taking him from the front of his division. They were forced to place him in prison to protect him from the rage of the populace, by whom he had already been most cruelly treated notwithstanding his escort.

Marshal Soult, seeing from the rejection of his propositions that force alone could decide the question, on the twenty-ninth of March, ordered an assault. Three columns carry the redoubts on the centre and two wings, while a fourth drives back the inhabitants who have sallied out of the city. They fire upon our troops from the houses and traverses constructed across the streets; but our troops surmount all obstacles, penetrate even to the superb bridge of boats across the Douro, on which the army of the archbishop precipitates itself pell-mell with the inhabitants. A ponton is broken under the weight of the flying mass, but is again repaired; our troops throw themselves on the opposing batteries, and carry the convent of La Serra, while the dispersed enemy flies to Coimbra. We are, perhaps, more disposed to look with pity on the fate of these fanatical people, who shot our soldiers from the roofs and windows of their houses, than on that of the brave troops who were exasperated to resort to severe but justifiable retaliation. A carnage of six hours was followed by a moment of pillage, which is but too commonly the price of such resistance; our troops, however, showed moderation instead of exceeding the limits allowed by the laws of war.

This feat of arms,—one of the finest in the whole war,—procured us immense booty: one hundred and ninety-seven pieces of ordnance, and a large quantity of military munitions. Only three hundred prisoners were taken.

Soult takes the left Bank of the Minho. — In any other country another such victory would have decided the fate, not only of Lisbon, but of Portugal : here, however, one success only rendered it necessary to gain another. The conquerors were now embarrassed by want of provisions, and actually ready to perish with famine in the richest country in Europe. Soult made every exertion in his power to restore tranquillity and reorganize the administrative service ; but how could order be expected in a country given up to all the furies of anarchy, where a Portuguese general massacres a corregidor for surrendering to the marshal !

Soult's first care was to capture Valenza and relieve Tuy, where the brave General Lamartinière had been besieged, with all the material of the army, by the fanatical bands of the Abbot Contho, and some Portuguese militia. General Heudelet, assisted by the dragoons of Lorges, had the good fortune to get possession of Valenza without opposition. He thus effected the junction, and succeeded in rescuing this precious convoy. Viana, and the strong places on the Minho, were surrendered, and a temporary pacification of the country effected.

Victories of Medellin and Cuidad-Real. — My departure from Spain at first seemed to produce no unfavorable change in our affairs in the Peninsula ; the very day previous to the triumph of Soult at Oporto, Victor preluded that victory in such a way as to induce me to hope for the entire success of his enterprise. Having gotten rid, at Ucles, of the army of Andalusia, Joseph had left to Sebastiani the care of holding it in check, while the first corps, established in the environs of Almaraz on the Tagus, was opposed to the army of Cuesta, or of Estramadura. My plan was for this corps to descend the valley of the Tagus, so as to assist the march of Soult on Lisbon, flattering myself that the victories of Almonacid and Ucles had destroyed all the chances of opposition from the Spanish armies. But this calculation was erroneous; the supreme junta had exerted all possible activity in reorganizing the army of Cuesta, an old general of mediocre talent, but endowed with presence of mind, courage, and perseverance. Emboldened by the inaction of our troops behind the Tagus, Cuesta took possession of Almaraz, and blew up the bridge. His audacity, however, ended here, and he took a defensive line behind the river.

The Duke of Belluno, having collected the necessary means, crossed the Tagus, and Cuesta retreated behind the Guadiana by Medellin. Victor followed in pursuit, crossing the river at Merida, and ascending the stream. A rencontre took place near Mengabriel, in rear of Medellin, and was one of the warmest contests that occurred during the war, at least with the Spaniards. The ephemeral success of driving back our first line for a moment, gave occasion for exultation and boasting to the enemy; but soon, charged by the divisions of Leval, Ruffin, and Villatte, assisted on the left by the cavalry of the redoubtable Lasalle, and on the right by Latour-Maubourg, the Spaniards were everywhere beaten. The rout was the more complete, as, menaced by the left, Cuesta was unable to maintain himself perpendicular to the Guadiana, without being turned and thrown upon the river. Our troops, exasperated by the insults received from the Spaniards in their moment of victory, were at first inclined to give no quarter. From six to seven thousand men, killed and wounded, were strewed over the field of battle, and five thousand were taken prioners. We paid pretty dearly for this success, which cost us not less than four thousand men *hors-de-combat.*

The day previous to this glorious victory (March 27th), Sebastiani had marched against the Duke of Infantado, completely defeating him at Cuidad-Real, and forced him to take refuge in the Sierra Morena, where the duke soon threw up his command and went to Seville.

The Spaniards were conquered, but they quickly sprung up again from their ashes ; a part of the prisoners, through the assistance of the inhabitants, escaped from our escorts ; and others, who had enrolled themselves under Joseph, deserted from us and rejoined their own colors. The junta pressed in the volunteers, or drafted men by lot, to fill up the skeletons of their regiments of the line. By the end of April, Cuesta had reorganized his army, and increased its numbers to about thirty thousand men, and Victor, cantoned between the Tagus and the Guadiana, was embarrassed to penetrate to Abrantes against the Anglo-Portuguese, while an army still more powerful than his own, debouching from Badajos on Alcantara, was coming to assail him in rear ;— he was in a precarious situation, and if he had now executed my orders, he would have been lost.

Difficult Position of Soult.—Having received at Oporto the materials which he had been forced to leave at Tuy, Soult applied himself to the pacification of the inhabitants of the province of Minho. By order and firmness, he was partially successful. It is said by some, that for the better success of his object, he thought to have himself declared sovereign of Portugal, as a kingdom independent both of France and England ; at least it is certain that proclamations of this character were issued by his chief of staff to the army. But from the good judgment and known patriotism of Soult, it must be believed that this project was designed merely as a means of creating a new party in Portugal : the idea of playing the part of a second Dumouriez, in my reign, was too absurd to be seriously entertained by a man of his judgment.*

---

* Alison conveys the impression that Soult was at this time intriguing to place himself on the throne of Portugal, with or without the authority of

Be this as it may Soult, before marching on Lisbon, waited to be joined by his brother who was bringing him four or five thousand convalescents from Astorga, and to hear from the

Napoleon, and that the plan went even so far as to contemplate a revolt against the French emperor. The statement is not sustained. Alison's account of Soult's operations at Oporto, and subsequently, is greatly discolored by prejudice. On the contrary, Napier's account is entirely fair and just. We copy his concluding remarks on Soult's conduct in this affair:

"Having repressed the disorders attendant on the battle, he adopted the same conciliatory policy which had marked his conduct at Chaves and Braga, and endeavored to remedy, as far as it was possible, the deplorable results of the soldier's fury; recovering and restoring a part of the plunder, he caused the inhabitants remaining in the town to be treated with respect, and invited, by proclamation, all those who had fled to return. He demanded no contributions, and restraining with a firm hand the violence of his men, contrived, from the captured public property, to support the army and even to succor the poorest and most distressed of the population.

"But his ability in the civil and political administration of the Entre Minho e Douro, produced an effect which he was not prepared for. The Prince Regent's desertion of the country was not forgotten. The national feeling was as adverse to Portugal being a dependency on the Brazils, as it was to the usurpation of the French, and the comparison between Soult's government and the horrible anarchy which preceded it, was all in favor of the former. His victories, and the evident vigor of his character, contrasted with the apparent supineness of the English, promised permanency for the French power, and the party, formerly noticed as being inimical to the house of Braganza, revived. The leaders, thinking this a favorable opportunity to execute their intention, waited upon the Duke of Dalmatia, and expressed their desire for a French prince and an independent government. They even intimated their good wishes toward the duke himself, and demanded his concurrence and protection, while, in the name of the people, they declared that the Braganza dynasty was at an end.

"Although unauthorized by the emperor to accede to this proposition, Soult was yet unwilling to reject a plan from which he could draw such immediate and important military advantages. Napoleon was not a man to be lightly dealt with on such an occasion, but the marshal, trusting that circumstances would justify him, encouraged the design, appointed men to civil employments and raised a Portuguese legion of five battalions. He acted with so much dexterity that in fifteen days, the cities of Oporto and Braga, and the towns of Bacellos, Viana, Villa-de-Conde, Povoa-de-Barcim, Feira and Avar, sent addresses, containing the expression of their sentiments, and bearing the signatures of thirty thousand persons, as well of the nobles, clergy, and merchants, as of the people. These addresses were burned when the French retreated from Oporto, but the fact that such a project was in agitation has never been denied; the regency even caused inquest to be made on the matter, and it was then asserted that very few persons were found to be implicated. That many

operations of Victor on the Tagus and of Lapisse's division which was to march by Almeida. He then hoped to be able to reach the capital, and to maintain himself there till he

of the signatures were forged by the leaders may readily be believed; but the policy of lessening the importance of the affair is also evident, and the Inquisitors, if willing, could not have probed it to the bottom.

"This transaction formed the ground-work of a tale, generally credited even by his own officers, that Soult perfidiously aimed at an independent crown. The circumstances were certainly such as might create suspicion; but that the conclusion was false, is shown, by the mode in which Napoleon treated both the rumor and the subject of it. Slighting the former, he yet made known to his lieutenant that it had reached his ears, adding, 'I remember nothing but Austerlitz,' and at the same time largely increased the Duke of Dalmatia's command. On the other hand, the policy of Soult's conduct on this occasion, and the great influence, if not the numbers of the Portuguese malcontents, were abundantly proved by the ameliorated relations between the army and the peasantry. The fierceness of the latter subsided; and even the priests abated of their hostility in the Entre Minho e Douro. The French soldiers were no longer assassinated in that province; whereas, previous to this intrigue, that cruel species of warfare had been carried on with infinite activity, and the most malignant passions called forth on both sides.

"Among other instances of Portuguese ferocity, and of the truculent violence of the French soldiers, the death of Colonel Lameth and the retaliation which followed, may be cited. That young officer, when returning from the marshal's quarters to his own, was waylaid, near the village of Arrifana, and murdered; his body was then stripped, and mutilated in a shocking manner. This assassination, committed within the French lines, and at a time when Soult enforced the strictest discipline, was justifiable neither by the laws of war nor by those of humanity. No general could neglect to punish such a proceeding. The protection due to the army, and even the welfare of the Portuguese within the French jurisdiction, demanded a severe example; for the violence of the troops had hitherto been with difficulty restrained by their commander, and if, at such a moment, he had appeared indifferent to their individual safety, his authority would have been set at nought, and the unmeasured indiscriminating vengeance of an insubordinate army executed.

"Impressed with this feeling, and afflicted at the unhappy death of a personal friend, Soult directed General Thomières to march, with a brigade of infantry, to Arrifana, and punish the criminals. Thomières was accompanied by a Portuguese civilian, and, after a judicial inquiry, shot five or six persons whose guilt was said to have been proved; but it is certain that the principal actor, a Portuguese major of militia, and some of his accomplices, escaped across the Vouga to Colonel Trant, who, disgusted at their conduct, sent them to Marshal Beresford. It would also appear, from the statement of a peasant, that Thomières, or those under him, exceeded Soult's orders; for, in that statement, attested by oath, it is said that twenty-four innocent persons were killed,

could receive my instructions respecting the means to be taken to sustain the place. But my departure for France, the war with Austria and the operations of the Anglo-Portuguese, soon destroyed this illusion.

The corps whose coöperation was indispensable for the success of his conquest could no longer act. Victor, as has just been explained, feared, with some reason to penetrate into Portugal. On the other side, Ney charged with the subjugation and organization of Galicia, and of guarding Coruña and Ferrol, had his hands full, with eighteen thousand men to cover a coast a hundred leagues in extent, and an entire kingdom from Orense to Ribadeo. He had on his left, the insurgent population of the bishopric of Orense; on his right, Romana held the Asturias, having retired there, on the retreat of Moore, and reënforced himself with the levies of that province. The occupation of Asturias was an important operation; for the English had made it a general depôt for the immense quantity of arms and equipments sent for the Spanish army, and for the militia which had been raised in the provinces of the north, notwithstanding the presence of our bayonets.

Ney was the only general at hand to subdue this province; but to act with his whole corps would have exposed Coruña and Ferrol, and left all Galicia open to insurrection; and, to act with only half of his troops, would not only have exposed him to defeat with a divided army, but, even in case of success, would have been too small for the occupation of the province. I ought to have placed under the orders of

and that the soldiers, after committing many atrocious excesses, burned the village.

"These details have been related partly because they throw a light upon the direful nature of this contest, but chiefly because the transaction has been adduced by other writers as proof of cruelty in Soult; a charge not to be sustained by the facts of this case. and belied by the general tenor of his conduct, which even his enemies, while they attributed it to an insidious policy, acknowledged, at the same time, to be mild and humane."

this marshal the troops of Biscay and Castile, so that he might himself have combined some concentric movements to fall on the organized corps of the enemy, and sweep the provinces in his rear. There were sufficient troops between Bayonne and Astorga for this purpose, but they did not act in concert; the result was that Ney could neither go to Oviedo nor assist the army of Portugal.

Soult, thus abandoned to his own resources, saw himself, like Junot, with a storm gathering on all sides. In advancing on Oporto he had separated, rather than removed, the obstacles in his way. Already, Silveira, reappearing in his rear, had captured Chaves and collected threatening forces on the Tamega. General Boutheilo, retook Braga and infested the country between the Minho and the Douro. As the waves of the sea, when separated by a ship, instantly close in its rear, so did the insurgents close around our troops and confine the army to the possession of the ground on which it encamped.

Combat of Amarante.—The party which favored us in Portugal, and ventured to declare for me and against the house of Braganza, was the most intelligent but not the most numerous. And the presence of Silveira on the Tamega and at Chaves, could not fail to rekindle the flames of insurrection in the country which we occupied. It was important to get rid of him before we could complete the work of pacification. Generals Delaborde and Loison, were sent to attack him at Amarante, where he had collected twelve thousand men. This corps had intrenched the stone bridge and placed themselves on the formidable heights near by, disputing the passage of the river which was no where fordable on account of its steep and rocky banks. All attempts to carry this bridge were unsuccessful, and Loison lost most precious time till the second of May, when he at last blew up the intrenchment and beat the enemy.

The Anglo-Portuguese derived much advantage from this delay of twelve days, to complete their organization; but it would be attributing too much importance to this circumstance to say that it alone decided the fate of the expedition. For Craddock and Beresford had thirty thousand good troops to oppose Soult, who, forced to guard Oporto, could appear at Coimbra with only eighteen thousand French troops.

New Descent of Wellington into Portugal.—More serious obstacles were now rising to ruin all my hopes in the Peninsula. England, instead of being discouraged by the ill-success of Moore's expedition, felt more sensibly than ever the importance of sustaining the Peninsula and delivering Portugal. Encouraged by the more than energetic measures ordered by the Prince Regent of Portugal, at her instigation, she resolved to second these measures with all her power. All the resources derived from her perfection in the mechanical arts were put in play to accelerate the manufacture of arms and military munitions. England now resembled the forges of Vulcan, filling Europe with the thunderbolts of war. But the cabinet of St. James did not limit themselves to these succors, but sent to Lisbon the same Wellington who had triumphed over Junot at Vimiera, and whose talents and fortune were destined to give a fatal direction to the war.

Wellington, who arrived at Lisbon with a reënforcement of English troops on the twenty-sixth of April, made preparations for falling upon his adversary and taking advantage of the nature of the country to cut off his retreat. He assembled twenty thousand troops at Coimbra, and advanced on the Vouga to keep Soult in check near Oporto; while Beresford, at the head of the Portuguese army, passed the Douro, near Lamego, and took the direction of Chaves, seconded by the partisan corps of Wilson. The plan was well conceived, and the disposition of the forces good. Soult's advanced guard, under the intrepid Franceschi, surprised and almost enveloped at Grijon, succeeded, by presence of mind, in regaining Oporto without any serious loss.

The position of Soult was critical; vague reports announced the coming tempest; but he could obtain no accurate information of the enemy; for, if the Spanish insurgents are good at keeping a secret, those of Portugal are still better. Hearing, however, on the eighth, of the arrival of Wellington at Coimbra, he begun to collect his scattered detachments, and prepare either for combat or retreat. The news of the war in Germany had shaken the *morale* of his army; for every one seemed to see an open abyss before him in Portugal, while all the glory and honors were to be won by the army in Germany. Daily contests in an insurgent country does not suit the character of the French soldier; he is brave, but sanguine and impatient, and soon becomes tired of this kind of hostilities. Moreover, the great triumphs which he had gained in the last few years made him negligent of the details of field service, thinking it sufficient for him to be brave in the battle-field.

Finally, as a climax to his anxiety, Soult now discovered, by the plot of Major d'Argenson, that he had traitors in his army, who were in secret communication with the enemy. He then resolved to unite his army behind the Tamega, in order to reach the vicinity of Almeida and of the division of Lapisse. Loison was already preceded at Amarante; Lorges received orders to evacuate the province of Minho, and direct himself on that city; but he could not reach there before the fifteenth of May. Soult, after having rallied his advanced guard, placed the division of Mermet intermediate between him and Loison, broke the bridge of the Douro, and withdrew the boats to the right bank, hoping to maintain his position under shelter of the river; but he was soon undeceived in this respect.

Wellington attacks Soult at Oporto.—Wellington, having passed the Vouga on the eleventh, advanced in three columns on the Douro. Murray's division was to cross the river two leagues above; those of Paget and Hill at Villanova, and the left on the quays of Oporto. By means of an understanding with the inhabitants, they obtained a few boats which were negligently guarded. General Paget passed to the right bank without being perceived, and established himself in a large building, from which he could protect the successive passage of the several battalions of General Hill. Soult, deceived by the reports of his generals and the negligence of his outposts, was tranquil at Oporto when the alarm was given. The Portuguese boatmen profited by this circumstance to escape with their boats and join the left of the English. Soult left Oporto with the division of Delaborde. He would have taken the direct road to Braga, had not the necessity of rallying on Mermet and Loison, in the direction of Amarante, induced him to retire in that direction. He encountered the columns of Paget and Hill, ready to debouch on his line of retreat. He attacked them, and drove them back far enough to facilitate the successive passage of his troops on the road to Penafiel and Valisa.

Soult's Retreat.—This surprise was the more fatal to Soult, as all his dispositions were made for a retreat on Loison's corps at Amarante, which place was no longer in our possession. Driven from Pavoa, on the tenth, by Beresford and Silveira, Loison had failed to inform his chief, and, on the night of the twelfth, had even decamped from Amarante on Guimarens. Soult's army was already on the road to Amarante when he heard this disastrous news. There was now but one means of escape: this was to throw all his material and baggage into the Souza, and march in all haste to Guimarens, by a path which was traveled only by the shepherds. He boldly decided to make this sacrifice, and had the good fortune to effect his junction with Loison. But he was not free from embarrassment; for it was probable that Wellington, taking the direct road from Oporto to Braga, would reach this city before the French. It was, therefore, not worth while to compromise the safety of the army in order to save ten or twelve pieces of artillery which belonged to Loison's division. Soult, therefore, directed his march across the mountains on the same field of Lanhoso, where he had defeated the Portuguese on the twentieth of March, thus reaching the great road in advance of the English. This desperate resolution saved his army. He continued his march on Salamonde and Ruivaens; but hearing that the bridge was cut, and guarded by infantry, and that large parties of the enemy were near Chaves, and that Beresford was marching on that place, he resolved to throw himself into the mountains of Montalégre. The great difficulties of this country were surmounted by our troops, whose march was facilitated by the entire destruction of their material and baggage train. After forcing the passage of the bridge of Misarella, near Villa de Pons, Soult reached Montalégre. These frightful precipices, where they were obliged to force the successive passages of two bridges, so impeded their march that they ham-strung their draft-horses and mules to get rid of the little baggage train that remained. The army finally reached Orense, with no further obstacle than being harassed by three or four thousand Anglo-Portuguese as far as Allariz; but it could not stop in this miserable country to punish the enemy, for fear of actual starvation; it, however, reached their rear-guard, and headed them off by Monterey and Abemides.

Notwithstanding the disasters of this retreat, Soult might deem himself fortunate in having effected his escape, even with the loss of his artillery, and two thousand men who had fallen in the several combats in which he had engaged since he left Oporto. In fact, he reached Lugo in a still worse condition than that in which Moore had traversed the same town six months before. Soult found here the army of Romana who was besieging the brigade of Fournier, while Ney was invading Asturias.

Ney's Operations in Asturias.—Uneasy at hearing no news of the sixth corps for the last four months, I had directed Kellerman to advance from Astorga to communicate with it by Lugo, and to act in concert with it for the subjugation of Asturias and the defeat of Romana. Ney, accordingly left Mondonedo with one half of his corps to reach the coast from the west side, while Kellerman marched by Leon on Oviedo, crossing the high chain of mountains which extends from the Pyrenees along the coast, or rather is the prolongation of that range. Marchand's division was left alone to guard all Galicia. At the very moment when Ney was valiantly forcing the passage of the Navia, and entering victorious into Gijon and Oviedo, Romana found it convenient to come and take his place in Galicia. Our movements were so well known to the enemy, while his were kept from us with such impenetrable secrecy, that Romana passed, as it were, in sight of our columns while on the march to Oviedo, and fell on Lugo when he was least expected. The brave sixty-ninth was valiantly defending itself in this city, determined to await the return of Ney, when Soult came to their relief. His return at this juncture was the more fortunate as the divisions of Carrera and Morillo had attacked General Maucune at Caldas-del-Rey, and taken possession of St. Jago and threatened Coruña. The return of Ney, and his junction with Soult toward Lugo, soon drove the enemy from Galicia.

Misunderstanding between Soult and Ney and consequent Evacuation of Galicia.—But these difficulties were dispersed, rather than conquered. Soult had supplied himself with arms, munitions and some light pieces of artillery in the arsenals of Galicia ; but as Romana was at Orense and the Anglo-Portuguese army were probably marching on Almeida or the Tagus, it was important to seek the enemy. Soult and Ney agreed to act in concert ; the former was to cross the mountains of Val-d'Ores to Zamora on the Douro, in order to hear something from King Joseph, and to oppose the English if they should debouch by Almeida. Ney, on his side, had driven back Carrera and Morillo on Vigo. But, supposing that Soult had agreed with him to remain near Orense, he was astonished to find that he was not there. Seeing himself thus left alone in Galicia, surrounded by enemies and ignorant of the operations of the victorious army of Wellington, Ney took it upon himself to march on Estremadura. This resolution was premature, but a natural one, if the circumstances had been such as he supposed. The Anglo-Portuguese army had been increased to forty-five thousand men ; Cuesta and Venegas commanded two other armies, making together more than sixty thousand combatants. The king had in the vicinity of Madrid, only forty thousand men ; he might be beaten and driven from his capital by one hundred thousand allies, if our generals did not rally to his assistance. Ney, therefore, resolved to leave Coruña where he had difficulty in subsisting his army. This voluntary abandonment of our maritime establishments at Ferrol was a serious affair, but Ney was advised to it by his generals ; and the battle at Talavera proved that there was at least some justice in their calculations. In presenting the subject to his generals, however, for their opinion, Ney concealed from them the agreement he had made with Soult, and represented the disappearance of that marshal from Orense as a new source of disquietude and danger ; whereas in fact, Soult's movements had been agreed upon between them.* In addition to other and more weighty reasons for his advance on Estremadura, Ney alleged the battle of Essling, the news of which he had just received; and my difficult position in the island of Lobau. By concentrating our forces so as to receive the orders of the king, he thought he manœuvred as a skillful general; for the divisions of Romana, who were continually patrolling the Val-d'Ores and Villa Franca, rendered it impossible to receive a dispatch unless it was protected by at least four thousand men. Moreover, his departure from this province would place it neither more nor less in the hands of the junta than it was already, for it was continually traversed by bands of insurgents even during Ney's occupation.

But whatever may be said in justification of this movement of the sixth corps, as a military manœuvre to give Joseph the means of crushing Wellington on the Tagus, it certainly was unwise in its political relations. I, myself, was far from satisfied with his hasty abandonment of Coruña and Ferrol. His chief of staff (Jomini) advised him to throw six battalions in the strongest fortresses of Galicia, and to march with the remainder of his army to Astorga, returning again to that province as soon as he should ascertain that the king did not require his assistance against Wellington. But Ney was too much attached to his heroes of Friedland, and too uncertain of returning, to risk, in this way, the safety of his battalions. It was unfortunate, however, that he neglected this advice, for Mortier and Soult were abundantly sufficient to enable Joseph to force Wellington into Portugal, and Ney might have returned into Galicia. But, isolated in this kingdom, and separated from the remainder of the army by a *coupe-gorge* of forty leagues,

---

* Documentary evidence more recently published, proves that the view taken by Jomini of Ney's conduct on this occasion, is entirely correct. Ney either acted from want of judgment, or from his well-known jealousy of Soult.

with Romana on his left and the Asturians on his right, he would not probably have been able to maintain this position for more than six months.

For these reasons, which Ney deemed sufficient to justify the course he pursued, he left Coruña on the twenty-second of June, and reached Astorga on the eighth of July, in the very best order. The enemy, however, have not blushed to pronounce as a disorderly retreat, what was, in reality, a voluntary manœuvre, founded on military principles, and executed without the loss of a single soldier, or even a single one of the sick.*

Advance of Wellington on Madrid. — Wellington, not deeming it best to waste his time in a vain pursuit of Soult in the mountains of Chaves, returned from Braga to the Tagus. After remaining more than a month at Abrantes to concert measures with the Spaniards, and complete his own preparations, he advanced towards Alcantara and Oropesa, where he effected, on the twentieth of July, his junction with Cuesta, who had united the *élite* of the Spanish forces to the number of thirty-seven thousand men, eight thousand of this number being cavalry. Their object was to march together on Madrid, to which place Venegas was to move with twenty thousand men by Toledo and Aranjuez; at the same time that Colonel Wilson, with his light corps, was to advance as partisans in the direction of the Escurial and Naval-Carnero, in order to threaten Joseph's line of communication with the north of Spain. The Portuguese, under Beresford, were to march on Almeida, and, by acting in concert with the Duke of Parque, who commanded about Ciudad-Rodrigo, to occupy the French on the Douro and at Salamanca.

This operation was skillfully conceived. It was natural to

---

* The order of relation in the preceding section has been slightly transposed in the translation; but the language of the original has been substantially preserved.

suppose that, in a country where we were kept in ignorance of operations beyond the view of our camps, Wellington might fall on our isolated corps and appear victorious at Madrid, before any efficacious measure could be taken to prevent him. The success of this plan would have been more certain, if it had been executed by the end of June; but Wellington did not command the Spaniards, and it was necessary to arrange his movements with two generals and the junta, which was not the affair of a day. Nor was it long before discord showed itself between these different chiefs; and, as usually happens between armies which are not agreed, each pretended to be in the right. If we are to believe the Spanish version of the affair, the primitive plan was to fall on Victor, before he could join Joseph, and Wellington, instead of hastening the operation, remained inactive at the very time when he was to have effected his junction with Cuesta. They thus reproach the English General with having paralyzed Vanega's corps, by forcing it to pass in rear of the Tagus to Toledo, instead of marching by Arganda direct to Madrid, which, they say, would have prevented the junction of Sebastiani and Victor. The English historians, on the contrary, affirm that Wellington wished to make the attack immediately after the junction, and that Cuesta opposed it. It is certain, however, that Victor having voluntarily left the Alberche at their approach, in order to unite with Sebastiani, the Spaniard animated by a noble ardor, put himself in pursuit as far as Torrijos. The dilatory movements of the English general, on this occasion, gave me no very exalted opinion of his talent and military character. I considered him brave and ready, but not bold. I was either deceived in him, or else his subsequent successes changed his character in this respect.

Joseph collects his Forces for an Attack.—The approach of the combined army created great alarm at Madrid—sure proof of the wisdom of the enterprise. Victor, at the head of the first corps, fell back from Talavera on Toledo. The king recalled Sebastiani from Aranjuez to Toledo, thus opening to Venegas the road to the capital. Joseph advanced with his guards and reserve to put himself at the head of forty-five thousand men; while Belliard, with only three battalions was left to guard Madrid, which was then a volcano ready to burst forth; he established himself in the Retiro.

The army leaves Toledo, and advances on the Alberche, two thousand men remaining to watch the movement of Venegas. Joseph now rests all his hopes on the union of the corps of Soult, Mortier, and Ney, to whom orders were given on the twenty-second of July, to march in all haste on Plasencia. On this important operation depends the fate of the campaign. Joseph now, blindly and in direct contradiction to the principles of the art, decides to take the offensive alone, and before he can rely upon the coöperation of fifty thousand men led by Soult! He should rather have moved back obliquely toward the sources of the Alberche to induce the enemy to follow in pursuit, and again have fallen impetuously on him as soon as our two armies could enter in concert into action. Joseph and Jourdan, under the advice, it is said, of Victor, took the absurd resolution to march alone against Wellington, and to attack him. The fear of exposing his capital, by refusing his left wing, was the reason assigned by my brother for this resolution.

On the twenty-sixth, the army passes the Guadarama, and overthrows Cuesta, who has advanced to Torrijos; he is driven back behind the Alberche. On the twenty-seventh, the army crosses this river at four o'clock in the afternoon, and reaches the enemy's position near the close of the day. Strange as it may seem, Victor, seeing the importance of the heights which supported Wellington's left, thought to carry them in the obscurity of the night, and directed Ruffin's division to assail them, at the same time that Lapisse threatened this left wing in front. The regiments of Ruffin, received by fresh and well-arranged troops, were beaten one after the other, as they successively arrived on the hillocks. This *début* was an unfavorable augury for the following day. Jourdan was of opinion that a battle should not be risked till they heard from Soult ; but Victor, hoping to obtain the honor of defeating an English army, objected that this circumspection would produce an unfavorable impression on soldiers accustomed to victory ; and this pitiful consideration induced my brother to renew an attack, condemned at the same time by reason, policy, and the rules of war.

Dispositions for Battle.—The only accessible point of the enemy's line being its left, it was necessary to assemble the mass of our army and the reserve on our right wing, to menace the position in front and to turn it by a deep valley, while sustaining the general movement to the right. By prolonging ourselves in this way in a line oblique to the Tagus, we would paralyze half of the enemy's army, or force it to make a change of front, and to fight with the river in its rear. We would base ourselves, in case of retreat on Avila and the Escurial, thus securing our communication with Soult. But instead of doing this, the king established his reserve on the left, near Sebastiani, and, with divisions in echelons coming successively into action without support, he attacked the hill where Wellington had placed his best troops and a numerous artillery. In accordance with these dispositions, Sebastiani, on our left, was to attack the point of the allied line where the troops of Wellington and Cuesta were united, thus assailing the left of the Spaniards and the right of the Anglo-Portuguese ; while Victor reserved to himself the honor of carrying the advantageous heights occupied by the extreme left of the allies. Their forces numbered sixty thousand men, while ours did not exceed forty thousand.

Wellington's System of Battle.—Wellington's system of combat was what is called the *defensive-offensive* ; awaiting his adversary on chosen ground, he fatigued his assailants with his artillery and a murderous fire of musketry, and when they were about to pierce his line, he avoided this formidable movement by falling on them with his united forces. This system, under certain circumstances, may be as good as any other ; it depends on the localities, the nature of the troops and the character of your opponent. I received defensive-offensive battles at Rivoli and Austerlitz.

Battle of Talavera.—Such was the system at Talavera ; the infantry of the first corps attacking successively one division after another. Our brave men attacked the enemy's position with admirable boldness ; but it only resulted in their destruction ; reaching the enemy's line, out of breath and in disorder, they were cut to pieces by the fire of sharpshooters and platoons, and then borne down with the bayonet. The action was begun by the division of Ruffin, which bravely ascended the height on the enemy's flank, while Lapisse directed his attack toward the centre of that wing. Our regiments, successively engaged, were easily repulsed. A new effort, and one better combined, though rather tardy, was made about four o'clock ;—three divisions advancing together to the attack. Never did our soldiers fight more bravely ; but the difficulty of the ground, the firmness and the deadly fire of the English triumphed over their efforts.

During this obstinate contest Sebastiani had assailed the enemy's right ; Leval's division was pushing before it a Spanish division, when Wellington directed his reserve of English to drive them back. Cut up by a concentric and deadly fire, and opposed by superior numbers, this division was obliged to fall back. The remainder of the day was passed by engagements of the sharpshooters, which produced no result on the line. Victor sought in vain to prolong his right by the valley, so as to turn Wellington, who opposed these efforts with his well-sustained reserve of cavalry. This partial and tardy movement was without success, and night finally put an end to this useless butchery. The two armies remained in each other's presence the following day; but Joseph, on hearing that Wilson was gaining the environs of Naval-Carnero and threatening his capital, finally ordered a retreat. Victor returned on the twenty-ninth, behind the Alberche; Joseph and Sebastiani marched to Illescas, and, on the thirtieth, threw a division into Toledo, which place was threatened by Venegas. Wellington, although reënforced by the arrival of Craufurd's division, did not advance from his position:* dissatisfied with the Spaniards, and paralyzed at his own losses, he wished to trust nothing to chance, and his circumspection was very natural. This battle, however, had restored the glory of the successors of Marlborough—a glory, which, for the last century, had been on the decline; and it was here shown that the English infantry was capable of contending with the best in Europe. Our

---

* The march of Craufurd's division is thus described by Napier: "On that day (the twenty-ninth), General Robert Craufurd reached the English camp, with the forty-third, fifty-second, and ninety-fifth regiments, and immediately took charge of the outposts. These troops, after a march of twenty miles, were in *bivouac* near Malpartida de Plasencia, when the alarm caused by the Spanish fugitives spread to that part. Craufurd, fearing that the army was pressed, allowed the men to rest for a few hours, and then, withdrawing about fifty of the weakest from the ranks, commenced his march with the resolution not to halt until he reached the field of battle. As the brigade advanced, crowds of runaways were met with, and although not all Spaniards, all propagating the vilest falsehoods:—'*The army was defeated,*'—'*Sir Arthur Wellesley was kil'ed,*'—'*The French were only a few miles distant;*' nay, some, blinded by their fears, affected even to point out the enemy's advanced posts on the nearest hills. Indignant at this shameful scene, the troops hasten'd, rather than slackened, the impetuosity of their pace, and leaving only seventeen stragglers behind, in twenty-six hours crossed the field of battle in a close and compact body, having, in that time, passed over sixty-two English miles, and in the hottest season of the year, each man carrying from fifty to sixty pounds weight upon his shoulders. Had the historian, Gibbon, known of such a march, he would have spared his sneer about the 'delicacy of modern soldiers!'"

loss in this battle was eight thousand, killed and wounded; and the allies confessed a loss of seven thousand.*

Operations of Soult, Ney and Mortier, to cut off Wellington's Retreat.—Joseph was wrong in fighting this battle,

---

* The following remarks of Napier on this battle are well worthy the attention of the military reader.

"1st. The moral courage evinced by Sir Arthur Wellesley, when with such a coadjutor as Cuesta, he accepted battle, was not less remarkable than the judicious disposition which, finally, rendered him master of the field. Yet, it is doubtful if he could have maintained his position had the French been well managed, and their strength reserved for the proper moment, instead of being wasted on isolated attacks during the night of the twenty-seventh, and the morning of the twenty-eighth.

"A pitched battle is a great affair. A good general must bring all the moral, as well as the physical, force of his army into play at the same time, if he means to win, and all may be too little. Marshal Jourdan's project was conceived in this spirit, and worthy of his reputation; and it is possible that he might have placed his army, unperceived, on the flank of the English, and then by a sudden and general attack, have carried the key of his position, thus commencing his battle well; but Sir Arthur Wellesley's resources would not then have been exhausted. He had foreseen such an occurrence, and was prepared by a change of front, to keep the enemy in check with his left wing and cavalry; while the right, marching upon the position abandoned by the French, should cut the latter off from the Alberche. In this movement the allies would have been reënforced by Wilson's corps, which was near Cazalegas, and the contending armies would then have exchanged lines of operation. The French could, however, have gained nothing, unless they won a complete victory, while the allies would, even though defeated, have insured their junction with Venegas. Madrid and Toledo would thus have fallen to them, and before Soult could unite with Joseph, a new line of operations, through the fertile country of La Mancha, might have been obtained. But these matters are only speculative.

"2d. The distribution of the French troops for the great attack cannot be praised. The attempt to turn the English left with a single division was puerile. The allied cavalry was plainly to be seen in the valley; how, then, could a single division hope to develop its attack upon the hill, when five thousand horsemen were hanging upon its flank? and, in fact, the whole of Ruffin's, and the half of Villatte's division, were paralyzed by the charge of a single regiment. To have rendered this movement formidable, the principal part of the French cavalry should have preceded the march of the infantry; but the great error was fighting at all before Soult reached Plasencia.

"3d. It has been said, that to complete the victory, Sir Arthur Wellesley should have caused the Spaniards to advance; this would, more probably, have led to a defeat. Neither Cuesta, nor his troops, were capable of an orderly movement. The infantry of the first and the fourth corps were still above twenty thousand strong, and, although a repulsed, by no means a dis-

inasmuch as Soult was marching by Plasencia on Almaraz, with fifty thousand men, and Wellington would have retired at his approach. But after he had decided to give battle, he ought to have left one of Sebastiani's divisions and three thousand horse to annoy the centre and right of the allies, and then have united all the remainder of his army and his reserve to assail the decisive point and turn the left. Perhaps even then he would have failed of success, considering the superiority of the enemy and the nature of the ground. But if success had been possible, it would have been won by this manœuvre, and by no other. In the mean time Soult was marching in the direction of Plasencia. He had not received the order for this movement till the twenty-seventh of July, and his troops were then extended over the country as far as the Douro, the fifth corps especially having a great distance to march in order to arrive in time. Soult satisfied himself with leaving a flying corps to watch Ciudad-Rodrigo, and, without troubling himself with the operations of Beresford and of the Duke del Parque, he marched on Plasencia, where his columns arrived successively between the first and fourth of August.

Retreat of the Allies.—Wellington heard of Soult's march

comfited force; the cavalry, the king's guards, and Dessolle's division, had not been engaged at all, and were alone sufficient to beat the Spaniards; a second panic, such as that of the twenty-seventh, would have led to the most deplorable consequences, as those, who know with what facility French soldiers recover from a repulse, will readily acknowledge.

"The battle of Talavera was one of hard honest fighting, and the exceeding gallantry of the troops honored the nations to which they belonged. The English owed much to the general's dispositions and something to fortune. The French owed nothing to their commander; but when it is considered that only the reserve of their infantry were withheld from the great attack on the twenty-eighth, and that, consequently, above thirty thousand men were closely and unsuccessfully engaged for three hours with sixteen thousand British, it must be confessed that the latter proved themselves to be truly formidable soldiers; yet the greatest part were raw men, so lately drafted from the militia regiments that many of them still bore the number of their former regiments on their accoutrements."

on the first of August, but incorrectly estimating his force at from twelve to fifteen thousand men, he at first marched against him, while Cuesta remained with twenty-five thousand before Victor, and removed five thousand wounded from Talavera. This false movement, and this important division of forces, were near proving fatal to the allies. In fact there was but one of two courses for them to pursue, to march against Soult with their whole army and attack him, or to promptly fall back behind the Tagus by Almaraz; in either case it would have been necessary for them to march to Casa-Tejada, to reach the junction of the road to Plasencia with the great road to Badajos. Learning from Cuesta at Naval-Moral, on the third, what the real force of Soult was, and the danger to which the allies were exposed, Wellington was afraid to venture alone on the road to Almaraz, and fell back from Naval-Moral to Arzobispo, instead of pushing on to Casa-Tejada, so as to be certain of his retreat on the road to Portugal. He might have reached this village on the fourth of August, whereas Soult did not present himself at that place till the following day. The idea of falling back on Arzobispo was good, on the supposition that Cuesta was still at Talavera; but this general, thinking that the English general would hasten his retreat on Almaraz, and that he himself would be compromised if he remained between Soult and Victor, resolved to fall back on Oropeza in order to follow Wellington. This *contre-temps* might have proved fatal to the combined army, if Victor had promptly directed himself on Arzobispo, which he unfortunately neglected to do; and the marshal hearing too late what was passing, and deeming himself fortunate that they had not attacked him on the Alberche after the departure of Joseph, did not venture to push an enemy who was superior in numbers to his own army.

The English army was very near paying dear for these

hesitations and indecisions; their allies, already dissatisfied with the affair of Torrijos, and reproaching the English with leaving them in danger, hastily repassed the bridge of Arzobispo, thus leaving the combined army, on the fifth, hemmed in against the impassable mountain of Guadalupe. This army would certainly have been lost, if Wellington had not sent a detachment, in all haste, to blow up the bridge of Almaraz, while another partly destroyed a portion of the bridge of Arzobispo. As Soult was, nevertheless, coming to attempt the passage of the Tagus, it was all important for the English to escape from the *cul-de-sac* in which they were engaged. With great labor, and by the aid of the Spanish peasants, they constructed a road for artillery, so as to reach the great highway to Truxillo. Soult finally reached the Tagus, with his three corps; he himself passed the river by a ford against the allies' right wing composed of Spanish troops, while Mortier forced the bridge of Arzobispo against the centre. Ney was to seek a ford near Almaraz, the bridge at that place having been destroyed; he would then manœuvre against Wellington's left, and cut off his communications by preceding him on the great road to Badajos. But Ney could find no ford; and the English, consequently, gained time to finish their cross-road and effect their retreat; and the Spaniards, after a warm engagement of cavalry fled, some to Naval-Moral and Toledo, and others to Deleytoza.*

---

* Napier's account of this combat of Arzobispo, and the military operations which followed are well worthy of perusal:

"The fifth and second corps and a division of the sixth were concentrated, to force this passage, early on the morning of the eighth; but Soult being just then informed of Victor's movement, and perceiving that Albuquerque had withdrawn the Spanish cavalry, leaving only a rear guard in the works, judged that the allies were retreating; wherefore, without relinquishing the attack of Arzobispo, he immediately sent the division of the sixth corps back to Naval-Moral, and, at the same time, transmitted a plan of the ford below Almaraz, directed Ney to cross the Tagus there, seize the Puerto de Mirabete, and be in readiness to fall upon the allies, as they came out from the defiles between Deleytoza and Truxillo. Meanwhile, the heat of the day had induced Albu-

This event completed the discord of the allies. Cuesta being disgusted with the operations, and, in fact, far too old for so difficult a command, resigned it to General Eguia,

querque to seek shelter for his horsemen in a wood, near Azutan, a village about five miles from the bridge; and the Spanish infantry, keeping a bad guard, were sleeping or loitering about without care or thought, when Mortier, who was charged with the direction of the attack, taking advantage of their want of vigilance, commenced the passage of the river.

COMBAT OF ARZOBISPO.

"The French cavalry, about six thousand in number, were secretly assembled near the ford, and about two o'clock in the day, General Caulaincourt's brigade suddenly entered the stream. The Spaniards, running to their arms, manned the batteries, and opened upon the leading squadrons, but Mortier, with a powerful concentric fire of artillery, immediately overwhelmed the Spanish gunners; and Caulaincourt having reached the other side of the river, turned to his right, and, taking the batteries in reverse, cut down the artillerymen, and dispersed the infantry who attempted to form. The Duke of Albuquerque, who had mounted at the first alarm, now came down with all his horsemen in one mass, but without order, upon Caulaincourt, and the latter was in imminent danger, when the rest of the French cavalry, passing rapidly, joined in the combat; one brigade of infantry followed at the ford, another burst the barriers on the bridge itself, and, by this time, the Spanish foot, were flying to the mountains. Albuquerque's effort was thus frustrated, a general route ensued, and five guns and about four hundred prisoners were taken.

"Soult's intention being to follow up this success, he directed that the first corps should move, in two columns, upon Guadalupe and Deleytoza, intending to support it with the second and fifth, while the sixth corps crossed at Almaraz, and seized the pass of Mirabete. This would undoubtedly have completed the ruin of the Spanish army, and forced Sir Arthur to make a rapid and disastrous retreat; for so complete was the surprise and so sudden the overthrow, that some of the English foragers also fell into the hands of the enemy; and that Cuesta's army was in no condition to have made any resistance, if the pursuit had been continued with vigor, is clear, from the following facts:

"First, when he withdrew his main body from the bridge of Arzobispo to Peralavla de Garbin, on the seventh, he left fifteen pieces of artillery by the road side, without a guard. The defeat of Albuquerque placed these guns at the mercy of the enemy, who were, however, ignorant of their situation, until a trumpeter attending an English flag of truce, either treacherously or foolishly, mentioned it in the French camp, from whence a detachment of cavalry was sent to fetch them off. Second, the British military agent placed at the Spanish head-quarters, was kept in ignorance of the action; and it was only by the arrival of the Duke of Albuquerque, at Deleytoza, on the evening of the ninth, that Sir Arthur Wellesley knew the bridge was lost. He had before advised Cuesta to withdraw behind the Ibor river, and even now contemplated a par-

who, with one half of his army, moved to the right on Toledo to assist Venegas, while the Duke of Albuquerque, with the left, rallied on Wellington. The latter gained Truxillo with

tial attack to keep the enemy in check; but when he repaired in person to that general's quarter, on the tenth, he found the country covered with fugitives and stragglers, and Cuesta as helpless and yet as haughty as ever. All his ammunition and guns (forty pieces) were on the right bank of the Ibor, and, of course, at the foot of the Meza, and within sight and cannon-shot of the enemy, on the right bank of the Tagus; they would have been taken by the first French patrols that approached, but that Sir Arthur Wellesley persuaded the Spanish staff officers to have them dragged up the hill, in the course of the tenth, without Cuesta's knowledge.

"In this state of affairs, the impending fate of the Peninsula was again averted by the king, who recalled the first corps to the support of the fourth, then opposed to Venegas. Marshal Ney, also, was unable to discover the ford below the bridge of Almaraz, and, by the eleventh, the allies had reëstablished their line of defense. The headquarters of the British were at Jaraicejo, and those of the Spanish at Deleytoza; the former guarding the ford of Almaraz, formed the left; the latter, occupying the Meza d'Ibor and Campillo, were on the right. The twelfth, Cuesta resigned. General Eguia succeeded to the command, and at first gave hopes of a better coöperation, but the evil was in the character of the people. The position of the allies was, however, compact and central; the reserves could easily support the advanced posts; the communication to the rear was open, and, if defended with courage, the Meza d'Ibor was impregnable; and to pass the Tagus at Almaraz, in itself a difficult operation, would, while the Mirabete and Meza d'Ibor were occupied, have been dangerous for the French, as they would be inclosed in the narrow space between those ridges and the river.

"The Duke of Dalmatia, thus thwarted, conceived that Sir Arthur Wellesley would endeavor to repass the Tagus by Alcantara, and so rejoin Beresford and the five thousand British troops under Catlin, Craufurd and Lightburn, which were, by this time, near the frontiers of Portugal. To prevent this he resolved to march at once upon Coria, with the second, fifth, and sixth corps, threaten both Beresford's and Sir Arthur's communication with Lisbon, and, at the same time, prepare for the siege of Ciudad-Rodrigo; but Marshal Ney absolutely refused to concur in this operation. He observed that Sir Arthur Wellesley was not yet in march for Alcantara; that it was exceedingly dangerous to invade Portugal in a hasty manner; and that the army could not be fed between Coria, Plasencia, and the Tagus; finally, that Salamanca, being again in possession of the Spaniards, it was more fitting that the sixth corps should retake that town, and occupy the line of the Tormes, to cover Castile. This reasoning was approved by Joseph, who dreaded the further fatigue and privations that would attend a continuance of the operations during the excessive heats, and in a wasted country; and he was strengthened in his opinion by the receipt of a dispatch from the emperor, dated Schönbrunn, the twenty-ninth of July, in which any further offensive operations were forbidden, until the reënforcements

difficulty, and afterward fell back on Badajos. General Wilson, compromised at Naval-Carnero, had the good fortune to escape in rear of Soult, and take refuge in the mountains of Gredos.

Battle of Almonacid.—Joseph, encouraged by the retreat of the enemy, returned to Toledo, at the moment when

which the recent victory of Wagram enabled him to send should arrive in Spain. The second corps was, consequently, directed to take post at Plasencia; the fifth corps relieved the first at Talavera, and the English wounded being, by Victor, given over to Marshal Mortier; the latter, with a chivalrous sense of honor, would not permit his own soldiers, although suffering severe privations themselves, to receive rations until the hospitals were first supplied; the sixth corps was directed upon Valladolid, for Joseph was alarmed lest a fresh insurrection, excited and supported by the Duke del Parque, should spread over the whole of Leon and Castile.

"Ney marched on the eleventh; but, to his surprise, found that Sir Robert Wilson, with about four thousand men, part Spaniards, part Portuguese, was in possession of the pass of Baños. To explain this, it must be observed, that when the British army marched from Talavera, on the third, Wilson, being at Nombella, was put in communication with Cuesta. He had sent his artillery to the army on the third, and on the fourth, finding that the Spaniards had abandoned Talavera, he fell back with his infantry to Vellada, a few miles north of Talavera. He was then twenty-four miles from Arzobispo, and, as Cuesta did not quit Oropesa until the fifth, a junction with Sir Arthur Wellesley might have been effected; but it was impossible to know this at the time, and Wilson, very prudently, crossing the Tietar, made for the mountains, trusting to his activity and local knowledge to escape the enemy. Villatte's division pursued him, on the fifth, to Nombella; a detachment from the garrison of Avila was watching for him in the passes of Arenas and Monbeltran; and General Foy waited for him in the Vera de Plasencia. Nevertheless, baffling his opponents, he broke through their circle at Viander, passed the Gredos at a ridge called the Sierra de Lanes, and, getting into the valley of the Tormes, reached Bejar;—from thence, thinking to recover his communications with the army, he marched toward Plasencia, by the pass of Baños, and thus, on the twelfth, met with Ney returning to the Salamanca country.

"The dust of the French column being seen from afar, and a retreat to Ciudad-Rodrigo open, it is not easy to comprehend why Sir Robert Wilson should have given battle to the sixth corps. His position, although difficult of approach, and strengthened by the piling of large stones in the narrowest parts, was not one in which he could hope to stop a whole army; and, accordingly, when the French, overcoming the local obstacles, got close upon his left, the fight was at an end; the first charge broke both the legion and the Spanish auxiliaries, and the whole dispersed. Ney continued his march, and, having recovered the line of the Tormes, resigned the command of the sixth corps to General Marchand, and returned to France."

Venegas was bombarding that city from the left bank of the Tagus, and seeking to get possession of the passage of the river; but the Spaniard's hopes, in this respect, were soon terminated. The corps of Sebastiani, seconded by Desolles' division, passed the Tagus on the ninth of August to punish the Spanish general for his untimely movement; he drove in his vanguard; and, on the eleventh of August, reached Venegas himself, at Almonacid, on the road to Mora and Madridejos. The Spanish forces amounted to about thirty thousand after receiving their reënforcements.* They occupied a well-selected position; a good reserve, supported by forty pieces of artillery, crowned the formidable heights, on which is situated the old chateau of Almonacid. Encouraged by the enthusiasm of his troops who requested, with loud cries, to be led against the enemy, and willing to give them all the honor of the victory, Sebastiani, without waiting for Desolles, directed his attack on the hill occupied by the Spanish left;—the Polish division, under Prince Sulkoski, attacked the position in front, while the German division, under Laval, turned it by the right. The French division, in order to favor this attack, assailed the centre on the plateau of Almonacid. The front line of the Spaniards is everywhere forced. Venegas, in order to disengage it, throws his cavalry on the right flank of Sebastiani, and drives it back. This movement gives the enemy a temporary success; but the arrival of Desolles' division soon restores the chances in our favor. New dispositions are made to complete the victory. Desolles is to attack the enemy's left in front, while its flank is turned by the Polish and German divisions; a brigade is at the same time to assail the right wing. Every thing falls before this well-combined effort;—the position is

---

* The number of this army is variously estimated at from fifteen to thirty-six thousand men. Napier says the force "was somewhat more than twenty-five thousand strong, with forty pieces of artillery."

carried; the chateau and the heights, occupied by the Spanish reserve, arrest our enthusiastic troops for scarcely a quarter of an hour; and the cavalry of Milhaud and Merlin carry terror and death into the broken battalions of the enemy. The Spaniards, routed with horrible slaughter, take the road to the Sierra Morena, leaving behind thirty-five pieces of artillery, two hundred carriages, four thousand prisoners, and an equal number *hors-de-combat*.

Ney defeats Wilson.—This brilliant feat of arms, which crowned the campaign of Talavera, was well calculated to encourage Joseph; but he had already deprived himself of the means of profiting by it, as he could otherwise have done, by too soon detaching Ney's corps and directing it to return toward Salamanca. While on this march, Ney's vanguard encountered the partisan Wilson, at the hill of Baños in the arid mountains of Gredos. The Anglo-Portuguese general, notwithstanding the natural strength of his position, which had been rendered still more impregnable by all the artificial means in his power, was defeated and driven, with the loss of a thousand men, into the mountains of Gata on the confines of Portugal.

Remarks on these Operations.—Thus ended the short campaign of Talavera, one of the most remarkable episodes in this war. The military talents of Joseph were far from brilliant. Having got rid of the English who retreated toward Badajos, but being still embarrassed by the danger with which the Spaniards threatened his capital, and not knowing how to profit by the imposing force which the union of five *corps-d'armée* had given him, his only thought was to despatch Sebastiani against Venegas; and Ney toward Salamanca! It is true that this point was without defense, and that Beresford, with the aid of the Duke del Parque, might, had he been of a more enterprising character, have threatened our communications in the north. But mere accessories like this, however important in themselves, must frequently be sacrificed in order to secure more important results. If Joseph had been a better general, and less anxious to return to his palace, he would not have given Wellington a moment's rest. Leaving a single *corps-d'armée* at Toledo, with his four others, he should have fallen on the English wherever they could be found, if it were even at Lisbon or Cadiz. Never was there so fine an opportunity for a decisive operation, during the whole war in Spain. One of the greatest regrets I have felt in leaving my stormy career, is that of not having been present at that time with my army on the Tagus. Even supposing Beresford had advanced to the Douro and Venegas had pushed forward to the capital, I should have troubled myself very little about their operations; for they would have deemed themselves exceedingly fortunate to escape safe and sound after the defeat of the principal army.

The news of my victory at Wagram, the armistice of Znaim, and the retreat of the English on the Guadiana, consoled Joseph for the loss of Galicia and his want of success at Talavera; but it was important not to sleep on the bosom of a negative victory. Marshal Soult, it is said, proposed to the king to advance on Lisbon by forced marches, at the moment when Wellington was seeking to repair, near Badajos, the losses which he had experienced in the defiles of Arzobispo and Guadalupe. The movement, indeed, seemed most favorable for anticipating the enemy in the capital of Portugal, and of thus overthrowing his whole system of defence. But why go to Lisbon, and leave Wellington an opportunity to base himself on Badajos and Cadiz? It was against *his* army that the king should have marched with four corps,—a force sufficient to force him in front, and, at the same time, to manœuvre so as to cut off his line of retreat. But the fear that Madrid might be exposed to the attacks of the

Spaniards closed the eyes of Joseph to every other consideration.

The most experienced military men have generally agreed in the opinion that this was the decisive moment in the whole war, and that the unfortunate issue of that war was attributable to allowing this opportunity to escape unimproved. It is certain that all probable conjectures on the resulting operations fully confirm this opinion; and, especially, if they had been so directed as to strike a mortal blow to Wellington's army before he could regain his vessels; but if he had succeeded in reaching Cadiz, and had based himself on that place and Gibraltar, he might still have prolonged the war. Although it would have been much easier for us to reduce him to the defensive in the island of Leon than at the mouth of the Tagus, still there would have been chances for him to carry on successful operations along the immense extent of coast from Coruña to Tarragona; and the contest might still have been continued, though under circumstances much more favorable for us.*

---

* The following remarks of Napier upon the operations of the French during this campaign are both able and just.

"Joseph was finally successful, yet it may be safely affirmed that, with the exception of uniting his three corps behind the Guadarama, on the evening of the twenty-fifth, his proceedings were an almost uninterrupted series of errors. He would not suffer Soult to besiege Ciudad-Rodrigo with seventy thousand men, in the end of July. To protect Madrid from the army of Venegas, overbalanced, in his mind, the advantages of this bold and grand project, which would inevitably have drawn Sir Arthur Wellesley from the Tagus, and which, interrupting all military communication between the northern and southern provinces, and insuring possession of Castile and Leon, would, by its success, have opened a broad way to Lisbon. Cuesta and Venegas, meanwhile, would have marched against Madrid! Cuesta and Venegas acting on external lines, and whose united force did not exceed sixty-five thousand men! The king, holding a central position, with fifty thousand French veterans, was alarmed at this prospect, and, rejecting Soult's plan, drew Mortier, with the fifth corps, to Villa Castin. Truly, this was to avoid the fruit-tree from fear of a nettle at its stem!

"Sir Arthur Wellesley's advance to Talavera was the result of this great error; but he having thus incautiously afforded Soult an opportunity of strik-

Soult succeeds Jourdan as Joseph's Chief of Staff.—All parties were dissatisfied with the results of the expedition on Talavera. Less displeased with the errors committed in the

ing a fatal blow, a fresh combination was concerted. The king, with equal judgment and activity, then united all his own forces near Toledo, separated Venegas from Cuesta, pushed back the latter upon the English army, and obliged both to stand on the defensive, with eyes attentively directed to their front, when the real point of danger was in the rear. This, indeed, was skillful; but the battle of Talavera, which followed, was a palpable, an enormous fault The allies could neither move forward nor backward, without being infinitely worse situated for success than in that strong position, which seemed marked out by fortune herself for their security. Until the thirty-first, the operations of Venegas were not even felt, hence, till the thirty-first, the French position on the Alberche might have been maintained without danger; and, on the first of August, the head of Soult's column was at Plasencia.

" Let us suppose that the French had merely made demonstrations on the twenty-eighth, and had retired behind the Alberche on the twenty-ninth, would the allies have dared to attack them in that position ? The conduct of the Spaniards, on the evening of the twenty-seventh, answers the question; and, moreover, Joseph, with an army compact, active, and experienced, could with ease have baffled any efforts of the combined forces to bring him to action; he might have covered himself by the Guadarama river and by the Tagus in succession, and the further he led his opponents from Talavera, without uncovering the line of La Mancha, the more certain the effect of Soult's operations; but here we have another proof that double external lines are essentially vicious.

" The combined movement of the French was desirable, from the greatness of the object to be gained, and safe, from the powerful force on each point : and the occasion was so favorable that, notwithstanding the imprudent heat of Victor, the reluctance of Ney, and the unsteady temper of the king, the fate of the allies was, up to the evening of the third, heavy in the scale. Nevertheless, as the central position held by the allies, cut the line of correspondence between Joseph and Soult, the king's despatches were intercepted, and the whole operation, even at the last hour, was thus baffled. The first element of success in war is, that every thing should emanate from a single head ; and it would have been preferable that the king, drawing the second and fifth corps to him by the pass of the Guadarama, or by that of Avila, should, with the eighty thousand men thus united, have fallen upon the allies in front. Such a combination, although of less brilliant promise than the one adopted, would have been a sure ; and the less a general trusts to fortune the better;—she is capricious!

" When one Spanish army was surprised at Arzobispo, another completely beaten at Almonacid, and when Wilson's Portuguese corps was dispersed at Baños, the junta had just completed the measure of their folly by quarreling with the British, which was the only force left that could protect them. The French were, in truth, therefore, the masters of the Peninsula, but they terminated their operations at the very moment when they should have pursued

battle itself than in the subsequent operations, I gave to Soult the office of major-general to Joseph, hoping that he would conduct his operations with more skill than his predecessor.

Combats of Tamames and Alba de Tormes.—On arriving at Salamanca, Marshal Ney, who, like many others, quarreled with his colleagues when placed under their orders, left the country and returned to France, rather than obey the orders of Soult. General Marchand, who, in Ney's absence, was charged with the command of the sixth corps, was disturbed

them with redoubled activity, because the general aspect of affairs and the particular circumstances of the campaign were alike favorable. For Napoleon was victorious in Germany; and of the British expeditions against Italy and Holland, the former had scarcely struggled into life,—the latter was already corrupting in death. Hence, Joseph might have been assured that he would receive reinforcements, but that none, of any consequence, could reach his adversaries; and, in the Peninsula, there was nothing to oppose him. Navarre, Biscay, Aragon, and the Castiles were subdued; Gerona closely beleaguered, and the rest of Catalonia, if not quiescent, totally unable to succor that noble city. Valencia was inert; the Asturians still trembling; in Galicia there was nothing but confusion. Romana, commanding fifteen thousand infantry, but neither cavalry nor artillery, was then at Coruña and dared not quit the mountains. The Duke del Parque held Ciudad-Rodrigo, but was in no condition to make head against more than a French division. The battle of Almonacid had cleared La Mancha of troops. Estremadura and Andalusia were, as we have seen, weak, distracted, and incapable of solid resistance. There remained only the English and Portuguese armies, the one being at Jaraceijo, the other at Moraleja.

"The line of resistance may, therefore, be said to have extended from the Sierra Morena to Coruña—weak from its length ; weaker, that the allied corps, being separated by mountains, by rivers, and by vast tracts of country, and having different bases of operation, such as Lisbon, Seville, and Ciudad-Rodrigo, could not act in concert, except offensively ; and with how little effect in that way the campaign of Talavera had proved. But the French were concentrated in a narrow space, and, having only Madrid to cover, were advantageously situated for offensive or defensive movements. The allied forces were, for the most part, imperfectly organized, and would not, altogether, have amounted to ninety thousand fighting men. The French were above one hundred thousand, dangerous from their discipline and experience, more dangerous that they held a central position, and that their numbers were unknown to their opponents; and, moreover, having, in four days, gained one general and two minor battles, their courage was high and eager."

in his cantonements about Salamanca by the corps of the Duke del Parque (formerly Romana's army), which, by means of the fortifications of Ciudad-Rodrigo and the proximity of the English army, was enabled to harass our troops almost incessantly. Marchand attacked him on the sixteenth of October, at Tamames, in a position difficult of access, where the efforts of the brave division of Maucune were of no avail against an enemy sheltered behind rocks. At the end of the combat the Duke del Parque gained possession of Salamanca. As it was incompatible with the safety of the army to suffer this slight success to go unpunished, General Kellerman, leaving Valladolid at the head of a division of dragoons, rejoined the sixth corps, and on the twenty-eighth of November, attacked and defeated the Duke del Parque at Alba de Tormes, without even waiting for a union of his own forces. He, therefore, was unable to cut up the beaten enemy, who escaped, during the night, from the resentment of the sixth corps, who were anxious to revenge the affront which they had received a few weeks before at Tamames.

Arrizaga beaten at Ocana.—The junta of Cadiz, dissatisfied with the dispersion of its armies and the failure of its project on Madrid, now ordered General Eguia to unite the army of Cuesta with the remains of Venegas' command. The Marquis of Arrizaga took command of these united forces, which numbered fifty thousand men. Proud of so imposing a force, the presumptuous Spaniard thought that he alone could accomplish what Wellington had failed to do. He advances on Aranjuez; a vanguard of the *élite*, preceding the Spanish army, debouches into the plain of Ocana, on the twelfth of November, and attacks Sebastiani. The Spanish cavalry even ventures to assail Milhaud, who draws it on to a square of a Polish regiment, whose fire makes terrible havoc in its ranks. Milhaud then throws himself on the enemy at the head of his dragoons, beats him, and destroys almost the entire corps of royal carabineers, the pride of Castile. By means of this success Sebastiani maintains himself audaciously between Ocana and the Tagus, and covers the bridge of Aranjuez till the arrival of reënforcements. Soult and Joseph, on hearing of this combat, fly to the assistance of Sebastiani, at the head of Mortier's corps; Victor, also, receives orders to march from Villamaurique on Ocana, where he will arrive on the eighteenth, until which time our troops are to suspend their attack. The Spanish army, united to its vanguard, either wishing to anticipate this junction, or taking our hesitation as an indication of fear, attack us on the morning of the eighteenth. Leval's division is obliged to fall back, and the presumptuous enemy pursues it across the ravine. Soult wishes to retire, in order to gain time for Victor to come up; but our troops are so eager for the fight, and Leval so seriously engaged, that all are directed to fall at once on the enemy, now puffed up with his temporary success. General Senarmont advances, as at Friedland, with a battery of thirty pieces of artillery, and thunders against the front, which Mortier attacks from his side. At this decisive moment the cavalry of Sebastiani charges the right of the Spaniards, whose squadrons, still terrified by the affair of the twelfth, remain quiet spectators of this movement; their infantry seek in vain to form squares in a wood of olive-trees, but are everywhere routed, sabred or taken prisoners. The division of Latour-Maubourg, belonging to Victor's corps, arrives at this opportune moment, and completes the total rout of the enemy, who flies even to Guardia, leaving behind him horrible traces of disorder and confusion. Fifty pieces of cannon, thirty stand of colors, and twenty thousand prisoners, are the brilliant trophies of their victory, and furnish, at the same time, a glorious and irrefragable proof of the superiority of our soldiers over the Spanish. The flying enemy does not rally till he reaches the defiles of the Sierra-Morena, where Joseph, troubled by the presence of Wellington's army on the confines of Portugal, thought he ought not to follow them.

Inaction of Wellington.—It is quite remarkable, that at this moment, when Spain was receiving such a terrible check, Wellington remained completely inactive on the confines of Portugal, although the dispersion of the second and third corps between the Tagus and Salamanca, offered an opportunity for a powerful diversion. The fault of this inaction is attributed to English policy, and an excessive care for the preservation of an army, on which, according to them, entirely depended the success of the war and the deliverance of the Peninsula. However excessive this prudence may appear in a military point of view, still it would be unjust to find fault with it; for it was, in fact, of very little importance to Wellington if the war should last for ten years, provided he did not hazard the safety of his own army; had it been *English* soil from which he was seeking to drive us, he should have risked everything to accomplish that object. But here the case was different. And to these plausible motives for inaction, there must be added others still more powerful. Wellington, dissatisfied at the hesitation of the supreme junta to place the Spanish troops formally under his own orders, had repaired to Seville after the retreat to Badajos, and consulted with his brother, the Marquis of Wellesley, then British embassador, for the purpose of establishing the basis of some system which would secure greater unity of action. The risk he had run at Arzobispo proved to the English general that, notwithstanding the great advantage derived from the *national* war in Spain, it would be dangerous for him to attempt any bold enterprises into the heart of the kingdom, until he had first secured a place of refuge, sufficient reënforcements, and a better system of coöperation on the part of the Spanish troops. Romana was called for this purpose to the junta of Seville, where it was hoped that his services and credit would give great additional support to the English influence.*

* When remonstrated with by Lord Wellesley for abandoning the Spaniards at this period, Wellington replied, that "Want had driven him to separate from them, but their shameful flight at Arzobispo would alone have justified him for doing so. To take up a defensive position behind the Guadiana would be useless, because that river was fordable, and the ground behind it weak. The line of the Tagus, occupied at the moment by Eguia, was so strong that if the Spaniards could defend anything they might defend that. His advice, then, was, that they should send the pontoon bridge to Badajos, and remain on the defensive at Deleytoza and Almaraz. But, it might be asked, he said, was there no chance of renewing the offensive? To what purpose? The French were as numerous, if not more so, than the allies; and, with respect to the Spaniards at least, superior in discipline and every military quality. To advance again was only to play the same losing game as before. Baños and Perales must be guarded, or the bands in Castile would again pour through upon the rear of the allied army; but who was to guard these passes. The British were too few to detach, and the Spaniards could not be trusted; and if they could, Avila and Guadarama passes remained, by which the enemy could reïnforce the army in front,—for there were no Spanish troops in the north of Spain capable of making a diversion.

"But there was a more serious consideration, namely, the constant and shameful misbehavior of the Spanish troops before the enemy. We, in England, never hear of their defeats and flights, but I have heard Spanish officers telling of nineteen or twenty actions of the description of that at the bridge of Arzobispo, accounts of which, I believe, have never been published. In the battle of Talavera, in which the Spanish army, with very trifling exception, was not engaged—whole corps threw away their arms, and ran off, when they were neither attacked nor threatened with an attack. When these dastardly soldiers run away they plunder everything they meet. In their flight from Talavera they plundered the baggage of the British army, which was, at that moment, bravely engaged in their cause.

"For these reasons he would not, he said, again coöperate with the Spaniards; yet, by taking post on the Portuguese frontier, he would hang upon the enemy's flank, and thus, unless the latter came with very great forces, prevent him from crossing the Guadiana. This reasoning was conclusive, but ere it reached Lord Wellesley, the latter found that, so far from his plans, relative to the supply, having been adopted, he could not even get an answer from the junta; that miserable body, at one moment shrinking with fear, at the next bursting with folly, now talked of the enemy's being about to retire to the Pyrenees, or even to the interior of France! and assuming the right to dispose of the Portuguese army as well as their own, importunately pressed for an immediate, combined, offensive operation, by the troops of the three nations to harass the enemy in his retreat! but, at the same time, they ordered Eguia to withdraw from Deleytoza, behind the Guadiana."

The expedition of Arrizaga was in no way connected with the defensive plan of the English general; to march again into Estremadura, in time to act in concert, was diametrically opposed to his present projects. In fact, instead of again ascending the Guadiana to act with Arrizaga, as soon as he had terminated the conferences of Seville, Wellington directed his army from Badajos by Albuquerque to the north of Portugal, to act in concert with the Duke del Parque, who was commanding the former corps of Romana, under Ciudad-Rodrigo, and with Beresford, who covered Almeida. This new plan of operations was not without merit, since it carried the English army on the most important point of our communications, which had been stripped of its means of defense by the concentration of our troops on the frontier of Andalusia. To this important advantage, it also added that of better covering Portugal, which constituted the essential base of all British operations for the deliverance of the Peninsula.

Intrenched Camp of Torres Vedras.—But Wellington did not stop here. He felt that a solid mass of forty thousand Anglo-Hanoverians, with as many more disciplined and devoted Portuguese, would contend with strong chances of success against an army like ours, compelled to greatly extend itself in order to procure provisions, cover its long line of communications, and repress insurrections; but the example of Moore proved to the English that, with adversaries so active and impetuous, they might encounter rude assaults. It was, therefore, important for Wellington to secure to his army a formidable place of refuge against a catastrophe like that of Coruña, to give him time to employ his forces to the best advantage, to enable him to receive reënforcements, and, in case of necessity, to embark his army in safety and descend again upon some other point of the vast Peninsula. For this purpose, immediately after his return from Seville, he directed an immense intrenched camp to be laid out on the heights of Torres Vedras, which constituted the base of a vast triangle, the sea coast and the Tagus forming the sides, with Lisbon for the vertex.

Romana and the Junta of Seville.—These measures seemed the more wise, as the presence of Romana at Seville failed to accomplish the desired object ; this general being soon involved in a controversy with the junta. The latter was jealous of the national independence, and treated the English as auxiliaries who affected a false disinterestedness for Spain. It thought, with reason, that it was less for Spain than for England herself that they exhibited so much *empressement ;* it had, therefore, refused to receive the English troops in Cadiz. Wellington attributed to this jealousy the conduct of Cuesta, and the ill-success of the enterprise against Madrid. Both had good reasons for their opinions ; but such a difference of interests might assist our cause as much as the force of bayonets. The English having obtained complete influence over the mind of Romana, they persuaded him that the junta would lose all through their ill-placed jealousy and national vanity, and determined him to dissolve that body and establish in its place a less numerous regency. He issued proclamations in which he reproached the junta for the same faults with which I had charged the Directory on my return from Egypt He seemed ready to effect a political revolution and seize on the helm of government ; but his trifling character ill-fitted him for playing the part of Cromwell, or even that which I had acted on the eighteenth Brumaire. Let us leave these intrigues as foreign from the object of the present narrative, and complete our hasty sketch of the military operations of the Peninsula.

Blake's Efforts to deliver Aragon. — The obstinate defense of Saragossa had given additional *eclat* to its fall ;— it was a second Numantia reduced. Satisfied with these results, my generals deemed the question decided, and that there was no need of great efforts to consolidate their success. But the more prompt we were to proclaim our success as decisive, the more active were the Spaniards to counteract its moral influence on the people. No sooner were they informed of my departure for France and that of Mortier's corps for Castile, than they perceived the advantages that would result from their falling in force on the third corps, which alone remained to guard Aragon. The regency took advantage, without delay, of this circumstance. Their troops in Catalonia and at Valencia were placed under the orders of General Blake, who was, at the same time, made commandant of Aragon. He soon collected a disposable *corps-d'armée*, and formed the bold and important plan of driving us from Aragon by raising and again arming the inhabitants of the country against us; if he should obtain complete success in this, he would afterward march by Navarre, reascending the Ebro toward Miranda, in order to establish himself between Bayonne and Madrid, threatening all our lines of operations and interrupting all communication between the capital and France. The latter part of this plan, although hazardous, will appear less rash, if we reflect that I was at this time engaged in a new contest with Austria, and that Marshal Soult was moving from Coruña toward the centre of Portugal, where the English were beginning to organize an army for the defense of the Peninsula. But Blake had first to fight the French corps who were defending Saragossa; and, if he failed in this attempt, he succeeded but too well in reviving the resistance of the populace. Levies and armaments were prepared in all parts of Aragon; Villa-Campa, Durand, Ramon, Gayan, on the right bank of the Ebro; Mina, on the frontier of Navarre; Renovalis, Sarrara, Perena, Pero-Duro, Cantarero, and others in Upper Aragon.—formed successively around the third *corps-d'armée*, a circle of partisans and guerilla bands which did not cease, till the end of the war, to fetter its movements and oppose its operations.

Operations of Suchet.—The troops of this corps were mainly composed of recruits collected from different nations, and the severe labors of the siege had both fatigued and disgusted them. They did not exceed fifteen or sixteen thousand combatants, and their moral force was still less than their numbers. Happily General Suchet had just replaced Junot in this important command. When this general reached Saragossa, on the nineteenth of May, his predecessor was still entirely ignorant of the movements and projects of Blake; but the next day after his arrival, he learned that General Leval had been attacked at Alcanitz, and obliged to retire before considerable forces; at the same time General Robert, posted on the Cinca, having passed eight companies of the *élite* to the left bank of that river, was prevented by the rise of water from going to their assistance, and reported that they had been surrounded and captured by the armed inhabitants with the aid of the garrison of Lerida, after a glorious combat of three days. The loss of these brave men was to be regretted, but could not be repaired. The movement of Blake on Alcanitz, demanded serious attention and prompt resolution; that general at the head of eighteen thousand men, was entering Aragon and menacing Saragossa. The third corps was scattered; General Suchet hastened to recall General Habert to the right bank of the Ebro; he took away all the reserve at Saragossa, and, marching on the Puebla of Ixar to the support of Leval's division, encountered the enemy on the twenty-third of May. The Spaniards had taken an advantageous position, and had a numerous and well-served artillery; and Suchet, notwithstanding all his efforts, could not bring his troops to the charge. He withdrew them at the close of the day, and a panic terror was near causing a total rout ; the authors of this were tried and shot ; order was restored and Suchet marched his army to Saragossa.

His position was critical ; if he should risk a decisive affair and be beaten, he would compromise all the centre of Spain ; if he should now abandon Saragossa, whose defense had covered the enemy with so much glory, Europe would not fail to contrast his conduct with the heroism of Palafox, without taking into consideration the difference of situations and of the elements of defense. Suchet encamped his troops on Mount Torero and caused them to manœuvre ; he excited their enthusiasm by presenting to them the disgrace of yielding in energy to the defenders of Saragossa, and merely waited for the return of the five battalions which had escorted the prisoners to France to punish Blake for his audacity. Fortunately, the Spanish general allowed him time for all his preparations ; either wishing to surround the third corps, or fearing to attack it in front, he took fifteen days to go round from Alcanitz by Ixar, Belchite, Botorte and Muela.

Combat of Maria.—The battalions from France were not expected to return till the fifteenth of June. But on the thirteenth, Blake, advancing by the valley of the Huerba, had separated from the *corps-d'armée* and driven on Epila a detachment commanded by General Fabre, thus threatening Alagon and our line of retreat. Suchet carried the brigades of Musnier and Habert with his cavalry to the convent of Santa-Fé, avoiding, however, a general action. General Leval was left on Mount Torero with a part of his division, and a reserve occupied Saragossa under Colonel Haxo. The interval till the fifteenth was occupied with skirmishes ; Blake then deployed twenty-five thousand men and offered battle. His position was taken in front of the village of Maria, his right resting on the Huerba and the great road

which, at this place, crosses by a bridge a small affluent of
the Huerba, his centre and his left resting on heights which
were cut up by ravines. A knowledge of the ground
instantly determined the dispositions of General Suchet.
After waiting till two o'clock in the afternoon for the arrival
of the troops returning from France, and hearing that they
were within a league of him, he determined to regard them
as a reserve and to engage all the troops he had on the
field of battle. He established his line parallel to that of
Blake, and attacked the left and centre; then, making a
vigorous charge on his right, he carried the bridge and road,
which was the only defile by which Blake could retire with
the artillery with which he had well furnished the front of
his line. The contest on the heights was prolonged by a
violent storm, but the retreat and flight of the Spanish
infantry closed it, leaving in our hands twenty-three pieces
of cannon and a small number of prisoners, among whom
were a colonel, and General O'Donoju.

Combat of Belchite.—The victory of Maria saved the third
corps and also Saragossa; but, in order to deliver all Aragon from the hands of the enemy, Suchet desired to cut up
and destroy the army of Blake; he, therefore, pushed it
with all possible rapidity in the direction of Belchite, to
which place it had retreated. Blake took position in front
of this little town on the eighteenth, and awaited his
approach; to attack the enemy in front, and to turn and
force his left, was only the work of an hour. The new levies
were seized with panic. The regiment of Valencia, in
attempting an orderly retreat, was sabred by our cavalry and
taken prisoners; the remainder fled to Alcanitz. Blake
reached Tortosa with the loss of twenty-three pieces of
cannon, and four or five thousand men killed and taken
prisoners.

St. Cyr's Operations in Catalonia.—Our troops had also

been successful in Catalonia, although the successes there had not been attended with the same results, on account of the magnitude of the obstacles to be overcome, and the immense resources furnished to the insurgents by sea. St. Cyr had been before Tarragona since the month of February; in the impossibility of holding out a long time before this place, he asked for the means of besieging Gerona, for without the possession of that place our position in Catalonia would always be precarious. It was almost impossible to maintain our communications; the correspondence was carried on by sea with the greatest difficulty, and not less than six or seven battalions were required to convey an order from Perpignan to Barcelona. St. Cyr, therefore, resolved to march toward Vich, both for the purpose of supplies and to facilitate the siege of Gerona. On learning the obstacles which opposed us in this province, I had resolved, near the end of 1808, to send there the fourth *corps-d'armée*, under the orders of Massena. He had already crossed the Rhine on his march to Spain when the war with Austria forced him to return to Germany, where the conquerors of Eylau proved themselves worthy of their ancient glory. This diversion was peculiarly unfortunate, and contributed not a little to the unfavorable issue of the war in Spain. However, measures were taken to supply the deficiency as soon as possible; a siege park was assembled at Perpignan; General Verdier replaced Reille at Figueras, and formed a corps of eighteen battalions destined to conduct the attack on this place.

Siege of Gerona.—Gerona has become illustrious in history for a defense no less extraordinary than that of Saragossa. It is true that this place was more regularly fortified than the capital of Aragon; but it is also indisputable that the obstinacy of its defense was due as much to the bravery of its inhabitants as to the resources of art. More fanatical still than their neighbors, the Geronians gave to St. Narcisse, the command not only of their battalions and the inhabitants of the place, but also of all Spain. Proud of the support of this generalissimo, the inhabitants and even the women, armed themselves against our attacks. If the resistance of the Spaniards had been the result of a patriotism, at the same time heroic and enlightened, they would undoubtedly have recurred to other means of resistance and have appointed different generals to command them! Fortunately for them St. Narcisse had a lieutenant worthy of the command; for General Alvarez was in every respect a brave man, and not less determined than Palafox, to render his name immortal by a desperate defense; the enthusiasm of the inhabitants assisted this natural resolution.

Gerona is situated on the Ter, at the foot of a gorge through which passes the road to Perpignan. The city has an enciente of mediocre character; but the mountains which surround it on the north and east, are crowned with four forts which render its investment difficult and of considerable extent. In order to attack it on the south side, it was necessary to open a road for the artillery; for the only practicable carriage road passes by the city. Men were wanting for such a work; moreover, it would have been difficult to maintain ourselves in the city, in case of its capture, against a hostile population, if the forts had not first been reduced. The most expeditious and natural plan was to take those first.

Verdier was reënforced to the number of eighteen thousand men, and St. Cyr remained at Vich to assist him. The Spaniards were not idle; Reding having died at Tarragona, the junta had confided to Blake the command of the kingdoms of Grenada, Valencia, and Catalonia. His first effort to justify the confidence thus reposed in him, was to deliver Saragossa. We have just seen how Suchet received him at

Santa Maria; Blake now sought to avenge himself for this, by delivering Gerona. He began by attempting to throw provisions into the place, and his very rich convoy fell into the hands of our soldiers. St. Cyr now saw the importance of taking from the insurgents the support of Port Palamos, which facilitated their receiving succors by sea; the place was carried by the Italians with great bravery. This capture rendered the provisioning of Gerona more difficult, and also enabled us to push forward our works with more security.

After a first assault had failed, and several efforts of the enemy to succor Gerona had been repelled, Blake himself finally appeared on the first of September, to provision the place. By pretending to attempt the deliverance of Gerona by open force, he succeeded in deceiving St. Cyr, and drawing away the mass of his army toward Bellona, while Brigadier Garcia-Condé introduced two thousand men, with a grand convoy of provisions and munitions. St. Cyr marched after Blake to offer him battle, but the latter fell back; our troops now returned to Gerona, but they were too late, for the enemy had deposited their convoy in the place and effected their escape. On the nineteenth of November, a practicable breach was effected in the enciente of the place, and an assault attempted; but it was unsuccessful. On the twenty-sixth, Blake made a third attempt to succor the place; but this time St. Cyr made his dispositions so well that the convoy, coming from Abisbal, was completely surrounded and captured. This brilliant affair, which cost the Spaniards three thousand men, took place in full view of Blake's army, which was encamped near San-Pelago.

The great length of the siege of Gerona appeared to me to argue against the energy and efficiency of St. Cyr, and I resolved to replace him by Augereau, who had rendered himself illustrious in this country by the celebrated battle of Figueras, in 1794. This general took command of the army a few days afterward, but he did nothing to justify my choice. He allowed O'Donnell to escape from Gerona where his presence had become superfluous after the loss of his convoy of provisions. On the eleventh of December, this place, pushed more and more warmly, and reduced to the last extremity, finally determined to capitulate. One half of its garrison and of its population had fallen in this glorious contest.

General Remarks on the Operations of the Campaign.— This event terminated the campaign of 1809, in which we had gained great successes and committed great errors. The worst error was, undoubtedly, that of leaving the command of the army to a king without energy and without military talents. Our forces should have been divided into three independent armies, with a reserve forming a corps of occupation on their rear. The king should have been empowered to order the junction of two of these armies, in case it had been necessary to attack the English, or, in case a serious check had required a concentration of forces. The most skillful of my marshals should have been given to the king as a major-general, to guide this mass to victory. In every other case each army should have acted independently within the limits assigned to it. But divided as our troops were into eight or ten isolated corps, their power was paralyzed by the jealousy and rivalry of their chiefs. Ney, for example, lay six months in Galicia with his arms folded, without being able to communicate either with Madrid or Bayonne, because he commanded neither at Valladolid, nor at Leon, nor in the Asturias, and could form no plan of coöperation. All the troops between Burgos and the ocean should have been put under the orders of a single chief. In the East there should have been an army of the Oriental Pyrenees, to operate in Aragon and in Catalonia.

The king was too anxious to enjoy the pleasures of royalty at Madrid; he should have waited till Spain was subjected to his power ; his capital should have been at the headquarters of the army of the centre, until his kingdom was conquered. But he wished, at every cost, to spare his country, and he rendered many of the military operations subordinate to this object. He acted the Spaniard more thoroughly than Philip V. in his war with the Regent. In truth, it was necessary to act well for Spain in order to create a party in his favor, and his only error was in beginning this course of policy two years too soon. Joseph had four or five thousand French guards ; but he wished an army ; regiments were organized from the Spanish prisoners taken in different parts of the kingdom, and armed and equipped. But this was merely giving arms and equipments to the insurgents, for all deserted on the first opportunity and rejoined their comrades. Instead of this course, all prisoners should have been sent to France, until the pacification of the country ; they could then have been employed to some purpose. The occupation of all the provinces at the same time, was also unfortunate, as it prevented the king from levying contributions ; this rendered it necessary for me to allow him an annual subsidy from the French treasury of six millions for the support of his household.

Soult was advanced into Portugal with insufficient forces ; the embarkation of Moore's army, had deceived me respecting the resistance we were likely to meet in Portugal ; I thought that the fame of our victories of Burgos, Tudela, Espinosa, and Coruña, and the slight assistance received from the English, would disgust the Portuguese with their destructive contest. But the inhabitants of the Peninsula knew nothing but what was told them by their priests, who took good care to represent our victories as so many reverses ; the war with Austria and my departure from the country were described to them as certain pledges of their speedy deliverance. Ten thousand English still remained in Portugal, and, when united with the regular and militia forces of the kingdom, were more powerful than Soult's army of twenty-six thousand men. This army should have been reënforced by the sixth corps, leaving some seven or eight thousand men to occupy Ferrol and Coruña. The plan to be pursued was to attack the enemy incessantly with movable armies, without stopping to administer the laws, till the whole country was conquered and its pacification completed; but my brother and his lieutenants did not comprehend the policy of such a course.

The unfortunate issue of this contest resulted mainly from the declaration of war by Austria, which effected more for the Peninsula than all the succors of England, both by the moral influence on the contending forces, and by compelling me to be absent from the theatre of the war, thus causing the most fatal results in the want of union among my generals, and in the false direction of their operations. As the Spaniards had driven the army of Joseph behind the Ebro before my arrival, they believed themselves capable of doing the same after my departure, considering my presence as the instrument of our victories.

Those who have compared this war with that of 1704–9, which Louis XIV. carried on in Spain, are but little acquainted with history. The French under Philip V. had three-quarters of the population of the kingdom in their favor; only Aragon, Catalonia and Valencia had declared in favor of the house of Austria. If I had had in my favor one half of the force which supported the arms of Louis XIV., my enemies and the English would have disappeared before my eagles like a breath, and the war would have ended in two campaigns. With such a party in our favor, and having plenty of provisions, and no reason for a military occupation of each province, we could have directed all our efforts against the English army and the few additional forces which Spain could have supplied; in a word, we could have conducted the war in strict accordance with the rules of military science; as Vendome and Berwick were able to do at their ease having never had more than thirty thousand Anglo-Austrians, and perhaps as many Spaniards, to contend with, while nearly eight millions of the Spanish people were in their favor.

Operations of Russia against Sweden.—While my arms were triumphing in Spain and Austria, those of the Emperor Alexander were not idle, and although their operations may appear somewhat foreign from the object of these commentaries, still they were so intimately connected with my policy as to justify a brief sketch of these several events.*

The little Russian army, which had entered Finland in 1808, and captured Sweaborg, had not been able to reduce that province; but when reënforced to forty thousand men, it finally succeeded in effecting the expulsion of the Swedes. But as it was necessary to menace the capital of Sweden, in order to effect the cession of this province, the Russians took advantage of the severe winter of 1809, to send across the frozen gulf two corps under Bagration and Barclay de Tolly. The former took Aland and menaced Stockholm, while the latter marched on Umeo to form a junction with Schuwalof. This double operation offers the new spectacle of an entire army crossing the sea on the ice, carrying with it its artillery, its magazines, and even wood for the fires of its bivouacs; a remarkable instance of audacity and devotion, for the slightest wind from the south-west would have engulfed its entire columns! Consternation spread to Stockholm at the news of the capture of Aland; the Swedish nobility, wearied with the rule of Gustavus IV., dethroned that king and

---

* As the relation of these events must be still less interesting to American than to French and Russian readers, the translator has considerably abreviated the matter of this article.

elected his uncle, the Duke of Sudermania in his place; this prince being a partisan of the French alliance, it was thought that he might save the monarchy from inevitable ruin. He was crowned with the title of Charles XIII., and, on the seventeenth of September, he purchased peace with Russia, by the cession of Swedish Finland. Peace with France, and the reconciliation between Sweden and Denmark soon followed. Sweden adopted the Continental System with the exception of the restrictions on salt. I restored to her Pomerania.

War between Russia and Turkey.—The affairs of Turkey now attracted the attention of Europe. Feeling at liberty after the conference of Erfurth to push her projects in that direction, Russia had employed the first part of 1808, in preparations for carrying on the war with vigor, if she did not succeed, by the negotiations of Jassy, in obtaining the Principalities. The Ottoman Empire at the end of the year, had become a prey to the most horrible convulsions. The party which had wished to subject the janissaries to discipline, and to shelter the throne from their insolence, by giving them a European organization, had not been discouraged by the imprisonment of Selim; Mustapha Bariactar, at the head of this party had overthrown the existing government, imprisoned the sultan, and proclaimed Mahmud in his place. But the janissaries soon effected a counter-revolution amidst the most horrible massacres and conflagrations. Constantinople became one vast field of carnage; the janissaries set fire every where, in hopes of enveloping their adversaries; men, women, and children, fell a prey to the flames, or to the rage of the combatants.

This state of things seemed to leave Constantinople exposed to the inroads of Russia; but the latter were not prepared to profit by the circumstance, and the Turks had the following winter in which to organize their resistance. The relations entered into between the Porte and England, and the result of the negotiations at Jassy leaving no hopes of effecting his objects without an appeal to arms, the Emperor Alexander reënforced his army with sixty battalions, and ordered it to pass the Danube.

Prince Prosorowski was not well suited for conducting this war, which was of a peculiar character, and more resembled than any other that which I was waging in Spain. The Turkish forces might be overthrown in the field, and their immense masses of cavalry be put to flight and apparently destroyed, but still it was found impossible to advance without besieging their fortresses, and their troops, so little to be feared in the open field, are the most redoubtable behind their ramparts, which they defend with the greatest tenacity. To this peculiar character of the Turks and the almost impossibility of obtaining supplies of provisions in their country, we must add the difficulties of the Balkan, and of the Danube, which is here like an arm of the sea ; and the configuration of the frontier, shut in by Transylvania on one side, but soon widening out to the confines of Dalmatia and Montenegro.

The assaults of Ismail and Oczakof had been so successful for the Russians that this system had become the fashion in their army ;—they thought to conquer the Turks by escalades and squares. These escalades, often ill-directed and always premature, cost them enormous losses—losses which might have been avoided by the expenditure of a hundred barrels of powder and a delay of a week for the operations of the miners ; for, in that time the engineers might have effected breaches practicable to an assault in any of the miserable works of the Turks ; and an assault under such circumstances is a very different affair from attempting an escalade as soon as the place has been reconnoitered.

The Russian army took the field with one hundred and

twenty-five battalions, ninety-five squadrons, and ten thousand Cossacks. Prosorowsky resolved to lay siege to Brahilov, but, while the preparations were making for this purpose, he directed the escalade of Giurgevo, which was fortified with a bastioned enciente that might readily have been reduced with heavy artillery. The escalade was unsuccessful, and the Russians lost from two to three thousand men in the attempt. The marshal next directed the escalade of Brahilov; but after the useless sacrifice of three or four thousand men more, he found it preferable to resort to the slower but more wise system of regular sieges. The passage of the Danube was effected in the early part of August near Galatz, and Ismail invested; but Prosorowsky now died, and Bagration was placed in temporary command of the army. After various unsuccessful operations against the enemy, this general directed Brahilov to be again attacked by ten thousand men under Essen, while, with twelve thousand men, he protected that operation from the direction of the rampart of Trajan, at the right of the Danube. The place, being battered and invested, capitulated on the twenty-first of November. The army then retired to winter-quarters on the left of the Danube, leaving only its advanced guards on the right bank.

In Asia the Russians, under Tormasof, had gained possession of Poti, notwithstanding the efforts of the Pacha of Trebisond to succor the place. This city, situated on the eastern shore of the Black Sea at the mouth of the Euphrates, was indispensable to the Russians for securing their possessions in Abasia, and protecting their relations with Persia.

CHAPTER XVI.

CAMPAIGN OF 1810;—CONTINUATION OF THE PENINSULAR
WAR.

Napoleon's Marriage with an Austrian Princess—He again offers Peace to England—Preparations for a new Campaign in Spain—Napoleon's Plan of Operations—Soult's Plan—Division of the Army—Invasion of Andalusia—Joseph's fatal Delay—Capture of Seville—Sebastiani takes Grenada and Malaga—Remarks on Joseph's Operations—His Return to Madrid—Internal Dissensions in Spain—The English Faction triumphs—Military Organization of the Provinces of the North—Soult neglects to take Badajos—Inaction of Wellington—Soult invests Cadiz—His Occupation of Andalusia—Operations in the North—Chances of Napoleon's Success—Massena's Expedition against Portugal—Sieges of Ciudad-Rodrigo and Almeida—Position of Wellington—Third Invasion of Portugal—Battle of Busaco—Massena turns the Position—Devastating System of the English General—Lines of Torres-Vedras—Massena's Position—Sufferings of his Army—Junction with Drouet—Remarks—Suchet's Success in Catalonia—Combat of Margalef—Sieges of Lerida and Mequinenza—Operations of Augereau—Siege of Tortosa—General Remarks on the War—Bernadotte elected Prince-Royal of Sweden—Reunion of Holland — Consequent Negotiations with England — Annexation of the Mouths of the Ems, the Elbe, and the Weser—Napoleon's Tour in Holland—Senatus-consultum on the Reunion of Rome—Council of Paris—Religious Fanaticism—Continuation of the War between Russia and Turkey.

Napoleon marries an Austrian Princess.—The result of the war of 1809, proved that I had not miscalculated in my attempt to carry on operations, at the same time, against Austria and the Anglo-Spaniards in the Peninsula. I had now to profit by these astonishing successes in order to consolidate my empire; a grand family alliance seemed to me the most certain means of securing this object. I had no children; and the restoration of the Bourbons seemed inevitable at my death; they alone had claims to it, and none of my brothers were capable of disputing them; even I, myself, in elevating Joseph, Jerome, and Louis to thrones, had been unable to give them the consideration and merit necessary for maintaining their position ; and Lucien had dishonored himself by a ridiculous opposition and a scandalous marriage. The entire male population of France were deeply interested in the preservation of my empire ; not that the princes of the house of Bourbon were not personally good men, but because their return would be attended by a *cortège* of men avaricious of power and wealth and hateful to the people. If the restoration of these princes at my death should produce intestine war, would not foreign powers be certain to profit by the circumstance to overthrow my edifice in Poland, Germany and Italy ? If, on the contrary, this restoration should be effected by foreign war, would not the consequences be still more dangerous for France ?

I thus foresaw the humiliation of France, and above all, of that million of brave men who had shed their blood in their country's cause. Of what importance was it to me personally, whether or not I left a dynasty after me ? Would that render my glory any more brilliant or lasting ? Was Alexander any the less great because he had no successor, and the empire of Macedonia was divided after him ? It was the good of France alone that I sought, and if I was deceived in this matter, not only my council, but the whole French nation partook of the same error.

My divorce having been completed, it was now necessary to decide between a Russian and an Austrian princess. As the Grand Duchess Catharine had been married to the Prince of Oldenbourg, negotiations were opened for her younger sister the Princess Anne ; here a difficulty arose ; it was the erection of a Russian chapel in the Tuileries, a condition strongly insisted on by the cabinet of St. Petersburg. I was never very orthodox, and even at this time was in a controtroversy with the clergy, and I wished no new subject for religious disputes. Moreover, the Russian cabinet asked for time on account of the youth of the princess and the repugnance of the empress-mother to the marriage; this was sufficient to determine my decision in favor of an Austrian alliance.

The question was both delicate and complicated, and the future of France perhaps depended on its solution. The first point to be considered was whether a distant and powerful ally would be more useful and lasting than one more near, but of a more limited character. If I had purposed conquests the first would be preferable, for the other would be rather an obstacle than an auxiliary. If, on the contrary, I purposed only defensive operations, the nearer power would be the most suitable, as it would cover our frontier and act in concert with our arms. But these axioms of general policy were subordinate to others not less powerful. In the first place we had both defeated Austria and stripped her of a portion of her territory; whereas Russia had by her relations with us gained Finland, Bialystok and Tarnopol. The Austrians were, therefore, not so likely to become our allies in good faith, unless we indemnified them for their losses, which was not an easy matter. The Russians had lost no province by us, and might gain much by a community of interest; they had fleets, sailors and seaports, and their frontiers on the Caspian Sea and Grand Bucharia opened to us the road to India, which was a great point against England. An alliance with Austria and war with Russia would render it necessary to decide the contest on the Dwina, or at least in Poland; whereas an alliance with the Russians against the Austrians would transfer the field of battle to the superb valley of the Danube and the centre of the Austrian monarchy. These motives were strong in favor of the Russian alliance; but on the other hand the maritime interest of the great landed proprietors and merchants of that empire were too seriously compromised by the closing of the ports to hope for a continuance of their friendship. The Russian nobility, devoted to the profession of arms, pretended that the treaty of Tilsit had been imposed by victory, and was therefore odious; and not the less so because it closed up the outlets of their agricultural products, the source of all their private wealth; it is not every one who is willing to suffer in private fortune, for a term of years, for the future prosperity of their country. I was not ignorant of this cause of opposition at St. Petersburg to my alliance, and was not a little piqued at the unfavorable dispositions toward me exhibited by a part of the royal family. I had on my side the Emperor Alexander, Count Romanzof, and a small number of the intelligent men of the empire; but even this influence had been somewhat weakened by the unfortunate dispositions of the treaty of Vienna, opposed to the stipulations of Tilsit.

In this relation there were less inconveniences in the alliance with Austria;—she had very little commerce; her manufactories were sufficient for her own wants; her cities offered a suitable market for her agricultural products, and Hungary and Moravia supplied her with wines. She had no military or commercial marine, and might remain in hostile relations with England without any sensible injury. In this respect I might calculate upon a more durable alliance with her than with Russia. France, within the limits of the Rhine, might be the natural ally of Russia, but an empire like mine, extending its influence to the Niemen, would find it difficult to maintain friendly relations with the Russian government. The unfortunate circumstance which had rendered this treaty of Vienna equally odious to Russia and Austria, placed me in an embarrassing situation toward these two powers, rendering the choice of alliance dependent upon the relative amount of hostility likely to be encountered.

Let us add to these considerations the influence this marriage was likely to produce on Spain. Russia was too distant from the Peninsula to take any active part in this war; Austria, on the contrary, when allied to my family, might become interested in it. Under Charles V., and in the war of the succession of Charles II., Austria had played an important part in the affairs of Spain. This motive alone appeared of much weight. If Austria reproached us for her losses, she might also console herself with the assurance that my alliance would give her a secure harbor against the tempest which, for the last fifteen years, had threatened her ship of state. We had antecedents for this alliance in the treaty of 1756, of which I have already spoken; if that treaty had been declaimed against at the beginning of the revolution, it was because, under Madame Pompadour, it had had a vicious application, and not because the primitive treaty was not wise and positively advantageous. But now, there could be little fear that my policy, like that of Louis XV., would become subordinate to the cabinet of Vienna. The motives which had then induced the cabinet of Versailles to secure a powerful ally against the rivalry of England, were now more powerful than ever. These motives influenced the majority of my council, and, finally, determined my own decision. There was one consideration, however, which made me hesitate for a moment; it was the idea that, after the intimate relations which I had so recently contracted at Erfurth with the Emperor Alexander, it might appear perfidious on my part to so abruptly abandon his friendship. But such scruples must yield to reasons of state. I, however, might consider myself secured from any such reproach by the slight inclination exhibited by the Russian government for the alliance, and the little importance attached to the preference I had given to it. I, therefore, resolved on a union with an Austrian princess.

Subsequent events have apparently authorized the opinion that I committed a fault in this decision, and that a Russian alliance would have been more advantageous. It is certain that it would have avoided the disastrous campaign of 1812; but was my march on Moscow a necessary result of my alliance with Austria? All things, however, taken into consideration, it must be confessed that the Russian alliance would probably have been the preferable one.

But I determined differently; and the negotiations entered into with Prince Schwartzenberg were soon terminated, for the Emperor Francis hastened to give me his daughter, Maria Louisa. Some have attributed this union with a daughter of the Cæsars to my inordinate pride; nothing could be more absurd. Josephine was no longer capable of child-bearing, and, in dissolving my connection with her and forming a new alliance, was it not important to France that I should form such a one as would effectually destroy the line of demarkation between the old dynasties and my own? It was of little use to have put the crown on my head, unless I could fix it there permanently; and nothing could consolidate it better than the ties of consanguinity with the noble houses of Hapsburg or Romanof. By leaving my dynasty isolated from the rest of Europe, I would have condemned it to a kind of reprobation, or to maintain its high position by new victories. There is no statesman who would not have approved a resolution which in no respect added to my glory or dignity, but which was calculated to consolidate my empire.*

---

* Alison thus describes the second empress and her unenviable fate:—
"Born in the highest rank, descended from the noblest ancestry, called to the most exalted destinies, the daughter of the Cæsars, the wife of Napoleon, the mother of his son, Marie Louise appeared to unite in her person all the grandeur and felicity of which human nature is susceptible. But her mind had received no lofty impress; her character was unworthy of the greatness of her fortune. She had the blood of Maria Theresa in her veins, but not her

My marriage took place at Paris on the second of April. The *fêtes* to which this great event gave rise eclipsed all those which had marked my reign; France saw the dawn of a happy future, and a pledge of that peace which she so much desired. The preponderance which this marriage gave me in Europe was well calculated to discourage my enemies, and every one believed that my throne was secure from all danger when Providence crowned my wishes by giving me a son on the twentieth of March, 1811. The Continent was tranquil, and had apparently become reconciled to my reign. The respect bore to the house of Hapsburg legitimatized my reign in the eyes of European sovereigns, and sanctioned it in the eyes of the different nations which had become a part of my empire. My dynasty now took rank with the highest

spirit in her soul. Her fair hair, blue eyes, and pleasing expression, bespoke the Gothic race; and the affability of her demeanor, and sweetness of her manners, at first produced a general prepossession in her favor. But she was adapted to the sunshine of prosperity only; the wind of adversity blew, and she sunk beneath its breath. Young, amiable, prepossessing, she won the emperor's affections by the *naiveté* and simplicity of her character; and he always said that she was innocence with all its sweetness, Josephine, grace with all its charms. All the attractions of art, says he, were employed by the first empress with such skill, that they were never perceived; all the charms of innocence displayed by the second with such simplicity, that their existence was never suspected. Both were benevolent, kind-hearted, affectionate both, to the last hour of his life, retained the warm regard of the emperor; and both possessed qualities worthy of his affection. If her husband had lived and died on the imperial throne, few empresses would have left a more blameless reputation; but she was unequal to the trials of the latter years of his life. If her dubious situation, the daughter of one emperor, the wife of another, both leaders in the strife, might serve her excuse for not taking any decided part in favor of the national independence on the invasion of France, the misfortunes of her husband and son had claims upon her fidelity which should never have been overlooked. The wife of the emperor should never have permitted him to go into exile alone; the mother of the King of Rome should never have forgotten to what destinies her son had been born. What an object would she, after such sacrifices, returning from St. Helena after his death, have formed in history! Force may have prevented her from discharging that sacred duty; but force did not compel her to appear at the Congress of Vienna, leaning on the arm of Wellington, nor oblige the widow of Napoleon to sink at last into the degraded wife of her own chamberlain."

in Europe, and I flattered myself that they would no longer dispute the throne with the son to which the empress had given birth. My marriage, and the erection of a new nobility, were the bonds to unite the revolution and the enemies of its doctrines;—that revolution now seemed to be completed, for, from this moment, France resumed her ancient line of intercourse with the other powers of Europe. But in the eyes of the French refugees in England, of the one hundred thousand broken down families of the old régime, and of the fanatics of the church, the quarrel was not yet ended. Such is the force of legitimacy that the Bourbons, of whom no one now spoke, gave me more trouble than the greatest power in Europe. I pity states who have pretenders in the ranks of their enemies.

He again offers Peace to England.—I now desired peace, and wished my empire to be recognized by the English government; for I desired to give some relaxation to my people, who had as yet been unable to enjoy the benefits they had derived from the revolution. We were no longer the protectors of propagandism or of popular insurrections, and to accustom Europe to the nature of my power, it was important to appear less in a hostile attitude. Moreover, my system of repression against the English supremacy had imposed great sacrifices by the closing of the ports. From St. Petersburg to Cadiz, and from Cadiz to Trieste, not a hamlet on the coast but had suffered from this restriction; the reaction which the closing of the ports had produced on our manufactures and agricultural products (wines), it was not in my power to avoid. My enemies took good care to profit by the advantages of this position; they proclaimed themselves the avengers of the independence of nations; and by an extravagance peculiar to the age, *the despots of the seas pretended to fight me, in order to restore the liberty of commerce!!!* These insinuations made dupes among the unreflecting part of community, and gradually diminished the popularity of my administration, by inducing people to believe that I did not desire peace. I nevertheless, proposed it every time that there was an occasion, but England persisted in her refusal. This obstinacy on her part showed her possessed of more resources than I had at first supposed.

In truth, a reconciliation was not easy. Since the treaty of Amiens, England had conquered twenty millions of subjects in India, which she was not disposed to surrender, while at the same time she was unwilling to allow us even Belgium, for fear of the use we might make of Antwerp! How had she yielded me the crown of Italy, and how had I resigned it, after I had placed it on my brow? The nature of the contest between us rendered it interminable. Instead of reducing my army, I was compelled to maintain it on a war footing and thus disturb the quiet of Europe. If I won the glory, my enemies gathered all the honor of the contest; for they assumed the innocent air of one fighting for legitimate objects; while I was made to appear the aggressor by destroying old institutions and building up new. I was thus made to bear the entire weight of the accusation. My personal enemies, the T———, the L———, and the C———, profited by this circumstance to represent me to France as the only cause of evils which were in reality the legitimate results of the revolution, and of the position in which it had placed the different nations of Europe toward each other, by destroying their most natural political relations. I defy my enemies to point out any epoch after the peace of Amiens, when it had been possible to make an honorable and durable peace with England. The negotiation of Lauderdale was the only occasion that gave the slightest hopes of such a result; and we have already seen that this was a mere lure, designed to involve us at the same time with Russia and Spain.

Preparations for a new Campaign in Spain. — England, although deprived of her most powerful allies, was not carrying on the war alone ; for she had on her side all the enemies of the revolution and of my power. We had plenty of room in Spain to fight out the contest. I sent there a part of the conquerors of Wagram, but did not go myself. If we are to judge from the appearance of things it was unfortunate that I did not return, for if I had terminated the war in Spain and avoided the contest with Russia, I should have died on my throne, feared and respected ; I should have given France time to breathe, and to recover her strength, so as to sustain my work. I fell, by attempting to finish the most difficult part myself before the proper time had arrived. I have said that twenty years were required, whereas I attempted to accelerate, by seven or eight years, the termination of this great drama. But appearances are often deceitful, and before deciding whether I committed an error in not returning to Madrid, it is but just to weigh the motives of my conduct.

In the first place, I did not expect that the affairs in Spain would take so unfavorable a turn ; the advantage gained by Wellington at Talavera had proved him a dangerous adversary ; but the promptitude with which he had retreated into Portugal and the victories of Joseph at Almonacid and Ocana over the Spanish army, had deceived me into the belief that Soult and Massena would be sufficient to oppose the English in the Peninsula, if I only sent them new reënforcements. Some have attributed this decision to the fear that *the Emperor Alexander, dissatisfied with my alliance with Austria, might fall on the Duchy of Warsaw, as soon as I should be engaged beyond the Pyrenees, and that he might draw after him Prussia and all the north of Germany.* This was his game, and, in his place, I should have hardly hesitated to adopt such a plan. And it was the more natural to expect him to seize upon such an opportunity, inasmuch as my marriage and the treaty of Schönbrunn, were grave subjects of dissatisfaction to Russia ; there was no very close union between us. But on the other hand the frank and loyal conduct of the Emperor Alexander at the time of our reverses in Spain, and the assurances of my ambassador, the Duke of Vicenza, were sufficient to dissipate such fears as chimerical. Moreover, Russia was at this time at war with Turkey, and Austria being now allied to my interests. Alexander could hardly trouble the north of Europe with the probability of success.

But there were other and less visionary reasons to prevent my return to Spain at this time. The country was filled with religious fanatics, who sought an opportunity to destroy my life in order to terminate the war ; this contest was now waged, not against large organized bodies, but against troops scattered throughout the whole Peninsula. Our forces moved in separate armies, the communications between them being frequently impossible, so that I could not myself have directed them all at the same time ; but I considered my lieutenants were capable of conducting an army, and they proved themselves so by the constant successes which they gained during the campaign. I, therefore, merely announced my intended return to Spain, and sent there a half of the old guard, and a part of the young guard, which had been increased by several regiments of voltigeurs and sharpshooters. The strength of this reserve already amounted to eight or nine thousand men ; I now increased it to twenty thousand, so as always to have a part of it disposable either at the north or at the south. This was a most valuable body in itself, and, at the same time, produced a good influence on the rest of the army, for this guard being an object of my special care, the French strove among themselves for the honor of forming a part of it. These troops formed the *élite* of the army of the north of Spain under the orders of Marshal Bessières ; in addition to the battalions of recruits which were sent to all the regiments to which they already belonged, I also sent there the entire eighth *corps-d'armée* under the orders of Junot.

Napoleon's new Plan of Campaign. — We have already seen how Joseph, after the affair of Arzobispo, neglected to profit by the union of eighty thousand men on the Tagus, in order to fall without delay on the English, who then had no fortified port to favor their reëmbarkation ; and, also, how successfully Wellington had profited, by the repose of eight months allowed him by my generals, to form a suitable system of defense for Portugal. I at first resolved to make a strong effort to repair this fault, and to intrust this task to Massena, who was to advance with three *corps-d'armée* by the right bank of the Tagus on Lisbon, while Joseph and Soult marched by the left bank with two or three other corps. The moment appeared the more propitious, as the English had just lost ten thousand men in the island of Walcheren ; and as they had now few troops to send to the Continent, another disastrous campaign might disgust them with the war.

Soult's Plan.—With this view I directed the king to collect his forces between the Tagus and the Guadiana, and prepare them for a renewal of operations early in the spring. Soult, anxious to distinguish himself in his new position of major-general, and fearing, perhaps, that he would be placed subordinate to Massena, thought to anticipate my wishes and begin the campaign with the subjugation of Andalusia. Joseph, who was more desirous to reduce the provinces of his own kingdom than to drive the English from Portugal, was easily persuaded to this plan. The decisive victory of Ocana rendered the success of this enterprise almost certain, and then, after the dispersion of the Spanish army of the south, the expedition would seem more easy and certain.

But, in order to do this, it would be necessary to fall with impetuosity on the Spaniards, and either cut off their retreat or enter pell-mell with them into the island of Leon and Cadiz, and then to immediately march the victorious army on Badajos and Evora. If Soult and the king had acted in this way, they would still have carried out the spirit of my plan of operations. But they deviated from my project to fail before Cadiz, and, by the untimely occupation of an immense territory, to lose the means of concentrating a sufficient force against Wellington.

Division of the Army.—The army in Spain was now organized as follows:—

> The 1st corps under Victor;
> " 2d " " Reynier;
> " 3d " " Suchet;
> " 4th " " Sebastiani;
> " 5th " " Mortier;
> " 6th " " Ney;
> " 7th " " Augereau and Macdonald;
> " 8th " " Junot.

There was also the army of Marshal Bessières, which occupied the north of Spain, and the ninth *corps-d'armée* which was organizing, at Bayonne, from the four battalions of the army of the south. The army of Andalusia, which Joseph united between the Guadiana and the Sierra Morena, was composed of the first, fourth, and fifth corps, King Joseph's guards, and the reserve of General Dessolles; the second, sixth, and eighth corps were to march on Portugal, and cover Madrid; while the other two corps were detached in Catalonia and Aragon. The army of Andalusia, with an effective force of fifty thousand men, took the field about the middle of January, to attack the remnant of Arrizaga's forces, which had escaped the disaster of Ocana and intrenched themselves in the defiles of the Sierra Morena.

Invasion of Andalusia.—Victor, on the right, debouched

by the mountains of Pedrehohes on Cordova; the king, with
Mortier and the reserve, at the centre, crossed the defile of
Despena-Perros, and followed the road to Andujar; Sebastiani, on the left, took the direction of Infantes on Ubeda. It
was here that Arrizaga had fixed his principal attention, and
had defended the intrenched heights of Montizon. Pierced
in the centre, and vigorously pushed by the right, he was
completely put to rout. Montizon was taken with its garrison of three thousand men, and the division of Castejon,
about five thousand strong, also laid down their arms at no
great distance from that place. The victorious Sebastiani
received orders at Jaen to direct himself on Grenada and
Malaga; he entered the former of these cities after a slight
combat at Alcala Real.

Joseph's fatal Delay.—Joseph, at the head of Mortier's
corps, the guard and the reserve, after having forced the
defile of Despena-Perros, descended, without any great
obstacle, by Carolina on Andujar, on the twenty-first of
January; Victor debouched the following day on Cordova.
These two corps had merely to hasten their march by Acija
directly on Seville, before the Spanish left, engaged near
Zafra, could reach that place. Instead of giving this order,
Joseph stopped at Andujar to issue proclamations, and plan
useless manœuvres, and then slowly resumed his march. The
left of the Spaniards, which was now isolated under the
Duke of Albuquerque between Badajos and Zafra, was thus
allowed time to reach San-Lucar and Cadiz, where it arrived
on the fourth of February.

My brother must have had his imagination strongly affected
by the catastrophe of Baylen, to act with so great circumspection. If I had commanded the expedition, I should
have presented myself, on the twenty-seventh of January,
before Santi-Petri and the island of Leon, and from what
was then passing within Cadiz, it is probable that I should

have entered that city without opposition. Terror reigned there; at the news of our march on Seville, the junta of government, forced to yield to a popular insurrection, resigned their powers, and fled to Cadiz. A portion of the members attempted to regain their power, but public opinion, incited by the proclamations of Romana, again put them down; there was no longer any regularly constituted authority; the most influential families in Andalusia, fled in disorder into Cadiz; and this place was without a garrison. What result then should we expect from an impetuous attack? But even suppose we should not have obtained an entrance into that city, had we not plenty of time to blockade it and to reduce Seville?

Capture of Seville.—Joseph, instead of marching rapidly from Cordova to Cadiz, directed all his forces on Seville, the entrance to which place was defended by intrenchments, armed with one hundred and twenty old pieces of artillery, served only by armed peasants. Nevertheless, Joseph stopped to negotiate with them until the thirty-first, without making any use of the thirty-six thousand men which he had uselessly collected on this point. At last our troops advanced to Chiclana the fifth of February, twenty-four hours after the arrival of the Duke of Albuquerque, who made active preparations for their reception.

Sebastiani takes Grenada and Malaga.—Sebastiani, on his side, entered Grenada on the twenty-eighth, and hotly pursued the enemy into the defile between Antequera and Malaga. A part of the *debris* of Arrizaga had taken the road to Murcia; seven or eight thousand fugitives, with two battalions of monks and the armed population of the country, sought in vain to dispute Sebastiani's passage; he drove every thing before him, and reached Malaga at the head of three thousand horse and six battalions of infantry. The enemy had the audacity to march out with six thousand men to give him battle. To charge upon this body, to overthrow it, and enter pell-mell with it into Malaga, was, for our dragoons, the affair of only a quarter of an hour. The enemy, however, made fight in the streets of the city until the arrival of our infantry put an end to all resistance. A part of the insurgents dispersed, and the remainder laid down their arms. The place was armed with one hundred and forty pieces of cannon, and was capable of a good defense.

Remarks on Joseph's Operations.—However brilliant and rapid these successes, our army had failed by the unpardonable slowness of its movements to secure the important key of all the southern provinces. It is not positively certain that Cadiz would have surrendered, if we had presented ourselves, some days sooner, before that place; but there was every probability that, in the stupor of a surprise, and an entire want of the means of defense, the operation would have been completely successful; and, in that case, we can hardly venture to fix a limit to the consequences that would have followed. In that rich city were the soul and the strength of the government; the columns of Hercules were at that epoch regarded as the palladium of Spanish liberty, and even if the regency had been removed to Carthagena, Alicante or Coruña, it would only have been the less powerful and the more easily attainable with our bayonets.

He returns to Madrid.—Joseph, after the capture of Seville, returned to Madrid, and left Soult in command of the army of the south. Notwithstanding the fatal delay that had allowed Cadiz to escape us, the conquest of Andalusia was important in its political as well as military relations. Seville had an artillery school of much celebrity, a superb arsenal, founderies, and powder-mills. We found here a considerable quantity of provisions and two hundred and forty pieces of artillery, exclusive of the armament of the intrenchments. Besides, this invasion was made at the proper moment, when anarchy was beginning to reign in the Spanish councils of administration.

Internal Dissensions in Spain.—The junta was dissolved, and the administration intrusted to a regency of five members—the bishop of Orense, General Castaños, the Ex-minister Saavedra, Admiral Escano, and Councillor Ardizabal; they also convoked the Cortes. Each party attributed to the other the evils which had befallen their country; and the germs of discord were becoming serious. The people attributed all their ills to their chiefs. In this respect the junta of Seville was rather to be pitied than blamed; the people were absurd enough to attribute to this body all the disasters of Spain, although it had contended against these disasters with all the firmness and activity possible in the generally disorganized condition of the kingdom. Nor could the new regency under these grave circustances direct the helm of state in a manner to satisfy all parties; it was already reproached with seeking to evade the convocation of the Cortes.

The English Faction triumphs.—These petty internal revolutions, to which no doubt Wellesley, the English ambassador, was privy, centralized for a moment all power in hands wholly devoted to the cabinet of London. The English troops were permitted to assist in the defense of Cadiz, and a division under General Graham was destined for this object. Romana, directed to return to Estremadura, placed himself without hesitation under the orders of Wellington; there was now more unity in the military operations; but Spain was not yet an auxilliary which the English general could direct at his pleasure.

Informed of the coming session of the Cortes at Cadiz, I authorized my brother to sound the views of that assembly; it would not have been impossible, by speaking to them of the future interests of Spain and by leaving them free arbiters in the choice of their king, and in the selection of their system of government, to calm their effervescence and to attach them to our party. It was a matter of little importance to me whether Joseph or Ferdinand was nominated king of Spain, provided Spain and Spanish America adopted the Continental System and closed their ports to the English.

Military Organization of the Provinces of the North.—While, on the one hand, I was offering them the hopes and the means of reconciliation, I thought it necessary, on the other, to show myself formidable, in case Spain persisted in repelling my advances. I then directed the organization of the provinces between the Pyrenees and the Ebro, into military governments, under French generals; thus giving them to understand that these provinces would be united to my empire, unless quiet should be restored in the Peninsula: this was arming my generals with temporary and dictatorial power over the provinces of Joseph. The measure was authorized by the laws of conquest, and might turn to the account of the inhabitants, by protecting them from the partial vexations of the crowd of civil vampires who followed the army, and by establishing order in these provinces by means more effectual than those employed by the king; in a word, this measure would prove to the Spaniards that the integrity of their soil would depend upon their own resolutions. Nor is it to be denied that the measure was also influenced in some degree by the consideration that these provinces, thus becoming accustomed to our government, might in time be exchanged for Portugal if Joseph should continue king, or become consolidated with my empire, in case it became necessary for us to give up the rest of Spain. In conformity with this system, Bonnet was made governor of the Asturias, Caffarelli of Biscay, Reille of Navarre, Baraguay d'Hilliers of Upper Catalonia, Maurice Mathieu of

Lower Catalonia, while Aragon remained under the direction of Suchet, who was there both feared and esteemed. Each of these generals commanded, in his department, a strong division of troops. Marshal Bessières commanded the army of the north ; and his active divisions guarded the country between the Ebro and the Douro. These measures, however, did not have the complete success that I anticipated; it required one or two more successful campaigns to give them their desired effect. They, however, caused loud cries against the partisans of Joseph, on the ground that they attacked the integrity of the Spanish soil.

Soult neglects to take Badajos.—Soult, who was now invested with the command of the three *corps-d'armée* in Andalusia, ought to have hastened to repair the error committed in not having, in the preceding October, fallen on Wellington and cut up his army, or at least have reduced Badajos before entering Andalusia. The garrison of that place, situated on the left bank of the Guadiana, not only threatened the rear of the army of the south, but also enabled the Spaniards to light up the fires of insurrection in the very heart of the kingdom. Such a fortified base, sustained as it was by the intact army of Wellington in its vicinity, demanded all the attention of Soult, for he could not remain quietly before Cadiz and guard the coast of ancient Bætica, so long as there remained on his line of communication so important a place of arms, from which the enemy might at any time debouch in force against his troops, which were necessarily divided in order to observe Cadiz and Gibraltar and occupy Grenada and Malaga ; but this marshal did not decide in time to act with vigor on the banks of the Guadiana ; he directed his attention to the submission of the country before he had destroyed the hostile masses which might dispute its possession. The want of a suitable park for the siege of Badajos might have been an admissable excuse, before the capture of the arsenal of Seville and the heavy artillery in the Sierra Morena.

Wellington remains inactive.— Wellington, on his side, did not take full advantage of this dispersion of our forces. His march to the environs of Ciudad-Rodrigo, which might have produced important results at the beginning of the campaign of 1810, if he had in time resumed the offensive, became of no importance when he decided to remain at that place. From his intermediary position it would seem that he might have acted with more vigor, either against Ney at Salamanca, or on the rear of Soult by debouching by Badajos. We have already mentioned the motives of this inaction which, for eight months, left the whole weight of the war on the Spaniards ; the system had been agreed upon at Seville between Wellington and his brother Wellesley ;— they asked of the cabinet of London a reënforcement of from twelve to fifteen thousand men, augmented the levies of Portugal, and pushed forward with activity the works of the vast intrenched camp of Lisbon. Until these objects were accomplished it suited Wellington's policy to remain inactive ; he had no object in bold and adventurous enterprises for the relief of a foreign soil, and waited for the force of events to display the advantages of his system. Soult, not comprehending the motives of his adversary's conduct, thought to profit by his distance and inaction to establish firmly his own position in Andalusia, adjourning, for the present, the reduction of Badajos.

Soult invests Cadiz.—His first care was to blockade by land the important place of Cadiz, which he had allowed to escape by his dilatory march. Three hundred pieces of cannon, taken in the Spanish depôts of Seville, and in the intrenchments of Sierra Morena, served to arm a line of contravallation, which was not less than ten leagues in length, extending from Rota to the tower of Bermeja. He flattered himself that, by the aid of these formidable lines, he could shut up the Anglo-Spanish forces within this narrow tongue of land; as though Gibraltar, Carthagena, and twenty other ports on the Mediterranean and the ocean did not permit the enemy to carry even the defenders of Cadiz to any point they might select for operating against our troops.

On learning what was passing in Andalusia, I deemed it best, as the error had been committed, not to evacuate where we had already experienced the check of Baylen, and where our reception by the population, who were already fatigued with revolutions and losses, had been more favorable than we expected. Nevertheless, as this occupation would change the nature of my projects against Portugal, I directed Massena to act with caution, and to first reduce the places of Ciudad-Rodrigo and Almeida; while Soult was to second these operations by pressing the reduction of Badajos, so as to make a diversion in Alemtejo.

Although I was well aware of the slight advantage likely to result from a land investment of Cadiz without the naval means required for the blockade of a place thus situated, still I thought it possible that a bombardment might induce the inhabitants, and, perhaps, the regency also, to surrender. I caused mortars of a new model (called *à la Villantroys*) to be cast and sent to Cadiz, which would carry shells to the distance of three thousand toises. A convoy of these mortars, with the shells and munitions, left Toulon, took in some troops at Porto Ferrajo, and sailed for Malaga; others were sent by land. I did not anticipate any great result from this attempt; but it was worth the trial. It was essential either to withdraw this army, or to take measures to consolidate its position in Andalusia; and one of the very first conditions for securing this consolidation was either to reduce Cadiz, or to mask it so as to prevent any sorties from the place against our scattered troops. Victor was charged with this task.

Mortier was to guard Seville and observe the road to Badajos; the old division of Desolles occupied Cordova and Jaen; Sebastiani had his hands full in occupying Grenada and Malaga, and in watching Gibraltar on the one side, and, on the other, the numerous assemblings which the enemy was forming in the kingdoms of Murcia and Valencia. Joseph had returned to Madrid with his guard.

His Occupation of Andalusia.—Soult employed the entire year of 1810, in seeking to obtain these several results; and it must be confessed that if Soult had neglected to employ his forces in a more useful manner against the English on the Tagus, he did every thing in his power to repair this fault, by the care he devoted to his establishments at Grenada and Seville, and to his preparations at Cadiz. There was a short time when our efforts appeared on the point of being crowned with success, and when the Spaniards themselves regarded our power as definitively consolidated in Andalusia. Soult at Seville, and Sebastiani at Grenada, maintained sumptuous courts; placed on the classic soil of the Moorish chivalry, they made every effort to revive the bright days of the Abencerages, and by *fêtes* to draw this voluptuous people of Andalusia, from the horrors of insurrection; but this seducing Bœtica, without being exactly a Capua for our army, nevertheless, paralyzed fifty thousand, or rather engaged them in mere accessaries, while Wellington was quietly laying the foundation of a defensive system which he ought never to have been allowed time to organize.

If the head-quarters of these two generals offered all the charms of peace and the *agrémcnts* of a happy conquest, their cantonments were not always thus tranquil. The dispersion of our troops necessary to secure the quiet of the country, gave the allied generals an opportunity to fall on our isolated brigades and to expose them to all the horrors of partisan warfare. Romana, Ballesteros, and Mendizabel, on the borders of Portugal and Estremadura, Blake and Ellio in the direction of Murcia, and lastly, Lasey and many others, leaving Cadiz to land on the coast near Moguer, engaged in numerous partial combats, in which they were at first successful against detached parties, but immediately after beaten and put to flight. The very names of these combats would occupy a space greater than can here be devoted to this particular subject; but the names of the heroes who fell in these contests are already written in the temple of fame.

Romana and Ballesteros, distinguished themselves by their activity and perseverance. The former had left to the convoked Cortes and the regency the reins of a state given up to anarchy, and returned to the army in the middle of 1810. Some have attributed to Romana the honor of forming the plan of Spanish resistance; without wishing to detract in any degree from the fame of that general, I am inclined to believe that that resistance was rather the result of circumstances, and of the character of the war; for the provincial juntas comprised, in all their different proclamations, the only system of resistance that was employed in the Peninsula.

The enemy, acting under the protection of Gibraltar, Cadiz, Badajos, and Ciudad Rodrigo, and aided by the inhabitants, continued to annoy and fatigue our troops with the harassing operations of partisan warfare. To aid these efforts, the English had planned an attack on Malaga in concert with the army of Murcia. Lord Blenheim landed, the thirteenth of August, on the coast of Almeria, but was himself captured with seven or eight hundred of his men by Sebastiani, while the remainder with difficulty regained their vessels.

Operations in the North.—During this time, nothing remarkable occurred in the north-west. The eighth corps, under Junot, had retaken the important post of Astorga, which Ney in his advance on Talavera had abandoned to the army of Galicia. General Bonnet, guarding the Asturias, was daily skirmishing with the corps reorganized by the Spaniards in Galicia immediately after the evacuation of that province. Porlier, a nephew of Romana, operated against this division in the Asturias, and those which guarded the kingdom of Leon. Other partisans successively attacked the several points of Navarre and Castile which were exposed, keeping the troops left to guard these provinces in continual watchfulness. Ney had returned from Paris to take command of the sixth *corps-d'armée*, after the affair of Tamames, and established himself at Salamanca to observe Beresford, who was soon joined by the entire army of Wellington. Reynier, at the head of the second *corps-d'armée*, was fighting against the English division of General Hill, and the troops of Romana, on the left of the Tagus.

Napoleon's Chances of Success.—Notwithstanding the presence of this army, which from day to day became more threatening, the brilliant successes of Soult and Suchet, the victories of Ocana, Sierra Morena, and Santa Maria, joined to the subjugation of the provinces of the south, confirmed me in the hope that success would crown our perseverance. I thought that the patience of the Spaniards would finally become exhausted; but I was deceived in the character of this people, and in the importance of the English army, estimating its efficiency from its operations in Holland and Flanders. Although the Spanish regency was shut up in Cadiz, it nevertheless, continued to give its orders throughout the monarchy. Priests were the staff officers who transmitted these orders, and watched over their execution ; speaking in the name of heaven, they were obeyed ; and even admirals were sent to serve in the insurgent infantry. Resistance sprung up every where, and although we were continually victorious, still, we were always engaged in partial combats, for no sooner was one place conquered, than we were obliged to put down the new forces that sprang up in another.

Massena's Expedition against Portugal.—In the meantime Massena prepared to execute his part of the project which I had formed for the overthrow of the English army, and which had been partially disarranged by the untimely invasion of Andalusia. I gave him the corps of Ney, Reynier, and Junot, numbering together about fifty thousand men.

Siege of Ciudad-Rodrigo.—Before advancing far in this expedition, it was necessary to reduce those fortifications behind which Wellington had been allowed for the last ten months to prepare his means of offense and defense. Junot had already captured Astorga, and it was now necessary to reduce Ciudad-Rodrigo and Almeida.. This task was confided to Ney, who, notwithstanding his want of proper means, succeeded beyond the most sanguine hopes. To collect and move his material for a siege two hundred leagues from his frontier, in the midst of an insurgent and hostile population, who pillaged the convoy, and massacred the escorts, was a most herculean task. The place was surrounded with an old and irregular enciente, but one capable of a pretty good resistance ; it also possessed one of those excellent artillery schools for which Spain was indebted to Charles III. The garrison of eight thousand men, under Brigadier Herasti, announced its intention of doing its duty, to which it was doubly incited by the fanaticism of the administrative junta. It sustained, for a long time, the destructive fire of our batteries, which caused great havoc in the city, and blew up the arsenal ; but these batteries were too distant to destroy the masonry of the fortifications ;—it, therefore, became necessary to establish them nearer. The breach was finally made practicable, and the ditch filled up by the explosion of the counterscarp; and, on the tenth of July, after an attack of forty-five days, the garrison capitulated as prisoners of war.

Siege of Almeida.—Our troops now marched to the investment of Almeida, and dislodged the English rear-guard which was posted in the vicinity. Six thousand Portuguese, half regulars, and half militia, prepared for a desperate defense; but the explosion of an immense powder magazine blew up the citadel and a part of the city, so that the governor surrendered the same day.* Massena, under the persuasion of the Marquis of Alorna, and forgetting what had already happened to Soult and Junot, had the misplaced generosity to release the Portuguese prisoners and incorporate the regulars into his own army. He remembered that a Portuguese brigade had been distinguished in our ranks in the Wagram campaign; and he now thought to gain over the Portuguese by good treatment. But the general hatred was too violent, and his misplaced confidence resulted in the virtual surrender to our enemies of four or five thousand of their captured soldiers.

Position of Wellington.—Wellington remained immovable during these two sieges, although the corps of Ney and

---

* Napier thus describes this terrible explosion:—"On the eighteenth, the trenches were begun under cover of a false attack, and on the twenty-sixth (the second parallel being commenced), sixty-five pieces of artillery, mounted on ten batteries, opened at once. Many houses were soon in flames, and the garrison was unable to extinguish them; the counter-fire was, however, briskly maintained, and little military damage was sustained. Toward evening the cannonade slackened on both sides; but just at dark the ground suddenly trembled, the castle bursting into a thousand pieces, gave vent to a column of smoke and fire, and with a prodigious noise the whole town sunk into a shapeless ruin. Treason or accident had caused the magazines to explode, and the devastation was incredible. The ramparts were breached, the greatest part of the guns thrown into the ditch, five hundred people were struck dead on the instant, and only six houses left standing; the stones thrown out hurt forty of the besiegers in the trenches, and the surviving garrison, aghast at the horrid commotion, disregarded all exhortations to rally."

Junot did not number over thirty-six thousand men, and half of these were engaged in the operations of the sieges. For some reason not known, the forces of the English general were divided; there were only thirty thousand men at Celorico, at the head of the valley of the Mondego; General Hill, with fifteen thousand men on the right, was at Portalegro, on the left bank of the Tagus, against Reynier's corps, which was observed by a light corps of Portuguese and that of Romana; the reserve of ten thousand men, under Leith, remained at Thomar, thirty leagues from the army, and twelve thousand Portuguese were thrown upon the frontiers as partisans. It would seem that Wellington might readily have united these means, and, by taking the initiative, have greatly troubled our operations, without compromising the system on which he had based his hopes. But he remained immovable in his position.

Third Invasion of Portugal.—Having completed all his preparations for invasion, Massena drew to himself the corps of Reynier, about the middle of September, and directed himself on Celorico. The enemy now fell back, descending the left of the Mondego, where ten affluents with deep ravines presented as many good lines of defense. But as Massena descended by the right bank on Viseu, the English general crossed the Mondego, marched rapidly on the mountains of Acobar, where he also directed, at the same time, the corps of Hill and Leith, by the road to Espinoha. He thus hoped to cover Coimbra and the road to Lisbon, by taking position with his united forces on the plateau of Busaco, at the summit of that chain, three hundred feet above the surrounding valleys. This important junction was effected on the twenty-sixth of September, at the very moment that the French army arrived at Busaco. Ney, who was the first to present himself, was inclined, it is said, to attack immediately, but was persuaded to await the arrival of the commander-in-chief. It is asserted that the junction of Hill and Leith was not then effected, nor even when Massena made his reconnoissance. If this be true, the delay was a deplorable fatality. However, the heroes of Essling and Genoa, accustomed in the Alps and Apennines not to fear rocks, however difficult of access, determined to make the attack the next day, although the union of the enemy's forces would then be consummated.

Battle of Busaco.—There were only two roads by which the English could be reached, that by the convent of Busaco, and that by San Antonio de Cantaro. The sixth corps took the first road in deep columns by echelons, the rocky escarpments not permitting them to attack in any other order, or even allowing the cannon to follow the infantry. Reynier attacked, in the same way, by San Antonio. Our troops ascended the heights with their accustomed impetuosity, but were exposed to a most horrible fire. After driving back the enemy's first line on the slope, they reached the summit by brigades, but out of breath and a little disordered by their vigorous effort. They were here exposed to a concentric fire of grape, from a numerous artillery, and of musketry from the enemy's battalions; and charged in front by fresh troops, and in flank by a crowd of Portuguese, they descended the mountains with a sensible loss and without inflicting much injury on the enemy. General Simon was killed, and General Ferrey wounded at the head of the column of the sixth corps. The intrepid Foy and the brave Graindorge, who led Reynier's corps, were severely wounded, without obtaining any better success. For a moment, they deemed themselves successful, when Hill's entire corps, acting as a reserve, assailed them, and, after a murderous combat, drove them back to the foot of the mountain. This butchery, which cost us six or seven thousand men, *hors-de-combat*, was the more to be regretted, as it changed the relative *morale* of the two armies, and might have been avoided, either by making the attack before the junction of Hill and Leith, or by manœuvring so as to dislodge the enemy.

Massena turns the Position of Wellington.—But the evil had now been committed, and the position of Massena was most critical; he could not remain without provisions at the foot of the mountain, nor could he retreat in the face of an enemy who was watching all his movements. To repass the Mondego, to act on the left bank, was also impracticable, since Wellington had a direct line there, by which he could anticipate him. Fortunately, a peasant pointed out to Massena a road two leagues further north, still better than the one he had attempted, which led to Coimbra by Avelans de Cinna and Soardo. Wellington had assigned the defense of this post to the Portuguese corps of Trant; but, for some reason not known, that corps had not arrived. Massena took this road without hesitation. This flank movement, executed between the English army and the sea was bold and audacious; but Wellington, satisfied with his victory, although a passive one and without results, preferred to regain his intrenched camp, rather than to venture an engagement with our troops in the open country, where he might be seriously cut up.

Devastating System of the English General.—The French army followed him by Coimbra. Here, as at Viseu, we found no inhabitants. These two rich and flourishing cities were deserted and abandoned, as was also the whole country. The unfortunate inhabitants had been forced to fly, under pain of death by the orders of the English general, the regency and an exasperated clergy. Wellington's orders of the twenty-fourth of August, directing this measure, are an historical monument of this cruel war.*

---

* To lay waste a country in this manner, is permitted by the severe rules of war, or, in other words, is within the extreme limits established by the laws of

Thus applying to a country mountainous, difficult of access, and possessing but little grain, the precepts given by Lloyd for the defense of England, Wellington had transformed the whole country from Celorico to Lisbon, into one vast artificial desert. Fortunately for us this vigorous order had not been literally executed ; the inhabitants had fled with a part of their provisions, but not having the means of transportation, they had buried the remainder ; a part of these were discovered by our soldiers, and, although an insufficient resource for the entire army, they served as a means of subsistence for some weeks.

Lines of Torres Vedras.—By a singular fatuity of which there is no other example in all the continental wars, Massena did not learn till he reached Leyria, the existence of these formidable lines on which Wellington had been laboring for the last ten months ! Two lines of redoubts, the greater part of which were closed at the gorge and palisaded ; and thus presenting eighty-seven separate forts, armed with two hundred and ninety pieces of heavy cannon, offered one of the most formidable positions mentioned in the annals of modern history ; a third line serving as a citadel to the other two, was so arranged as to cover an embarkation in case the others were forced. Taking refuge in this redoubtable asylum, resting on the sea (which for the English alone was a good base), and therefore certain of provisions, he could brave all our attacks.*

---

war ; but such measures are justifiable only by the extreme necessity of the case. Vattel characterizes them, as " savage and monstrous excesses, when committed without necessity." We are to understand by the word *necessity*, a military necessity, or great military advantage to be gained toward accomplishing the object of the campaign or of the war. The laying waste of a district of country, or the destroying of a city, sometimes produces a greater result than a victory gained. Napoleon's campaign in Russia furnishes a striking illustration. The general must decide according to the circumstances of each particular case. *Halleck's Int. Law, and Laws of War.* Ch. xix., § 23.

* The defenses of Torres Vedras, from the important influence which they

Ch. XVI.]   CAMPAIGN OF 1810 IN SPAIN   229

Embarrassing Position of Massena.—Although Massena was no more fond of retreating than I was, still he did not dare to risk an attack, as it would have been too hazardous.

had upon the Peninsular war, deserve a more full description than that given in the text. We copy the following from Napier:
"The lines of Torres Vedras," he says, "consisted of three distinct ranges of defense.

"The first, extending from Alhandra on the Tagus, to the mouth of the Zizandro on the sea-coast, was, following the inflections of the hills, twenty-nine miles long.

"The second, traced at a distance varying from six to ten miles in rear of the first, stretched from Quintella on the Tagus to the mouth of the St. Lorenza, being twenty-four miles in length.

"The third, intended to cover a forced embarkation, extended from Passo-d'Arcos on the Tagus, to the tower of Junquera on the coast. Here an outer line, constructed on an opening of three thousand yards, inclosed an intrenched camp designed to cover the embarkation with fewer troops, should the operation be delayed by bad weather; within the second camp, Fort St. Julians (whose high ramparts and deep ditches defied an escalade), was armed and strengthened to enable a rear-guard to protect both itself and the army.

"The nearest part of the second line was twenty-four miles from these works at Passo-d'Arcos, and some parts of the first line were two long marches distant; but the principal routes led through Lisbon, where measures were taken to retard the enemy and give time for the embarkation.

"Of these stupendous lines, the second, whether regarded for its strength or importance, was undoubtedly the principal; the others were only appendages. the one as a final place of refuge, the other as an advanced work to stem the first violence of the enemy, and to enable the army to take up its ground on the second line without hurry or pressure. Massena having, however, wasted the summer season on the frontiers, the first line acquired such strength, both from labor and from the fall of rain, that Lord Wellington resolved to abide his opponent's charge there.

"The ground presented to the French being, as it were, divided into five parts or positions, shall be described in succession from right to left.

"1st. *From Alhandra to the head of the valley of Calandrix.* This distance, of about five miles, was a continuous and lofty ridge, defended by thirteen redoubts, and for two miles rendered inaccessible by a scarp fifteen to twenty feet high, executed along the brow. It was guarded by the British and Portuguese division under General Hill, and flanked from the Tagus by a strong flotilla of gun-boats, manned by British seamen.

"2d. *From the head of the vale of Calandrix to the Pé-de-Monte.* This position, also five miles in length, consisted of two salient mountains forming the valley of Aruda, that town being exactly in the mouth of the pass. Only three feeble redoubts, totally incapable of stopping an enemy for an instant, were constructed here, and the defense of the ground was intrusted to General Crawfurd and the light division.

The enemy had taken at Coimbra some four thousand of our sick and wounded, so that our army was reduced to forty thousand combatants, while the enemy numbered more than

"3d. *The Monte Agraca.* This lofty mountain overtopped the adjacent country in such a manner, that from its summit the whole of the first line could be distinctly observed. The right was separated from the Aruda position, by a deep ravine which led to nothing; the left overlooked the village and valley of Zibreira; the centre overhung the town of Sobral. The summit of this mountain was crowned by an immense redoubt, mounting twenty-five guns, and having three smaller works, containing nineteeen guns, clustered around it. The garrisons, amounting to two thousand men, were supplied by Pack's brigade; and on the reverse of the position, which might be about four miles in length, the fifth division, under General Leith, was posted in reserve.

4th. *From the valley of Zibreira to Torres Vedras.* This position, seven miles long, was at first without works; because it was only when the rains had set in, that the resolution to defend the first line permanently, was adopted. But the ground being rough and well-defined, the valley in front, deep, and watered by the Zizandre, now become a considerable river, it presented a fine field of battle for a small army. The first and fourth, and a sixth division formed of troops just arrived from England and from Cadiz, were there posted, under the immediate command of Lord Wellington himself, whose head-quarters were fixed at Pedro Negro, near the Socorra. a rock, on which a telegraph was erected, communicating with every part of the lines.

5th. *From the heights of Torres Vedras to the mouth of the Zizandre.* The right flank of this position and the pass in front of the town of Torres Vedras were secured, first, by one great redoubt, mounting forty guns; secondly, by several smaller forts, judiciously planted so as to command all the approaches. From these works to the sea a range of moderate heights were crowned with small forts; but the chief defense there, after the rains had set in, was to be found in the Zizandre, which was not only unfordable, but overflowed its banks, and formed an impassable marsh. A paved road, parallel to the foot of the hills, ran along the whole front; that is, from Torres Vedras, by Runa Sobral and Aruda, to Alhandra. This was the nature of the *first* line of defense; the second was still more formidable.

"1st. *From the mouth of the St. Lourenca to Mafra.* In this distance of seven miles, there was a range of hills naturally steep, artificially scarped, and covered by a deep, and in many parts impracticable ravine. The salient points were secured by forts, which flanked and commanded the few accessible points; but as this line was extensive, a secondary post was fortified a few miles in the rear, to secure a road leading from Ereceira to Cintra.

"2d. *On the right of the above line the Tapada, or royal park of Mafra.* Here there was some open ground for an attack. Yet it was strong, and, together with the pass of Mafra, was defended by a system of fourteen redoubts, constructed with great labor and care, well considered with respect to the natural disposition of the ground, and, in some degree, connected with the secondary

sixty thousand. Massena sent to me, by General Foy, for orders and reënforcements. In the mean time he hoped to fatigue his adversary by his perseverance. In this he mis-

post spoken of above; in front, the Sierra-de-Chypre, covered with redoubts, obstructed all approaches to Mafra itself.

"3d. *From the Tapada to the pass of Bucellas.* In this space of ten or twelve miles, which formed the middle of the second line, the country is choked by the Monte Chique, the Cabeca, or head of which, is in the centre of, and over-topping, all the other mountain masses. A road, conducted along a chain of hills, high and salient, but less bold than any other parts of the line, connected Mafra with the Cabeca, and was secured by a number of forts. The country in front was extremely difficult, and a second and stronger range of heights, parallel to and behind the first, offered a good fighting position, which could only be approached with artillery by the connecting road in front; and to reach that, either the Sierra-de-Chypre, on the left, or the pass of the Cabeca-de-Monte-Chique, on the right, must have been carried. Now the works covering the latter, consisted of a cluster of redoubts constructed on the inferior rocky heads in advance of the Cabeca, and completely commanding all the approaches, and both from their artificial and natural strength, nearly impregnable to open force. The Cabeca and its immediate flanks were considered secure in their natural precipitous strength; and, in like manner, the ridges connecting the Cabeca with the pass of Bucellas, being impregnable, were left untouched, save the blocking of one bad mule road that led over them.

"3d. *From Bucellas to the low ground about the Tagus.* The pass of Bucellas was difficult, and strongly defended by redoubts on each side. A ridge, or rather a collection of impassable rocks, called the Sierra-de-Serves, stretched to the right for two miles without a break, and then died away by gradual slopes in the low ground about the Tagus. These declivities and the flat banks of the river offered an opening two miles and a half wide, which was laboriously and carefully strengthened by redoubts, water-cuts, and retrenchments, and connected by a system of forts with the heights of Alhandra; but it was the weakest part of the whole line in itself, and the most dangerous from its proximity to the valleys of Calandrix and Aruda.

There were five roads practicable for artillery piercing the *first line* of defense, namely, two at Torres Vedras, two at Sobral, and one at Alhandra; but as two of these united again at the Cabeca, there were, in fact, only four points of passage through the *second line*, that is to say, at Mafra, Monte-Chique, Bucellas, and Quintella in the flat ground. The aim and scope of all the works was to bar these passes and to strengthen the favorable fighting positions between them, without impeding the movements of the army. Those objects were attained, and it is certain that the loss of the *first line* would not have been injurious, save in reputation, because the retreat was secure upon the *second and stronger line;* and the guns of the first were all inferior calibre, mounted on common truck-carriages, and consequently immovable and useless to the enemy.

"The movements of the allies were free and unfettered by the works. The

calculated; but he could do no better under the circumstances. The English army, having two hundred vessels at its disposal, had always an abundance; it passed five months in its camp, completing its intrenchments and exercising and instructing its troops. The Portuguese militia were here instructed and disciplined till they rivaled the regulars; so that the army came out of the camp more formidable than ever. Massena, on the contrary, was ruining his army in order to subsist it; his troops were divided into movable columns, and exposed to attacks by the inhabitants and the Portuguese partisans. They ravaged the country through which they were soon to make their retreat; sickness, daily combats, and assassinations, diminished their numbers, while the obstacles were increasing before them. In a word, they were so situated as to render it necessary to either attack the enemy immediately or to retreat. Informed of these circumstances by General Foy, I advised Massena to attack the enemy if the thing was practicable, and if not, to keep him within his lines. I promised to send him the ninth corps, under Drouet, which had just entered Spain, and gave him hopes of being seconded by Soult, who was operating on the Guadiana. Being so far from the theatre of the war, I could not presume to give any definitive orders, and, therefore, left

<small>movements of the French army were impeded and cramped by the great Monte-Junta, which, rising opposite the centre of the first line, sent forth a spur called the Sierra-de-Baragueda in a slanting direction, so close up to the heights of Torres Vedras, that the narrow pass of Runa alone separated them. As this pass was commanded by heavy redoubts, Massena was of necessity obliged to dispose his forces on one or other side of the Baragueda, and he could not transfer his army to either without danger; because the Sierra, although not impassable, was difficult; and the movement, which would require time and arrangement, could always be overlooked from the Monte-Agraca, whence, in a few hours, the allied forces could pour down upon the head, flank, or rear of the French while on the march. And this could be done with the utmost rapidity, because communications had been cut by the engineers to all important points of the lines, and a system of signals was established, by which orders were transmitted from the centre to the extremities in a few minutes."</small>

Massena to act according to his own judgment. In the mean time Wellington had completed his works and armed them with additional batteries, while his force had been increased by fifteen thousand additional English and Spanish troops.

There was but one means left by which we could operate against Lisbon; this was to construct a bridge at Santarem, to cover it with a strong *tête-de-pont*, draw Soult from Badajos on Setuval, and to bombard Lisbon from the heights on the opposite bank of the river. To accomplish this object, there was required not only great activity and unity of action, but also means which we did not possess. Massena fortified Punhete near the mouth of the Zezere, and devoted all his efforts to the construction of a bridge-equipage that would enable him to manœuvre on either side of the Tagus. The pontoniers and sappers, with the assistance of a battalion of sailors which he had with the army, succeeded, at the end of six weeks, in completing this task to the satisfaction of the commander-in-chief. But these equipages had now become unnecessary, for Soult did not appear on the Tagus, and Massena could not venture alone to attempt so perilous a passage in the presence of Hill and Romana. It is evident that if Soult had reduced Badajos at the same time that Massena took Almeida, and the two armies had advanced in concert on Lisbon by both banks of the Tagus, the chances of success would have been greatly in our favor. But without the possession of Badajos, and without a suitable bridge-equipage on the Tagus, it is not so certain that Soult's coöperation would have been entirely successful. Even allowing that Soult's march in Alemtejo had not decided the evacuation of Lisbon, it however cannot be doubted that that march would have effected a favorable diversion, and afforded Massena an opportunity to attack the lines of Torres Vedras, by drawing off a part of Wellington's troops. The bombardment of Lisbon from the heights of Almada might have caused great damage to the city, but could hardly have induced Wellington to abandon his formidable camp, which was situated at the distance of four leagues from the city, and out of the reach of batteries on the left bank of the Tagus.

Sufferings of his Army.—Modern history offers no example of an army in such a condition as that of Massena. Placed two hundred leagues from its own frontiers, in the midst of two warlike and insurgent nations, deprived of all maritime means of subsistence in a country deserted by its inhabitants, it could subsist only like a nomadic horde, devouring every thing within the reach of its camp, and then moving to some other place. In all preceding wars, an army, even in a hostile country, could procure provisions by paying for them their weight in gold. Neutral commerce, avaricious of large profits, is ever ready to carry its grains and provisions necessary for the support of life wherever the chances of want promise certain gain. But in our contest, so great was the preponderance of the English marine, and so stringent and arbitrary the rules which this tyrant of the ocean had imposed on neutrals, that she had destroyed all neutral rights of commerce and liberty of the seas; and, on a coast of eight hundred leagues in extent, not a single coaster had ventured to make its appearance.

His Junction with Drouet.—After having sojourned a month near Alenquer opposite the enemy's lines, Massena moved toward Santarem, the middle of November, in order to facilitate the subsistence of his army which he drew from the valley of the Zezere; this also favored his junction with Drouet who was coming by Celorico and Castel Franco. This junction was effected near Leyria on the twenty-sixth of December. Wellington, reënforced by the troops of Romana, advanced as far as Cartaxo, and the two armies secured themselves behind their intrenchments.

Remarks on the Position of Affairs.—It was certainly very unfortunate that the strength of this position was such as to prevent our expelling the English from the Peninsula by a single decisive blow; but the situation of affairs was such as to leave us but few combinations from which to choose. It may be said that when we found an assault impossible we might either have blockaded his lines or have manœuvred to draw him into the interior of Spain. But there were other positions on the frontier of Portugal as strong as that of Torres Vedras ; and by retiring we would merely have extended the sphere of his activity from the Ebro to the Guadalquiver. A larger force would have been necessary to hold him in check behind the Agueda than to observe his lines ; he could always keep the field with advantage, against troops which were now under the necessity of extending themselves so as to cover the immense space between Salamanca and Cadiz, and which he might threaten on any part of this line, by operating from his intrenched camp, either to the right or to the left. If beaten, he could always take refuge behind the works of Torres Vedras ; so that, under any circumstances, this would be the point from which he was finally to be driven. As we now held him at this point, it was evidently our policy to keep him there. Fifty thousand French troops holding the Anglo-Portuguese in close blockade, would demonstrate the incapability of that army's delivering the Peninsula ; it was the same as if that army did not exist, if we deduct the offset of fifty thousand men from our forces, or what was the same thing, add that number to the army required for the reduction of Spain. Some unworthy Frenchmen who have undertaken the task of undervaluing my glory, in order to elevate to the clouds that of the enemies of France, and to make Wellington *the man of Providence*, have not been able to comprehend this simple question, and have consequently represented Massena as an imbecile ; and me as a madman, who lost all through his violence and obstinacy.

In fine we may lay this down as positive ; we were obliged either to attack Wellington two days after our arrival, or to act precisely as we did. And if we had had the means of supplying our army in their position in this devastated and insurgent country, Wellington would never have left his lines, except to embark his troops and land them again in some other point of the Peninsula.

Suchet's brilliant Success in Catalonia. — My army in Aragon was more fortunate. Having returned to Saragossa in triumph after the victory of Santa Maria over the corps of Blake, Suchet had succeeded, by his wise administration, in restoring abundant supplies as well as discipline among his troops, which were composed of different nations as well as new levies. He regulated the pay of the troops, and forbade any person in this army becoming a charge to the inhabitants, and, what was still more extraordinary, succeeded in reducing to quiet submission those same Aragonese who had exhibited so much energy and ferocity in the defense of Saragossa. Provided with every thing requisite for this object, and being able to descend the Ebro with his convoys, he was silently preparing to attack the places on the lower Ebro, which alone would decide the fate of Catalonia, when Joseph, in marching for Andalusia, directed him to advance to Valencia in order to support that movement. The king, relying on the understanding he had with some of the Valencians, announced that the gates would be opened at our approach. The army of Aragon moved, the early part of March, in two columns which united at Murviedro ; it defeated the advanced guard of the Valencian army, captured nine pieces of cannon, and occupied the faubourgs of the city ; but the gates did not open, notwithstanding a summons supported by threatening demonstrations.

Combat of Margalef.—Convinced that this enterprise was immature, Suchet hastened to return to Saragossa to commence an operation from which he hoped greater success, and rapidly completed his preparation against Lerida. On the twelfth of April, he presented himself before that place, and effected its investment. He did not open the trenches, because he had received information of the approach of a corps of the enemy from Tarragona under the orders of General Henry O'Donnel. On the twenty-third, this general thought to surprise our troops on the left bank of the Ebro, and advanced boldly toward the *tête-de-pont* of Lerida, by the plains of Margalef. The garrison of the place at the same time made an unsuccessful effort at a sortie; and while General Harispe was repelling the head of O'Donnel's column, the thirteenth cuirassiers, sustained by Musnier's division, charged the first Spanish division in flank and forced it, after a hot combat, to lay down its arms; the other division took to flight. The enemy lost five thousand prisoners, in addition to those killed and wounded.

Siege of Lerida.—The operations of the siege were now begun with vigor. The trenches were opened on the twenty-ninth of April, and on the seventh of May, the batteries opened against the north front of the place. The assault was made on the thirteenth, and the city and bridge carried by the bayonet. In the mean time Suchet, seeing that the garrison took refuge in the citadel directed that all the population should be driven in there also. By driving them from street to street and from house to house, this adroit manœuvre succeeded. The citadel became filled with a useless crowd, who not only consumed their provisions but also became more terrified at the sight of our shells than at the fanatical discourses of their priests. Embarrassed and intimidated by this useless multitude, the governor found himself forced to capitulate. General Suchet thus avoided a second siege, which, in 1807, had cost the Duke of Orleans twenty-five days. The garrison were taken prisoners, to the number of seven thousand men. We found in the place large magazines, and one hundred and five pieces of cannon. The occupation of Lerida rendered us masters of the vast and fertile plain of Urgel, which procured us great resources for provisioning the army.*

Siege of Mequinenza.—The siege of Mequinenza was undertaken immediately after that of Lerida. It was necessary to construct a road across the mountains, at the extremity of which this fort is situated. The trenches were opened on the 1st of June, and the assault made on the 8th, when the fort capitulated. We took there fourteen hundred men, and forty-five pieces of cannon; and, what was most important of all, made ourselves masters of the navigation of the Ebro from Saragossa to Tortosa.

Augereau's Operations in Catalonia.—But if I was satisfied with the operations of Suchet, the submission of Aragon, and the taking Lerida, I was the less so with Augereau, who did nothing in Catalonia, notwithstanding the advantages he derived from the possession of Gerona. His first operation had been to approach Barcelona, and invest Hostalrich: the Spaniards made useless attempts to supply this fort, and the garrison finally took advantage of the negligence of the investing corps to effect their escape. The taking of this fort rendered us masters of the road so indispensable for our communications and the transportation of our material. But Augereau seemed to derive no advantages from this important

---

* The conduct of Suchet in driving the inhabitants at Lerida into the citadel along with the garrison, can be justified only by the overruling necessity of the case. It, however, was not contrary to the laws of war. It is a singular circumstance that while Alison and Napier so severely condemn Suchet's conduct on this occasion, they are silent in regard to Wellington's devastation of the country in front of Torres Vedras. Both are to be justified, if justified at all, upon the same grounds,—the necessities of the war.

acquisition. He made demonstrations in the direction of Lerida, when that place was besieged by Suchet, but he did not carry out the operation. In fact, the want of provisions, and the difficulty of communications, added to the general insurrection of the province, fettered all his movements, and rendered them dangerous. I neglected nothing in my power to assist him: a great convoy which I sent him from Provence by sea, could not enter Barcelona; it was captured and dispersed, and the three ships of the line which escorted it, had to run ashore to avoid being taken by the English. The troops of Augereau having been beaten in two rencounters, I saw plainly that the conqueror of the Monga and of Castiglione, was not suited to this kind of war, in which talent and activity were more requisite than courage. I therefore replaced him by Macdonald.*

Siege of Tortosa.—The success of Suchet induced me to intrust him with an important operation, on which, in my opinion, depended the reduction of Catalonia. There are only two great roads in this province, the one running from

---

* Napier, in speaking of the siege of Lerida, and the opportunity presented to the Spaniards to attack Suchet, says:

"It was to obviate this danger that Napoleon directed the seventh corps to take such a position on the Lower Ebro as would keep both O'Donnel and the Valencians in check. Augereau, as we have seen, failed to do this; and St. Cyr asserts that the seventh corps could never safely venture to pass the mountains, and enter the valley of the Ebro. On the other hand, Suchet affirms that Napoleon's instructions could have been obeyed without difficulty. St. Cyr himself, under somewhat similar circumstances, blockaded Tarragona for a month; Augereau, who had more troops and fewer enemies, might have done the same, and yet spared six thousand men to pass the mountains. Suchet would then have been tranquil with respect to O'Donnel, would have had a covering army to protect the siege, and the succors, fed from the resources of Aragon, would have relieved Catalonia.

"Augereau has been justified, on the ground that the blockade of Hostalrich would have been raised while he was on the Ebro. The danger of this could not have escaped the emperor, yet his military judgment, unerring in principle, was often false in application, because men measure difficulties by the standard of their own capacity, and Napoleon's standard only suited the heroic proportions. One thing is, however, certain, that Catalonia presented

Barcelona to Saragossa, and the other from Perpignan to Valencia, by Tarragona, Tortosa and Peniscola, all of which were fortified sea-ports. It was important for us to get possession of this direct route, so as at the same time to cut off the communication of the insurgents with the sea, and to secure ours between the Ebro and France. Suchet, being charged with this task, preluded it by the siege of Tortosa, while Macdonald, acting as a corps of observation, was to hold in check the hostile divisions which were scattered among the mountains, from Cerdagne and the confines of Aragon to the limits of the kingdom of Valencia. All the upper valleys of Vic, Manresa, Cervera, and Puicerda, however often passed over by our columns, still remained in the power of the Spaniards, and their chiefs, far from suffering themselves to be discouraged by our success on the Ebro, often appeared in a threatening attitude in the French Cerdagne, at the gates of Mont-Louis and in the Ampurdan.

The difficulty of drawing our convoys from France across a country so full of obstacles, rendered all the operations of our troops exceedingly hazardous. Having collected at Lerida the material necessary for the siege of Tortosa, Suchet resolved to hasten this operation, for fear that Macdonald might not be able to hold, for a long time, the positions necessary for covering this siege. He opened a practicable road from Mequinenza and Carpe to Batea and Gandesa, and then established himself before Tortosa, the last of the month. But the army of Catalonia was not ready to act in concert

---

the most extraordinary difficulties to the invaders. The powerful military organization of the Migueletes and Somatenes,—the well-arranged system of fortresses,—the ruggedness and sterility of the country,—the ingenuity and readiness of a manufacturing population thrown out of work,—and, finally, the aid of an English fleet, combined to render the conquest of this province a gigantic task. Nevertheless, the French made progress, each step planted slowly indeed and with pain, but firmly, and insuring the power of making another."

with that of Aragon. Macdonald held an interview with his colleague at Lerida near the end of August, and immediately afterwards moved with his corps in the direction of Barcelona and Gerona, to meet a convoy coming from France, which was necessary for the combined operations with Suchet. The latter now regretted having so soon established himself before Tortosa, but fearing the influence of a retrograde movement, he determined to continue the blockade on the right bank of the Ebro. During this interval, a continual contest was waged against the Valencians and the garrison, who attempted numerous attacks on the blockading troops, or against the enemy's corps from Tarragona or the camp at Falcet and its environs, or against the parties which were spread along the Ebro to intercept our convoys of artillery. The long-expected coöperation was not effected until the month of December. Marshal Macdonald to whom Suchet had given Lerida and its magazines, established himself with the main body of his forces between Tarragona, Tortosa, and Mora, and one of his divisions passed temporarily under the orders of Suchet, to take part in the siege. Thus reënforced, this general invested Tortosa on both banks of the river, and occupied the hill of Alba on the fifteenth of December. The attack was directed against the front of the place between the Ebro and Fort Orleans inclusively. The works of the engineers were pushed forward with extraordinary rapidity, notwithstanding the sorties of the garrison. The covered-way was crowned on the first of January, and the descent of the ditch executed at the same time that the work was battered in breach. The governor proposed a capitulation, which he afterwards hesitated to conclude, although he could not have been ignorant that our miners were about to attack the body of the place. The following day (January 2d), everything was prepared early for the assault. The white flag reappeared, although neither the governor nor his messenger presented themselves. The negotiations of the previous day had already affected the garrison so that they advanced from all sides to the glaçis, and entered into conversation with our soldiers. Seizing upon this opportunity to prevent a useless effusion of blood, General Suchet, followed by some officers, rode to the first group of Spaniards and caused the barrier-gate to be opened; seeing some officers he went to them, and complained of the hesitation of the governor and the fate to which he exposed the city. At his words the cannoneers left their pieces, the French collected on the ramparts, and the governor, a little confused, was brought before him, and the capitulation of the previous day was concluded, signed, and executed at the same instant. The garrison numbering over eight thousand men were sent into France by Saragossa, as prisoners of war; and a hundred and seventy-seven pieces of artillery were found in the place and captured. This conquest separated the Valencians from the Catalans, and, by this division, greatly weakened their means of defense. No sooner was Suchet in possession of Tortosa than he prepared to attack Fort St. Philip on the hill of Belaguer. General Habert made a successful attempt to carry the place by a *coup-de-main:* our voltigeurs intimidated the garrison, scaled the walls, and took the fort. This was a most valuable *point-d'appui* for ulterior operations against Tarragona.

General Remarks on the War.—Notwithstanding these disasters, the Spanish government was very far from regarding their cause as desperate. The Cortes of the nation, convoked as has been already remarked, at the moment of the dissolution of the central junta, finally assembled at Cadiz in September, 1810. From the spirit manifested by this assembly, it was evident that they could not long agree with the regency: in fact this body was soon dissolved, and a new one appointed in its place, at the head of which figured the duke of Infantado and General Blake, who, like Romana, enjoyed more popularity than his colleagues, without being any more successful in his military operations. Under this new organization, some efforts were made to obtain success in the East under the protection of Tarragona; in the South, by the aid of Carthagena, Murcia, and Cadiz; in the West, by means of Badajos and Wellington's army, which still lay behind their intrenchments at Lisbon. Romana had here joined the English general with a force of seven or eight thousand men.

The cabinet of London, on its side, encouraged by the success of its arms and the influence which the appointment of Wellesley to the ministry had given to the war party, obtained from parliament subsidies for the succor of Spain! The efforts of my enemies were naturally calculated to increase mine also: and after the success of Suchet in the East, and of Soult in the South, I hoped to see the resistance of Spain cease sooner or later: this war did not give me much uneasiness, for I had resolved to be still more obstinate than the Spaniards, and I was certain of ultimate success. The empire was strong enough to sustain such a contest, with the aid of its powerful allies, without being exhausted by it. This war did not prevent me from undertaking such enterprises as I deemed beneficial to the prosperity of France. I improved the administration of the government; I organized new institutions which were calculated to give permanency to the empire by raising up a generation interested in sustaining it. Maritime commerce alone was wanting to revive the prosperity of our ports, and draw upon me benedictions greater than any other mortal ever received.

Bernadotte elected Prince Royal of Sweden.—With the exception of the Peninsular war, France enjoyed, in profound quiet, the fruits of my labors. My Continental System had been embraced by nearly all Europe. Sweden had adopted it on the accession of Charles XIII.; this prince, having no heirs, had adopted the Prince of Augustenbourg of the Holstein branch, which connected him, at the same time, with the houses of Russia and Denmark. But no sooner was he recognized as the prince royal than he died a sudden and violent death. The people accused General Fersen of this act and massacred him in a riot. They required a successor to the throne of Sweden, and thought to strengthen their bonds of connection with France by nominating a member of my family. Bernadotte was very remotely connected with me by being the brother-in-law of King Joseph; this was a very frail bond of connection, but, in addition to it, Bernadotte had gained the esteem of many Swedes in his different commands in Pomerania and at Rugen. The diet, assembled at Oerebro, proclaimed him the adopted son of Charles XIII. and prince royal. We had not been on good terms since the campaign of Wagram; although I did not provoke his nomination, yet I readily gave it my assent, when the proposition was made to me, and it must be acknowledged by all parties that he was entirely indebted for it to his connection with my brother. I flattered myself that if he did not have for me the devotion of a Seide, he would at least remember that he was a Frenchman, and that in this capacity as well as that of a Swede, he would appreciate the value of the alliance with France, since all the kings of Sweden, with the exception of Gustavus IV., had followed this system for the last two centuries. But I was deceived; Bernadotte retained for me the rancor of the eighteenth Brumaire, and Sweden was less attached to me under him than it would have been under a Swedish prince Even supposing that my policy was too rigorous, and that he left my system to return to a neutrality toward England, I was far from expecting to see him at the head of the armies of the enemy at a time when we were defending the national independence on the banks of the Rhine and even on the soil of France.*

Reunion of Holland.—Four events, equally remarkable, signalized the year 1810 ; the first was the donation of the

---

* The course pursued by Bernadotte during the invasions of his native country in 1814 and 1815, has made his name odious in France. Although made crown prince of Sweden through French influence, it by no means followed that he was not bound to do every thing in his power to promote the interests of his adopted country. But it by no means followed that the interests of the two were incompatible, or that, as a Swede by adoption, he was bound to oppose his native country and do all in his power to injure the man to whom he was mainly indebted for his elevation. History will judge of Bernadotte by his course before, as well as after, he became crown prince of Sweden.

After Napoleon's return from Egypt, Bernadotte, while pretending great friendship, was engaged in various intrigues against him. These were afterward discovered and their author was at one time disgraced and exiled. But through the influence of his wife and his brother-in-law, Joseph Bonaparte, Napoleon forgave and restored him to a command. He afterward made him a marshal of France and prince of Ponte-Corvo. At the battle of Austerlitz, his corps did good service, and he was complimented by the emperor. But in the campaigns of 1806 and 1807, and at the battle of Wagram, his course was such as to cause him to be several times reprimanded, and to raise strong suspicions of his good faith. Nevertheless, his connection by marriage with the Bonaparte family, caused all these offenses to be forgiven, and when offered the rank of crown prince of Sweden, Napoleon not only gave his consent, but gave him large sums of money as an outfit for his new position, saying that a prince of his family and government, should not appear in Sweden as a beggar. Bernadotte seemed very grateful for the compliment, but no sooner did he reach Sweden, than he renewed his intrigues against Napoleon. The Swedes elected Bernadotte as a compliment to Bonaparte, and as a pledge of future friendly relations, and it was so regarded by Napoleon. But the enemies of France who influenced the arrangement, had a very different object in view.

Bernadotte had always been more popular with the northern and German soldiers than with the French. In most of his campaigns he had commanded foreign troops. Neither the French marshals nor the French troops liked him. This was particularly the case after the campaign of Wagram. At the same time he was popular with the allies, and on every occasion courted their good-will. He moreover sought the friendship of Fouché and other old republican enemies of Napoleon. These facts should have been sufficient for the emperor to distrust him Where a general is popular with the enemies of a government either at home or abroad, there is good cause to distrust his loyalty to that government. It is now incontestable that while Bernadotte was serving under Napoleon, he was already intriguing for his overthrow, and the restoration of the Bourbons, conduct which can be justified in no possible way.

grand-duchy of Frankfort, to Prince Eugene, in reversion at the death of the Prince Primate. If I should have a second son I projected giving him the crown of Italy and Rome; but Europe, not knowing my intentions, did not understand the object of this new arrangement, and supposed that I intended Germany, or at least the Confederation of the Rhine, for my adopted son. A still more important affair was the re-annexation to the French Empire of Holland and the mouths of the Ems, of the Weser and of the Elbe, as far as Lubec.

The contest with England daily becoming more complicated by the chances of the war in Spain, I looked around me for means to force the cabinet of St. James to dispositions more pacific, and adopted the project of annexing territory to the empire as a means of retrocession to be offered as an inducement for peace. Of all those who were the temporary victims of the Continental System, none complained more than the Dutch. This nation, whose industrious, speculating, and enterprising character, rendered its prosperity dependent on the advantages of commerce, could not submit to our maritime code without the ruin of these interests. It was necessary to close our eyes to the daily infractions of this code committed by the inhabitants, or to restore to the sea the land which they had conquered, and still defended with so much care and so many sacrifices. My brother Louis had not hesitated to espouse the interests of the Batavian commerce; he felt that he could not have the love of his people unless he acted with them and for them. He published my decrees, but openly allowed them to be violated. This state of things was destroying my system. Of what use was it that I had conquered the coast of Europe, and closed its ports to the English, if the members of my own family were to become the brokers of the enemy's commerce? My representations of this abuse not producing the desired effect, I was forced to interdict all importation into Holland : my brother retaliated by interdicting the admission of all French merchandise into his kingdom. This manner of governing Holland did not at all suit my policy : by taking the helm of the government myself, I might direct its resources wholly towards my object. Holland would suffer by it for some years, perhaps ten or twenty, but it would be amply repaid for these sacrifices, if we should succeed.

Consequent Negotiations with England.—Independently of these powerful considerations, I wished to prove to England that in the course which she forced me to pursue, every year in which she delayed to make peace, would lead to the aggrandizement of my empire : no power in Europe was now prepared to oppose my project. Nevertheless, before deciding on it, I resolved to make one more effort to negotiate peace with the cabinet of London.

My brother Louis came to Paris, in the early part of 1810. After declaring to him that he had carried out my intentions in Holland even less than the old Batavian government, I assured him that I would allow no deviation from the system I had formed against England, and hinted to him the possibility of re-annexation. I gave him to understand that the only means of avoiding the overthrow of his throne, was to induce England to make peace. In accordance with these instructions, Louis informed his ministers of the danger which threatened Holland ; and directed them to send a reliable man to England to induce the cabinet of London to enter into negotiations in order to avoid a catastrophe equally injurious to both countries. He solicited that government to make some modification in its maritime code which might be the first step towards a treaty of peace.

The Marquis of Wellesley was at this time minister of foreign affairs ; and M. Labouchère, who was charged with this important embassy, failed to effect any negotiations. A singular circumstance came to light during this discussion. Fouché, tormented with the spirit of intrigue which formed a part of his composition, had also attempted, on his own account, to open negotiations for peace with England, the bases of which did not agree with the assurances given by Labouchère. Wellesley made this a pretext for rejecting propositions which he accused of being insincere. The brother of Wellington was the most decided advocate for the continuance of the war : he carried his hatred of me to the extent of wishing to emancipate the Irish Catholics, not only to dispose of the English troops necessary for guarding that island, but also to embody the Irish militia itself. He thus hoped to send fifty thousand of these Irish troops to his brother in Spain, so as to push the war with vigor, and to attach to his party the religious opinion of Spain, by showing them an entire army of Catholics under British colors. I do not mention these things as matters of reproach or blame against an English minister, but merely as a proof that between me and the men who had resolved upon possessing the trident of the seas, or the sceptre of the world, there was little possibility of a treaty of peace : it was necessary that one of these two parties should succumb to the other.

Informed by the English of Fouché's intrigue, I replaced him in office by Savary ; but instead of bringing him to trial, as he deserved, I sent him away in a sort of disgrace as governor of the Roman states. However, in order to give the English ministry time for reflection, I determined to postpone the reunion of Holland, and to try another means which would lead to the same result in case the cabinet of St. James remained inflexible. I therefore concluded, in March, a treaty with Louis, by which he ceded to me Zealand and Dutch Brabant to the first arm of the Meuse, and consented to the establishment of the French customs in his kingdom. This condition, so severe upon the interests of the

Dutch, was near effecting a revolt; the suite of my ambassador was insulted; and I therefore resolved to end the matter by sending into Holland a corps of twenty thousand men. My brother hesitated whether he should not imitate the example of the Regent of Portugal, by retiring to Batavia; but was persuaded from it by General Tarayre, the commandant of his guard; he abdicated and retired to Austria. On the ninth of July, I declared the reunion of Holland to the French empire, but this reunion was not consummated by a *senatus-consultum*, till the thirteenth of December, when the silence of the English government proved that she would not be influenced by the ruin of her ancient allies.

Annexation of the Mouths of the Ems, the Elbe and the Weser.—In order to complete this great measure, I also decreed the reannexation of Oldenburg and a part of Westphalia as far as Lubec, including the cities of Hamburg and Bremen. The object of this measure was to put an end to the illicit commerce which was here carried on. The English had got possession of the island of Heligoland belonging to the Danes, and situated some leagues from the coast of Holstein. Although of limited extent, this island had been transformed into an immense magazine, where the coasters of the Baltic and the North Sea supplied themselves with English and colonial merchandise. This was a sufficient motive to justify a military occupation of the country, but not for its formal annexation to the empire. I, however, did not intend to retain this as a permanent acquisition, but to restore it as soon as I could force England to confine herself within the limits of moderation. It was evident that, after the restoration of the independence of Holland, the departments beyond that country could no longer remain as French provinces. In the mean time, I would destroy these nests of smugglers of English goods, augment my maritime means, and my Continental System, and, by gaining a footing in the Baltic, increase my influence over Denmark and Sweden. But in order to connect these departments of the Ems, the Weser and the Elbe to the empire, I had also decreed the annexation of the states of the Duke of Oldenburg, the brother-in-law of the Emperor of Russia. It was to be expected that the Emperor Alexander would demand an explanation for so high handed an act of authority. As we were already punctilious and formal in explanations, there was reason to believe that if he did not object to the reunion of Holland and the Hanseatic towns, he would at least expect some explanation for this encroachment on the states of his sister.

Napoleon's Tour in Holland.—In the mean time I sought to deceive Europe respecting my real projects, and to give an idea of my confidence and security. Not being able to restore to the Belgians and the Dutch the advantages of maritime commerce, I thought to turn their attention to works of internal improvement, and to dazzle them with the spectacle of my glory, by visiting their provinces. No time in my whole career was employed to greater advantage than this tour. I inspected the superb works of Antwerp, and encouraged the commerce of Amsterdam to still sustain with firmness the last efforts of a contest which would finally give liberty to all. I proved to them that by my perseverance and vast solicitude, we might construct twenty-five large vessels per annum, so that in six years I should have one hundred and fifty ships of the line at Genoa, Venice, Toulon, Brest, Cherbourg, Antwerp, and the Texel, and that if the continent would continue to second my efforts, we would soon restore the freedom of the seas. Canals, roads, and public works of all kinds were equally the objects of my solicitude. I employed numerous Spanish prisoners in the construction of the canal of Napoleon, which was to connect the Soane with the Rhine, and the Mediterranean with the North Sea. In order to complete this work, I ordered the opening of the canal of the North, which connected the navigation of the Rhine with Hamburg, and thence, by Lubec, with the Baltic sea; important works calculated to secure, in time of war, the transportation of our products into the north of Europe, and, in return, the products of the north necessary for the navy. The canal of St. Quintin, which Louis XVI. had abandoned on account of the difficulties of its construction, was completed, and immense tunnels, securing the navigation of the Scheldt to the Seine by the Oise, proved to Belgium and France that, to me, nothing was impossible which was calculated to promote their prosperity.

Senatus-Consultum on the Incorporation of Rome.—I, at this time, had some difficulties with the Pope; although wholly at my discretion at Savona, the pontiff was firmly opposed to all reconciliation. The principles which he manifested in his bull of excommunication, showed that, although a prisoner, he still arrogated to himself the right to dispose of thrones. It was necessary to oppose to these pretensions solemn acts of state calculated to destroy their effect. The senate accomplished this object by the act of February 17th, 1810, which contained the following stipulations:

1st. The Roman States were to form two departments, and be entitled to be represented by seven deputies in the legislative body;

2d. Rome was to be regarded as the second city of the empire;

3d. The Prince-Imperial was to bear the title of King of Rome;

4th. Rome was to have a resident imperial prince holding there the court of the empire;

5th. The emperors were to be crowned at Paris, and also at Rome;

6th. All sovereignty was declared incompatible with the spiritual authority in the interior of the empire ;

7th. On their exaltation, the Popes were to take an oath never to act contrary to the four propositions of the Gallican Church ;

8th. These propositions were declared common to all the churches of the empire.

The remaining articles established a palace for the Pope at Paris, and another at Rome ; fixed his salary at two millions per annum ; and directed the expenses of the Sacred College and of the Propaganda, to be paid from the imperial treasury. Conformably to these measures, all the archives of the Vatican were to be transferred to Paris. *The grand project of making this city the capital of Catholic Europe was half accomplished : I would by the same act reinforce the empire with all theocratic influence, and free religion of all ultramontane jesuitism. Europe would have been for ever secured from religious fanaticism : the pure religion of the early Christians would only have been the more venerated, and the more useful both to the people and to their governments.*

The profession of these doctrines so conservative of the rights of the throne, was not of a nature calculated to calm the hostility of the Pope, who, not being able to defend his temporal power, attempted to revive the absolute privileges of the Holy See. I was excommunicated, and my nominations to the vacant sees, not confirmed : the canonical institution was refused. Being thus engaged in a new kind of warfare, I appointed for my guide an ecclesiastic council composed of the most worthy prelates, among whom figured the Cardinal Maury, and the bishop of Nantes. As the Pope persisted in refusing the canonical institution, I was obliged to provide for the vacant sees by spiritual administrators, designated by the name of *bishops capitulaires*. Pius VII.

forbade their exercising the office, and appointed vicars apostolic in their places. Such an act of authority, establishing in my empire a power superior to my own, was well calculated to irritate me ; the cardinals who instigated this assumption of authority were conducted to Vincennes, and also P. Fontana, one of the members of my council.

Council of Paris.—This state of schism could not long continue. To make an end of the matter, I assembled, in the early part of 1811, a council of the bishops of France; the ostensible object of this council was to provide for the canonical institutions, but in reality I wished to establish an ecclesiastic authority superior to that of the Pope, in order that the one might counterbalance the other. My new ecclesiastic council, feeling the necessity of a reconciliation with the Holy See, sent a solemn deputation to him at Savona, to ask his blessing, and to offer a reconciliation. The Pope, being free from his perfidious counselors, and influenced solely by his own philanthropic feeling, promised the institution, and authorized the council. It assembled on the ninth of July, 1811. The bishops did not comprehend my policy, and declined the very power which they had so often sought. They declared themselves incompetent. I was under the necessity of immediately dissolving this council, to avoid the appearance of yielding the point. A second council, which was assembled only to pronounce on the canonical institution, decided it. The Pope sanctioned their resolutions, and sent me letters of reconciliation.

Religious Fanaticism.—Nevertheless, the impression which I wished to avoid had been made. The zeal of devotees became more active than ever ; a little church which had ventured to form itself even in France, after I had been crowned by the Pope, and which then put itself above the pontiff whose authority it contested, had again rallied itself to the Pope as soon as it thought he could be made to serve its own ambitious views. This church again raised the banners of opposition, as soon as he appeared to yield to my ascendancy. Thus, in the nineteenth century, France also had her fanatics; and if we are astonished at the apostolic junta of Spain, what shall we say of this *ultra catholic* sect, in the very bosom of the most enlightened nation! At its voice the Jesuits resumed their activity; it was a secret action, but quick, active and powerful against me. Notwithstanding all my precautions, these devotees succeeded in communicating with Savona, and in receiving instructions from that place. The Trappists of Fribourg served as the agents in this correspondence; they printed pamphlets among themselves and circulated them, from curate to curate, throughout the whole empire. The focus of these troubles had ramifications in France, Switzerland, Italy, and Spain. The clergy, the malcontents of all kinds, the partisans of the old *régime*, were everywhere intriguing against my authority and seeking to embarrass my administration. They no longer appeared in the shape of conspirators; they had borrowed the banners of the church, the most formidable of all against the throne; they fought with its thunders, and not with cannon; they had their secret signs and rallying words. It was a kind of orthodox masonry, whose compact structure and polished surface presented nothing by which I could grasp it. It attained its object the more securely as it could not be attacked without the appearance of religious persecution. To act by force against disarmed men, would have given them the character of martyrs.

Continuation of the War between Russia and Turkey.—
While I was extending the limits of my empire from the Tiber to the Baltic, the Russians were slowly operating in the Balkan and in Roumelia. The campaign of 1810, had been active at the mouth of the Danube. General Kamenski (the younger), had succeeded Bagration in the command;

he was a man in the flower of life, well-informed, but without experience. A fine army of one hundred and forty-three battalions, one hundred and twenty-two squadrons, and twenty-seven regiments of Cossacks, forming a line of one hundred thousand combatants, constituted a force more considerable than Russia had ever before sent against the Ottoman empire. This seemed sufficient to march to Constantinople; I would have asked no more to deliver it from the Bosphorus to Moscow.

Kamenski resolved to direct his efforts by Hirsova on Shumla, while, on his right, forces were directed to besiege Silistria and Roudschouck. Bazardjik was carried after a vigorous resistance, and Silistria, Tourtonkai and Rasgrad also fell into the hands of the Russians. While these cities were falling before the enemy, the grand-vizir remained, with Ottoman gravity, in his camp at Shumla. Kamenski advanced to this place on the twenty-second of June. An attempt was made to storm this fortified city from the rocky heights above, but it proved unsuccessful. The place was now invested, but as the Turks succeeded in introducing a large convoy by the road to Constantinople, all hopes of starving out the garrison were at an end. Raising the investment of Shumla, and leaving his brother with thirty thousand combatants in observation before the grand-vizir, Kamenski joined in the siege of Roudschouck with twelve thousand men. Without waiting to breach the walls of the place, an assault, or rather an escalade, was ordered on the fourth of August, but, after a useless loss of eight thousand men killed and wounded, the attempt was given up, and Kamenski resolved to proceed more methodically. The Seraskier of Sophia attempted to raise this siege with an army of thirty thousand men, but was met and totally defeated at Batin on the seventh of September. The capture of Sistow was the immediate result of this victory.

Being reënforced by a new division under General Suwarrow (the younger), the Russian general renewed the sieges of Roudschouck and Giorgevo, which are situated on the Danube almost in the same way as Mayence and Cassel on the Rhine. The sides of the two cities bordering the river were not fortified, and the Russians, by getting possession of the island which divides the river at this point, succeeded in cutting off all communication between them, and finally forced them to surrender. After having also reduced Nicopoli and Loweza, near the end of October, the Russian army went into winter-quarters.

In Servia, Czerni-Georges also defeated the Turks on the Dwina. In Asia, Tormassof took Soukoum-Kalé and Soudjouk-Kalé; a landing was also attempted near Trebisond, but without result. Notwithstanding these successes, I saw that this war was advancing but slowly and at great cost, both in blood and treasure. As my relations with Russia seemed on the point of changing, I was not displeased at the slow progress of its arms against the Turks, for, in case of difficulty with that power, the Ottomans would make a useful diversion in my favor.

CHAPTER XVII.

CAMPAIGN OF 1811;—CONTINUATION OF THE PENINSULAR WAR.

General Review of the Foreign Relations of France—Faulty Relations with Prussia—Proposed Alliance—New Difficulties with Russia—Prospects of closing the War in Spain—Dissensions between Joseph and my Generals—New Cortes to be assembled at Madrid—Critical Situation of Massena—Soult marches on Badajoz and Olivenza—Siege of Badajoz—Remarks on the Operations of Soult—Attempt to raise the Siege of Cadiz—Affair of Chiclana—Retreat of the Allies—Soult marches to the Support of Victor—Massena evacuates Portugal—Battle of Fuente di Honor—Massena retires to Salamanca—Remarks on Massena's Retreat—Beresford threatens Badajoz—He captures Olivenza and lays Siege to Badajoz—Soult marches to its Succor—Battle of Albuera—Napoleon directs the Junction of Soult and Marmont—Wellington renews the Siege of Badajoz—He is again forced to retire into Portugal—Operations of the Spaniards in Andalusia—They are defeated by Soult—Wellington and Marmont near Ciudad Rodrigo—Hill surprises Girard—Suchet on the Ebro—Figueras surprised by the Catalans—Suchet prepares to attack Tarragona—Memorable Siege of that City—Further Operations of Suchet—He prepares to attack Valencia—Siege of Saguntum—Battle of Saguntum—Investment of Valencia—Siege of that Place—Reduction of Peniscola and Gandia—Remarks on Soult's Operations in the South—Winter-campaign of Wellington in Estremadura—He captures Ciudad Rodrigo and Badajoz—Remarks on these Operations—Insurrection in Spanish America—General State of Affairs in Spain—Continuation of the War between Russia and Turkey.

Foreign Relations of France.—Notwithstanding our success in Aragon and Andalusia, and the retreat of the Anglo-Spaniards under the walls of Lisbon and Cadiz, the position of Europe was far from offering the result which I had hoped from the treaty of Tilsit, and especially from my marriage. While I was seeking to interdict the English commerce from the North Sea and the Baltic, they opened a vast outlet on the American continent, and, by the insurrection of America, inundated the Peninsula ; they reduced the islands of France and of Bourbon, after a long blockade and a formal attack which the inhabitants sustained with great glory; they also took possession of Amboin, and even of Batavia. Equally fortunate in the West Indies, they captured Guadaloupe, St. Eustacia, and St. Martin. For more than two years St. Domingo had been lost to us, and divided between the black empire of Christophe and Dessalines, and the mulatto republic of Pethion and Boyer. Our only possession here was Martinique; all our colonial hopes had long since been destroyed.

On the other hand my federative system seemed to embrace the whole European continent: I was now connected with Austria by the ties of blood; but she had entered into my system as a power of the first rank, without any alliance offensive or defensive. My temporary connections with Russia were weakened; Prussia had made at Tilsit only a nominal peace; Spain had escaped from my hands to throw herself into the front rank of my enemies. I ruled on the Vistula, but the country between that river and the Rhine was exasperated against me; the South had risen in mass, and from the North a violent storm had threatened my Empire.

Faulty Relations with Prussia.—My whole system was defective, because I had alienated Prussia, when I might so easily have attached her to me, and when her geographical position was most advantageous for restoring the kingdom of Poland, and paralyzing the power of Austria. Possessing Dantzic and Graudentz on one side, and Schweidnitz and Glatz on the other, Prussia formed the corner-stone on which might have been based all my operations, either against Bohemia or Lithuania. With the aid of Prussia, Saxony, Bavaria, and the kingdom of Italy, I might have embraced Austria like a new Anteus, and after having reduced it to the impossibility of injuring me, I might have dictated law to the North. But the fault of 1806 was now irreparable; being placed in a false position towards Frederick William and his nation, without the ability of now gaining their good will, it was necessary to chain them to my car. The rising generation of Prussia, brought up in the school of adversity, with a liberal, solid and patriotic education, had imbibed as strong a hatred for the destroyer of the public liberties, as for the conqueror who had destroyed the heritage of the great Frederick. It was not enough that some represented me as a Tarquin to these new Brutuses, and others invoked the names of the first sons of Teuton in favor of Germanic liberty; all the living interests of commerce were raised up against me. I was, according to their representations, a new Gengiskhan, who swept over Europe to bind it in chains, without any real utility to France, or advantage to my crown, and against all the interests of other nations. Secret societies, under the title of *Fédérés de la Vertu,* daily made proselytes; and the resistance of Spain encouraged them in their projects to throw off the yoke. If their efforts had failed in 1809, it was only a motive for additional precaution in their future projects. The skillful artificer of this conspiracy was only waiting for a favorable moment to bring it out into action; he was watching for the opportune moment to light up the general conflagration, whose progress and result no one could predict.

The King proposes an Alliance with France.—It was under these circumstances that the king of Prussia proposed to me an alliance offensive and defensive. I eluded giving a direct answer to this offer, which, under other circumstances, I would have accepted with eagerness, because I did not wish to give offense to Prussia by a treaty which could only have had reference to that power; moreover, the alliance would merely have given me Frederick William, for his people would have been none the less hostile to me; in fine, I was quite certain to find the disposition of the king the same when the time should arrive for using this alliance. If the Prussians hated me I reciprocated their dislike, and instead of wishing to bind myself by a treaty which would have been beneficial to them, I would have been delighted to injure them ; for our hatred had arrived at that pitch when reconciliation seemed impossible. All these circumstances prove at least the following truths :

1st. That after the great coalition of 1805, the idea of becoming preponderant in Europe by my federative system was legitimate and natural.

2d. That to succeed in this object it was necessary to attach to myself, by benefits conferred, a population of twelve or fifteen millions in the north of Europe, and that, in default of Austria, who had been stripped at Campo-Formio, Luneville and Presbourg, of a portion of her territory, Prussia was the only power who could satisfy this condition.

3d. That if the passions which divided us in 1806, have been as fatal to France as to Prussia, and if I initiated this division by my negotiation with Lauderdale in relation to Hanover, it is not the less true that our enmity rose more from the inconsiderate exaltation of the Prussians against me in 1806, than from all other causes.

4th. That after that fatal war, I was never in position to find *an ally of twelve or fifteen millions of people, who derived their prosperity from me, and was thus irrevocably attached to my cause ;* and

5th. That for want of such an auxiliary, I was obliged to connect myself with Austria, although she was far from being attached to me by any benefits which I had conferred on her.

New Difficulties with Russia.—In the mean time a storm was beginning to rise in the North. The obligation of maintaining the Continental System led to numerous difficulties with Russia, difficulties which were daily increasing ; she was in want of manufactured articles, which, brought over land, were sold at exorbitant prices ; while the products of her own soil, being of too bulky a nature to be transported otherwise than by water, encumbered the ports of the empire without finding sale, even at the lowest prices. I, nevertheless, insisted that all which had touched the English soil or which had submitted to her visit, should be prohibited ; in the eyes of the Russians this rigor was an absurdity, but it was indispensable to the success of the system. There was a moment when the silks of France found their way into London by the Archangel and the Frozen Ocean. Afterward, however, the contraband system was regularly organized ; I had foreseen this, because the Russian government could not well watch her whole coast, and it was too much interested in allowing contraband to have done so, had it been possible ; but as it is always easier to pass free ports than those which are closed, the amount of contraband merchandise was less than what would have been introduced through the same ports, if they had been free. I, therefore, partly accomplished my object. I, nevertheless, complained to Russia of these violations of the treaty ; she justified herself, punished the smugglers, but the smuggling itself was continued. These complaints and rejoinders were mutually calculated to irritate ; and it was evident that this state of things could not long continue.

In fact, our relations had not been very amicable since my alliance with Austria. It was evident to Russia, from the moment that this alliance was contracted, that she must either lose her rank and influence in Europe, or fight ; she was too powerful to consent to the former, and therefore determined to risk the result of a war. The annexation of Holland and Lübeck, giving me footing on the Baltic, and especially the augmentation of the Duchy of Warsaw, were sufficient ostensible causes for declaring war against me.*

I therefore had good reason to expect the coolness which soon manifested itself in my relations with the court of St. Petersburg: they refused to prohibit their ports to neutrals loaded with colonial goods for English commerce; they complained, and with justice, of the occupation of Oldenburg; finally, on the thirtieth of December, 1810, they imposed on French commerce a series of prohibitions, which put us on about the same footing as the English. It was, therefore, evident that hostilities must ensue between us, for we were both ready for the contest: the affairs of Spain gave me about the same occupation as those of Turkey gave to Russia.

Prospects of closing the War in Spain.—The campaign of 1811 in the Peninsula was begun under the most favorable auspices. If the expeditions against Portugal and Cadiz had not entirely attained the object I had proposed, the success of Suchet on the Ebro, and of Soult in Andalusia had compensated for this disappointment, which might be only temporary. It was natural to suppose that after having reduced the provinces of the East and South, they would unite all their forces towards Estremadura for the expulsion of the English.

Dissensions continued to exist between the different parties; the proceedings of the Cortes were opposed both by the apostolic junta and by the grandees. The regency, at the head of which was placed the Duke de l'Infantado, did not agree with the projects of the Spanish reformers; and it was possible that, in time, the dissenters would unite with the party of King Joseph.

* Jomini here combats with much warmth the opinions of Mr. Fain on the causes of the rupture with Russia. As the discussion is repeated at the beginning of the next chapter the contents of this article have been slightly condensed.

Dissensions between Joseph and my Generals.—Unfortunately, the best understanding did not, at this time, exist between my brother and my generals. Joseph, dissatisfied with seeing his authority daily passing into the hands of my lieutenants, sent me, by the Marquis of Almenara, his formal abdication, if I persisted in making the chiefs of the French army independent of his authority. A party was formed in his favor even in the Cortes, and he deceived himself into the belief that by warmly espousing the interests of the Spaniards, he would so increase the number of his partisans as to end the war, and dispense with the further assistance of my troops.

Napoleon advises the assembling of new Cortes at Madrid.—I had induced my brother to treat with the Cortes of Cadiz ; but from what I had now learned of their composition and debates, I was convinced that they could not long enjoy the consideration of men of reflection, who were really more numerous in Spain than has been supposed. I flattered myself with the hope that we might oppose to this collection of fanatics, an assembly of intelligent men whose public deliberations, being circulated throughout the kingdom, might gradually calm the effervescence of the Spaniards, by enlightening them with these solemn debates on the general interests of the nation, and by giving them assurances on the future destiny of the monarchy, and my intentions respecting it.

Joseph adopted this advice ; but the order for the convocation of this assembly was not transmitted to the provinces till the middle of the following year, the battle of Salamanca having then rendered it illusory.

This delay was not the least error in the administration of my brother : it did not require a whole year to promulgate a decree with the necessary instructions for conducting the elections. It is now impossible to say positively what would have been the result of such an assembly; but I am persuaded that it would have improved our affairs, and accelerated our reconciliation with the Cortes of Cadiz, of which we shall speak hereafter.

Critical Situation of Massena.—Massena, after having laid five months before the lines of Torres Vedras, and exhausted all the resources of patience, resignation and obstinacy, saw the critical moment approaching when he must either fight or retreat. His troops had thus far supported themselves by prodigies of industry, activity and individual bravery; but they had now ravaged the country for fifty leagues round, and there was no further resource; moreover, the soldiers, by being habituated to this organized marauding, had dissolved the bonds of discipline. While this system of subsistence was occupying the attention of our army, Wellington had not once attempted to trouble us, although his forces had been increased in December, by reënforcements from Sicily, England and Malta, to forty thousand English and forty thousand Portuguese regulars, exclusive of the several corps of Ordonanzas, who acted on our rear.*

In truth, he himself was not without anxiety respecting his provisions, for if the supplies of his own army were abundant, the numerous population of Lisbon, doubled by the forced emigration from the country, suffered much from famine, and could obtain supplies only by sea. England was obliged to provide for these wants, and succeeded by her activity and money. But so considerable was the crowd col-

---

* Jomini says, that an English pamphlet published at the time in London, estimates the forces of Wellington, at forty thousand Anglo-Hanoverians, forty-five thousand regular Portuguese, and thirty-five thousand militia. M. de Montverran, estimates the Anglo-Portuguese regulars at one hundred thousand and the militia at fifty thousand. Napier, who is the most reliable authority in this matter, gives the total English and Portuguese cavalry and infantry on the first of October, 1811, at ninety-two thousand, of which, over fifty-eight thousand were for duty. The artillery force is not included.

lected behind the lines of Torres Vedras, that a horrible epidemic broke out during the winter, and carried off, it is said, more than one hundred thousand persons :—the deplorable result of the rigor with which the English general had ordered the depopulation of the surrounding country !

Soult marches on Badajos and Olivenza.—The double motive of seconding Massena by the left bank of the Tagus, and of delivering the armies of Portugal and Andalusia from the important and troublesome influence of the fortifications of Badajos, had induced me to advise Soult to turn his whole attention in the direction of the Guadiana ; he himself felt too deeply interested in repairing the precious time which he had lost, to neglect any longer the reduction of this place. After augmenting his reserves (consisting of the ancient division of Dessolles and the cavalry division of Latour-Maubourg) with all possible reënforcements, he directed it with Mortier's corps on Olivenza, leaving Sebastiani to observe the army of Murcia and Gibraltar, and Victor to contine the blockade of Cadiz, watch Tarifa, and guard Seville.

The corps of Ballesteros and Mendizabal, being too weak to hold out against the twenty thousand troops which Soult was bringing against them, took refuge in the mountains ; the latter imprudently threw four thousand men into Olivenza, without provisions ; and when attacked by Soult, the garrison, in less than ten days (January 22d,) were compelled to lay down their arms. The siege-equipage having in the mean time arrived from Seville, it was immediately directed against Badajos.

Siege of Badajos.—This city was then, by its position, the most important place of arms in the theatre of the war ; it served as the principal arsenal of the Spaniards in Estremadura, and the base of all the enterprises of the combined forces against the centre of the monarchy ; it contained a garrison of ten thousand men under the orders of the brave Manecho, who was determined to resist whatever efforts the French might direct against him. Mortier was charged with the investment of the place ; while they pressed, with great activity, the arrival of the enormous equipage indispensable for beginning the siege. Romana, who had joined Wellington on the Tagus, on hearing the danger which threatened his lieutenants on the Guadiana, was about marching to their succor, when he died at Cartaxo, the twenty-third of January, from apoplexy. Mendizabal, who was appointed to succeed him, advanced at the head of ten thousand men to deliver Badajos.

Soult's position now became embarrassing. While all his convoys of provisions and munitions were coming from Seville across the rough and inhospitable country of the Sierra-d'Arroche, he was forced to send out detachments to protect its arrival and reconnoitre on his flanks, so that he had only fifteen thousand combatants left to form and cover the siege. The Spaniards, emboldened by the arrival of re-enforcements which increased their numbers to more than twenty thousand men, made a general sortie against the trenches. After a temporary success, they were forced to retire again within the place. Fearful of exhausting the magazines of the garrison, and perhaps of being invested if he remained in the city, Mendizabel determined to encamp on the right bank of the Guadiana, behind the Gehora, three hundred toises from Fort San Christoval. Soult immediately conceived the audacious project of passing the Guadiana in two columns, on the night of the nineteenth of February, so as to crush the right flank of the enemy which rested on the fort, and to turn the opposite wing with three thousand horse under General Latour-Maubourg. These dispositions were executed with rare accuracy and crowned with complete success. Girard's division assailed the right of the Spaniards, and precipitated them into the half-ruined lines of Berwick; it thus cut off all retreat on the *tête-de-pont*, while Latour-Maubourg turned their left and took the line in reverse. Mendizabel escaped to Elvas with only a thousand men; as many more fell on the field of battle, and eight thousand were taken prisoners.

Governor Monecho, instead of being discouraged by this disaster, prepared to imitate the example of Saragossa and Gerona; but he was killed some days after on the rampart where he was directing a sortie, and his successor, being in want of provisions, or perhaps being of a less determined character, capitulated the eleventh of March with a garrison of nine thousand men.

Remarks on the Operations of Soult.—Thus in less than two months, Soult had destroyed or captured more of the enemy than he himself had combatants on his departure from Seville, and had reduced two important places. The departure of Massena from Portugal at the very time that Badajos fell, did not allow him to reap the fruits of this success; and some hypercritics have taken occasion to blame the time consumed in a regular attack of that place. They pretend that Soult should have marched on Abrantes, without stopping to take a city, which, a year later, he did not hesitate to leave behind him. The reproach is more specious than just. It is true that Massena, thus seconded, might have crossed the Tagus, and avoided a difficult retreat, have threatened Lisbon from the heights of Almada, have subsisted his troops some months in Alemtejo, and fought Wellington with advantage, if he had presented himself. But was this project without its dangers? If Wellington, ascending the right bank of the Tagus, had destroyed our bridge-equipages, would he not have manœuvred at his ease into the heart of Castile, and destroyed all our establishments at the north of Sierra Morena? Against whom could the united forces of Massena and Soult have been employed? Of what use had been this imposing union on the plains of Evora? Would they not have been under the necessity of marching in all haste to the succor of Joseph, Madrid, and Castile, as in 1812? Moreover, Soult having left two of his corps in Andalusia, could not penetrate, with the third alone, into the midst of the whole army of Wellington and Romana, leaving behind him garrisons as numerous as his own *corps-d'armée.*

It is true that after the surrender of Olivenza on the twenty-second of January, with four thousand men, it was possible to march direct by Jurumenha to Abrantes, but what would have been the result? Would he not have been crushed by the superior forces of Hill and Romana, who were certain of being sustained, if necessary, by Wellington's *corps-de-bataille?* No movement could have been better, if Soult had had his whole fifty thousand men, and felt certain that his march would have induced Wellington to leave the right bank of the Tagus, and the lines of Torres-Vedras, and receive a decisive battle in Alemtejo against the two French armies united. But was such a step at all probable, considering the character and manifest interest of the English general? Soult did much better to reduce Badajos than to run off on such Quixotic adventures.

It was in the beginning of 1810, and not at this period, that a concentrated movement of the two should have been made to bombard Lisbon, and attack the enemy before the completion of the lines of Torres-Vedras, and of the defensive system of Wellington.

In March, 1811, things had changed: it no longer appeared reasonable to evacuate the lines of Cadiz, abandon three hundred pieces of canon, and give up Seville, Grenada, Cordova, and Malaga to the regency, in order to march into Alemtejo, without the slightest hope of bringing Wellington to a decisive battle. To leave an enemy, equal in numbers, master of the right bank of the Tagus, and, in a considerable degree, on our line of retreat, would have been a hazardous manœuvre in an ordinary war, with a neutral population, but in a national war, where a vast kingdom was to be reduced, the operation was the more rash, as it would have required the evacuation of a considerable portion of the conquered country.

Attempt to raise the Siege of Cadiz.—The events which actually occurred in the early part of March, proves the correctness of these views, and the extent of the obstacles which we would have encountered. Hardly had Soult reached Badajos when he heard that Victor and the first corps were seriously assailed before Cadiz. Generals Graham, La Pena, and Zayas, wishing to profit by the departure of Soult for Estremadura, thought to raise the siege of Cadiz, by landing at Tarifa, and taking our lines in reverse. Ten thousand Spaniards, and six thousand English were thus to act in concert with a sortie of six or seven thousand men from the Island of Leon, while Ballesteros, crossing the Rio Tinto at Niebla, threatened Seville.

Affair of Chiclana.—After a fatiguing march, the troops of Graham and La Rena left Conil, on the morning of the fifth of March, directing themselves along the coast on the heights of Chiclana. Victor, forced to leave Villatte with two thousand men to guard his lines, had thought it prudent to also establish some battalions at Medina Sidonia, for reconnoitring in the direction of Gibraltar, so that he could unite only seven thousand men under Ruffin and Leval. With this handful of men, he had no other course than to fall on the enemy's right and rear, and drive them into the sea, by cutting them off from the heights of Barrosa, where he threw the brigade of Ruffin. General Graham saw the danger to which he was exposed, and attacked with impetuosity the French columns, which, astonished at so much vigor, fell back. General Leval, charged with the double task of sustaining Ruffin, and maintaining his communications with Villatte, could not join in the engagement till his colleague had been mortally wounded and his troops driven back; he fought in an olive wood with firmness, and retired in good order to the heights of Chiclana. Thinking that Villatte might be surrounded before Cadiz, Victor ordered him to join the main body, thus leaving the enemy at liberty to open his communications with the island of Leon.

During this time the main body of La Peña's forces had remained near the town of Barmeja, undecided whether to advance on the canal of Santi Petri, or to return to the support of Graham. Zayas, on his side, favored by the squadron of Admiral Keith, had landed near Puerto-Real and Santa Maria, and gained possession of a redoubt, without any other result. The combat did much honor to the English general and his infantry; but it must be confessed that the English, sustained by one Spanish brigade, had more battalions engaged on the decisive point than the French, the troops of Ruffin and Leval, not being both engaged at the same time.

Retreat of the Allies.—The position of Victor was a critical one; he was hesitating whether to retreat on Seville or to give battle with his united forces behind Puerto-Real, when his reconnoitring parties announced that the enemy was retiring into the island of Leon. An impenetrable mystery still covers the action of Graham. It is true that his infantry had suffered cruelly and had reason to complain of La Peña for not having joined him and completed the victory; on the other side, Sebastiani, on hearing his debarkation, had assembled troops on the Guadiaro, and might restore the chances in favor of the French. Nevertheless, the English general was victorious, and, on the sixth and seventh, might have brought La Pena into action before the arrival of Sebastiani ; it is therefore impossible to conceive the motive of his retreat.*

Soult marches to the Support of Victor.— Soult, on hearing at Badajos the first result of this contest, left to Mortier the care of reducing Campo Mayor and Albuquerque, and took, in haste, the road to Seville, with some battalions of the reserve. He there learned at the same time the danger of his lieutenant and his fortunate escape ; and also that Darricaud had arrested Ballesteros at Niebla. Nevertheless, the arrival of the general-in-chief at Seville was not useless ; for a few days afterward, the Spanish government, not discouraged by the ill-success of this enterprise, again pushed forward the corps of Lardizabal and Ballesteros, on the capital of Andalusia ; General Maranzin forced the first to reëmbark at Moguer, and afterward completely defeated the second at Frencjal, on the twelfth of April.

In the mean time a more threatening storm was rising in the direction of Badajos. Mortier, after the reduction of Campo Mayor and Albuquerque, was expecting to quietly enjoy his conquests, when he heard of Massena's retreat from Portugal, and the approach of a considerable portion of Wellington's army.

Massena evacuates Portugal.—Massena, whose critical position we have already described, had but two courses from which to choose—to see his army perish by famine and the arms of the Anglo-Portuguese, or to resign himself to the humiliation of a voluntary retreat. This retreat was rendered difficult from the nature of the country, the general

---

* Jomini's remarks on this battle are based on the supposition that Graham was in chief command, and that La Pena was subject to his orders. On the contrary, La Pena was the ranking officer, and Graham had consented to obey his orders. The conduct of the Spanish general on this occasion was highly censurable. For a full account of these operations, the reader is referred to Napier, who entirely exculpates Graham. He calls it the battle of Barosa.

insurrection of the inhabitants, the absolute destitution of his army, and the numerical superiority of the enemy. Massena might direct his retreat by Coimbra, by the valley of the Zezere on Sabugal, or by that of Castel-Franco. He had also the means of floating his bridge-equipage down the Zezere into the Tagus, of crossing this river, and of marching by Portalegro on Badajos. He had been advised to this last course, but the fear that Hill might dispute the passage of the Tagus had deterred him from it. He had not time to attempt the operation, for if unsuccessful, he would have exposed his army. The road by Castel-Franco was too difficult, and, moreover, ran across a sterile country. Massena decided to take the same road by which he had advanced, fearing that those by Sabugal and Castel-Franco might not offer the same facilities for his material.

Thus far the conduct of Massena had been without reproach; he had shown all the tenacity which formed so prominent a trait of his character; but he suddenly seemed to act without any well-digested project. The Coimbra road, running at first from south to north and inclining to the east along the Mondego, forms a right-angled triangle, of which the road from Espinhal to Ponte-Murcella by the slope of the Estrella mountains is the hypothenuse. This cross road was, therefore, much shorter than the grand route, and we might have been anticipated on the Alva if it had been left uncovered. The *corps-de-bataille* and the material took the Coimbra road, while the rear-guard followed this cross road. The second corps under Reynier, was directed by this route.

Massena remained at Pombal, either to impose on the enemy, or with the design of really accepting battle; the fault of this delay is, however, attributed to his lieutenants, who asked for more time to rally their troops and equipages, and regulate the order of their movement; in the mean time the enemy manœuvred by his right to precede him on the Ceira. To this first *contre-temps* was soon added a second. On hearing that the English had reïnforced the garrison of Coimbra, and were marching in that direction another corps which had been landed at Figueras, and not venturing to risk an attack on that city with an enemy close on his rear, Massena decided to turn aside by Miranda-del-Corvo. This information was false, and there is every reason to believe that he might easily have forced Coimbra. This fatal resolution tended to break the *morale* of his troops, and to introduce disorder in their movements. Forced to return toward the enemy, he was near being anticipated on the Ceira and seriously cut to pieces at Foz-d'Aronce, where a panic terror got possession of the best regiments of his rear guard. The firmness of Ney at the head of the rear brigade, saved the army from total rout. Thus closely pressed, he finally reached the sources of the Mondego, but in a situation truly deplorable. The stragglers who fell into the hands of the English, inspired them with respect for the heroic firmness of their adversaries, by showing the condition to which famine had reduced them.

On reaching Celorico, Massena resolved to retire on Guarda; the hope of maintaining himself in this intermediate position by the aid of the troops with which Soult and Joseph might act between the Tagus and the Guadiana, and the advantage of putting himself into more immediate contact with Madrid and Seville, militated strangely in favor of this project. But Ney flatly refused to comply, directing the march of his own army on Almeida, where he could more easily find shelter, provisions, and time to reorganize his troops. The general-in-chief, irritated by a refusal which compromised his authority, deemed it his duty to order that marshal to leave the army, in order to reëstablish subordination by an example of severity against one of his highest officers.

Wellington closely pursued the army in the new direction which it had taken; after a warm combat near Sabugal between the enemy and Reynier's corps, this army decided to regain Ciudad-Rodrigo, both to avoid disastrous engagements, and to put an end to the frightful want of provisions from which they were still suffering. Massena afterward retired to Salmanaca, the better to accomplish this object and recover his troops from their fatigues.

Battle of Fuente di Honore.—This new retreat proved that Ney was right in opinion, though censurable for the manner of his conduct. By the circuit which our army had taken, so much time was lost that the enemy had preceded us to Almeida, and immediately invested the place which had been dismantled during Massena's operations before Lisbon, and which we had not been able to occupy since his retreat. The brave General Brenier commanded here; but being unexpectedly invested, he was without a supply of provisions: the place must now be revictualed or lost. Massena, who had found in Estremadura some reënforcements for his regiments, and a fine cavalry division of my guard, finally determined to advance to its relief, with the apparent resolution of revenging his affront. Wellington placed himself in advance of the Coa to cover the siege. This river, which is a considerable stream, runs through a deep ravine with high and very steep banks. With such a ravine in his rear, the position of the English general, though advantageous by the difficulties in front, would have become fatal in case of a reverse. His left, composed of two divisions, was lodged in the ruins of Concepcion, which place had been captured; the centre, composed of a single English division, held the plateau of Almeida; the main body, composed of three strong divisions, occupied the plateau of Fuente di Honore. A Spanish corps covered the right flank at Naval-di-Avar, near the head of the ravine of Duas-Casas where the heights, being less elevated and less steep, offered a more easy access. Loison, who had taken the command of Ney's corps, burning to wipe off the disgrace of a retreat, unhesitatingly ordered the attack on the third of May. He had only reconnoitered the position of the English directly in his front, and made his attack on this point, as if he feared they might escape him, if he delayed to manœuvre. In a word he took the bull by the horns, without waiting for Massena's orders.

The sixth corps succeeded in carrying the lower part of Fuente di Honore; but three English divisions, formed in rear of the village on a slope which was difficult of access, and defended by fifty pieces of cannon, repelled all their efforts against the upper post. As at Brisac, they fought against the main body of the English forces in close column, and were exposed to the fire of the enemy's whole line, without the slightest result. Massena, after reconnoitering the enemy's position, directed different dispositions for the following day; he ordered the sixth corps to the left, to fall on Naval-di-Avar, and force the English right in concert with the cavalry of Montbrun and the guard; while the ninth corps attacked Fuente di Honore, and the second corps under Reynier held in check the enemy's left from Almeida to Concepcion.

Although these dispositions were defective, in as much as too many forces were employed in observation, and the flank movement to our left was executed in full view of the enemy, they were nevertheless crowned with success. The sixth corps carried Posabella, drove back the enemy's flankers, and forced the Spanish corps into an eccentric retreat: Montbrun overthrew the Anglo-Portuguese cavalry, and hotly pursued it to a distance from the line. The seventh English division at the centre which had marched parallel to our left, seeing its first brigade driven back, held firm with the second which had distinguished itself by its immovable firmness. It required but one more effort to drive back the enemy's left on the ravine of the Coa. The soldiers of the sixth corps were the same who three years before had precipitated themselves into Friedland against adversaries more numerous and not less formidable. A charge like that which Ney executed on Bagration's corps in 1807, would inevitably have destroyed the army of Wellington; but Ney no longer commanded these men, and they were no longer animated by his presence. Instead of falling on the half beaten enemy, our left halted, and the chiefs hesitated how to act: Massena who remained at the centre was absent from the decisive point; the Spaniards had time to rejoin Wellington's right by a detour; the English reserve came to the support of this wing which formed *en potence*, and presented a front of iron at a point where the plateau forms a defile difficult of access in front. The favorable moment had now escaped; and Massena, who, instead of supporting his left, had made vain efforts to carry Fuente di Honore at the centre, came to this point too late, and saw himself forced to renounce his project.

Although Massena had committed a real fault in not himself taking the direction of the wing which was to strike the decisive blow, it must be confessed that fortune was against him in this battle; General Loison, who commanded the sixth corps, was to be replaced by Marmont, and recalled to Paris; he was aware of this, and did not display the same zeal which he had exhibited on a hundred other occasions. The ninth corps which attacked Fuente di Honore, was going to join the army of Andalusia, of which it formed a part: finally the dispute between Ney and Massena had rendered the latter unpopular with the soldiers; there was neither unity nor enthusiasm in their attacks.*

---

* Napier says: "Both sides claimed the victory. The French, because they won the passage at Poco Velho, cleared the wood, turned our right flank,

Massena retires to Salamanca.—The Prince of Essling disliked to return to Salamanca and sacrifice the brave garrison of Almeida. A few brave men offered to penetrate into the place; one of these succeeded in passing the English and Spanish lines amidst a shower of bullets, and gaining the ditches of the fort. He took an order to Brenier to attempt to cut his way through. Having completed the preparations for blowing up the place, the garrison set fire to the trains of the mines which were to destroy the ramparts, and taking advantage of the darkness, threw themselves upon the least guarded point of the camp of the besiegers; placed

obliged the cavalry to retire, and forced Lord Wellington to relinquish three miles of ground, and to change his front. The English, because the village of Fuentes so often attacked, was successfully defended, and because the principal object (the covering the blockade of Almeida) was attained.

"Certain it is, that Massena at first gained great advantages. Napoleon would have made them fatal! but it is also certain that, with an overwhelming cavalry, on ground particularly suitable to that arm, the Prince of Essling having, as it were, indicated all the errors of the English general's position, stopped short at the very moment when he should have sprung forward. By some this has been attributed to extreme negligence, by others to disgust at being superseded by Marmont; but the true reason seems to be, that discord in his army had arisen to actual insubordination. The imperial guards would not charge at his order—Junot did not second him cordially—Loison disregarded his instructions—Drouet sought to spare his own divisions in the fight, and Reynier remained perfectly inactive. Thus the machinery of battle was shaken, and would not work.

"General Pelet censures Lord Wellington for not sending his cavalry against Reynier after the second position was taken up. He asserts that any danger, on that side, would have forced the French to retreat. This criticism is, however, unsustainable, being based on the notion that the allies had fifty thousand men in the field, whereas, including Sanchez Partida, they had not thirty-five thousand. It may be, with more justice, objected to Massena that he did not launch some of his numerous horsemen, by the bridge of Secerias, or Sabugal, against Guarda and Celorico, to destroy the magazines, cut the communication, and capture the mules and other means of transport belonging to the allied army. The vice of the English general's position would then have been clearly exposed, for, although the second regiment of German hussars was on the march from Lisbon, it had not passed Coimbra at this period, and could not have protected the depôts. But it can never be too often repeated that war, however adorned by splendid strokes of skill, is commonly a series of errors and accidents. All the operations, on both sides, for six weeks, furnished illustrations of this truth."

between the bayonets of the enemy and a volcano ready to explode in his rear, Brenier directed his movement so well as to drive every thing before him and reach the Coa at the very moment that a *corps-d'armée* had advanced to receive him. He effected his junction amidst the acclamations of the army. This feat of arms not less glorious than a victory, deserves to be recorded on the pages of history.

Remarks on Massena's Retreat.—Although Massena's retreat from Portugal had been attended with some sad results, it is certain that these might have been worse. If it had been delayed two days longer, it might have resulted in the entire ruin of his army.* Its most injurious effect was the reaction produced on the public mind of the Spaniards; the approach of Wellington relighted the flames of insurrection. The guerillas of Porlier, Mina, Empécinado, Longa, &c., kept our troops continually on the alert, carried off our best escorted convoys, and spread terror amongst the inhabitants of the cities which were most disposed to give in their submission. Nevertheless, the armed regulars of the Cortes which were recruited with great difficulty, were neither more formidable, nor more disciplined; they were bands of soldiers without experience; and I would still have had the means of overcoming these obstacles, if my relations with Russia had allowed me to direct all the efforts of my empire against Wellington, and expel him from his last refuge.

Beresford threatens Badajos.—The English general, when he had heard of the fall of Badajos, and the subsequent dis-

---

* Napier says: "Massena entered Portugal with sixty-five thousand men, his reënforcements while at Santarem were about ten thousand, and he repassed the frontier with forty-five thousand: hence the invasion of Portugal cost him about thirty thousand men, of which fourteen thousand might have fallen by the sword or been taken. Not more than six thousand were lost during the retreat; but had Lord Wellington, unrestrained by political considerations, attacked him vigorously at Redinha, Condeixa, Casal Nova, and Miranda-de-Corvo, half the French army would have been lost. It is unquestionable that a retreating army should fight as little as possible."

asters of the Spaniards, and was convinced that Massena would return to Estremadura without giving battle, determined to turn his attention to Soult. For this purpose he had detached General Beresford with three divisions of Anglo-Portuguese, which left the main army at the heights of Villa-Velha, and, on the twentieth of March, directed themselves by Portalegro on Elvas. His vanguard reached Campo-Mayor, on the twenty-third of March, at the very time that Mortier had directed the evacuation and dismantling of the place. Latour-Maubourg had not time to complete this operation, and with difficulty saved his convoy. Mortier, who had some days before been recalled to France, now resigned the command of the fifth corps to this general ; the circumstances were critical, and there seemed but one course to pursue—to throw a garrison into Badajos and march toward Seville for reënforcements. Accordingly Latour-Maubourg, left a garrison of two thousand five hundred men in Badajos, and a detachment of four hundred in Olivenza to attract the enemy's attention toward this paltry town, while, with the remaining nine thousand combatants, he retired in good order on Llerena.

He captures Olivenza and lays Siege to Badajos.—On learning his superiority over his adversaries, Beresford formed a junction with the troops of Castaños and Ballesteros, and decided to cross the Guadiana. He left an entire division to act against Olivenza, directed another against Badajos, and pursued the fifth corps with eighteen thousand men on Zafra, Usagre and Fuente-de-Cantos, but soon returned toward Elvas, when the fall of Olivenza gave him the means of continuing the offensive, or of directing his efforts against Badajos. Wellington came in person to preside at this siege ; having reconnoitred the place with his lieutenant, he directed its investment, which, after a delay of some days from rains, took place on the third of May. Having assisted at the opening of the trenches, he departed on the seventh, for his army which was still opposed to Massena on the Agueda.

Soult comes to the Succor of that Place.—Soult, on his side, was too much disquieted by these events to remain inactive ; but to succor Badajos required an army of at least thirty thousand men, and to collect this number of troops required the evacuation of his important positions in Andalusia. To present himself, on the contrary, with inferior forces on the Guadiana, was to release at the same time Badajos, Seville, and Grenada. Soult did every thing in his power to avoid these two dangers. He succeeded in forming two strong brigades of Sebastiani's corps, from the different commands in the interior and the reserve. Immediately after the union of these forces and the necessary material, he left Seville on the tenth of May, and having joined General Latour-Maubourg at Fuente-de-Cantos on the thirteenth, he presented himself at Santa Maria on the fifteenth, within six leagues of Badajos, at the head of eighteen thousand foot and five thousand horse.

Battle of Albuera.—Although the enemy's forces was reported at thirty-six thousand, Soult did not believe that he would give battle before the arrival of a reënforcement of ten thousand Spaniards, which Blake was to bring from Murcia by the mouth of the Guadiana. Soult, however, afterward learned that this junction had just taken place, and in reconnoitering, he found the Anglo-Spaniards drawn up on the plateau of Albuera ; having examined their position the marshal did not hesitate to make the attack.

There was every reason for this resolution ; he could not expect any further reënforcements without raising the blockade of Cadiz, and withdrawing all his forces from Andalusia ; whereas he supposed that the enemy were still waiting for the junction of ten thousand Spanish troops. Moreover, Badajos was not well supplied with provisions, and the sooner he raised the blockade the less liable would he be to lose the place and the garrison. The enemy's left was supported on the village of Albuera, the right and centre being prolonged on a chain of heights which were steep on the side toward the French, but of a gentle slope on the opposite side. This local advantage was more than counterbalanced by a serious fault of position, the line of battle being formed on the prolongation of the road to Olivenza, which was Beresford's only line of retreat in case of defeat. The least success on the enemy's right wing would be decisive, and necessarily secure the loss of the left and centre which would be thrown back on Badajos. It is true that the English had thrown temporary bridges across the river near this place; but in case of our success the garrison, with the aid of the army, would be most likely to render the passage disastrous.

Soult's plan of attack was to make a feint by his right against the village of Albuera, on the morning of the sixteenth, in order to draw the attention of Beresford on this point, at the moment when the mass of our forces were falling on the right of the English and carrying their line of retreat. The plan was skillfully formed, but unfortunately, it failed in the execution. Godinot debouched against Albuera too late to attract the attention of the English, while the principal attack moved with too much precipitation; for Godinot had hardly reached this village, when Girard crossed the rivulet with the fifth corps, and precipitated himself at the head of his two divisions in deep columns on the right of Beresford.

The first line of the English yielded to this vigorous effort; but being soon sustained by three brigades of reserve, it opposed a murderous fire of musketry to our columns, to which only the first battalion of each column could reply. The same cause which had proved fatal at Vimiera, Busaco, and Fuente-di-Honore, was still more disastrous on this occasion. The troops of Girard fought with the utmost bravery under the direction of this valiant officer ; but it was in vain that Brayer, Maransin, and the chief-of-staff—the impassible Gazan—were wounded at the head of their brave men ; nothing could counterbalance the effect of a false position ; disorder already began to make its appearance. Girard now attempted to deploy his columns under the enemy's fire of grape and ball ; the movement could only be effected by the flank, thus exposing our men to the concentric fire of the English musketry and cannon. Our two massive columns experience the same fate as the famous Anglo-Hanoverian column of Fontenoy ; the different regiments became mingled together and soon form a confused mass ; retreat is now attempted ; but the difficulties of recrossing the stream which they had passed in the morning, renders the disorder complete. Fortunately, Soult brought up the reserve in time to sustain the combat and arrest the success of the enemy. This circumstance relieves our troops for a moment, but does not restore victory. This brigade drawn away by the *débris* of Girard, and partially broken by the enemy's fire, and discouraged by the death of its chief, General Werlé, also beats a retreat, which, however, is conducted in better order. The French artillery, concentrated on this point, was now unmasked, and by its admirable conduct arrested the advance of the English, by sowing death in their ranks. Godinot still held fast in the village of Albuera, but this was a secondary point and its occupation no longer of any use. Two hours after the engagement commenced, the victory was decided, and Soult led back the wreck of his army into the position which it had occupied in the morning.

This murderous combat, costing us one-third of the troops engaged, that is a loss of six thousand men out of twenty thousand combatants, ought to have decided for ever the superiority of infantry deployed in line and well-practiced in firing, over troops drawn up in very deep columns. But failing to profit by experience, we afterwards made still further proof of this truth. After such a check, the only course left for Soult to pursue, was to approach Seville, and rally on him all his disposable troops.

After an unfortunate cavalry combat at Usagre, brought about by the ill-directed impetuosity of General Bron, Soult took up his position at Llerena.*

* Napier's criticism on the battle of Albuera is worthy the attention of the military reader. We give the following extract:
"No general ever gained a great battle with so little increase of military reputation as Marshal Beresford. His personal intrepidity and strength, qualities so attractive for the multitude, were conspicuously displayed, yet the breath of his own army withered his laurels, and his triumph was disputed by the very soldiers who followed his car. Their censures have been reiterated, without change and without abatement, even to this hour; and a close examination of his operations, while it detects many ill-founded objections, and others tainted with malice, leaves little doubt that the general feeling was right.'
"When he had passed the Guardiana, and driven the fifth corps upon Guadalcanal, the delay that intervened, before he invested Badajos, was unjustly attributed to him; it was Lord Wellington's order, resulting from the tardiness of the Spanish generals, that paralyzed his operations.
"But when the time for action arrived, the want of concert in the investment, and the ill-matured attack on San Christoval belonged to Beresford's arrangements; and he is especially responsible in reputation for the latter, because Captain Squire earnestly warned him of the inevitable result, and his words were unheeded.
"During the progress of the siege, either the want of correct intelligence, or a blunted judgment, misled the marshal. It was remarked that, at all times, he too readily believed the idle tales of distress and difficulties in the French armies, with which the spies generally, and the deserters always, interlarded their information; thus he was incredulous of Soult's enterprise, and that officer was actually over the Morena before the orders were given to commence the main attack of the Castle of Badajos. However, the firmness with which Beresford resisted the importunities of the engineers to continue the siege, and the quick and orderly removal of the stores and battering-train, were alike remarkable and praiseworthy. It would have been happy if he had shown as much magnanimity in what followed.
"When he met Blake and Castaños at Valverde, the alternative of fighting or retiring behind the Guadiana was the subject of consideration. The Spanish generals were both in favor of giving battle. Blake, who could not retire the way he had arrived, without danger of having his march intercepted, was par-

Napoleon directs the Junction of Soult and Marmont.—But seeing the inefficiency of Soult's measures to restore matters, I myself directed my attention to the application of more efficacious remedies. As soon as I heard of these events I directed the march of the ninth corps, composed of the fourth battalions of each division of Soult's army, and which had gone to the assistance of Massena in Portugal. This corps, reduced to eight thousand men, succeeded in gaining the camp of Llerena, and in supplying the losses in Soult's army. But this reënforcement was not sufficient; I therefore directed Marmont, who had just succeeded Massena in

ticularly earnest to fight, affirming that his troops, who were already in a miserable state, would disperse entirely if they were obliged to enter Portugal. Castaños was of the same opinion. Beresford also argued that it was unwise to relinquish the hope of taking Badajos, and ungenerous to desert the people of Estremadura; that a retreat would endanger Elvas, lay open the Alemtejo, and encourage the enemy to push his incursions further, which he could safely do, having such a fortress as Badajos with its bridge over the Guadiana, in his rear. A battle must then be fought in the Alemtejo, with fewer troops and after a dispiriting retreat; there was also a greater scarcity of food in the Portuguese than in the Spanish province, and finally, as the weather was menacing, the Guadiana might again rise before the stores were carried over, when the latter must be abandoned, or the army endangered to protect their passage.

"But these plausible reasons were but a mask. The true cause why the English general adopted Blake's proposals was the impatient temper of the British troops. None of them had been engaged in the late battles under Lord Wellington. At Busaco the regiments of the fourth division were idle spectators on the left, as those of the second division were on the right, while the action was in the centre. During Massena's retreat they had not been employed under fire, and the combats of Sabugal and Fuentes Onore had been fought without them. Thus a burning thirst for battle was general, and Beresford had not the art either of conciliating or of exacting the confidence of his troops. It is certain that if he had retreated, a very violent and unjust clamor would have been raised against him, and this was so strongly and unceremoniously represented to him, by an officer on his own staff, that he gave way. These are what may be termed the moral obstacles of war. Such men as Lord Wellington or Sir John Moore can stride over them, but to secondrate minds they are insuperable. Practice and study may make a good general as far as the handling of troops and the designing of a campaign, but that ascendency of spirit which leads the wise, and controls the insolence of folly, is a rare gift of nature."

the command of the army of Portugal, to manœuvre by his left on the Tagus, so as to connect himself more intimately with Soult, and to operate in concert with him for the relief of Badajos.

Wellington renews the Siege of Badajos.—Wellington on his side, deemed it necessary, notwithstanding the success of Beresford at Albuera, to march with the main body of his army on the Guadiana, leaving General Spencer with eighteen thousand Anglo-Portuguese in observation near Sabugal. This resolution, influenced by the importance of Badajos and the probability that Soult would collect the army of Andalusia to revenge the check he had suffered, merits the approbation of all judges of military operations.

All the preparations being completed, and the parallel opened, on the second of June, the siege of Badajos was pushed with all possible vigor. The English established their batteries on a rock, and for want of earth they used sacks of wool for forming the epaulements of their works,— an operation of rare occurrence in the history of sieges.* The siege of Badajos is also remarkable for furnishing full proof of the superiority of iron cannon over those of brass, the latter becoming sooner heated, and consequently not sustaining so rapid and continuous a fire. The intrepid Philippon defended the place with valor and intelligence; while the siege was pressed with no less energy by Wellington. Impatient at the slow progress of the siege, and learning the movements of our troops preparatory to the relief of the place, the English general directed an assault to be made on Fort San Christoval, which is situated on an eminence on the right of the Guadiana; but the attack was repelled with a considerable and useless loss of life on the part of the assailants.

* The use of bales of cotton at New Orleans by General Jackson is a parallel case.

He is again forced to retire into Portugal.—Marmont had but just relieved Massena in the command of the army of Portugal, after the battle of Fuente-di-Honore, when he received orders to unite with Soult for the succor of Badajos. On hearing that Wellington had moved in that direction, leaving behind him only the corps of Spencer, Marmont marched with two divisions on the upper valley of the Coa to reprovision Ciudad-Rodrigo, and mask the movement which the rest of the army was executing at the same time by Placencia on Almaraz. This marshal soon took the same road and advanced on Merida, while Soult, hearing of this movement, left Llerena and moved toward Almendralejo, in order to open the communication. This important junction was effected on the seventeenth of June, and the two armies, numbering from fifty-five to sixty thousand combatants, advanced against the enemy. But Wellington, *always anxious to hazard nothing, had raised the siege of Badajos on the night* of the sixteenth, (after having vainly attempted a second assault on the side of the citadel), and retired into Portugal by Olivenza and Campo-Mayor.

It would, of course, have been imprudent for Wellington to remain at Albuera while Marmont was advancing from Albuquerque on Badajos; but it is difficult to conceive a reason why the English general did not throw himself by Campo-Mayor on Albuquerque against Marmont, in concert with Spencer, who had advanced from Almeida parallel with the Duke of Ragusa. If Wellington had manœuvred as I did at Castiglione, he would have successively beaten Marmont and Soult, as I did Wurmser and Quasdanowich. Badajos would, perhaps, have been succored as Mantua was in 1796, but victory would soon have reëstablished the allies within its walls.

Operations of the Spanish in Andalusia.—Soult's withdrawal of the mass of his forces from Andalusia, in order to maintain himself at Llerena after the defeat of Albuera, had decided the Spanish generals to attempt to crush our scattered detachments and reconquer that province. Cadiz, Seville, and Grenada were the first objects of their attention. Encouraged by the success at Albuera, Blake descended on the lower Guadiana, near Mogner, and attempted to carry the post of Niebla which covered the passage of the Rio Tinto and Seville; but the noble defense of a Swiss battalion defeated all his efforts. Ballesteros at the same time manœuvred on the left of the Guadalquiver, and threw himself into the mountains of Ronda, to raise these ferocious mountaineers, and cut off all communication between Seville and Grenada; a multitude of partisans soon inundated the environs of Seville and were reënforced by all the malcontents of the province. General Darricaud took refuge in a monastery, and found himself blockaded in the capital. Sebastiani's corps had been reduced, by the troops sent to the succor of Badajos, to seven or eight thousand men who were scattered in Malaga, Grenada, and Jaen; so that instead of being able to march to the relief of Darricaud, he found himself shut up in Grenada by a multitude of insurgents, who were sustained by troops from the army of Murcia or from Ballesteros.

They are defeated by Soult. — The junction of our armies, and Wellington's retreat into Portugal, changed the face of affairs in Andalusia. Soult now hastened to carry his reserve, under Godinot and Latour-Maubourg, to the assistance of his cantonments. Blake, after his unsuccessful attempt at the escalade of Niebla, menaced by the return of our forces, reëmbarked at Ayamonte for Cadiz; Ballesteros took refuge in the mountains of Ronda. Having thus delivered Seville, Soult had now to succor Sebastiani's corps, which was exposed to a threatening storm near Grenada. The regency of Cadiz, without being discouraged at their unsuccessful efforts against Soult's right, directed Blake, in concert with the corps of Murcia, to make a similar attempt against the left. Having formed a junction with the corps of Murcia at Baza, Blake now found himself at the head of eighteen or twenty thousand good troops. Soult marched against him by Guadix, and encountered him at the Venta-de-Bahul, in a position apparently impregnable. The marshal was to approach him in front with the fourth corps, and the cavalry of Latour-Maubourg, while that of Godinot, coming from Jean by Meda, would take him in reverse. The attack took place on the ninth of August; but Godinot, instead of imitating the example of Ney at Friedland and Richepanse at Hohenlinden, feared to throw himself in the midst of the enemy, and moved round by Baza. Blake now perceived his danger and hastened to retreat on Lorca, hotly pursued by Soult. Having returned to Seville, the marshal directed his attention to Gibraltar, where Ballesteros was threatening our communications with the blockading corps of Cadiz. Godinot, who had been detached against him, drove him back on the camp of St. Roque. On the approach of three brigades of Soult, Ballesteros evacuated this position and took refuge under the cannon of Gibraltar. The enemy now landed at Tarifa to disengage Ballesteros. Godinot marched against this city, but after a useless loss of many brave men, he fell back again on Seville; where, being warmly blamed by Soult, he committed suicide. Ballesteros returned to St. Roque and resumed the offensive; but Leval soon forced him to again seek refuge under the fire of the English at Gibraltar. As the enemy from his position at Tarifa, continued to threaten our corps at Cadiz and our cantonments from Gibraltar to the Guadiaro and Ronda, Leval received orders to reduce that place. He arrived there with some siege pieces, and opened the trenches on the twenty-fifth of December; after an unsuccessful assault, he received orders to abandon the enterprise.

Operations of Wellington and Marmont near Ciudad Rodrigo.—In the mean time the army of Marmont, returning from Badajos towards Salamanca, had encountered enemies still more dangerous than those of Soult. Wellington, on his return towards Almeida, had invested Ciudad Rodrigo, on the fifth of September, and was waiting the arrival of his siege artillery, which had been ordered from Lisbon by Oporto and the Douro. This place was the key of our positions in Estremadura. Marmont had left one of his divisions near Alcantara to communicate with the fifth corps which remained on the Guadiana, to guard the space between Olivenza and the mountains of Caceres. Having decided to succor Ciudad Rodrigo, Marmont recalled this division, and also opened a communication with the army of the North of Spain. This army had passed under the orders of General Dorsenne after the departure of Marshal Bessières, who brought back to France a part of the guard destined for the army of Russia. This general had been operating between the Douro, Astorga, and the mountains of Asturias, in order to second General Bonnet, and drive the army of Galicia into the mountains of Lugo.

Marmont and Dorsenne effected their junction at Tamames on the twenty-second of September; their united forces advanced to the succor of Ciudad Rodrigo; Wellington fell back with his advanced corps on Guinaldo. Marmont now presented himself before this intrenched camp, but Wellington withdrew his forces to Sabugal; and the former, proud of having his offer of battle declined by the enemy, and deeming it proper not to pursue him further into these desolate and inaccessible countries, established his army in cantonments, to give his troops some repose. He received orders, however, a few days after, to detach a thousand men under General Montbrun, to second the enterprise of Suchet on Valencia.

Hill surprises the Division of Girard.—The valley of the Tagus being stripped of its defense by Marmont, in order to offer battle to Wellington, the English right, under Hill, profited by this circumstance to attack the divisions of the fifth corps which had remained between the Tagus and the Guadiana; he surprised a brigade of Girard's division at Aroyo de Molinos, and was on the point of capturing that general himself with all his troops. Girard, however, saved himself by a great detour on Merida, where he crossed the Guadiana, but, for want of proper precautions, lost a thousand men. A series of uninterrupted successess, and the security which they had formerly enjoyed in the cantonments of Germany and Italy, had rendered our troops careless of their laurels, and all our corps-d'armée had some loss of this kind, which was to be attributed to an excess of self-confidence. This event was the only one of importance that occurred in the West during the autumn; if we except the operations of the divisions of Biscay, Navarre, and Castile, against the guerillas of Porlier, Mina, and Empecinado.*

---

* Napier gives a detailed account of the operations of the armies of Marmont and Wellington about Ciudad Rodrigo, and closes with the following observations:

"1st. Lord Wellington's position behind Soita has been noticed by two recent authors. The one condemns the imprudence of offering battle on ground whence there was no retreat; the other intimates that it was assumed in contempt of the adversary's prowess. This last appears a mere shift to evade what was not understood, for if Lord Wellington had despised Marmont, he would have fought him beyond the Agueda. But sixty thousand French soldiers were never to be despised, neither was Wellington a man to put an army in jeopardy from an overweening confidence; and it is not difficult to show that his position was chosen well, without imprudence, and without presumption.

"The space between the Sierra de Mesas and the Coa was less than six miles, and the part open to attack was very much reduced by the rugged bed of a torrent which covered the left. Forty thousand men were quite able to defend this line, which was scarcely more than one-third of their full front; and as the roads were bad, the country hilly and much broken with woods

Operations of Suchet on the Ebro.—Our affairs succeeded better in the East. Suchet, who had returned to Saragossa after the taking of Tortosa, arranged with Guilleminot,

and ravines, the superiority of the enemy's horse and guns would have availed him little. Lord Wellington had a right to be bold against an adversary who had not molested him at Guinaldo, and it is always of importance to show a menacing front. It was also certain that great combinations must have been made by Marmont, before he could fight a general battle on such ground; it was equally certain that he could only have a few days' provisions with his army, and that the neighborhood could not supply him. It was, therefore, reasonable to expect that he would retire rather than fight, and he did so.

"Let us, however, take the other side, and suppose that Marmont was prepared and resolute to bring on a great battle. The position behind Soita would still have been good. The French were indeed too strong to be fought with on a plain, yet not strong enough to warrant a retreat indicating fear; hence the allies had retired slowly for three days, each day engaged, and the enemy's powerful horse and artillery was always close upon their rear. Now the bed of the Coa, which was extremely rugged, furnished only a few points for crossing, of which the principal were, the ford of Serraleira behind the right of the allies; the ford of Rapoulha de Coa, behind their left; and the bridge of Sabugal, behind their centre. The ways to those points were narrow, and the passage of the river, with all the baggage, could not have been easily effected in face of an enemy without some loss and perhaps dishonor: and had Lord Wellington been unable to hold his position in a battle, the difficulty of passing the river would not have been very much increased, because his incumbrances would all have been at the other side, and there was a second range of heights half a mile in front of Sabugal favorable for a rear guard. The position of Soita appears therefore to have been chosen with good judgment in regard to the immediate object of opposing the enemy; but it is certain that the battering-train, then between Pinhel and Villa Ponte, was completely exposed to the enemy. Marmont, however, had not sufficiently considered his enterprise, and knew not where or how to strike.

"2d. The position of Aldea Ponte was equally well chosen. Had the allies retreated at once from Guinaldo, to Soita, baggage and stores would have been lost, and the retrograde movement have had the appearance of a flight; the road from Payo would have been uncovered, and the junction of the fifth division endangered. But in the position taken up, the points of junction of all the roads were occupied, and as each point was strong in itself, it was not difficult for a quick-sighted general, perfectly acquainted with the country, and having excellent troops, to check the heads of the enemy's columns, until the baggage had gained a sufficient offing, and the fifth division had taken its place in line.

"3d. The position at Guinaldo was very different from the others. The previous intrenching of it proved Lord Wellington's foresight, and he remained there thirty-six hours, that is, from mid-day of the twenty-fifth until midnight of the twenty-sixth, which proved his firmness. It is said that Sir George

Macdonald's chief of staff, the means of securing the siege of Tarragona : it was agreed between them that Macdonald's corps should conduct the siege, while Suchet both reënforced

Murray advised him to abandon it in the night of the twenty-fifth, and that arrangements were actually made in that view, yet anxious for the safety of the light division, he would not stir. The object was certainly one of an importance sufficient to justify the resolution, but the resolution itself was one of those daring strokes of genius which the ordinary rules of art were never made to control. The position was contracted, of no great natural strength in front, and easily to be turned; the intrenchments constructed were only a few breastworks and two weak field redoubts, open in rear, and without palisades; not more than fourteen thousand British and Portuguese troops were in line, and sixty thousand French veterans with a hundred pieces of artillery were before them! When Marmont heard of the escape of the light division, and discovered the deceit, he prophetically exclaimed, alluding to Napoleon's fortune, "*And Wellington's star, it also is bright!*"

"4th. The positions of Aldea Ponte and Soita are to be commended, that at Guinaldo to be admired rather than imitated, but the preceding operations are censurable. The country immediately beyond Ciudad Rodrigo offered no covering position for a siege or blockade; and the sudden floods, to which the Agueda is subject, rendered the communications with the left bank precarious. Nor though bridges had been secured, could Wellington have ventured to encamp round the place with lines of contravallation and circumvallation, on both sides of the river; because Marmont's army would then have advanced from Placencia to Castello Branco, having seized the passage over the Tagus at Villa Velha, and, in concert with the fifth corps, endangered the safety of Hill. This would have obliged the allies to quit their intrenched camp, and Dorsenne could then have revictualled the place. It was, therefore, necessary to hold a strong central position with respect to Marmont and Dorsenne, to keep both in check while separate, and to oppose them when united. This position was on the Coa, and as Salamanca or Bejar, the nearest points where convoys could be collected for Ciudad Rodrigo, were from fifty to sixty miles distant, Lord Wellington's object, namely, the forcing the French to assemble in large bodies without any adequate result, could be, and was obtained by a distant as well as by a close investment.

"So far all was well calculated, but when Marmont and Dorsenne arrived with sixty thousand men at Ciudad Rodrigo, the aspect of affairs entirely changed, and as the English general could not dispute the entrance of the convoy, he should have concentrated his army at once behind Guinaldo. Instead of doing this, he kept it extended on a line of many miles, and the right wing separated from the centre by a difficult river. In his dispatch, he says, that, from some uncertainty in his estimate of the enemy's numbers, it was necessary to ascertain their exact strength by actual observation ; but this is rather an excuse than a valid reason, because, for this object, which could be obtained by other means, he risked the loss of his whole army, and violated two vital rules of war which forbid—

and covered his operations. Guilleminot came to me at Paris to ask for the means of pushing this siege with vigor: but I preferred intrusting this enterprise to Suchet, who had

"1st. The parcelling of an army before a concentrated enemy.

"2d. The fixing of your own point of concentration within the enemy's reach.

"Now Lord Wellington's position on the twenty-fourth and twenty-fifth, extended from the ford of the Vadillo on the right of the Agueda, to Marialva on the Azava; the distance either from the Vadillo, or Marialva, to Guinaldo, was as great as that from Ciudad to Guinaldo, and by worse roads; and the distance from Ciudad to Elbodon was as nothing, compared to the distance of the wings from the same place. Wherefore, when Montbrun attacked, at Elbodon, the allies' wings were cut off, and the escape of the third and light divisions, and of the troops at Pastores, was a matter of fortune and gallantry, rather than of generalship; that is, in the enlarged sense of the last word, for it can not be denied that the actual movements of the troops were conducted with consummate skill.

But what if Marmont, instead of being drawn by circumstances into a series of ill-combined, and partial attacks, had previously made dispositions for a great battle? He certainly knew, through the garrison, the real situation of the allies, and he also knew of the camp at Guinaldo, which being on their line of retreat was the important point. If he had issued from the fortress before day-break on the twenty-fifth, with the whole or even half of his forces, he could have reached Campillo in two hours with one column, while another fell on the position at Pastores and Elbodon; the third division, thus attacked, would have been enveloped and captured, or broken and driven over the Agueda, by the ford of Zamara, and would have been irretrievably separated from Guinaldo. And if this division had even reached Guinaldo, the French army would have arrived with it in such overwhelming numbers, that the fourth division could not have restored the battle; meanwhile a few thousand men thrown across the ford of Caros near Robleda, would have sufficed to keep the light division at bay, because the channel of the Robleda torrent, over which their retreat lay, was a very deep and rugged ravine. The centre being broken the French could, at choice, have either surrounded the light division, or directed the mass of their forces against the reserves, and then the left wing under Graham would have had to retreat from the Azava over the plains toward Almeida.

"It may be said that all the French were not up on the twenty-fifth, but they might have been so, and as Lord Wellington was resolved to see their number he would have been in the same position the twenty-sixth. It is, however, sufficient to remark that the allies, exclusive of the fifth division, which was at Payo, did not exceed thirty-five thousand men of all arms; that they were on an irregular line of at least twenty miles, and mostly in an open country; that at no point were the troops more than eight, and at the principal point, namely, Pastores, only three miles, from a fortress from whence sixty thousand infantry and six thousand cavalry, with one hundred and twenty guns were ready to issue. Finally the point of concentration at Guinaldo was thus far perfectly accomplished my wishes; I, therefore, decided that the army of Aragon should form a new siege-park of the artillery of Lerida and Tortosa, and attack Tarragona; I also ordered this army to be reënforced by a French and Italian division of the army of Catalonia. But hardly had they began to execute these new dispositions, when Marshal Macdonald returned from Lerida to Barcelona, and announced that Figueras had just been surprised by the Spaniards.

The Catalans take Figueras.—The junta and the captain-general of Catalonia, encouraged by the success of their petty operations, and certain of the assistance of the inhabitants of the cities against which they might operate, now redoubled

only twelve miles from that fortress. The allies escaped because their adversary was blind! Lord Wellington's conduct at Guinaldo was above rules, but at Elbodon it was against rules, which is just the difference between genius and error.

"4th. In these operations Marmont gave proof that as a general he was rather shining than great. He was in error throughout. Before he commenced his march, he had desired Girard to advance on the side of the Alemtejo, assuring him that the whole of the allied army, and even the Spanish troops under Castaños, had crossed the Tagus to operate against Rodrigo; but in fact only one brigade of Hill's corps had moved, and Girard would have been destroyed, if, fortunately for him, the allies had not intercepted the original and duplicate of the letter containing this false information.

"5th. When Marmont brought his convoy into Ciudad, it would appear he had no intention of fighting, but tempted by the false position of the allies, and angry at the repulse of his cavalry on the Lower Azava, he turned his scouting troops into columns of attack. And yet he permitted his adversary to throw dust in his eyes for thirty-six hours at Guinaldo; and at Aldea Ponte his attack was a useless waste of men, because there was no local advantage offered, and he did not intend a great battle.

"6th. The loss incurred in the different combats was not great. About three hundred men and officers fell on the part of the allies, and on that of the French rather more, because of the fire of the squares and artillery at Elbodon. But the movements during the three days were full of interest, and instruction, and diversified also by brilliant examples of heroism. Ridge's daring charge has been already noticed, and it was in one of the cavalry rencounters, that a French officer in the act of striking at the gallant Felton Harvey of the Fourteenth Dragoons perceived that he had only one arm, and with a rapid movement brought down his sword into a salute, and passed on."

their activity and audacity, in hopes of wearying out our patience, and forcing us finally to evacuate the province. O'Donnel had already fallen, with his united forces, on an isolated brigade at the Abisbal and captured it, without the army's being able to save it.

While Macdonald was concentrating his forces towards the Ebro for the projected expedition, General Campo-Verde, on the night of the nineteenth and twentieth of March, attempted to surprise Fort Montejouy. Maurice Matthieu allowed the enemy's grenadiers to descend into the ditch, and then opened upon them a fire of grape and musketry. Eight hundred men were killed in the ditches, while others took to flight, but were pursued by a sortie party, and several hundreds brought back prisoners. This reception, however, did not entirely discourage the enemy: a few weeks after, a troop of *Miguelets* surprised General Guillot in the city of Figueras, and got possession of the citadel by a *coup-de-main*.

On hearing of these events, Macdonald renounced his projects and returned in haste to Gerona, in order to invest Figueras, before the Spaniards could provision the detachment which had been thrown into that place. General Baraguay d'Hilliers left Gerona with all the forces which he could collect in Upper Catalonia, but he could not prevent Campo-Verde from reënforcing the place with three thousand men, although he had defeated him on the third of May. Macdonald informed General Suchet of this event, insisted on the return of the two divisions which he had lent him, and even asked for his assistance with the army of Aragon.

Preparations of Suchet to attack Taragona.—But Suchet very properly refused to comply with this demand, deeming it useless to collect so many troops for a simple blockade, and in a part of the country destitute of resources: he even considered it dangerous to remove his active forces from the important valley of the Ebro, at a moment when the enemy, multiplying his efforts around Tarragona, might become the assailant, and take from us not only a part of Catalonia, but also of Aragon. In fact, at the moment when the junta placed a garrison of twelve thousand chosen men in Tarragona, and General Contreras, former director of the artillery school of Segovia, and a man of skill and energy, was making every disposition for a long resistance, Campo-Verde collected an army of twenty thousand men between that city and Gerona, and the corps of Valencia and the partisans of Navarre were preparing to disquiet the garrisons left by Suchet in Aragon.

Notwithstanding the unexpected loss of Figueras, the vigor of the enemy's preparations and the imperfect state of his own, Suchet formed his resolution without hesitation. After consulting his chiefs of engineers, artillery, and administration, examining his resources, and calculating his forces, and leaving in Aragon troops necessary for maintaining our establishments there, he sent to Tortosa orders for forming the siege-park, and directing it by Balaguer on Cambrils, established magazines of provisions, and secured the means of transportation to Caspe and Mora: finally, he marched with all his disposable forces on Lerida, where he rallied the divisions of Freyre and Palombini, and, instead of marching in the direction of Figueras, moved rapidly on Tarragona, and invested the place on the fourth of May. This resolution was a wise one, and was crowned with the most happy result: Campo-Verde, not knowing whether he ought to deliver a place which was simply blockaded, or fly to the assistance of one which was more seriously attacked, did neither one thing nor the other; and Contreras, instead of completing his means of defense, saw his resources and his troops daily diminish.

Memorable Siege of that City.—Tarragona, strong in its natural position and by its ancient defenses, had been connected by a line of new works with the port and lower town. Mount Olivo, which had been fortified, covered the approaches on one side ; while on the other the sea always furnished them the means of succor or retreat. An English fleet, carrying two thousand troops, was lying in the harbor for this purpose, to annoy the flank of the besieging army. But Suchet commenced by establishing a strong redoubt on the shore, from which, with a few mortars, he soon drove the shipping to a distance, and then directed his attack upon Mount Olivo.

But this last was a difficult operation, for the trenches had to be constructed on a bare rock, and against a numerous garrison which was daily renewed, and which disputed the ground inch by inch. We lost in these combats General Salm and numerous officers and soldiers killed or wounded. When the batteries had breached the walls of the fort, an assault was made, on the night of the twenty-ninth of May, at the moment when a detachment from the city had come to relieve the garrison of the place. This circumstance, instead of being favorable to the defense, was decidedly injurious, by crowding within a small space a greater number of men than could be employed to advantage. The fort was carried, and the enemy lost one hundred and eighty men killed or taken prisoners. Suchet now resolved to push his attack by the Francoli against the lower town, as he would thus separate the main defenses of the place from the port, and at the same time cut off all succor from the garrison and all means of retreat. The works were, consequently, pushed with great vigor ; a second assault was made, on the seventh of June, against Fort Francoli ; a third, on the fourteenth, against the bastion of the Chanoines ; a fourth, on the twenty-first, against Fort Royal, and the remainder of the lower town. These several successes greatly increased the ardor of our soldiers ; for without the stimulus which the success of one night gave to the perils of the following day, they must have yielded to the fatigues of the siege and the heat of the weather. The works were not only of a fatiguing character, but required incessant labor ; chosen sharpshooters were continually occupied in the trenches firing upon the cannoneers of the place, while the garrison, on its side, kept up an incessant fire on our batteries ; for fifty-four days there was one continual engagement, like a long continued battle. The governor, astonished at so much perseverance, and despairing of any assistance from the Spanish army, which lay inactive in the field, wrote to the junta that he could not answer any longer for the place if they did not send him succor. Campo-Verde, who had failed in his attempt to succor Figueras, now yielded to the solicitations of the junta and of Contreras, and approached Tarragona, at the moment when we had opened the third parallel and established our breaching batteries against the body of the place. Our firmness imposed on him, and he retired without any effort to raise the siege, although his attack would have placed us between two fires. The English Colonel Skerret, landed from the fleet for the purpose of reënforcing the garrison with his two thousand troops, but, on seeing that the taking of the lower town would cut off his line of retreat, he renounced his project. The garrison, therefore, after a momentary hope of being delivered, saw itself abandoned to its fate.

The moment seemed favorable for a final blow. On the twenty-eighth of June, Suchet deemed the breach practicable, and threw against the ramparts of Tarragona sixteen companies of the *élite*, commanded by General Habert, and supported by numerous reserves. A most furious contest followed ; but nothing could arrest the impetuosity of our soldiers; a bloody combat was waged on the ramparts, in the streets, and even in the houses; it ended in the massacre of a part of the garrison. The remainder, to the number of ten thousand, cut off from retreat by sea, attempted in vain to escape by the gate of Barcelona; but being pursued, surrounded, and driven upon the shore, they finally laid down their arms. The Governor, Contreras, wounded with a bayonet, surrendered with all his staff; three hundred and twenty-two pieces of cannon fell into our hands. The sack of this unfortunate city was the inevitable result of such a resistance. Party spirit, the deplorable infirmity of human nature, has made every effort to detract from the glory which the French arms won on this occasion, by unworthy declamations against our brave men, because some excesses succeeded to an assault without example in the history of the war. Where have these philanthropic writers seen cities taken after five separate assaults, without any loss to the inhabitants, especially when these inhabitants join with the garrison in the defense of their ramparts.*

---

* The accounts which were at first published of this affair by English writers were exceedingly unjust to Suchet and his officers. The resistance of the inhabitants after the breach was carried, necessarily led to numerous excesses on both sides; but these were stopped as soon as possible under the circumstances.

The following is Napier's account of the final assault:

"At five o'clock in the evening, the French fire suddenly ceased, and fifteen hundred men led by General Habert passing out from the parallel, went at full speed up against the breach: twelve hundred under General Ficartier followed in support, General Montmarie led a brigade round the left, to the bastion of Rosario, with a view to break the gates there during the assault, and thus penetrating, to turn the interior defense of the Rambla. Harispe took post on the Barcelona road, to cut off the retreat of the garrison.

"The columns of attack had to pass over an open space of more than a hundred yards before they could reach the foot of the breach; and when within twenty yards of it, the hedge of aloes obliged them to turn to the right, and left, under a terrible fire of musketry and of grape, which the Spaniards, who were crowding on the breach with apparent desperation, poured unceasingly upon them. The destruction was great, the head of the French column got into confusion, gave back, and was beginning to fly, when the reserves rushed

Further Operations of Suchet.—The fall of Tarragona produced the same effect in Catalonia as that of Saragossa in Aragon. To make this influence still more decisive, Suchet marched rapidly on Barcelona and Vich. This movement served both to coöperate with the blockade of Figueras, and to favor a project which he had formed against Mont Serrat.

up, and a great many officers coming forward in a body, renewed the attack. At that moment one Bianchini, an Italian soldier, who had obtained leave to join the column as a volunteer, and whose white clothes, amidst the blue uniforms of the French, gave him a supernatural appearance, went forth alone from the ranks, and gliding silently and sternly up the breach, notwithstanding many wounds, reached the top, and there fell dead. Then the multitude bounded forward with a shout, the first line of the Spaniards fled, and the ramparts were darkened by the following masses of the French.

"Meanwhile Montmarie's sappers cut away the palisades at Rosario, and his light troops finding a rope hanging from the wall, mounted by it, at the moment when the assailants at the breach broke the Spanish reserves with one shock, and poured into the town like a devastating torrent. At the Rambla a momentary stand was indeed made, but the impulse of victory was too strong to be longer resisted, and a dreadful scene of slaughter and violence ensued. Citizens and soldiers, maddened with fear, rushed out in crowds by the Barcelona gate, while others, throwing themselves over the ramparts, made for the landing-places within the Milagro; but that way also had been intercepted by General Rogniat with his sappers, and then numbers throwing themselves down the steep rocks were dashed to pieces, while they who gained the shore were still exposed to the sword of the enemy. Those that went out by the Barcelona gate were met by Harispe's men, and some being killed, the rest, three thousand in number, were made prisoners. But within the town all was horror; fire had been set to many houses; Gonzales, fighting manfully, was killed; Contreras, wounded with the stroke of a bayonet, was only saved by a French officer; and though the hospitals were respected by the soldiers, in every other part their fury was unbounded. When the assault first commenced, the ship-launches had come close into the Milagro, and now saved some of the fugitives, but their guns swept the open space beyond, killing friends and enemies, as, mixed together, they rushed to the shore; and the French dragoons, passing through the flaming streets at a trot, rode upon the fugitives, sabring those who had outstripped the infantry. In every quarter there was great rage and cruelty, and although most of the women and children had, during the siege, been removed from Tarragona by the English shipping, and though the richest citizens had all gone to Sitjes, this assault was memorable as a day of blood. Only seven or eight hundred miserable creatures, principally soldiers, escaped on board the vessels; nine thousand, including the sick and wounded, were made prisoners; more than five thousand persons were slain, and a great part of the city was reduced to ashes."

Leaving Harispe's division in the environs of Vich, he returned to organize the garrisons and government of Tarragona and Tortosa; then, directing the mass of his forces on Lerida as though he intended to remain in Aragon, he marched with a detached division on Igualada, while General Harispe, on the appointed day, executed a similar movement. He thus enveloped and attacked the celebrated mountain of Serrat, where the Baron of Eroles had intrenched himself in a position reputed impregnable. The redoubts and convent were turned and carried; the Spaniards effected their escape across the precipices.

We established a garrison in this defensive point, which completed the reduction of southern Catalonia.

He is made Marshal.—Fully satisfied with the operations of Suchet, I sent him the bâton of Marshal of France, and gave him the command of southern Catalonia; Macdonald was called to the army of Russia which was organizing, and the command of the corps of occupation of Upper Catalonia was given to General Decaen. This officer had served with distinction in the army of Moreau in 1800, and at the peace of Amiens was appointed governor of our public possessions in India, which he had defended with all the means in his power.

He prepares to attack Valencia.—The resistance of the Catalans was now weakened; Andalusia was reduced, and I thought that if we should succeed in reducing Valencia and Murcia, we might unite all our means against Wellington. No one was more capable than Suchet of directing the important operations in the East; I therefore ordered him to take Valencia.

His preparations were made with wisdom; he deemed it necessary to strike a sudden and decisive blow, so as not to exhaust the provinces from which he was to draw his resources; while at the same time he might envelop and capture the army which the enemy had assembled for the defense of that place.

To accomplish this double object the army of Aragon required reënforcements, having been considerably reduced by the severe operations of the sieges it had carried on, and by the detachments required for the new garrison ; but while strongly soliciting reënforcements, Suchet prepared to obey my orders ; he rapidly collected his disposable forces, and on the twentieth of September, marched before Saguntum.

Siege of Saguntum.—At four leagues from Valencia, and at the junction of the roads to that city from Saragossa by Terruel and from Barcelona by Tortosa, lie the ancient and numerous ruins of the celebrated Saguntum, which is situated on a steep and isolated rock above the town and the river of Murviedro. Some recent works had strengthened this post sufficiently to intercept the passage. It was large enough to receive a garrison of two or three thousand men, and to reduce it required a regular siege. Valencia had also been covered by a vast line of intrenchments in front of the *enciente* of the place ; its bridges had been cut, its faubourgs raised, and a good intrenched camp behind the Guadalaviar secured the defense of the place, which the regency had intrusted to General Blake. To his title of captain-general were added unlimited powers, and the command of all the Spanish forces in the east of the Peninsula. These forces were composed of the remains of the old regiments of the line. Blake had stationed General Andriani at Saguntum, while he himself remained in his intrenched camp watching our movements.

On arriving before Saguntum, Marshal Suchet immediately occupied Murviedro ; and, as a part of the *enciente* of Saguntum appeared incomplete, he directed an escalade to be attempted in the night, in hopes of avoiding a siege ; but the enemy was on the alert and repelled our columns. It was now necessary to establish batteries on the only accessible side of the mountain ; but there was no earth here except what was carried by our troops, and the plunging fire of the fort rendered our trenches scarcely tenable. A breach was opened on the eighteenth of October, and an assault attempted ; but the steep rock and the obstinate resistance of the Spaniards rendered this attempt also unsuccessful. The batteries were now doubled and established nearer the place, and every thing prepared for renewing the attack, when General Blake left his intrenchments in order to succor the place, and on the twenty-fifth of October offered us battle.

Battle of Saguntum.—To take from the enemy the moral advantage of the initiative, Suchet resolved to march against him, leaving some battalions to continue the siege. Blake's line extended from the heights of Puch toward the two little mountains of Germanel. He charged with vigor by the road and gained possession of a height on which we had placed some field-pieces. Suchet at this moment discovered that the enemy had too much extended his front in order to manœuvre by both wings. In imitation of my movements at Rivoli and Austerlitz, he ordered a rapid attack on the Spanish centre, pierced it and put to flight the left wing ; the right sustained an obstinate combat on the heights of Puch ; but was finally forced to yield, and retreated with the others in disorder to Valencia, in full view of the English squadron and the garrison who remained impassible spectators of the battle. Saguntum capitulated the next day, surrendering to us nineteen pieces of cannon, and two thousand five hundred men. We had taken in the battle four thousand prisoners, four stand of colors, and twelve pieces of cannon. Nothing now prevented our march on Valencia ; Oropesa was in our power ; Peniscola was masked, but still held out.

Investment of Valencia.—But Suchet now waited for the

promised reënforcements, and did not yet approach Valencia; during the month of November, he defeated the two corps of the enemy which showed themselves, one in advance of Gaudalaviar near Betera, and the other on the road to Segorbia. Near the middle of December, he was informed that General Reille was bringing him a French and an Italian division from Pampeluna by Terruel, and that Marshal Marmont had received orders, at the same time, to detach a division across Castile on Valencia. He immediately made his dispositions to manœuvre against Blake. These dispositions bear the stamp of a skillful and experienced *coup-d'œil*. Seeing that the enemy's forces were extended in their lines from Manisses to the sea-shore, and that Valencia was too far from the water to favor an embarkation, for which, however, no preparations had been made, he deemed that a successful attack against their left, would be decisive. Their only line of retreat was on Alicante, which however could be reached by the French before them.

The corps of General Reille having arrived, three divisions of cavalry crossed the river, on the twenty-sixth of December, two leagues above the city; while on the left bank the whole camp of Blake from Manisses to the sea-shore was attacked in front. This attack gave place to a warm and bloody combat; but in the mean time the marshal had passed the river, gained the extreme left of the enemy, defeated and driven back all the troops which were successively brought to oppose him, so that the whole Spanish army found itself driven within the fortifications of Valencia, except a corps which escaped between Albufera and the sea, and which was pursued to St. Philip.

Siege of that Place.—The siege commenced immediately after the investment. Under the circumstances, it could not be of long duration; the exterior *enciente*, being a mere field-work of earth, and having too much development for a regular defense, was abandoned after eight days' resistance, with eighty pieces of cannon. Blake, shut up in Valencia, now attempted a sortie, but only a small column under cover of the night escaped into the mountains. Shells were now thrown into the city in order to intimidate the inhabitants; and Blake, being summoned to surrender and threatened with the fate of Tarragona, if he exposed this rich city to the consequences of an assault, finally capitulated on the ninth of January, surrendering to us himself and staff, his army of nineteen thousand men, twenty-one stand of colors, three hundred and seventy-four pieces of cannon, besides immense magazines and military munitions. The Spanish general did not sustain on this occasion the reputation which he had previously acquired; to surrender a city in order to save it is certainly an act of weakness; but to surrender it with an army within its walls is an act of cowardice.

Reduction of Peniscola and Gandia.—Suchet employed three days in establishing order within the city, and afterward moved the mass of his forces in the direction of Alicante. On the eleventh of January, he learned of General Montbrun's march on this point with the division from Portugal, and recommended this general to return immediately to Marmont, his assistance being no longer required. Montbrun, being disgusted with marching entirely across Spain for no purpose, and not wishing to return without doing something, presented himself before Alicante, and threatened to bombard the place. But as the Spaniards did not allow themselves to be imposed on by the few howitzers which he carried in his train, he resumed his march to Estremadura, where his absence had been disastrous to Marmont. Soon after this the capture of Peniscola and Gandia completed the submission of the kingdom of Valencia.*

---

* Napier's observations on these events are brief and instructive.

"1st. The events which led to the capitulation of Valencia, were but a con-

So many successes merited a recompense and an encouragement; I therefore conferred on Suchet the title of Duke of Albufera, and gave to his army a donation of two hundred millions of francs, levied on the provinces which they had conquered with so much glory.*

Remarks on Soult's Operations in the South.—These events formed a contrast with what was passing in the rest of the Peninsula; nevertheless, it must be said in Soult's praise, that he had skillfully maintained himself in his delicate position. Arrested in front by two impregnable cities—Cadiz and Gibraltar—one of which served as the focus of the

---

tinuation of those faults which had before ruined the Spanish cause in every part of the Peninsula, namely, the neglect of all good military usages, and the mania for fighting great battles with bad troops.

"2d. Blake needed not to have fought a serious action during any part of the campaign. He might have succored Saguntum without a dangerous battle, and might have retreated in safety behind the Guadalaviar; he might have defended that river without risking his whole army, and then have retreated behind the Xucar. He should never have shut up his army in Valencia, but having done so he should never have capitulated. Eighteen thousand men, well conducted, could always have broken through the thin circle of investment, drawn by Suchet, especially as the Spaniards had the power of operating on both banks of the river. But the campaign was one huge error throughout, and was pithily summed up in one sentence by the Duke of Wellington. Being accused by the regency at Cadiz of having caused the catastrophe, by permitting the army of the North and that of Portugal to send reenforcements to Suchet, he replied thus—' The misfortunes of Valencia are to be attributed to Blake's ignorance of his profession, and to Mahi's cowardice and treachery.'"

* Napier says of this general:

"On the fourteenth of January, Suchet made his triumphal entry into Valencia, having completed a series of campaigns in which the feebleness of his adversaries somewhat diminished his glory, but in which his own activity and skill, were not the less conspicuous. Napoleon created him Duke of Albufera, and his civil administration was strictly in unison with his conduct in the field, that is to say, vigorous and prudent. He arrested all dangerous persons, especially the friars, and sent them to France, and he rigorously deprived the people of their military resources; but he proportioned his demands to their real ability, kept his troops in perfect discipline, was careful not to offend the citizens by violating their customs, or shocking their religious prejudices, and endeavored, as much as possible, to govern through the native authorities. The archbishop and many of the clergy aided him, and the submission of the people was secured."

whole Spanish resistance; menaced on the left by the army of Murcia, and in rear by Wellington and Badajos, he had, nevertheless, extricated himself by his activity. Viewed, however, in their strategic relations, his operations were open to criticisms; he should have operated more on his wings, especially by the right. On learning the affair of Chiclana, I had recommended him to attach less importance to the occupation of the territory, and to concentrate all his attention on Cadiz, Seville and Badajos, the occupation of Malaga and Grenada, being only accessories which could be accomplished by movable columns. But the hope of preserving these superb provinces induced him to not abandon them. He thus had a hundred leagues of territory to protect against indefatigable guerillas and organized forces, which, having nothing to cover, could concentrate any where and operate in any direction, while any movement of Soult's forces seriously interfered with his occupation of the conquered provinces.

Taking all things into consideration, our affairs in the Peninsula had been improved during this campaign, notwithstanding the unfortunate retreat from Portugal. There seemed no doubt that, if successful in my enterprise against Russia, I might soon terminate the war in Spain by going there myself. But the events of 1812, and the double disaster of Moscow and Salamanca, entirely changed the face of affairs, and broke the double sceptre of Charles V. and of Charlemagne.

Winter Campaign of Wellington in Estremadura.—The satisfaction which I derived from the brilliant successes of Tarragona, Saguntum and Valencia, was destined to be of short duration. It has already been said, that, after the momentary junction of Soult and Marmont for the relief of Badajos, these two armies had again separated, the former returning to Andalusia, and the latter to Ciudad-Rodrigo, where

Wellington was threatening a serious attack. I had in the mean time taken efficacious measures for the reënforcement of my army; on hearing the news of Massena's retreat, and the events of Chiclana and Albuera, I had sent into Spain all the troops which I could spare without seriously interfering with my preparations against Russia. A corps of reserve, formed in old Castile under Count Dorsenne, was ordered to march on Salamanca to second Marmont, while their place in the north was temporarily supplied by the detachments destined for the reënforcement of the regiments of the different arms.

By the aid of these powerful reënforcements, Marmont had no difficulty in raising the siege of Ciudad-Rodrigo. Wellington was not a man to engage his troops unless the chances were in his favor. He retreated to the impregnable position of Guinaldo and Sabugal. Marmont's advance to offer him battle, and his retirement to his own cantonments, when a battle was declined by the English; and finally his detachment of Montbrun's division in the direction of Alicante to second Suchet, have already been mentioned. Wellington who was promptly informed of all our movements, determined to profit by the detachment of Montbrun, and the retirement of Marmont's troops into their cantonments, to strike some decisive blows in Estramadura.

My lieutenant had supposed that his adversary would not attempt a campaign at a season of the year which is always exceedingly rigorous in this latitude, especially among the mountains, and consequently he was not prepared to repel his attack.

He captures Ciudad-Rodrigo and Badajos.—But notwithstanding the great depth of the snow, the cold was not so great as to prevent the English army, which was abundantly supplied with every thing, from taking the field. Wellington passed the Agueda on the eighth of January, approached

Ciudad-Rodrigo, and pushed forward the siege so that two breaches were made practicable by the twenty-first. The masonry of the body of the place was uncovered, so as to expose it to be breached by the English artillery, which threw against it solid shot of large size and ninety-six pounder shells fired horizontally from iron carronades. The assault was made the next day, and sustained by the garrison with a bravery worthy of a better fate; the place, however, was carried, and the garrison of seventeen hundred men taken prisoners. Marmont, who in the mean time had laid quiet in his cantonments, advanced toward Salamanca a few days after the capture of Ciudad-Rodrigo; but the English had in the mean time repaired the breaches and garrisoned the place. This loss was the more to be regretted as Marmont had no means of carrying on a siege.

Wellington now retired behind the Agueda, passed the Guadiana the sixteenth of March, and appeared before Badajos. It was hardly to be supposed that Soult would be as dilatory in securing this place, as Marmont had been in relieving Ciudad-Rodrigo. Wellington's project was based on the possibility of carrying Fort Picurina, opening the second parallel at its base and breaching the masonry in the same way as at Ciudad-Rodrigo. The place was defended by four thousand men under the same Philippon who had covered himself with so much glory in the first siege. Fort Picurina was attacked on the night of the twenty-fourth and twenty-fifth of March, and, after a heavy bombardment, carried without opposition; the second parallel was immediately established and the breach batteries opened with so much success, that, on the fifth of April, three large breaches were made practicable; the assault was made the next day. Two divisions assailed the breaches, while two others attempted an escalade on the opposite side toward the castle; the latter, however, was intended as a feint to divide the attention of the garrison rather than with any expectation of success on this point.

The attention of the commandant and of the garrison, was wholly directed toward the side of the breaches; all their preparations were made with skill, and the English after two murderous assaults saw themselves forced to retreat. But, by a most unexpected chance, the columns which were to attempt an escalade on the opposite side, which had been deemed invulnerable, succeeded in making a lodgment on the rampart, and in suddenly assailing our brave men who had just covered themselves with so much glory. A severe combat was engaged hand to hand; but as the enemy had already penetrated in considerable numbers and as our men fought without order or concert, the garrison was finally forced to surrender. The brave Philippon was above all suspicion; but either his measures were not well taken or one of his officers failed in his duty. If he had had a suitable and well-disposed reserve, it is probable that this misfortune would not have happened. The English, however, lost two hundred officers and three thousand four hundred men killed and wounded, which is an incontestable proof of the vigor and brilliancy of the defense.

Soult arrived the next day at the head of his army, and, on hearing the fate of the place, fell back on Seville, which place had again been threatened by the Spaniards during his absence.

Remarks on these Operations.—The loss of these two places, which covered the centre of our immense line of operations from Bayonne to Cadiz, was a bad omen. Marmont, supposing that Soult had sufficient forces for the protection of Badajos without his assistance, as in the first siege, had preferred to remain, and seek to repair the affront which he himself had just received. He consequently invested Ciudad-Rodrigo and Almeida, and then advanced into Portugal as far as Castel-Franco. He intended either to destroy the bridge of Villa-Ucha, or to pass the river at that place and coöperate with Soult in the rescue of Badajos, by threatening Wellington's line of retreat. If this movement had been concerted with Soult, it would have been wise; but, being isolated, it could effect nothing. On hearing that Badajos had fallen, and that his adversary was returning upon the Tagus, Marmont again fell back upon his depôts.

Insurrection in Spanish America.—Many other memorable events occurred in 1811; the insurrection of Spanish America by Miranda, the creation of the Republic of Venezuela and Carraccas, the preliminary acts of the independence of Mexico and Peru, announced in all parts of this hemisphere the dawn of a new political era. A formidable counterpoise was forming in the new world, and threatening the overthrow of the colonial system of the Europeans. Europe was at this time so occupied with me, that it could give but little attention to these important events, which were calculated to eventually effect a complete revolution in the maritime, commercial, and political affairs of the old world.

General State of Affairs in Spain.—The loss of Ciudad-Rodrigo and Badajos annoyed me, less by the real importance of the places themselves, than by the talent displayed by my new adversary in their capture, and the manifest negligence of my lieutenants in obeying my instructions. I had directed the two marshals to furnish these places with sufficient garrisons and provisions for six months; Marmont, in particular, was inexcusable for leaving Ciudad-Rodrigo with too feeble a garrison. I felt these reverses the more sensibly, as I was on the eve of my expedition against Russia. Fortunately, Suchet's successes amply compensated for these disasters, and I flattered myself that after disposing of the enemy in the east of Spain and north of Europe, I would be able to take my revenge by concentrating all our means for a decisive blow against the English in the Peninsula. Many skillful judges, however, are of opinion that I would have done better to repair to Spain myself, recapture our lost fortresses, and drive Wellington from the Peninsula, rather than to engage in the expedition to Russia. I will explain hereafter the reasons which decided my course.

Continuation of the War between Russia and Turkey.— The events of the latter part of the campaign of 1811 in Turkey, were not calculated to authorize me to hope as much from this diversion as I had previously expected. I was not ignorant of the famous Roman maxim, *never to undertake two wars at the same time.* If Spain furnished occupation for a half of my army, Turkey also occupied one hundred thousand Russians.

Kamenski, being reënforced during the winter by twenty-five thousand recruits, took Loweza in the month of February, the Turks having lost in its defense four thousand men killed and prisoners. The Emperor Alexander now ordered five divisions of this army to return to the frontiers of Poland, and Kutusof, on the death of Kamenski, took command of the remaining fifty thousand. After several undecisive battles, this general dismantled the works which had cost his predecessor so much blood, and retired behind the Danube. The Vizir passed the Danube above Roudschouck, but found himself opposed to a line of field-works which Kutusof had constructed to intercept his advance. Seeing himself opposed in front by a well-defended line of fortifications, with the Danube and the corps of Markof in his rear, the Vizir abandoned his army and effected his escape in a boat. Ismael-Bey had crossed the river at Widden, but on seeing that Zass had also erected a line of intrenchments to prevent his advance, he retired behind the Danube. Russia profited by the perilous position of the Vizir's army to negotiate for peace, which had now become necessary on account of mysterious preparations in the north. An armistice was concluded ; and, during the negotiations for peace, the remains of the army of the Vizir capitulated, and were carried prisoners into Russia. I hoped to intercept these negotiations by declaring war against Russia ; but unfortunately Sebastiani, who enjoyed the full confidence of the Turks, had left Constantinople, and the Sultan, whose capital he had saved in 1807, had perished, the victim of fanaticism and anarchy. My new minister, Latour-Maubourg, neglected nothing to carry out my instructions, but he had not the same title to the confidence of the Ottomans. Informed by my enemies of the stipulations of Erfurth, and by Austria of the project of partition, the Turks abandoned themselves without reserve to the counsels of England. The British minister became all powerful with the divan, and every effort was resorted to to induce it to make peace with Russia ; while I sought to prevent this consummation by a declaration of war against the enemy of the Porte.

The campaign against Persia had been attended with success ; the Russians, who had for three years been in possession of Anapa, captured the allies' camp at Ascholkalaki on the seventeenth of September, 1810, and carried their victorious banners to the walls of Poti and the mouth of the Euphrates ; while in the east, they pushed their success along the borders of the Caspian Sea to the walls of Lankaran. This war was for them a relaxation rather than a serious diversion.

It is time to turn from these distant countries to the grand enterprise which was to put Europe at my feet, or to wholly ruin the immense edifice which I had erected with so much care and labor.

CHAPTER XVIII.

WAR OF 1812, OR CAMPAIGN IN RUSSIA.

Part I.—Advance to Moscow.

Causes of the War with Russia—Opinions of Napoleon's Counselors—Military Chances of Success—Negotiations with Russia—Fruits of the Continental System—Occupation of Swedish Pomerania—Alliance with Prussia—Pacific Proposals to the Emperor Alexander—Offensive and Defensive Alliance with Austria—Result of the Negotiations with Russia—Proposals of Peace to England—Ultimatum of Russia—Napoleon repairs to Dresden—Return of Narbonne—Pradt's Mission to Warsaw—Lauriston's Mission to Sweden—Preparations for opening the Campaign—Diversion of the Turks—Dispositions of the Russian Army—Its Organization—French and Allied Army—Plans of Napoleon—Passage of the Niemen—The Russians retreat on Drissa—Napoleon's Delay at Wilna—Mission of Balaschof—Reply of Napoleon—Poland—War between England and the United States—Operations against Bagration—Napoleon advances on Polotsk—Camp of Drissa—Alexander retires to St. Petersburg—Operations of Barclay—Combats of Ostrowno—Operations of Bagration—Affair of Mohilew—Halt at Witepsk—Operations of Napoleon's Wings—Tormassof defeats the Saxons—Operations of Oudinot—Turkey, Sweden and England—Council of War—Barclay takes the Offensive—Napoleon's March on Smolensk—Battles of Smolensk—Retreat of Barclay—Results of the Campaign—Ney passes the Dnieper—Hazardous March of Barclay—Pursuit of Ney and Murat—Battle of Valoutina—Retreat of the Russians—Position of Napoleon—Battle of Gorodeczno—Affairs of Polotsk—Napoleon resolves to advance—Character of the Country—New Generalissimo of the Russian Armies—Preparations for Battle—Position of the Enemy—Plan of Attack—Battle of Borodino or the Moscowa—Remarks on this Battle—Napoleon enters Moscow—The Russians burn the City—New Projects of Napoleon—The Russians march on Taroutina—Embarrassing Position of the French.

Causes of the War with Russia.—The great enterprise which was to decide the fate of Europe, or rather the empire of the world, was preparing amid songs of victory. The cannon on the tower of London, were announcing the success of Wellington at Ciudad-Rodrigo and Badajos; while the

Russians were celebrating the success of Kutusof on the Danube, and the French were consoling themselves with the victories of Suchet at Valencia. Negotiations still continued with Russia, but the discussion of merely incidental questions tended to embarrass, rather than clear up the main causes of the dispute.

I have already partially explained the motives which drew the two countries into this war. It is not exactly true that the Russian and French cabinets were in favor of war, while the two Emperors were opposed to it, for it is well known that Alexander constituted his own cabinet, while I directed that of the Tuileries. The alleged motives of the war, on both sides, were pretexts; the real objects were different. It must be confessed, however, that if the two sovereigns had consulted their own individual wishes, they would have prefered to avoid, or at least to postpone, this contest. But, unfortunately, the interests at stake were so great that such a result was scarcely possible; to attempt any thing like a permanent reconciliation, it would have been necessary to go back to the treaty of Vienna in 1809, and to the union of the mouths of the Weser, the Elbe, and the Trave with the French Empire.

I had long felt that this war was inevitable, but I wished to postpone it till a favorable opportunity occurred for carrying it on.* It was, in my opinion, the only means of terminating for ever, the contest to which I devoted my life. It was evident to the most simple, that Russia was too powerful to ever adhere to the European system of which France was the

---

* The reader will not find in this chapter the exact impartiality which characterizes the preceding portions of this work. It would be too much to expect that Jomini's opinion of this war should not be somewhat discolored by his attachment to the cause, as well as to the person of the Emperor Alexander. Nevertheless, it must be admitted, that these opinions are expressed with a moderation and candor seldom to be found in the writings of those who were opposed to Napoleon.

pivot. My edifice had risen too high for its base; Russia pressed with all her immense weight upon its summit; Alexander, younger than myself and full of energy, would probably outlive me, and on my death the French Empire would be dismembered. It was, therefore, necessary to place Russia in such a condition that she could not destroy the unity of my system, and to give new political boundaries to my frontiers sufficiently strong to resist the weight of the entire power of the Czars. Such an attempt would require not only the strength of my own empire, but also that of my allies. It was not without its dangers; but at the same time there were, at least, many chances of success; and, moreover, it was the only means of consolidating my work.

To render this plan successful, it was necessary to reconstruct Poland, and to compel the Russians to accept the new frontiers thus traced with the point of the sword. Russia might then renew her alliance with England without danger to my empire, which would be separated from the power of the Czars by an immense extent of country and a guard of two hundred thousand men. Our success would, therefore, not only consolidate the present, but also serve as a sure guarantee of the future. This would be my last war, and decide the political fate of Europe. Some have attributed to me the project of marching into India through Persia. I do not deny having thought of the possibility of sending an expedition there; but it would have been only a secondary object, totally subordinate to such arrangements as we might make with the cabinet of St. Petersburg. I had no idea of going there in person. No great force was required to destroy the monstrous edifice of the English company; twenty thousand good soldiers, a large number of officers, a little money, and a good understanding with the Mahratta chiefs, would have been sufficient to accomplish this object.

The essential base of my project was the resurrection of

Poland, a subject as delicate to treat upon with Austria as with Russia. It was necessary to guarantee Galicia to the former, or to offer her ample indemnities in Italy and Germany. But this was to abandon possessions useful, certain, and contiguous to my empire, for distant and uncertain acquisitions,—a sacrifice which I made dependent on the success of the war. It was so arranged in the secret articles of the treaty with Austria. I knew that a formal proclamation of the reëstablishment of Poland would form an insurmountable obstacle to any arrangement with Russia; if I took away from her, by a public act, Lithuania, Podolia, and Volhynia, it made it necessary to carry on the war till the cession should be sanctioned by a treaty of peace, and at the same time announce to Alexander that he must conquer or die. In attacking a colossal power like Russia, it would have been madness to destroy in advance all chance of a reconciliation, and to dispose of provinces which were as yet unconquered. All that I could do was to prepare this emancipation and to tranquillize Austria, reserving to myself the right to exchange the remainder of Galicia for the Illyrian provinces; this was to admit the principle of the future reunion of ancient Poland into one consolidated power; which would have been an immense step in favor of the Poles, but they did not appreciate it, and a hundred pamphlets have reproached me with having sacrificed them to my own private views and interests. This project was the cause of all my disasters, and posterity will blame me for having undertaken it; but, even now, I do not well see how the war could have been avoided, and I preferred conducting it myself to leaving it for my successor.

If it had depended on me to determine the time of this war with Russia, every thing continuing as had been arranged at Tilsit, I should certainly have delayed it for two or three years, till I could end the war in Spain. But in these three years, Russia might entirely destroy my Continental System —the ruling motive of my policy. If she should augment her forces and overthrow my power in the north of Germany, while I was personally engaged in Spain, I should lose more than I gained by postponing the war. It seemed better to delay for a couple of years the termination of the war in Spain ; for by this time the grand question of the north would be settled, and we might then definitely arrange the affairs of the south. By sending an annual reïnforcement of twenty-five thousand recruits to my army in Spain, I hoped to enable it to maintain its present position in the defensive ; this was all I required. The question was, therefore, reduced to these two points : " If I first directed my efforts to the north, the south could give me no serious cause for fear ; but if I first went to the south, the north might rise and render the condition of affairs still more doubtful than in 1809. By deferring the subjugation of Spain for two years, I was merely prolonging a guerilla war which could have no dangerous consequences ; but by deferring for two years the war in the north, I could gain no advantage which would be decisive in determining the main question at issue ; even had I become master of Lisbon, Cadiz, Carthagena, and Oporto, it would still have been necessary to hold them militarily, and no additional troops could have been drawn from the army of occupation in Spain to march against Russia ; whereas, in the mean time, the English policy, dominant at St. Petersburg and Stockholm, might have reached Berlin ; it might even have shaken Vienna at the moment when I was attacking Torres Vedras."

I held Prussia by her propositions of an alliance. Fear, my marriage, and the hope of gaining new indemnities, gave me a temporary assurance of Austria ; Sweden still hesitated ; although Bernadotte and myself were not the best of friends, still he was a Frenchman, and the interests of

Sweden and France had been identical for a century past; with our aid, he might reconquer Finland and restore it to his kingdom. The rather abrupt occupation of Pomerania was indeed a temporary grief, but not one for which the Swedish interests should be sacrificed, or still less the French sentiments of this government. I had every reason to believe that I had only to show to Sweden the road to Abo and Sweaborg, to make certain of her coöperation! Turkey had recently sustained reverses and entered into a treaty; but there was no reason to think that when the Porte should be certain of our armaments against Russia, it would not resume a hostile attitude toward that power.

By deferring this enterprise in order to go myself to the Spanish Peninsula, I might lose all these advantages; and the new chances of the war might change my doubtful allies into open enemies, and render the others but lukewarm in their friendship. Independently of these motives I had full confidence in the issue of this war,—a confidence which was authorized by all the preceding events of my history.

Opinions of Napoleon's Counselors.—But there was no want of objections to my project; if many of the public functionaries and generals whom I consulted adopted my opinion, by far the greatest number recoiled from the difficulties of the enterprise. The grand-usher, Caulaincourt, who had recently been ambassador to the court of Russia, was not the least ardent in opposing it. He endeavored to demonstrate that it was authorized neither by interest nor necessity, and drew a frightful picture of the obstacles which the climate and the immense extent of the Russian Empire would oppose to our success. He represented the advantage which the Russian soldier, inured to that rigorous climate, would have over our southern soldiers, one half of whom would encumber our hospitals before the termination of the enterprise. Even the Muscovite horses, by their half savage

training, would be found superior to those of Germany and
Normandy, which were accustomed to an abundant and
regular supply of food, and were, therefore, less fitted for the
fatigues and privations of such an enterprise. The severe
discipline, the impassible character, the constancy and firmness of those soldiers who have no country or friends but
their colors, give to the Russian army a solidity which is
elsewhere sought for in vain. Of course they are subject,
like ourselves, to the chances of war; but with them sickness is more rare than with any other army; desertion is
with them unknown; and the dispersion of organized corps
is prevented by an instinct which makes them huddle together
like sheep in case of danger,—an instinct originating partly
in the docile character and severe discipline of the soldier,
and partly in the habit of never separating from their colors,
which they had formed in their wars with the Turks, where
every straggler was certain to be cut off by the enemy's
cavalry. The grand master of ceremonies, M. de Segur, who
had been the French ambassador to Russia in the reign of
Catherine, and who was the author of the advantageous
commercial treaty of 1787, supported with all his eloquence
the party that opposed the war; Duroc also joined in the
opposition.

Those of my counselors who approved the enterprise,
said: "If we neglect to profit by the ascendency of the
Emperor Napoleon over his adversaries, and the military
superiority which he has exhibited in all his battles, from
the Niemen to the Nile;—if we now defer taking from
Russia the power to injure us, who will dare, after Napoleon's
death to oppose the efforts of that empire to destroy his
work? What captain can be found capable of sustaining,
with a French army, the feeble Duchy of Warsaw, against
which Austria herself will then conspire, the alliance of that
power being entirely dependent on the life of the emperor?

Austria has too many losses to repair, and too many injuries to avenge, not to turn against us on his death. Why should we defer consolidating this immense edifice and placing it on an immovable base, now that there is a fit occasion? It is no augmentation of this power that is sought, but merely a consolidation of that which exists and a guarantee of the future. What is now required to complete this glorious edifice? Would not a second Friedland on the fields of Wilna suffice? And are we not certain of victory, if we but look at the past, and consider the numerous phalanxes that march under our colors?"

To these arguments the opponents of the war replied: "Who will compel the Russians to give us battle in the old Polish provinces, when it is evidently their interest to fight only on the Dwina? Lithuania is little better than the deserts of Asia. Unlike Courland and Samogitia, it is covered with vast forests and marshes, and human habitations are there as scarce as cultivated fields. The enemy can surrender to us such provinces, without in the least compromising his safety; we shall be as ill-at-ease in the marshes of the Beresina, the Lepel, and the Pripetz, as in the mud of Pultusk and Ostrolenka. Obstacles will multiply in our way if the enemy, led by a second Fabius, only temporizes, and falls back on the centre of his power and resources. The first war of 1807 owed its success, in a considerable degree, to the numerous cities and immense resources of old Prussia; it was Dantzic, Elbing, Thorn, Braunsberg, Osterode, Allenstein, Eylau, Gustadt, Holland, Bischofswerder, the Island of Nogat, that enabled us to support an army of a hundred and fifty thousand men. But the hamlets of Lithuania, peopled by miserable Jews, can furnish us no supplies for our troops, our hospitals or depôts; cantonments will there be nothing better than miserable bivouacs. Will it be prudent to throw our army into these distant deserts, across countries made insurgent by this invasion, or by the ravages of preceding campaigns?—to support our base on Prussia already humiliated and trodden upon? Is it wise to trace a line of operations five hundred leagues in extent through a hostile country, where the embers of ill-extinguished fires are ready to burst forth into a volcano? And during all this long and perilous enterprise, shall we leave France exposed to the attacks of her enemies, and endanger her security and internal tranquillity, by again rousing from sleep the tiger of party spirit?"

Military Chances of Success.—All these arguments were not sufficient to deter me from the enterprise. I could not dispute the existence of numerous obstacles, but my genius consisted in comprehending the difficulties of an affair, and in seeing, at the same time, the means by which these difficulties could be overcome. I must confess, however, that fifteen years of uninterrupted success had made me overconfident in my own resources. I saw all the obstacles, but I did not attach to them sufficient importance. I was not ignorant that Russia, based on the Frozen Ocean, and the deserts of Great Tartary, was difficult to subjugate, and that it would be impossible to pursue her army and her government, if they should retreat before our eagles to the Oural; but, at the same time, I was aware that the very extent of her empire rendered it the more dependent on the centre of its vitality, and that this source, or centre of vitality, was Moscow, St. Petersburg, and the army.

I held the Russian army in the highest estimation; and if the contrary opinions are drawn from my bulletins and the *Moniteur*, it must be remembered that such expressions were intended for a particular object. But the greater my estimation of that army, the more was I convinced that it constituted the real strength of Russia. I thought that the self-esteem of the Russians would not suffer them to evacuate

Lithuania without a general battle ; and if I could gain, at
Wilna, Smolensk, or Witepsk, a victory like that of Friedland, all Europe would be at my disposal. Could I ever
give battle with a greater object, where the probabilities of
success were so positive, or the results of that success so immense ? I had decided the fate of Europe at Austerlitz and
Friedland, with eighty thousand men, and now was it not
still more probable that, with four hundred and fifty thousand, I would definitely fix that destiny ? Even if the first
battle should be undecisive, like that of Eylau, and I should
lose an equal number of brave men without result, would I
not still have an army of four hundred thousand men with
which to retrieve a fortune which had attended me for the
last twenty years ?

With so many probabilities in my favor, ought I to leave
to my successor the task of sustaining, on the Vistula, an
imperfectly organized Poland, and to contend, at the same
time, with England and the other powers who, at my death,
would attempt the restoration of the Bourbons? Undoubtedly it would have been better to leave to my son the
chance of this uncertain contest in the North, than the destiny which I finally bequeathed him ; but, in judging of my
conduct in this case, it is necessary to consider all the chances
which militated in my favor. I certainly deemed the result
less doubtful, with Austria and Prussia on my side, than it
was at Eylau in 1807, when Austria might have fallen on
my rear, between the Elbe and the Oder, have revived the
sinking courage of the Prussians, and cut off all hopes of
retreat. Now, based on Dantzic, Graudentz, Modlin, and
Warsaw, and at the head of the armies of all Europe, how
could I anticipate such a result !

With respect to the other objections to the war, I will add
that I felt very little apprehension from party spirit in
France ; that I expected to direct the affairs of the empire

from my head-quarters, as in my preceding wars ; the Empress assisting in my councils ; that the whole nation, being organized into three *bans* or classes, would give for the first *ban* one hundred and twenty thousand men in the flower of their age, who, formed into cohorts, and disciplined in the *cadres* or skeletons detached from the line, would supply the places of veterans in guarding our fortifications, our harbors, and the interior of France. I had nothing to fear from Germany, since I took with me the élite corps of Austria and Prussia ; and I had no apprehensions of another maritime expedition by the English, who were sufficiently occupied in Spain, and not disposed to repeat the disasters of Antwerp. With respect to provisions, I could purchase an abundance of grain of the Poles, and deposit it at Dantzic ; and, in return for this money, the Poles would furnish me fifty thousand good soldiers ; beef could be procured in Galicia ; and I could organize twenty new battalions of the provision train to increase our means of transportation.* Prussia had owed us several millions since the treaty of Tilsit, and would pay us in the magazines which she had laid up : thus affording me a year's supply of provisions in the rear of my army. I had no desire to imitate Cambyses, or the Emperor Julian, or Crassus ; all my measures were adopted with care, and every possible precaution taken to provide against disasters like theirs. It was possible that I might be defeated, and forced to fall back on the Vistula ; but I regarded this as the extent of the evil which could happen to me. The chances of the enterprise being decidedly in my favor, I had only to determine whether the proper time had come for its commencement, or whether it could be any longer postponed.

* Battalions of military equipages were organized after the battle of Eylau, the caissons being arranged and drawn like a train of artillery.

Negotiations with Russia.—Thus far, our discussions with Russia had been limited to vague complaints and imperfect explanations, while both parties were collecting troops. Causes of complaint were not wanting, but they were rather alluded to, than pressed for negotiation, each party fearing to hasten a rupture, which might be so important in its consequences, and which there were so many reasons for postponing. I only knew that Russia complained of the increase of the Duchy of Warsaw, of the additions made to my empire, and especially of the annexation of Oldenburg : she desired Dantzic in exchange for that principality, but she did not say positively what were her views with respect to Poland, leaving me to infer that nothing but the literal execution of the treaty of Tilsit would satisfy her. On my side, I complained of the infractions of the Continental System, of new laws calculated to injure French commerce, and of the raising of new troops.

Fruits of the Continental System.—If Russia had consented to adhere to the Continental System, I could have asked nothing better than the continuance of our friendly relations ; for the fruits of this system were beginning to appear. The distress of the English manufactories was manifesting itself in the rising of the workmen against the use of machinery, and the sufferings of this class of men were becoming matters of serious importance. In the Parliament, even Brougham declared the British Orders in Council to be the cause of the public distress. Notes of the Bank of England had considerably depreciated in value, and the exchange on London had fallen to seventy per cent. It was too much to expect me to renounce this system, just as I was beginning to reap its fruits. If my adherence to this system should produce an alliance between Russia and England, this was unavoidable, for war was preferable to its renunciation. By this war I hoped to accomplish two objects at the same time: first, to effect the reëstablishment of Poland, and second, to force the return of Russia to the Continental System. I flattered myself that the Cabinet of St. Petersburg, surprised at the numerous forces which I would bring into the field, at a time when it supposed my means were exhausted, would yield to my conditions, and that all our difficulties would be compromised. But matters had gone too far to be easily arranged: I might consent to abstain from any coöperation in the restoration of Poland, but to place things on the footing agreed upon at Tilsit was difficult, after the annexation of Galicia.

Occupation of Swedish Pomerania.—While we were discussing these causes of mutual complaint, circumstances occurred which were calculated to increase them. The English depôt on the rock of Heligoland had become one of the richest bazaars of the old world—a real political and military arsenal. Colonial merchandise from this place found its way into the north under the neutral flag of America, and on the coast between Holland and Lubec by the little contraband coasters. The occupation of the Hanseatic cities had closed all the commercial avenues; but the port of Stralsund and Swedish Pomerania, notwithstanding the official declarations of the cabinet of Stockholm, still carried on a considerable fraudulent traffic. I was not more pleased with the political course of Bernadotte than with this clandestine commerce, and I consequently ordered Davoust to occupy Pomerania in the early part of January. It would have been perfectly absurd for me to induce Russia, Denmark, Prussia, Austria and Spain to close their ports, while contraband articles were admitted into the ports of Sweden, a country which was entirely at our discretion. Bernadotte, irritated at this measure, sought the support of Russia, and complained at the court of St. Petersburg of an aggression which his own conduct had provoked. Considering the existing relations between France and Russia, this step was calculated to produce a sensation. The Emperor Alexander, who, since 1809, had been persuaded that I designed to attack him, regarded this as preliminary to the opening of hostilities. In the unsettled state of our affairs, I had deemed it necessary to increase the garrison of Dantzic to twenty thousand men, and, at the same time, to reënforce those of Stettin, Custrin and Glogau. These measures in the eyes of Russia, were so many additional proofs of hostility, and only tended to aggravate the wound which had already been inflicted by the augmentation of the Duchy of Warsaw, and the annexation of Oldenburg.

Alliance with Prussia.—While my propositions and the responses of Russia were being exchanged, and it was announced at St. Petersburg, that Count Nesselrode was about to be sent to France with new proposals, I directed my attention to forming the alliance with Prussia, which had been offered to me a year before. It has been said by some that, not being able to fully trust this power, I ought to have overthrown the monarchy of the Great Frederick, which was already surrounded by my troops. This opinion, though specious, is not entirely correct. Frederick William had always exhibited a character of perfect rectitude; and if the humiliation of the peace of Tilsit had incited him against me, it was, nevertheless, possible to induce him to enter fully into my system, by showing him the possibility of the restoration of his kingdom to what it was in 1806. If he had more to hope from me than from my enemies, he might attach himself sincerely to my cause. The army and people might not have been so easily persuaded; nevertheless, they also would have been attached to my cause by the plan proposed in 1806 by Jomini, that is, by giving to Prussia, either the kingdom of Poland or the Presidency of the Confederation of the Rhine, with indemnities. The former would probably have been the most wise; for if it had not been so advantageous as the complete reëstablishment of the throne of Sobieski, it would, nevertheless, have been preferable to an imperfect restoration of Poland, surrounded by enemies anxious for a new partition. This would have been a strong inducement to Prussia to remain faithful to my cause, and would have afforded to the Poles hopes of a better future. The king of Saxony could have been easily indemnified. If I had followed the advice to destroy Prussia at the beginning of hostilities, it would have required one hundred thousand soldiers to guard the monarchy; moreover, I might have found a German Vendée in the mountains of Silesia, and the forests of La Marche. I took a middle course; to attach the king to my cause by hopes of indemnities in Courland, and at the same time to observe his country with a reserve of fifty thousand men, which would supply my army with recruits and guard my magazines. The fear of doing too much for a country which was ill-disposed toward me, prevented me from giving ample satisfaction to the cabinet of Berlin; and the fear of embarrassing myself with new enemies, prevented me from acting in a hostile manner toward her. It was, however, no small advantage to obtain from a country ready to join the ranks of the enemy, an auxiliary force of twenty thousand men and abundant supplies; and I hoped that my victories would soon attach them firmly to my cause. I therefore, directed the Duke of Bassano to negotiate with Krusemarck, on the proposals of the cabinet of Berlin; the affair was soon arranged and the treaty signed, on the twenty-sixth of February. Frederick William made numerous efforts to arrange the difficulties between France and Russia, but his efforts produced no effect.

Pacific Mission of Czernitscheff.—As soon as I had completed this alliance with the cabinet of Berlin, I resolved to make a final effort to arrange our difficulties with Russia and thus avoid war. As the discussions of our ambassadors led to no satisfactory result, and the promised mission of Count Nesselrode had been postponed, I called Colonel Czernitscheff, the *aide-de-camp* of the Emperor Alexander, who had resided near my court since the campaign of 1809, and directed him to bear to his master the following proposals for a pacific arrangement of our differences, viz. : *I am ready to agree to make no further increase to the Duchy of Warsaw, and to give an indemnity for Oldenburg ; but as I have occupied that country solely for the purpose of cutting off all clandestine communication with England, I can not concede Dantzic, which would soon become an English entrepôt ! I offer in exchange Erfurth and its territory. Finally, if the emperor will adhere to the Continental System, I will give my assent to the system of licenses to Russian merchants, provided the new commercial laws against France are modified by a new treaty.*

With these propositions Czernitscheff took also the returns of our troops which he obtained through the treachery of one of the clerks of the war-office ; this was important information for the Emperor Alexander, but information which he would probably have soon obtained from other sources, had it not been procured by Czernitscheff, so difficult is it to conceal such matters from the diplomatic agents of an enemy.

Offensive and defensive Alliance with Austria. — In the mean time, Austria signed a treaty of alliance more close than that of our family relations. My political position made me feel the importance of connecting this power more closely to my enterprise, for I was well aware that my marriage would not prevent her from an armed mediation, as soon as I had penetrated into the interior of Russia. The cabinet of Vienna anticipated my wishes by voluntarily offering to share with me the chances of the war; it proposed even more than I could have ventured to ask, and the treaty was signed on the fourteenth of March.

Result of the Mission of Czernitscheff.—Czernitscheff had reached St. Petersburg on the tenth of March; but the Emperor Alexander did not find in my proposals anything to induce him to change the course of conduct which he had marked out to himself.* A whole month passed without any response being made to these propositions. To the natural distrust of my pacific intentions caused by the affairs of Poland, and Oldenburg, and the increase of the garrison of Dantzic, was, at this time, added one of those intrigues to which the Russian court is so often subject. Alexander's most intimate counselor was suddenly arrested and banished to Siberia, on the charge of a connection with me and my ministers. These charges were afterwards found to be utterly false, and the minister was appointed governor of Siberia,— a reparation as honorable to the monarch as to his counselor. It is probable that this intrigue of a coterie had some little influence on external politics, but far less than was supposed at the time. The causes which have already been mentioned were sufficient to determine the course of the Emperor Alexander, without attributing it to any influence of petty coteries.

Proposals of Peace to England.—While the Cabinet of St. Petersburg were deliberating on my propositions, I opened negotiations with England. Strong in the advantageous position in which I was now placed by my alliances with Austria and Prussia, I nevertheless wished, before throwing down the gauntlet and again drawing the sword, to make a final appeal to England. She was the first cause of my contest in the north, and, if I could treat with her, I

---

* The author here repeats the causes of the war as given at the beginning of the chapter—a repetition which is omitted in the translation.

might renounce my Continental System, and give up my plan of the restoration of Poland. I therefore directed the duke of Bassano to dispatch, on the seventeenth of April, a note to Lord Castlereagh with proposals of peace.

Our colonial differences had been swallowed up in the immense naval superiority of England, and in important continental questions. All our present difficulties had reference to Spain, Portugal, and the Two Sicilies. I proposed to proclaim the independence of Spain under the reigning dynasty, to restore Portugal to the House of Braganza, to leave Naples to Murat, and Sicily to Ferdinand. It seemed easy to decide these questions, which were nevertheless as important to England as to us. To propose to the Cabinet of London to recognize Joseph, when Wellington had taken Ciudad-Rodrigo and Badajos, and when a war with Russia promised still more important successes, was to risk the chance of a refusal. Castlereagh naturally asked whether I meant by the *reigning dynasty* in Spain, my brother Joseph or Ferdinand VII.? If it was impossible for the Prince Regent to recognize the former, it was equally difficult for me to consent to the restoration of the latter. It has been absurdly said that the peace of the world at this time depended upon the simple question of *Joseph or Ferdinand*, and that my decision was influenced by the interests of my brother. The real question to be decided in the recognition of Ferdinand, was, whether Spain should belong to us or to England. To recognize that prince in 1812, after refusing to do so in 1808, and after keeping him captive for some years, would have placed Spain more decidedly than ever in the ranks of my enemies. It was not as the brother of Joseph, but as the chief of the French nation and of its interests, that I opposed the return of Ferdinand. To have *no more Pyrenees*, it was necessary that none of my enemies should occupy the throne of Spain. It is an unjust accusation to charge me with precipitating France into an interminable war, for the sake of my own family interests ; and this charge of *nepotism* is the more absurd as Joseph had never given any convincing proofs of his attachment to my interests, and as I knew very well that Philip V. had declared war against the successor of Louis XIV, ten years after the latter had compromised the existence of France in order to place Philip on the Spanish throne.

Ultimatum of Russia.—The messenger who brought the response of Castlereagh, was preceded only a few hours by the messenger who brought the *ultimatum* of Russia (April 24th.) Prince Kourakin, the *chargé*, demanded the evacuation of Prussia and the places of the Oder, the reduction of the garrison of Dantzic, the conclusion of an arrangement with Sweden, and the evacuation of Pomerania. On these conditions Russia would agree to cut off all direct relations with England, but would not discontinue this intercourse through neutrals ; commercial licenses would be given to Russian merchants, the same as was given in France ; the Russian custom-house duties would be modified for the advantage of French commerce ; and pacific negotiations would be entered into to fix upon an indemnity for Oldenburg.

These conditions were in themselves less objectionable than the manner in which they were proposed, that is, as an *ultimatum*. They certainly formed a striking contrast with my political position after the important alliances which I had just formed with Austria and Prussia ; but in examining them at this day dispassionately, I must confess that they were the natural result of the position of Russia since 1807. It was a harsh requisition on the part of the Emperor Alexander to ask that I should retract the donation of Galicia to the Duchy of Warsaw, and restore to Holland and the mouths of the Weser their independence, although the tenure of our treaties authorized this demand. To require, for the security of his empire, the evacuation of Prussia was moderate on his part; but to demand this evacuation as a preliminary to any definitive arrangement, was to draw around me the circle of Popilius and subject me to a gratuitous humiliation.

The evacuation of the Prussian fortresses was a most serious matter: By such a measure I should have thrown Prussia into the ranks of my enemies; Frederick William would have unhesitatingly thrown himself into the arms of Alexander. He had already offered to do so, in 1811, if the Russians would take the offensive and advance upon the Oder. This circumstance was sufficient to prove that the moment I surrendered the Prussian fortresses, she would join the ranks of the enemy. Moreover, I should thereby compromise the Duchy of Warsaw which would have been invaded and destroyed in fifteen days. It may be said that as Prussia was now my ally this fear was chimerical; but the motives of this alliance having ceased, of course the policy of the cabinet of Berlin would have changed. It is possible that Alexander, satisfied with some modifications in his maritime system, would not have taken advantage of the evacuation of Prussia to regain his superiority in the north; it is possible that he would have been satisfied with the restoration of his commerce and the tranquillity of his empire, and the increase of his territories by Finland and several districts of Poland; while, on the other hand, he could have occupied the Turkish Principalities which he so reasonably desired to possess: But what guarantee had I that he would be thus moderate, and that Prussia, with his assistance, would not rekindle the flames of war? Perhaps it was my misfortune on this occasion to have been too thoughtful of the future, and to have been too cautious in the arrangement of existing differences.

With respect to the Duchy of Warsaw, it had now become

almost impossible for me to restore things to the footing agreed upon at Tilsit; to revoke the annexation of Galicia would have given the death blow to Poland. Russia did not peremptorily demand this, but it was evident that nothing short of this would entirely satisfy her.

But, as has already been said, it was less the character of the demands of Kourakin, than the manner in which they were made that astonished me. If they had proposed a definitive treaty in which the evacuation of Prussia had been stipulated as an indemnity for sacrifices specified in the same treaty, I might have accepted the proposal; but to make this a condition preliminary to any arrangement of our differences, was to place me in the condition of a man challenged to a duel and required to beg the pardon of his antagonist before entering into any explanation of the cause of the quarrel. This course was so contrary to the usual urbanity of the Emperor Alexander, that I could not help thinking that some intrigue had caused so complete a change in his character and manner of acting. Anxious to obtain some direct explanation from him, I resolved to dispatch M. de Narbonne, on a special mission to Russia. This ancient courtier, reputed for his agreeable and captivating manners, had sufficient finesse and penetration to qualify him for so delicate a mission. He received orders to repair to St. Petersburg on the twenty-sixth of April; the pretext of his journey was to communicate to the emperor the nature of my recent negotiation with England, while its real object was to penetrate the mystery of Alexander's recent conduct, and to ascertain if there were any means of inducing him to adhere to the Continental System.

Napoleon repairs to Dresden.—In the mean time my army had been on the march for two months; it had crossed the Prussian territory and was already on the Oder. The time had now come to give the finishing hand to my preparations.

I set out for Dresden, where I had appointed to meet my father-in-law, the King of Prussia, and the several German princes, who marched under our banners. Never had my superiority been displayed in an assembly so august, and never, since the middle ages, had there been so imposing a meeting of sovereigns. Who could have believed that two years after, the same sovereigns, assembled at Vienna, would have put me under the ban of nations? . . . Nothing was neglected that could increase the splendor of this assembly. The *élite* of the Parisian theatres were there; and *fêtes*, concerts, and plays, served as a prelude to the great tragedy which we were preparing to act.

It is the present object to explain my political and military acts, rather than to describe the splendor of courts, or the anecdotes and adventures of the salons. I can not, however, omit to mention the interview between Maria-Louisa and her father,—the first since her marriage. He had sent her to my court as an expiatory victim; he found her radiant with satisfaction and glory, and proud of my power, which had placed her on the first throne in the universe,—not an usurped throne—as some fools have asserted, but a throne erected by my genius and my sword. Animated by sentiments very different from those of his son-in-law, this proud descendant of the courts of Hapsburg, perceived none of that glory with which I illumined the brow of his daughter; but told her with transport, that as I was a descendant of the Princess of Treviso, she need not blush at having given me her hand ! ! ! I left him the petty satisfaction of believing the doubtful genealogies which his courtiers had discovered in old parchments, convinced myself that if there were really any descendants of the Bonaparte who once reigned at Treviso, they would one day pride themselves less in being his descendants, than in being mine.*

---

* Napoleon, in the St. Helena Memoirs, discusses this reputed genealogy, show-

I learned at Dresden that the Emperor Alexander had left his capital to repair to Wilna. Fearing that Narbonne might be too late to meet him, I directed to Maret a letter for Lauriston, my ambassador at St. Petersburg, charging him to repair to the emperor with all possible haste, and to endeavor to revive his former sentiments of friendship for me, and to discover the true cause of his change—a change which I then attributed more to petty intrigues than to considerations of high political policy. Less credit is due to these pacific measures on my part than has been attributed to them by my friends; but they were nevertheless sincere: for, if I could have induced Alexander, by an advantageous treaty of commerce, to maintain the Continental System, and thus avoid a war, I could instantly fly to Spain: and, in case of refusal, I could then pursue the enterprise which I had undertaken, as my troops, which had been collected from the four corners of Europe, were already assembling on the Vistula.

Return of Narbonne.—I waited with impatience for the return of Narbonne, who at length arrived on the twenty-eighth of May. He had found the Emperor Alexander at Wilna, who exhibited neither a spirit of boasting nor of apprehension, but refused to add to, or to retrench in any respect, the proposals made by Kourakin. War was therefore inevitable.

Pradt's Mission to Warsaw.—The news received from Wilna announced that the Emperor of Russia was seeking to attach to himself the Poles of the Russian provinces by benefits and conciliatory measures. It was, therefore, more urgent than ever that I should immediately act upon my project of declaring the independence of Poland. Towards

---

ing that he did not attach to it the slightest importance. The discussion, however, is interesting to those who attach importance to such investigations, or their results.

the end of 1811, I had designed sending Talleyrand to Warsaw, to arrange with the Polish provinces the necessary measures for the restoration of their country. Since the reprimand which I gave him on my return from Spain, he had had no connection with the affairs of state, but was burning to be again employed. This mission was one of cunning and intrigue, and well-suited to his talent. But the vindictive diplomatist, charmed at having an opportunity to thwart my projects, took the first opportunity to divulge them to the Court of Vienna, where, of all places, he ought to have been the most careful to conceal them. I could hardly restrain my indignation at such a procedure, which was in reality high-treason against the interests of France. I was on the point of pronouncing his exile; but as he had been intrusted with the most important secrets of state, it would have been necessary to condemn him to death or to imprisonment for life: this I was unwilling to do. The excitement caused by these developments of Talleyrand, forced me to postpone the mission till after the alliance with Austria. I finally charged M. de Pradt, Archbishop of Mechlin, with it. He was a man more ambitious than shrewd, and still more vain than ambitious. He had, however, eloquence and a poetical imagination, and I hoped that he would be able to rouse the enthusiasm of the Polish nation. I unbosomed to him that I hoped to gain two battles, and dictate peace at Moscow; but that, if the war was prolonged, I would leave the Poles an auxiliary force of one hundred thousand men with which they could themselves complete their work of restoration. It was important to excite their patriotism to the highest degree, and to determine them to make the greatest sacrifices; for it was for their existence that I had taken up arms.*

---

* Dominique Dufour de Pradt, known as Abbé De Pradt, was born in the province of Auvergne, in 1759, and early entered the church under the patron-

Mission of Ligneul to Sweden.—I left Dresden, the twenty-ninth of May, to reach, by Posen, the head-quarters of my army at Thorn. Hardly had I left the capital of

age of the Archbishop of Rouen. In the early part of the revolution he took a prominent position in politics, and was elected deputy to the States-General. He opposed the revolution, and fled from France among the first *émigrés*. He became a strong partisan of the Bourbon cause in Europe, and during his exile published anonymously several books and pamphlets against the government of his own country. Considering the hopes of the Bourbons destroyed by the eighteenth Brumaire, he applied through his relative, General Duroc, for permission to return to France, which, through Duroc's influence, was granted by Napoleon, who afterwards appointed him his First Almoner, and afterwards made him Archbishop of Mechlin.

By his talents as a writer, and his great conversational powers, he at one time acquired considerable influence with the emperor, but was much disliked by the generals on account of his sycophancy and character for intrigue. Having successfully filled several unimportant missions, Napoleon selected him in 1812, as his agent or ambassador to Warsaw. Either through incapacity, or, as it was charged, a desire to keep on good terms with Austria and Prussia, he accomplished none of the objects of his mission, and, on Napoleon's return from Moscow, was dismissed and sent back to France.

Napoleon, at St. Helena, thus speaks of him: "The Abbé did not fulfil at Warsaw any of the objects which had been intended. On the contrary, he did a great deal of mischief. Reports against him poured in from every quarter. Even the young men, the clerks attached to the embassy, were surprised at his conduct, and went so far as to accuse him of maintaining an understanding with the enemy, which I by no means believed. But he certainly had a long talk with me, which he misrepresents, as might have been expected; and it was at the very moment when he was delivering a long, prosy speech, which appeared to me a mere string of absurdity and impertinence, that I scrawled on the corner of the chimney-piece the order to withdraw him from his embassy, and to send him, as soon as possible, to France; a circumstance which was the cause of a good deal of merriment at the time, and which the Abbé seems very desirous of concealing."

On his return to France, the Abbé commenced his intrigues for the restoration of the Bourbons, but so adroitly as to escape prosecution. In 1814, when the allies reached the vicinity of Paris, he resumed all his activity, and excelled even the ultra-royalists in bitterness against Napoleon.

An anecdote is related of his interview with Caulaincourt at the gate of the Court of the allied sovereigns, around which the priest was hovering, and rubbing his hands with delight at the news of the abdication. After vainly seeking to obtain more favorable terms, Caulaincourt was retiring in deep dejection when he encountered the Abbé at the door. The latter made some insulting remarks in regard to the fall of his former patron, when the Duke, losing all self-control, seized the sycophantic and ungrateful priest by the collar, and, after almost shaking the breath out of his body, turned him around upon his

Frederick-Augustus when M. Ligneul returned there from Stockholm. He was an intimate friend of Bernadotte whom I had sent to arrange our difficulties with Sweden. He reported that the Prince-Royal was ready to forget all that had passed, and join my banners; but that he required a subsidy to aid him in carrying on the war, and Norway as an indemnity for the sacrifices made by Sweden! I was not in the situation, nor the humor, to purchase a doubtful ally at the expense of one that had always proved itself faithful. A Swedish diversion by Torneo could not have sufficient influence upon the great question at issue to induce me to subscribe to conditions which were calculated only to incite my anger.

Preparations for opening the Campaign. — Thoroughly persuaded of the immense importance of the contest in which I was about to engage, I had assembled the most numerous army that had ever fought in Europe. The great invasions of the Cimbrians and Huns have never presented a mass of combatants like that of the army of 1812. Reënforced by the troops of Prussia, Austria, and the Princes of the Confederation, I had, in April and May, an army of nearly half a million of men, crossing Prussia and the Duchy of Warsaw to their rendezvous on the Niemen. I hoped that the Russians would defend Lithuania, and I felt certain of gaining the battle, if they would accept one; but those who think that I had previously determined, any further than this, on my plan of campaign, are in error: my operations were to depend upon those of the enemy.

Diversion of the Turks. — I had counted on a powerful

---

heels like a top. and then contemptuously turning his back upon him, walked away. The Abbé did not easily forget this rude pirouette, and it required the balm of many honors from the restored Bourbons to soothe his wounded pride.

He was a voluminous writer, but diffuse and inaccurate, utterly disregarding the facts of history and geography, whenever it suited his purpose to misstate them.

diversion of the Turks ; and as soon as the treaty of alliance with Austria had guaranteed the integrity of the Ottoman Empire, 'I directed Andréossi, my ambassador at Vienna, to repair to Constantinople for the purpose of forming an alliance there, and of arranging a common plan of operations. He was retained a long time upon the frontier waiting the firman of the Grand-Seignior, and had hardly reached the capital when I crossed the Niemen. It was now too late: the gold of England and the intrigues of the Morouzzi had corrupted the divan, and even the vizir ; and these ignorant disciples of Mahomet made peace at the very moment when they might have repaired the losses of a century of disastrous wars. This peace was signed on the twenty-fifth of May, at the Russian head-quarters at Bucharest, and was not known when I crossed the Niemen. Some have attempted to justify the course of the Turks at my expense, and have accused me of wishing to sacrifice them. The affairs of Spain forced me to abandon the Mussulman interests at Erfurth, in order to conciliate Russia ; but now when I was about to strike at the heart of this rival empire, I necessarily became the natural ally of the Turks. It required no great genius to comprehend this truth, and to profit by the occasion which I offered them of regaining at a single blow all that they had lost since the reign of Peter the Great. It was not to gratify me that they were to renew the war, but for their own manifest interest. On the contrary, they signed a disgraceful peace, yielding Bessarabia at the most favorable moment ever presented for carrying on the war with certain chances of success. I evidently relied too much on the Turks pursuing their own manifest interest ; for, if I had known the influence of their petty intrigues, I might have scattered two or three millions of francs among the counselors of Mahmoud, and have thus obtained a diversion of a hundred thousand Turks on the Dnieper. I, at one time, thought of sending the Viceroy of Italy with an army by the Illyrian provinces on Servia, in order to act in concert with that of the Turks. By this means I hoped to encourage them, and destroy the impression which had been produced by my temporary alliance with Russia. Sebastiani had negotiated, in 1807, the passage of a corps of twenty-five thousand men; but now I would have sent fifty thousand. Unfortunately times had changed, and the difficulty of arranging such an operation with these barbarians induced me to renounce a project which would have secured a powerful diversion for the invasion of Podolia.

Dispositions of the Russian Army.—If I had previously formed a definitive plan of campaign, the present dispositions of the Russians would have forced me to deviate from it, for how could I have supposed it possible that the Russian army would remain divided and scattered along their entire frontier? They had organized their forces into separate armies: The first, commanded by General Barclay, about a hundred and thirty thousand strong (exclusive of Platof's Cossacks), was cantoned behind the Niemen from Rossieny to Lida: Wittgenstein, on the right near Rossieny; Bagawouth, between Wilia and that city; Tuczkoff at Troki; the fourth corps at Olkeniki on the road to Merecz; Doctorof at Lida; the guards and reserves about Wilna; with the light troops bordering the Niemen. The second, commanded by Prince Bagration, fifty thousand strong, was cantoned in the environs of Wolkowisk, opposite the gap between the Niemen and the Bug. A third, commanded by General Tomassof, forty thousand combatants, was in rear of the Bug in the environs of Loutsk. Platof with his Cossacks was opposite Grodno. There was a great difference of opinion among the Russian generals. Admiral Tchichagof, who had succeeded Kutusof in Moldavia, had thought to penetrate by Servia and the valley of the Danube into Illyria and Italy: Prince

Bagration wished to invade the Duchy of Warsaw, dissolve the Polish army, destroy our establishments, and dispute the country between the Vistula and the Niemen : Barclay wished to await the enemy : Fuhl wished to allow us to advance into Lithuania, to fall back upon Drissa, and act on our flanks with the armies of Bagration and Tormassof, one on the Bug, and the other on the Pinsk. They were still discussing these projects when my army was collecting from all directions on the Niemen, like a threatening tempest. My forces were crossing old Prussia about the middle of June. I passed successively in review in the environs of Königsberg, Insterburg, and Gumbinnen the splendid troops which were collecting from all directions, and concentrated my principal mass on Wilkowisk and Kowno.

Organization of the Russian Army.—The following was the composition of the Russian armies in this campaign :

I. THE ARMY OF BARCLAY.

				bats.	Cossack sqds.	regts.
1st corps, commanded by *Wittgenstein;* division of Berg, Sazonof, and Kakowskoi.........				28	16	3
2d " " *Baguwouth;* divisions of Olsousief, and Prince Eugene of Wurtemberg				24	8	
3d " " *Tourzkof;* divisions of Kanownitzin and Strogonof............				26	6	
4th " " *Schouwalof* and *Osterman;* divisions of Tschaglokof and Bachmetief.....................				22	8	
5th " " *Grand-Duke Constantine;* guards and reserves, under Yermolof, Depreradowich and Galitzin.....				26	20	
6th " " *Doctorof;* divisions of Kopsewicz and Likatschef...............				24	8	
Cavalry, 1st corps under Ouwarof...................					24	
" 2d " " Korf....................					24	
" 3d " " Pahlen................,.........					24	
Platof's Cossacks...........................						14
				Total 150	138	17

Making in all about one hundred and thirty-eight thousand men, of whom eight thousand were Cossacks under Platof.

CH. XVIII.] INVASION OF RUSSIA. 343

II. ARMY OF BAGRATION.

	bats.	sqds.	regts.
7th corps under Raefsky; Paskiewicz, Kolubakin. and Wassiltchikof	24	8	
8th " Borosdin; Prince Charles of Mechlenberg, Warrusof, and Newerowski	22	20	
Cavalry, 4th corps under Siewers		24	
Cossacks			9
Total	46	52	9

This army numbered from forty-five to fifty thousand men.

III. ARMY OF TORMASSOF.

	bats.	sqds.	regts.
Corps of Kamenski; divisions of Scherbalof	18	8	
" Markof; two divisions	24	8	
" Saken; divisions of Sorokin and Laskin	12	24	
Cavalry of Lambert		36	
Cossacks			9
Total	54	76	9

Making in all about forty thousand men.

IV. ARMY OF ADMIRAL TCHICHAGOF.

	bats.	sqds.
Division of Langeron	12	8
" " Essen	12	8
" " Woinof	11	12
" " Servia	9	8
Corps of Sabaneef, in observation	9	8
Total	53	44

V. CORPS OF FINLAND, ... 16 bats. 63 sqds.

This organization was changed towards the close of the campaign. The army of Wittgenstein united to the corps of Finland, was composed of three corps, seventy-five battalions and thirty-eight squadrons; while Tchichagof's army was composed of six corps, one hundred and two battalions, and one hundred and sixteen squadrons.

French and Allied Army.—The following was the organization of the French and allied army in this campaign :

344 LIFE OF NAPOLEON. [CH. XVIII.

Old Guard under *Lefèvre*		divisions of Laborde, Curial, Raquet, Young Guard under *Mortier* and Clarapède; cavalry of Woither	40,000
1st corps under *Davoust*; divisions of Gudin, Friant, Morand, Dessaix, and Compans; cavalry of Doumerc, Castel, and Corbineau...			70,000
2d	"	"	*Oudinot*; divisions of Legrand, Verdier, and Merle; cavalry of Doumerc, Castel, and Corbineau.........	42,000
3d	"	"	*Ney*; divisions of Ledru, Rozant, Marchand, and the Wurtemburgers; cavalry of Wolworth, and Mounier	40,000
4th	"	"	The *Viceroy (Eugene)*; divisions of Broussier, Delzons, Levchi, and Pino; cavalry of Guyon.........	45,000
5th	"	(Poles), under *Poniatowski*; divisions of Zayonskeck, Donsdrowsky, and Kniasewich; cavalry of Kamensky...		35,000
6th	"	(Bavarians), under *St. Cyr*; divisions of Wrede, Deroi, and Lieben......................		22,000
7th	"	(Saxons), under *Reynier*; divisions of Lecoq, and Funk; cavalry of Gablentz		16,000
8th	"	(Westphalians), under *Junot*; divisions of Warreau and Ochs; cavalry of Wolff...........................		16,000
9th	"	under *Belluno*; divisions of Partouneaux, Daendels, and Girard; cavalry of Delaitre and Fournier..........		32,000
10th	"	"	*Macdonald*; composed of the troops of Yorck, Moessenbach, and Grandjean.............................	32,000
11th	"	(Reserve), under *Augereau*; divisions of Heudelet, Loison, Durutte, Destres, and Morand; cavalry of Cavoignac		50,000
Cavalry, 1st corps, under *Nansouty*; Bruyères, St. Germain, and Volence...			12,000
	2d	"	"	*Montbrun*: Pajol, Wathier, and Defrance.	10,000
	3d	"	"	*Grouchy*; Chartel, Doumerc, and Lahoussaye............................	7,700
	4th	"	"	*Latour-Maubourg*; Raswiecky and Lorges	8,000
Austrian Contingent under *Schwartzenberg*; Frimont, Bianchi, Siegenthal, and Trautenberg..............			32,000
		Total	509,700

These numbers exhibit the army organization, rather than
the forces which actually made the campaign. About four
hundred and eighty thousand crossed Prussia, but not more
than three hundred and forty thousand advanced on the
Dwina. Changes were also made in some of the corps:
Doumerc was detached from Grouchy to Oudinot with a
division of cuirassiers.

Napoleon determines to pierce the Enemy's Centre.—
Time is all-important in war, as is also the faculty of profit-

ing by the faults of an enemy. The Russians being divided into separate and distant corps, it seemed possible to take them *en flagrant délit*. But as they had never in their former wars followed this fatal system of extended lines of isolated bodies, I was led to believe that the extension had been made merely for the purpose of subsistence, and that they would hasten to concentrate, on the approach of our troops. When, however, I learned that nothing of this kind was done, I deemed it of the greatest importance to anticipate any such movements. I resolved to cross the Niemen at Kowno, a salient point extremely favorable to my project. It was necessary to strike quickly and promptly, without waiting for our magazines, which were coming slowly from Dantzic by the Curish Haff to Königsberg; I, therefore directed my troops to take with them provisions for fifteen days in their march across the territories of Prussia. This rigorous, but necessary measure, led to a multitude of excesses, by which Prussia most severely suffered. This country, rich in horses, was completely stripped of these animals under the pretext of transporting these provisions, the greater part of which, accumulated in immense parks, two or three days' march from the columns, could not keep pace with the troops, and fell a prey to the teamsters.

In order to derive the utmost advantage from my great superiority of forces, I formed the project of attacking the enemy along his entire front, taking care, however, to direct my principal effort upon the decisive point. For this purpose my army was divided into three grand masses. The principal one, two hundred and twenty thousand strong, under my own immediate orders, was to attack the first Russian army and pierce the centre of their line; the King of Westphalia, with sixty-five thousand men, forming my right, was to act against the army of Prince Bagration; the viceroy, with seventy thousand combatants, was to throw himself between these two Russian armies, to prevent their union; while, on the left, Macdonald, at the head of some thirty thousand men, mostly Prussians, received orders to take the road to Riga.

It was a great operation to concentrate, at the exact time and place, forces so formidable and which had been brought from Pomerania, Mayence, Paris, Boulogne, Valladolid, Milan, and even from Naples ; to form such an assemblage in the forests of the Niemen, required not a little care and foresight in directing the march of the columns, and in arranging supplies for an army whose horses alone numbered two hundred thousand, and whose carriages numbered not less than twenty thousand. We might here, without exaggeration, use the hyperbole employed to describe the army of Xerxes ; *after its passage, they endeavored to find the countries which it had passed over !*

Passage of the Niemen.—On the twenty-fourth of June, I passed the Niemen near Kowno, on three bridges constructed, in a few hours, by General Eblé ; the Russians did not oppose this passage. It would be difficult to describe my feelings at that moment. My splendid phalanxes now trod the soil of Russia, which no enemy had ventured to touch, since the time of Peter the Great, and, if the war should prove successful, all Europe would be irrevocably subject to my power ! There was something gigantic in our enterprise, which struck us all ; it was said that, like the Titans, we were going to scale the walls of Heaven ; but we were far from foreseeing that their fate was also to be ours !

I advanced on the road to Wilna and Trocki, at the head of the corps of Davoust, the cavalry of Murat, and my guards. On my right, Eugene passed to Piloni and was to direct himself on Roudnicki ; on the left, Oudinot marched by the left of the Wilia and Janowo ; he attacked, at Develtowno, the rear guard of Wittgenstein, coming from Keidoni, and took several hundred prisoners.

Retreat of the Russians on Drissa.—Barclay had collected at Wilna only two corps and the guards ; he seemed, for a moment, to wish to defend the advantageous position of Trocki, in order to concentrate the army about Wilna. But he soon saw the critical nature of his position. If he remained at Wilna, he would, with seventy thousand men, have to contend with the mass of my army ; if he joined Bagawouth and Wittgenstein on the right of the Wilia, he might be cut off on his left, which was extended to Lida ; if he fell back on the road to Polotsk, his right would be greatly exposed. He had no other course than to pass the Wilia, to burn the bridges and to destroy the magazines which had been collected at great expense, so as to gain Nementschin and march by Swenziany on Drissa, in order to rally his army there, under the protection of the intrenched camp. The left, and especially Doctorof, had to make a forced march to gain, from Lida, the road to Michaeliski, and to rejoin him, if the thing was still possible. Bagration was to march from his side on the Dwina from Slonim, by Wileika or Minsk.

I entered Wilna on the twenty-eighth of June, at the head of my guards, the cavalry and the first *corps-d'armée* ; my first attention was naturally directed to the military operations resulting from my combinations to pierce the enemy's centre, and afterward, to fall upon his wings. The King of Westphalia, who had reached Grodno, toward the end of June, followed the traces of Bagration. The viceroy, who had passed the Niemen at Piloni, being delayed by the bad roads and the difficult nature of the country, sought to gain Rondnicki. Being uncertain whether he would succeed in anticipating the enemy, I thought to make sure of this, by pushing Davoust on Minsk, with two divisions of infantry, and his light cavalry, sustained by Grouchy's corps of cavalry; he reached the road to Smolensko before the enemy. Swartzenberg, who was in the direction of Slonim, would gain the extreme left of Bagration. Murat, with two divisions of Davoust's corps and his reserve of cavalry, put himself on the traces of Barclay on Swenziany, followed by Ney. Morand's division and the corps of Nansouty, directed their march on Michaeliski, in order to form a corps intermediate between Murat and Davoust. Finally, Oudinot pursued Wittgenstein on the road to Dunaburg, and Macdonald drove the flying enemy on Mittau and Riga. My army, thus divided, pursued the enemy in every direction.

Doctorof, in seeking to gain Ozmiana, found there the light cavalry of Davoust. Being called by Barclay in the direction of Drissa, he was near falling into the midst of the columns of the King of Naples. The Russian general, however, marched with so much rapidity, that he succeeded in gaining Swir before us. The similarity of his name to that of General Dorakof, who commanded a brigade of light cavalry in the army of Bagration, deceived our columns which had been directed to intercept him. Nevertheless, it must be confessed, that he very skillfully extricated himself from his difficult situation.

When I saw the Russian armies falling back in all directions, I began to have some fears of the possibility of bringing them to a general action; still I hoped to envelope Bagration, and afterward to overthrow Barclay, if he should attempt for an instant to hold out alone. His absurd retreat on the Lower Dwina, revived my hopes; he evidently wished to manœuvre, like Benningsen in 1807; he threw himself in a false direction where I might readily find him after having destroyed his colleague. If they should both retreat to the Borysthenese, I would pursue them, and thus disengage Poland; at Smolensko, I would determine upon my subsequent operations. I had already announced my intention of halting at that place, if the enemy should escape me unhurt. I had a double motive in giving publicity to this intention— to encourage my own forces, by giving them some fixed point of termination for their severe privations, and perpetual marching, and to induce the Russians to risk a battle to prevent my thus forming a permanent establisment in the very heart of their empire.

Napoleon's Delay at Wilna.—I remained at Wilna for fifteen days ; some have regarded this delay as an error. I had sufficient motives for it. In the first place, I wished to learn the result of the operations directed against the enemy's columns on my right and against the army of Bagration ; secondly, to make arrangements for bringing up our magazines from Königsberg ; thirdly, to organize a provisional government in Lithuania ; and fourthly, to give time to the viceroy and the Bavarians to join us and put themselves in line on the Dwina.*

Our entrance into Lithuania had been attended by unfavorable circumstances ; our horses could get no other forage than green rye, and were continually exposed to the most terrible rains ; our artillery horses perished by entire teams ; one hundred pieces of cannon and five hundred caissons were left without draught-animals ; the suburbs of Wilna were encumbered with four or five thousand dead horses ! The difficulties of procuring provisions, and the disorders of a rapid passage of three hundred thousand men, had occasioned a multitude of stragglers ; these already numbered more than thirty thousand. All these circumstances rendered a short delay necessary in order to regulate affairs.

Mission of Balaschof.—A few days after our entrance into Wilna, the Emperor Alexander sent me General Balaschof,

---

* Jomini thinks there may have been other, and still more important causes for this delay, which are not known.

his aid-de-camp and minister of police, a man who had been pointed out to me as one of the warmest partisans of the English alliance. He brought the response to the advances of Lauriston. The emperor announced his disposition to adhere to the Continental System, and to arrange the other points of dispute ; but he required, as a preliminary step to any arrangement, that we should first retire behind the Niemen, being resolved to conquer or die, rather than to negotiate, so long as a foreign soldier stood upon his territory. There was certainly greatness in this resolution, at a moment when the chances appeared evidently in my favor!

Response of Napoleon.—I gave Balaschof to understand that I could not renounce the fruits of my manœuvres and go back, without some positive certainty of peace. Bagration was cut off and pursued, and I hoped to destroy him ; it was manifestly for my interest to push forward to the Dwina, where I could better discuss our affairs and require guarantees. In fact I attributed this mission of Balaschof mainly to a desire to gain time in order to unite the scattered Russian forces, and I permitted him to see that I regarded it in that light.

Some have thought that if Balaschof had arrived eight days sooner, he would have negotiated a peace ; that the Russians would have retired behind the Dwina while I remained behind the Niemen, making Wilna neutral ; that new combinations would here have been formed that would have changed the face of the world. These are mere conjectures. There is little reason to believe that the Russians would have consented to evacuate Lithuania, with four hundred thousand hostile troops on the Niemen, nor is it at all probable that Alexander and myself could have come to an understanding respecting the principal causes of our difference. The treaty of Vienna had so destroyed his confidence that my most sincere promises seemed to him mere lures, and his distrust had been still further augmented by the intrigues which I have already mentioned. Be this as it may, the return of Balaschof to Drissa, instead of tending to a pacific arrangement, became a kind of signal for an unrelenting war. Reports which reached me in my exile have led me to believe that he exaggerated to the Emperor Alexander the expressions which I used on that occasion. I do not know that these reports were well founded, but I suppose that this adventure, and the affair of Speranski, tended to fan, in the mind of Alexander, the hatred against me which influenced all his conduct, and which he was far from exhibiting after our intercourse at Tilsit and Erfuth.

The Re-establishment of Poland proclaimed. — I also received at Wilna the deputation of the kingdom of Poland. My ambassador, Pradt, had experienced very little difficulty in inducing them to the decisive step, of themselves proclaiming the restoration of their country. The Diet proclaimed the reëstablishment of the Polish Confederation; but they confined themselves to mere declarations; the provinces occupied by the Russians did not act, and they all limited themselves to the tardy levy of some Lithuanian regiments, and the sending to Wilna of an executive commission of the kingdom, for the organization of the province. I could not make a formal and definitive recognition of the kingdom without offending Austria, and without destroying the last hope of a reconciliation with Russia. I, however, promised to interest myself in its fate, when I should make a treaty of peace; it was not prudent, under the circumstances, for me to promise more, although I was determined to do every thing in my power to effect this reëstablishment.*

---

* The following is Thiers' account of Napoleon's reply to the Polish deputation at Wilna, and its effect:

"Gentlemen," he said in reply to the address of the deputation, "Gentlemen, deputies of the Confederation of Poland. I have listened with much inter-

War between England and the United States.—Another event of considerable importance occurred during my stay at Wilna,—the declaration of war between the United States

est to all that you have just addressed to me! Poles, I should have thought and acted in your place as you have done; I should have acted as you have acted in the assembly at Warsaw. The love of country is the first virtue of civilized humanity.

"In my position I have many interests to conciliate, many duties to fulfill. Had I reigned in the time of the first, the second, or the third division of Poland, I would have armed all my people in your support. As soon as victory enabled me to restore your ancient laws to your capital and a portion of your provinces, I eagerly seized the opportunity.

"I love your nation. During sixteen years I have been accustomed to see its soldiers fighting by my side, on the battle-fields of Italy and Spain.

"I applaud all that you have done; I sanction the efforts which you have made; all that I can do to second them I will do.

"If your efforts be unanimous you may well hope to succeed in compelling your enemies to recognize your rights; but in these distant and vast countries it is on the unanimous efforts of their peoples alone that such hopes of success can be founded.

"I addressed you in the same terms on my first appearance in Poland. I must add, that I have guaranteed to the Emperor of Austria the integrity of his states, and that I cannot authorize any manœuvre or movement tending to disturb him in the peaceable possession of what remains to him of the Polish provinces. But let Lithuania, Samogitia, Witebsk, Polotsk, Mohilew, Volhynia, the Ukraine, and Podolia, be animated with the same spirit which I have found to exist in Great Poland, and Providence will crown with success the sanctity of your cause, and will recompense you for that devotion to your country which renders you so interesting, and has given you so many claims upon my esteem and protection, upon which, in all circumstances, you may always rely."

This address had no particularly unfavorable effect on the Polish deputies, for they were previously aware that Napoleon entertained the sentiments which it expressed, but its effect at Wilna, in spite of the enthusiasm caused by the presence of the victorious French troops, was most disastrous.

"How can Napoleon," said the Lithuanians, "demand that we should lavish our blood, and our resources in his service, when he is unwilling on his part, to declare the reconstitution of the kingdom of Poland? And what withholds him from this course? Prussia is at his feet; Austria is dependent on his will, and might readily, moreover, be recompensed by Illyria; and Russia is already flying before his armies. Is it the truth, that he is not willing to restore us to existence as a nation? Is it the truth, that he has come here only to gain a victory over the Russians, intending then to retreat without having effected anything with regard to us, save having added half a million of Poles to the Grand Duchy, and exposed the greater number of us to exile and sequestration?" To these doubts it was replied, that Napoleon was in a

and Great Britian. Annoyed by the execution of the British Orders in Council, as well as by our system of reprisals, the United States had obtained from me a promise of withdrawing so much of the decrees of Berlin and Milan as affected the Americans; the cabinet of London refused to modify their system, and continued their hostile acts, till, at last, the Americans became indignant and, on the nineteenth of June, proclaimed war.*

If I had not already begun the war with Russia, this new event might have had a most important influence upon the destinies of the world. A ministerial revolution had already occurred in England; Perceval had been assassinated by a man partially insane, on the eleventh of May; his death did not necessarily bring with it any political combinations; but under such circumstances, it was possible that he would have been replaced by a minister less hostile to me. In fact, however, a war with the United States was not deemed of sufficient importance to counterbalance the advantages to be gained from the successes of Wellington and the war with Russia, or to incline the ambitious cabinet of London to a more pacific policy. The new ministry, at the head of which was Lord Liverpool, with Castlereagh for foreign affairs, Bathurst, Harrowby, etc., pursued the same policy as that which preceded it. Things had now gone too far to expect any change before the close of the campaign.

Operations against Bagration.—These unfruitful diplo-

---

delicate position, that it was absolutely necessary that he should act with caution, but that it was easy to see through his caution, that his real intention was to reconstitute Poland, should he be seriously aided;—that it was necessary, therefore, for the Polish people to rise *en masse*, and furnish him with the means of accomplishing the undertaking upon which he had entered. But the party which held these latter opinions was by far the least numerous, and the large body of people made Napoleon's caution an excuse for want of energy, avarice, and selfish calculations."

* The act declaring hostilities passed on the eighteenth, and the proclamation of the president was signed, on the nineteenth of June, 1812.

VOL. III.—23.

matic discussions, however, produced no influence upon military operations. The army of Barclay having taken refuge in the camp of Drissa, I directed my attention to the army of Bagration. Davoust, who was at Minsk with two divisions, would be ready to attack him in front, while the King of Westphalia, who entered Grodno the thirtieth of June, with the Poles and Westphalians, and the Saxons marching to join, making in all sixty-five thousand men, attacked him in rear, seconded by Schwartzenberg, who in reality belonged to the centre, but was now on the right, marching by Proujani on Slonim. Prince Bagration, hearing at Walkowisk of the passage of the Niemen, and the intention of concentrating the army in the environs of Wilna, at first determined to take the road to that city by Mosty, so as to act in conformity with the plan of operations formed previous to the campaign; but the order to march on the Dwina induced him to take the road to Nowogrodeck and Nicolajeff so as to gain Vileika. Davoust having already preceded him, he was obliged to fall back by Mir, whence he marched again in the direction of Minsk by Kaidanow. This was a faulty movement; for Davoust was ready to enter Minsk before him. When he learned this fact, he fell back again to the south-east, so as to reach Neswije before the Poles; he arrived there on the eighth. Jerome left Grodno on the first of July, and did not reach Bielitza till the seventh. His march was a difficult one, but unnecessarily slow. His advanced guard of Poles having passed the Niemen a second time at Bielitza, advanced on Mir, where their cavalry, on the ninth and tenth, had two engagements with Platof and Wassiltchikof, in which they fought bravely but experienced considerable loss. Davoust had reached Minsk on the eighth, but not knowing the position of the enemy he did not venture to march on Igumen, lest he might open the passage of Minsk, nor upon Kaidanow or Glutzk for fear that Bagration might take him in rear. On the eleventh of July, the latter decided to take the road to Bobrouisk, and Davoust being still at Minsk, that prince found himself relieved from his embarrassment.

Dissatisfied with the slow movements of Jerome, I ordered Davoust to take command of all his army and to march on Mohilew, which he might reach in eight days, whereas the Russians would require at least ten or twelve to arrive at the same place. Jerome received orders to push on more rapidly, while Schwartzenberg was to establish himself on the enemy's flank between Bobrouisk and Pinsk. The Saxons were deemed sufficient for observing the enemy's corps remaining at Volhynia.

But, in so vast an empire, the manœuvres of strategy are less certain than in a country hemmed in by seas or neutral territory; practicable roads run in all directions, so that our best founded hopes frequently failed. We committed some faults in this operation it is true, but then there were a thousand unforeseen obstacles which seemed to spring up to baffle our calculations. From Minsk, Davoust might hope to anticipate Bagration at Bobrouisk or at Glutzk. The first of these cities, being more distant from Bagration, was the most advantageous direction. But it was a fortress, and although singularly situated, it, on this occasion, played a most important part. The head of Bagration's column reached Glutzk on the fifteenth of July; Davoust could not anticipate him at that place without destroying the efficiency of his troops; if he had moved on without hesitation he might readily have fallen perpendicularly upon the flank of the long column of the Russians, and it is impossible to say what would have been the result. But, to have gained Glutzk, Davoust should not have remained a single day at Minsk. The marshal, however, on arriving at that city learned that Bagration had rallied the light corps of Dorokof in the direction of Kaidanow, and did not deem it prudent to leave Minsk unprotected. If he had had his whole five divisions, he would undoubtedly have marched to Glutzk with three, leaving the other two in echelon on Minsk; but the dispersion of our forces, which were sent in all directions in pursuit of the enemy, caused the failure of an operation which was much better planned than executed.

Napoleon advances on Polotsk.—The fifteen days which I had spent at Wilna, waiting for the result of my operations against Bagration, were, therefore, virtually lost; this delay, however, allowed the viceroy and the Bavarians to come into line. The former, having crossed the country between Trocki and the Niemen, directed his march on Vileika, whence he took the road to Polotsk. The Bavarians took the road to Gloubokoe. The manœuvres against Bagration no longer requiring my presence at Wilna, I determined to take command myself of the forces which were closing in on the Dwina. I consequently left Wilna on the sixteenth of July, after a sojourn which some, as has already been said, without knowing the cause of this delay, have endeavored to contrast with my activity at Ulm, Abensburg, etc. I left at Wilna the Duke of Bassano, the minister of foreign affairs, with the diplomatic agents who had followed my head-quarters. He was to watch over the relations with our allies, and the Polish authorities; he was also to serve as a medium of communication with my lieutenants who were still in rear, and to give to the administration and military operations all the vigor that could be imparted by cabinet orders. If some of my plans had failed to produce the expected results, I now hoped to indemnify myself for the loss of time.

Camp of Drissa.—The camp which the first Russian army occupied at Drissa was a manifest proof that their generals did not understand their position, and a still more positive

proof that the pretended project of Barclay to draw us into
Russia was a mere romance. My sojourn at Wilna had
unfortunately prevented me from profiting by the capital
fault of their operations. In limiting themselves to the
defense of the single road from Wilna to St. Petersburg, the
Russians had left without defense the roads that led to the
very heart of their empire. They had so little apprehension
of the danger of their eccentric manœuvre, that at the very
moment when they abandoned the centre road to Witebesk
and Borisof, they directed Prince Bagration to join them by
the road from Slonim to Drissa, by a long march which could
be executed only through the midst of our columns. Fortunately for him, he saw from the first the impossibility of
obeying this order. Not having succeeded in cutting off his
forces, I now resolved to profit by the double fault of the
enemy, by throwing myself in mass on Polotsk. After having gained the extreme left of their principal army I would
fall back on their line, which had been forced to effect a
change of front and to fight with the sea in their rear. By
gaining a single battle I would have driven them back on
Courland, forcing them to cut their way out, to lay down
their arms, or be driven into the sea. I arrived at Gloubokoe
on the eighteenth of July. I intended to march immediately
on Polotsk where I had also directed the King of Naples to
repair, defiling by his right along the Dwina.

**Alexander retires from Drissa to Moscow and St. Peters-
burg.**—There was now no apparent obstacle to the entire
success of my projects. It seemed, however, throughout the
whole of this war that all my operations were under the
spell of some evil genius, for new obstacles, entirely without
the ordinary calculations of probabilities, were continually
springing up to destroy my best conceived combinations.
Could I foresee that the Russian army would not remain
three days in a camp which had cost them several months'

work and immense sums of money? Such, however, was the fact. The Emperor Alexander, who had adopted this camp at the instance of a general ignorant of his profession, now perceived the danger of his position. He saw that two armies, so very inferior in numbers to ours, and so divided as to have no hope of a union, would be utterly incompetent to save Russia. It now appeared evident to him that this could only be effected by a general levy of the whole nation. He ordered Barclay to march on Smolensko, and to do every thing in his power to effect a junction with Bagration. The emperor himself first repaired to Polotsk, and afterward went to Moscow and St. Petersburg, to incite the nobility and the people to a general arming in defense of their country. He designated positions for vast intrenched camps, where these levies were to be assembled and organized. Considerable works were ordered for this purpose at Nijeni-Nowogorod, on the confines of Europe.

Barclay's Operations to gain Smolensko.—In accordance with the plans formed at Drissa, Barclay, having left in the environs of that city a corps of twenty-five thousand men under Count Wittgenstein, in order to cover the direct road to St. Petersburg, began his march to Smolensko, ascending the left bank of the Dwina. He had reached Polotsk when we arrived at Groubokoe. I, nevertheless, still had hopes of being able to turn his left; the least delay in his march would enable us to precede him to Witepsk. I, therefore, directed my march on that city. We reached the Dwina on the twenty-fourth of July, at Bechenkowizi. Finding here that the enemy had already passed on his way to Witepsk, I ascended the river by the left bank. I now saw little chance of interrupting him, and became fully sensible of the losses due to my unfortunate delay at Wilna. Nevertheless, in order to regain Smolensko, Barclay was obliged to pass to the left bank of the Dwina so as to reach Witepsk and the road to Roudnia. This was a hazardous operation, for, if we should arrive in time, he would be obliged to give battle with a river in his rear, as Benningsen did at Friedland. He, in consequence, hastened to direct on Bechenkowizi an advanced guard of about twelve thousand men, in order to retard our march and thus gain time to rally the corps of General Doctorof, who, being the rear guard of his army on the road to Polotsk, was still on the right bank of the river.

Combats of Ostrowno.—On the twenty-fifth and twenty-sixth, Murat had some sharp engagements with the enemy's rear-guard near Ostrowno. Murat was destitute of infantry, while the woody nature of the country favored the corps of Ostermann; some brilliant charges, however, were made to repel the attacks of the Russian columns. On the arrival of the division of Delzons, Ostermann fell back in good order. Night separated the combatants. The next day Murat renewed the attack; being seconded by the viceroy, he now hoped to be able to defeat the enemy's troops; but Barclay had reënforced them during the night by the fresh corps of Konownitzin. This combat was still more warm than the preceding; the Russians held their ground firmly; in attempting to turn them, our left was assailed by their reserve and driven back; but the right, under Roussel, having turned the enemy, Konownitzin retreated in good order, and, at Komarki, was reënforced by Touczkof, who had been sent to his assistance. These new troops again succeeded in checking the ardor of our advanced guard. Impatient at so many checks, I put myself at the head of the column and threw the fourth corps across the wood. The enemy retreated in echelon and we arrived in sight of Witepsk without further obstacle.

Barclay concentrated his army near Witepsk behind the river Louchetza, and appointed a rendezvous with Bagration near Orcha. To reach that city, it was necessary to march to the south by Babinowitchi in a line parallel to my army and with their flank exposed. The Russian general thought that it would be impossible to execute this movement without fighting, and prepared to give us battle so as to dispute the passage of the Louchetza. Fortunately for him he learned the same evening that Bagration, not being able to pierce his way to Mohilew, had marched by Mestilow on Smolensko. This incident saved Barclay a probable defeat, for he could not oppose more than eighty thousand men to my army of one hundred and twenty thousand. I myself made a reconnoisance of the enemy's position behind the Louchetza, near mid-day of the twenty-seventh; but, as it was impolitic to risk a partial engagement, the affair was postponed till the next day in order that our troops might come up. But, in the evening, Barclay received information which rendered it unnecessary for him to give battle, and he decamped during the night on Smolensko, where he was certain of effecting a junction with Bagration. His march was covered by Pahlen with the *élite* of the Russian cavalry. At the break of day on the twenty-eighth of July, the enemy had entirely disappeared and we entered Witepsk, more disgusted than ever that the Russians had again escaped us. If Barclay had injudiciously placed his army on the Niemen, and had imprudently directed his retreat on the Lower Dwina, he had certainly manœuvred with sagacity after leaving Drissa.

Operations of Bagration.—The second Russian army had also continued its retreat with more good fortune than it had reason to expect. Davoust transmitted the order to my brother, in which he was directed to assume the command; Jerome took offense at being placed under the orders of another, resigned the command of the Westphalians to General Tharreau, directed Poniatowski to obey the orders of Davoust, and left the army on the sixteenth of July. This

foolish anger tended for a moment to diminish the vigor of
our pursuit. Nevertheless, Davoust, forced to act on Orcha
on the left, and to watch the Beresina on the right, marched
with twenty thousand men on Mohilew, calling to him the
corps of Poniatowski, and directing the Westphalians to
follow alone in the trail of the enemy's columns. The Russian general, having reached Nowoy-Bichow, on the Borysthenese, by Bobrouisk, had the choice either to continue his
march on Mestilow or to attack Davoust. He had been
invited to direct his march on Orcha ; but the road to that
city passes Mohilew, and if, to avoid the hostile forces, he
had deviated from the direct road, Davoust would have
preceded him at Mestilow. He then resolved to open a
passage with the sword, and marched direct on Mohilew.

Affair of Mohilew.—Considering the disposition of the
forces it would probably have been more wise for Davoust to
move on Orcha ; but this marshal determined to give the
enemy battle, and bravely establish himself in advance of
Mohilew on the road from that city to Staro-Bichow, at the
risk of being crushed. Fortunately Prince Bagration, who
attacked him on the twenty-third, brought only one of his
corps d'armée into action, the other being still in rear. The
combat was a warm one. The position of Davoust, very
strong in front, was susceptible of being turned by his right.
The enemy, fearing, probably, to expose his communications,
preferred to take the bull by the horns. He was repelled
with considerable loss. Discouraged by this check, Bagration
fell back on Nowoy-Bichow where he crossed the Borysthenese on the twenty-sixth, and continued his march by Mestilow on Smolensko. Davoust deemed himself fortunate in
being able to sustain his position at Mohilew, and did not
venture to throw himself alone on the left of the Borysthenese. The two Russian armies had no further obstacles to

prevent their junction, which was effected on the third of August, at Smolensko.

Halt at Witepsk.—The month of July had been extremely rainy. My troops had suffered much from bad weather during their march from the Niemen to the Dwina and the Borysthenese. Our scanty supplies and coarse food had propagated diseases among the soldiers; our magazines were still on their way from Königsberg to Kowno; we were greatly in want of flour and the means of grinding it; the soldiers were obliged to subsist on boiled rye which produced horrible dysenteries. I ordered portable hand-mills to be forwarded from Paris; but these could not arrive before winter. In the mean time half of our troops were in the same situation as those of the Duke of Brunswick in Champagne. It was important to give them some repose. Having no farther hopes of cutting off Barclay, I halted at Witepsk, and my army, reënforced by the junction of the corps of Davoust, Poniatowski, and the Westphalians, was cantoned with its left at Sourage on the Dwina, the right at Mohilew on the Borysthenese, and the advanced guard at Doubrowna.

Operations of the Wings of the Army.—In opening the campaign I had supposed that our success in the centre would involve the retreat of the enemy's wings. The Russians, however, had persisted in holding firmly their ground on the two extremities of the line. Under the circumstances this was natural. Riga and the vicinity of the Baltic on Revel secured the retreat of their right. Their left, superior to us in Volhynia, had its rear free to Odessa, and was expecting to be reënforced by the entire army of Moldavia, which Tschichagof had commanded since the departure of Kutusof. We had not estimated this army at more than half its real strength, which was not less than forty thousand men. I had detached against it only the corps of the Saxons, intending to reënforce them by the Poles as soon as Schwartzenberg rejoined my army. The Poles, after assisting Davoust in the pursuit of Bagration, were to return into Volhynia by Mozyr, and, threatening the retreat of Tormasof with an army reënforced by the insurrection of the province, they would easily free our right from all apprehension in that direction. The delay of Schwartzenberg, and the operations in the centre, prevented the execution of this project, which misfortune was not the least fatal one in this campaign.

Tormassof defeats the Saxons.—On the march of the Westphalians and Schwartzenberg, Tormassof took the offensive on the rear of Jerome, by the orders of the emperor Alexander, and conformably to the plan of operations, in case of the invasion of Lithuania. The Saxons, not being in condition to oppose an efficient resistance, were attacked by Tormassof at the head of thirty-five thousand men, and an entire brigade at Kobrin was taken prisoners on the twenty-third of July. Reynier called loudly for aid, and Schwartzenberg was detached to his assistance. This prince left Nishnije on the first of August by Slonim where he met Reynier, who had easily effected his retreat.

Operations of Oudinot.—My left wing was not more fortunate: in marching on Witepsk, I had left Oudinot at Polotsk with twenty-seven or twenty-eight thousand men to secure my base against Wittgenstein, whom Barclay had left to cover the road to St. Petersburg with twenty-five thousand Russians. Oudinot advanced, on the thirtieth of July, on the road to Sebeje with two divisions, leaving the third in echelons on the Drissa. Wittgenstein not finding himself threatened by Macdonald in the direction of Donaberg, at the same time had taken the offensive against the second corps. The rencontre took place at Kliastitzi. Oudinot was driven back on the Drissa, where he rallied his forces. The Russians ventured to cross this river, on the first of August, and paid for their imprudence with the loss of a thousand men. Oudinot now committed the same error, by pursuing the enemy across the river with the division of Verdier ; he was driven back with loss. He returned to Polotsk, on the second of August, after two warm engagements in which his momentary success scarcely compensated for his losses. Deeming this marshal too weak to oppose Wittgenstein, I reënforced him with the corps of Bavarians, which famine and sickness had already reduced to twelve thousand combatants.

Turkey, Sweden, and England.—In addition to the ill-success of my military projects, I was at this time annoyed by the news of unexpected and most vexatious political events, which were calculated to have no little influence on the results of the war. While I was at Witepsk I learned that the treaty of peace between Russia and the Turks had been ratified. This was a most extraordinary error on the part of the Turks, and one which I might have prevented, had I foreseen it. The gold and intrigues which had gained the vizir at Bucharest, also triumphed over the scruples of the divan, which had at first hesitated to ratify the treaty. The Sultan had decided the question on the fourteenth of July ; afterwards seeing his error he caused the vizir and the Moruzzi to be decapitated ; but the evil was none the less irreparable for us. I also at this time received a copy of the treaty, which had been signed on the twenty-fourth of March, between Russia and Sweden. This had been kept a profound secret for two months, (till the twenty-ninth of May), after it had been signed. Bernadotte was still offering to form an alliance with me to make war against Russia. About the same time, (the eighteenth of July), Russia had signed at Orebro a treaty of alliance and subsidy with England : the latter paid a subsidy of eighteen millions, and as the invasion of the French endangered the Russian fleet if it should be frozen up in the Gulf, it was stipulated that it should be placed in depôt in one of the ports of Great Britain.

Council of War at Witepsk.—The Emperor Alexander had gone to Abo in Finland to confer with Bernadotte on the conditions of a more close alliance. He then returned to Moscow to incite the people to a levy *en masse*. All these circumstances were of a nature to convince me of the necessity of some more decisive movement. The importance of the crisis induced me to call a kind of council of war, in which the opinions of my generals were consulted. This was the first council of the kind which I had held since the battle of Castiglione. At Essling I had discussed certain questions with Massena and Davoust, but had not formally consulted them in council. I never repelled the advice of individuals; but I attached very little importance to the debates of councils. Nor did I on this occasion derive much profit from the discussions of my generals. Some wished to halt on the Dwina and the Borysthenese; others deemed it more wise to continue our operations. I was also of this opinion. To take a position between two rivers which would soon be frozen over, and expose us to the harassing attacks of the enemy's light troops was not a kind of warfare which suited my army. It was necessary to conquer a peace: this was the only favorable issue which we could hope, and this could be attained only at Moscow. At any rate the capture of Smolensko was necessary before my ulterior operations could be formed.

Barclay takes the Offensive.—The junction of the Russian armies near Smolensko had encouraged Barclay to undertake an offensive movement. The project was not without merit, but was poorly executed. Leaving Smolensko on the seventh of August for Roudnia their advanced guard of ten thousand men surprised our cavalry near Inkowo. Sebastiani saved himself by a firm stand and a well-ordered retreat. The Russians made no further serious attacks ; and it was well for them that they did not ; for a partial engagement might have brought on a general battle, as at Friedland, which was of all things what I most desired.

Napoleon marches on Smolensko.—On the fourteenth of August, I crossed the Borysthenese at Passasna and Khomino, and marched on Krasnoi. The corps which had been cantoned at Orcha and Mohilew, crossed the river at those places, and also marched on Krasnoi. I proposed to move rapidly on Smolensko, surprise that place, and take in reverse the enemy's troops which had ventured to threaten me at Roudnia. The Russian armies, being thus turned by their left would be compromised, cut off from Moscow, and thrown back on the Lower Dwina. This was the third grand manœuvre of the campaign, and was the last on our side.

A detachment of eight or nine thousand men, which the Russians had left in observation on the left bank of the Borysthenese, was driven out of Krasnoi by our advanced guard and hotly pursued toward Smolensko by my numerous cavalry. But these brave men succeeded in reaching Smolensko without being seriously cut up, although they had been obliged to leave a part of their cannon, near a thousand killed, and many wounded.

Battles of Smolensko.—The city of Smolensko, situated in amphitheatre on both banks of the Dnieper, presents a fine appearance. Its enciente, which enclosed twenty thousand inhabitants, was large enough to contain eighty thousand ; it was surrounded by a brick wall of extraordinary thickness and flanked by towers. The citadel, which formed a regular pentagon, was the weakest side, for the parapets, which were not revetted, had so fallen down as to form an accessible slope. The enciente of the city, on the contrary, being surrounded by a wall twenty-five feet high

and fifteen feet thick between the towers, was secure from
escalade and almost impregnable to field artillery. The
weak part of this enciente was secured by these same towers
which were only three or four feet thick and exposed to be
battered in breach by twelve pounders. A few yards from
the place were deep ravines which had been cut out by the
rains. The Russians directed their defense to these ravines
on the weak side of the town, rather than to the citadel;
Generals Rayewski and Paskiewicz, defended the place with
twenty thousand men.

Ney reached Smolensko on the morning of the sixteenth,
at the head of my advanced guard. I followed soon after,
and having made a reconnoisance of the weak point, I
directed Ney to make the assault. His columns advanced
with rare intrepidity; the enemy received them with admirable
coolness. Twice Ney's brave soldiers penetrated to the counterscarp of the citadel; and twice were they driven back by
the reserves of Rayewski and Paskiewicz. This resistance
gave time for two other Russian armies to come to their
assistance toward noon; my corps also came up one after
another, so that by night we had one hundred and fifty thousand men bivouacked under the walls of Smolensko. Not
having succeeded in surprising that city, I now hoped to
surround it. I directed General Guilleminot to find a passage above, in order to throw a bridge across and cut the
enemy from the road to Moscow. Junot, with the Westphalians, undertook this operation, but lost his way and
failed of success. In the mean time the combat was continued under the walls of Smolensko, but unfortunately these
operations led to no decisive results. Perhaps it would have
been difficult to force a passage, on account of the vicinity
of Bagration's army, which covered the road to Moscow;
but as it was the most feasible plan that presented itself, it
was necessary to make the attempt.

The affair of the seventeenth, was warmly contested. The Russian generals deployed their forces on the heights to the right of the Borysthenese, and sent into the city a fresh corps of thirty thousand men to relieve Rayewski; I made preparations to receive them; but seeing that they were not disposed to take the offensive, I ordered an attack. Ney directed the attack on our left against the citadel, Poniatowski on our right ascended the Dnieper, while Davoust at the centre assailed the faubourgs of Roslaw. The attack on the extremities was difficult, exposed as our men were to the hundred pieces of artillery which the enemy placed along the Dnieper. Nevertheless, Poniatowski, under the protection of our counter-batteries, succeeded in reaching the foot of a practicable breach in the walls, and Ney was again on the point of penetrating the citadel. At the centre we succeeded, after a furious combat, in dislodging Doctorof from the faubourgs; but all our efforts failed against the body of the place which the enemy defended with great obstinacy. I directed my reserve to batter in breach the curtain, but it proved a useless attempt, our balls producing no effect upon those immense walls of brick. The only means of effecting a practicable breach was to concentrate our fire upon the two round towers; but we were then ignorant of the difference in the thickness of the walls.

Barclay evacuates Smolensko.—But as our shells had set fire to a part of the town, and as the enemy had sustained considerable losses in the defense, Barclay determined to evacuate it in the night, leaving Korf to cover the retreat, which he did by increasing the fire which had been kindled by our shells.

General Review of the Results of the Campaign.—Our entrance into Smolensko was under still more discouraging presages than that into Wilna, notwithstanding the destructive storms with which the latter was accompanied

Our army had expected here to terminate their march, and they now hoped to find a fertile country and enjoy some repose. The vulgar look upon great and hazardous enterprises in different lights. My troops, astonished at the extent and difficulty of their marches, and discouraged by constantly seeing the fruit of their efforts and sacrifices escape them, began to look with disquietude upon the distance that separated them from France. As I had given them to understand that this would be my stopping-place, it was natural that they should be discouraged at seeing no prospect of their efforts terminating here. This city, towards which I had directed all my hopes, and which the Russians had regarded as the palladium of the empire, was now one vast funeral pile strewed with the dead and dying, one half of the town had been devastated by fire, for which it was difficult to assign a cause. The principal inhabitants had fled to escape the ravages of war, abandoning their effects to the imprudence of our soldiers, and the excesses of an exasperated populace. It is said that many of the inhabitants set fire to their own houses during the excitement of the assault. A city, carried, as it were, by the point of the sword, and abandoned by its own inhabitants, cannot escape pillage, and the little that was left by the enemy fell a prey to our soldiers, their appetites being sharpened by long privations. A single priest, who had remained behind through his love for his flock, showed by his answers to what a degree the people had been prejudiced against us, painting us in the blackest colors.* All the religious and patriotic passions had been

---

* This venerable man had been taught that Napoleon was a fiend incarnate, recklessly deluging the world in blood and woe. He was brought before the emperor, and in fearless tones he reproached Napoleon with the destruction of the city.

Napoleon listened to him attentively and respectfully.

"But," said he to him at last, "has your church been burned?" "No, s. e," the priest replied; "God will be more powerful than you. He will

excited against us, and it was easily seen that to the privations of Lithuania were to be added all the bitterness and rage of a national war; we were about to find here a new Spain, but a Spain without boundaries, and destitute of cities, provisions, or resources. We were not likely to encounter new Saragossas where all the buildings are constructed of wood, and at the mercy of the torch or the shell; but there were before us obstacles of another kind and not less formidable.

My heart felt oppressed when I reflected upon the interval which separated me from Moscow, and that which was likely to intervene between my magazines and my army, which sickness and want had already diminished one-third. Although I had so often announced my intention of halting here, I soon saw the inconvenience and difficulty of doing so. The harvest of 1811 had been light, and the crops of 1812, still ungathered, had been greatly injured and neglected by the ravages of war, and the flight of the inhabitants. Moreover, to subsist two hundred thousand men in a depopulated

---

protect it, for I have opened it to all the unfortunate people whom the destruction of the city has deprived of a home." "You are right," rejoined Napoleon, with emotion. "Yes! God will watch over the innocent victims of war. He will reward you for your courage. Go, worthy priest, return to your post. Had all the clergy followed your example, they had not basely betrayed the mission of peace they have received from Heaven. If they had not deserted the temples which their presence alone renders sacred, my soldiers would have spared your holy edifices. We are all Christians. Your God is our God."

Saying this Napoleon sent the priest back to his church with an escort and some succors. A shriek of terror arose from the inmates of the church when they saw the French soldiers entering. But the priest immediately quieted their alarm.

"Be not afraid," said he; "I have seen Napoleon. I have spoken to him. Oh, how have we been deceived, my children! The Emperor of France is not the man he has been represented to you. He and his soldiers worship the same God that we do. The war that he wages is not religious; it is a political quarrel with our emperor. His soldiers fight only against our soldiers. They do not slaughter, as we have been told, women and children." The priest then commenced a hymn of thanksgiving, in which they all joined with tearful eyes.

country, and in the face of a numerous and well-supplied army, is not without difficulty at any time. To retreat was now impossible: my army would have starved in crossing Lithuania, or have been swallowed up in the marshes of Prépecz; or, if directed on Warsaw, my retreat would have been the signal for the desertion of my allies, and the attack of my enemies. Prussia would have risen *en masse ;* the North of Germany would have followed her example; my whole edifice would have fallen without my having, as it were, once drawn the sword in its defense. We had not undertaken this war merely to march to Smolensko and then return to canton within the limits of the Duchy of Warsaw. To march on Moscow, to force the Russians to a battle, and to dictate peace in the ancient capital of the Czars, which was still the heart of the grand arteries of the empire,—such was the only means of safety that now remained.

I, however, still encouraged my soldiers with the hope of a near termination to their sufferings, and flattered my marshals with the idea of taking up their winter quarters between Witepsk, Smolensko and Mohilew; and I ordered the passage of the Dnieper merely to avoid the neighborhood of the enemy's army! But I gave some of my confidential friends to understand that my army was an army of operation, and not an army of position; that its composition, (being made up of twenty different peoples), and moral character required that I should maintain an active offense;—in a word, that I had no other course than to march upon Moscow. Some ultra critics and detractors have pretended to find in this conduct an unjustifiable deception and falsehood! As if a general was under obligations to make known his real intentions and designs!

My marshals were divided in opinion on this great question. Murat, who had at first accused the Russians of pusillanimity, now trembled at the danger of penetrating so far into the interior of their country. Others contended that we could hope for no repose till we had gained one decisive battle. I was also of this opinion. But how were we to obtain this battle? Certainly not by remaining at Smolensko, without provisions or other resources. There was no third choice; we must march upon Moscow, or retreat upon the Niemen.

I was not sufficiently presumptuous to suppose there were no serious difficulties to be surmounted in selecting a new objective point a hundred leagues from my natural base of operations, leaving behind me Riga and Bobrouisk, supported by the armies of Wittgenstein and Volhynia; moreover, the conclusion of peace between Russia and the Porte, would enable the army of Moldavia to ascend the Dnieper. But if the enemy still held two threatening points on my flank, I could oppose to them the armies of Macdonald, St. Cyr and Schwartzenberg. Belluno, with a fine reserve of thirty-two thousand combatants, was on the Niemen, ready to sustain my right on the Bug, or my left on the Dwina. Not only were these armies superior to the forces which the enemy could bring against them, but I had besides fifty thousand men in Prussia, and as many marching from the interior, ready to reënforce my army and replace any losses which I might sustain in battle. Never had I taken more care and foresight in preparing the means of securing the success of a great enterprise; Europe seemed to have placed her whole population in echelons toward the pole. Already the fine divisions of Loison and Durutte were guarding Königsberg and Warsaw; others were forming on the Oder; the cohorts of the first ban were collecting on the Elbe;—nothing was neglected to secure the success of the expedition.

The experience of ten campaigns had taught me what was the most decisive point; and I did not doubt but a blow struck at the heart of the Russian Empire would instantly destroy the accessory resistance of isolated corps. This blow I hoped to strike as soon as I could force the enemy to give me battle. I had a diminished force it is true, but what remained under our flags was the very *élite* of our army.

Ney crosses the Dnieper.—After having reconnoitered the smoking ruins of Smolensko, its extraordinary enciente, and its ill-planned citadel, I pressed forward our preparations for the passage of the Dnieper, the enemy having burnt the bridge. Morand's division crossed over in boats to protect the passage against the rear-guard of Barclay. Ney directed this operation, but, notwithstanding all his efforts, it was not completed till the night of the eighteenth and nineteenth. In the mean time Junot, at the head of the eighth corps, received orders to pass at my extreme right near Proudichewo. It would have been better if I had directed the main body of my army on this point, as it was the most direct line for reaching the position of the enemy.

Hazardous March of Barclay.—Before the evacuation of the city, the army of Bagration had been detached on Dorogobuje, in order to prevent our gaining the road to Moscow. Barclay himself first took the road to St. Petersburg, and then by a circuitous route regained that leading to Moscow. thus moving upon the arc of a circle of which we held the chord. The alleged motive of this *détour* was, that the direct road along the Dnieper, was exposed to our batteries. This, however, was choosing the greater of the two evils, and, to avoid exposure to our cannon, risking the destruction of their entire army. If I had known this in time, they would have paid dearly for their fault, for it exposed them in a worse position than after the retreat on Drissa and the separation of their two armies.

Pursuit of Ney and Murat.—Convinced that the Russians were not disposed to give us battle, I satisfied myself with sending in pursuit of their rear-guard, Murat and Ney, seconded by Junot, who crossed the river higher up, so as to manœuvre on their left. Ney crossed the Dnieper at four o'clock on the morning of the nineteenth, amid the flames of the faubourg of Smolensko. The army of Barclay was first seen encamped on the heights of the road to St. Petersburg, and his rear-guard under General Korf was still there. We hoped for a moment to cut him off from the road to Moscow, and drive him back to the north; but some of the enemy's troops were seen in that direction. Ney and Murat were ordered to examine these two roads. Grouchy at first took the direction of Doukowtschina. Our columns of the left now observed a division of infantry in an intermediate position near the Stabna. Ney immediately ordered it to be attacked. This was unfortunate; for, if he had marched directly to Loubino on the road to Moscow, we should have reached that place as soon as the enemy, and have engaged the Russians while they were making an extended flank movement.

Barclay now saw the perilous nature of his manœuvre, and directed Touczkof to march with a division of infantry in all haste to the assistance of the Cossacks who covered the road to Moscow; he placed Prince Eugene of Wurtemberg at Gredeonowo, to flank the march of the nearest column, and to give the rear guard of Korf time to reach Gorbounowo and Loubino. The first column of the army, under Bagawouth, was also directed upon the same point. It was this division of Eugene that Ney first encountered and vigorously attacked. It was about to fall under our blows, when twenty squadrons came to its assistance. Reënforced still further by a part of the column of Korf, it succeeded in reaching Gorbounowo, after having for three hours lost sight of the most important point on the road to Moscow. Ney followed in pursuit, taking five or six hundred prisoners of the rear-guard of Korf, and their cannon; it was relieved by

Potemkin, who arrived just in time to save the rear of their columns.

Battle of Valoutina.—In the mean time Touczkof had reached the heights of Valoutina, and formed a junction with the Cossacks of Karpof. Ney, who had been drawn too far to the left by the combats of Staba and Gedeonowo, now received orders to incline further to the right, and soon arrived in presence of the enemy. A furious combat was engaged near Kosina. As soon as I learned the retreat of the Prince of Wurtemberg and Korf, I returned to Smolensko, thinking to push forward Davoust to the assistance of Murat and Ney. The latter, though now left alone, nevertheless, pressed Touczkof with vigor; but this general defended his ground inch by inch to the rear of the creek of Strachan, where the *corps-d'armée* of his brother and the cavalry of Orlof-Denisof came to his aid.* The Russians, feeling that the safety of the army depended upon the defense of this position, fought with desperation. An hour sooner, and with a few divisions more, Ney would have cut the enemy in two and decided the success of the campaign. It was, however, the last time that such an advantage presented itself.

Far from expecting so serious a combat, I had gone back to Smolensko, when Barclay returned with his third and fourth corps of infantry and his first corps of cavalry. Ney did every thing which heroism could do under such circumstances, and both parties may well boast of the courage displayed on that occasion. Murat was so embarrassed on the right and left by the wood and marshes, that he could not manœuvre his cavalry to advantage. Orlof-Denisof showed, on this occasion, as much firmness as the king of Naples displayed activity and bravery. Not being able to penetrate

* Major General Touczkof commanded the rear-guard, while his brother, Lieutenant General Touczkof, commanded the third *corps-d'armée*.

in advance of Latichino against the left of the Russians, Murat hoped to be more successful with the troops of Junot, and moved in that direction. He first charged with his advanced guard, then returned to his reserve ; but Junot remained stationary between the woods and the Dnieper only a few hundred yards from the enemy's left ; he seemed paralyzed by the delicate nature of his position, or what is more probable, had partially lost his mind.

The division of Gudin, of Davoust's corps, which had been sent to the assistance of Ney, arrived about five o'clock, and the marshal immediately renewed his efforts to carry the heights of Kosina. The enemy was repulsed, his centre pierced, and his whole line on the point of being driven into the muddy stream of Samile when Konownitzin, arriving with a division of infantry, several battalions of grenadiers, and three thousand horse, restored the equilibrium. Gudin being killed by a cannon ball, his division was repelled notwithstanding its prodigies of valor.

At dark the Russian corps of battle was rejoined by the columns of Bagawouth and Korf ; ignorant of this circumstance, our people renewed their efforts to carry the position. The division of Gudin crossed the Strachan, and crowned the heights ; but as it had fallen into the midst of the enemy's columns, it was driven back, notwithstanding the most glorious efforts. Night separated the combatants who disputed the honor of this vast field of carnage, covered with twelve or thirteen thousand killed or wounded, of which each party might claim an equal number. To this deplorable and almost useless loss was to be added the death of the lamented Gudin. This brave and skillful general, who had well deserved a marshal's baton, perished a victim to the fatality which seemed to preside over the fortunes of the day. Although this affair had taken place contrary to my expectations, and contrary to all probabilities, he at least was free from reproach. Notwithstanding the false direction of our first movements we could have gained important results, if Junot had acted with vigor. This conduct was probably a prelude to the mental alienation with which he was affected after the retreat. His character from this time seemed strange and changeable ; he never possessed great merit, but heretofore he had displayed an energy almost bordering on rashness. Murat was not entirely free from reproach ; his cavalry might have acted with more vigor on the Cossacks of Karpof and the little rear guard of Touczkof ; he should also have thrown a part of this cavalry with Junot on Proudichewo, on the night of the eighteenth.

Retreat of the Russians.—Learning at midnight, on the return of my aid-de-camp, Gourgaud, the state of the battle which my generals were fighting without my knowledge, I immediately mounted my horse, and at three o'clock was on the field of combat. But everything was ours and the enemy in retreat. Seeing the proofs of the efforts of my brave men in the bloody and mangled bodies which covered the field, I lavished on them praises and rewards, and returned to Smolensko, my heart being sad at having allowed so fine an opportunity to escape me. My first impulse was to severely reprimand Junot, and to replace him in the command by Rapp ; but feelings of kindness toward this old companion in arms induced me to forgive him.

The king of Naples, on the twentieth of August, pursued the enemy on Dorogobouje ; as Ney's corps had greatly suffered in the battle, and as its chief had not been on good terms with my brother-in-law since their quarrel before Ulm in 1805, I caused it to be replaced by the corps of Davoust ; unfortunately Murat was on no better terms with Davoust than with Ney.

Reflections of Napoleon on his Position.—On my return to Smolensko from the camp of Ney, on the twentieth, my mind was filled with sadness. The useless results of three bloody battles, the ruins of Smolensko, the reduced and impoverished state of our battalions and our squadrons,—were all calculated to produce sad and melancholy reflections. To supply the wants of our men, I ordered administrative establishments to be formed ; and directed an intelligent officer with a body of light troops to explore the fertile banks of the Kmora, celebrated for its mills and extensive trade in flour. He was directed to collect provisions sufficient for the troops on the return of our columns, which had to make but one more effort to cover their asylum.

Battle of Gorodeczno.—After my arrival at Smolensko the affairs on the wings of my army took a more favorable turn. Conformably to my orders, Schwartzenberg had been charged with the general command in the south against Tormassof, whom he encountered on the twelfth of August at Gorodeczno. The Russian general had so scattered his forces that he had not more than twenty-five thousand men in line, while the Austrians and Saxons numbered about forty thousand combatants. But Schwartzenberg failed to profit either by the superiority of his own forces, or the bad position of the enemy : yielding to the advice of Reynier he manœuvred to turn the left wing of the Russians with his Saxons. But he failed to sustain them with sufficient vigor, and the enemy had time to oppose a parallel manœuvre, although obliged to give battle with his left completely turned. Tormassof escaped with considerable loss, and continued his retreat by Kobrin and Kowel on Loutsk behind the Styr. Schwartzenberg and Reynier established themselves opposite his position on the other side of that river.

Affairs of Polotsk.—My left had also been successful, but had derived no advantages from their success. Certain of being soon reënforced by the Bavarians, Oudinot had again marched on Swolna to drive the enemy from the Dwina, and prevent him from again troubling Polotsk. This was manifestly imprudent, for Wittgenstein was disposed to pursue the offensive, and would be prepared to meet him before the Bavarians could come to his aid ; which was actually the case. The advanced guard of Oudinot, being attacked on the Swolna, the twelfth of August, and receiving a check, the main body fell back on the plain of Polotsk, and formed a junction with the Bavarians. Ignorant of this reënforcement, Wittgenstein continued to advance, and, deploying his twenty-four thousand men, hoped to pierce our centre by directing his principal effort along the ravine of the Polota. The combat took place on the seventeenth, but had no other result than the mutual loss of two thousand men. Oudinot being wounded, the command devolved on St. Cyr.

The Russian general now saw that he had to contend with a superior force, but fearing to fall back lest his retreat might become disastrous, he thought to impose on us by a firm countenance. St. Cyr determined to attack him the next day, and concentrated his principal efforts towards Spass against the Russian left and centre. The Bavarians and Legrand's division, concentrated about Spass, overthrew every opposition, and penetrated to Presmenistza, notwithstanding the strong resistance of the enemy, and the destructive fire of the Russian artillery. Wittgenstein's reserve finally arrested their impetuous advance, while the audacious charges of his cavalry drove ours back to the very faubourg of Polotsk : St. Cyr himself was obliged to take shelter in a ravine. His reserves finally disengaged his cavalry, and the combat ended in the position which the enemy's reserve had occupied in the morning. The Russian general retired during the night on Gomselewo.

Ten pieces of artillery and a thousand prisoners were the only trophies of this battle ; our inferiority in cavalry had prevented us from profiting by our success. St. Cyr had left

Merle's division inactive on the left of the Polota ; if he had directed it so as to take Wittgenstein's line in reverse, the victory would have been more easily gained and more complete. Nevertheless it was a success, and the baton of marshal was given to St. Cyr, who had already deserved this honor. The brave General Deroy had been slain in battle. I assigned his family, from my private purse, a pension of twenty thousand francs, and dotations ; thus, at the same time repaying a debt of gratitude to a good ally, and stimulating the zeal of those who had reluctantly espoused our cause.

Napoleon determines to advance.—The successes of Gorodeczno and Polotsk, had given temporary security to my wings. My right, however, was still seriously threatened by the army of Moldavia. In an extensive country like Russia where there is so great a space for the manœuvres of armies, the accessories may become principals, and the operations of lateral corps may seriously endanger the communications of the main army ; and especially in this case, as we had but a single line of communication while the enemy had for his base the whole width of Europe from the Baltic to the Black Sea.

The tranquil state of affairs on my wings, and the reports of my lieutenants, now determined me to advance ; they announced to me that it was not impossible to bring the enemy to a battle. The king of Naples had found the Russians formed behind the Loujea, and had no doubt but they wished to accept battle. Barclay had, in fact, that intention. Informed of this circumstance on the night of the twenty-fourth, I immediately departed at the head of my guards who marched twelve leagues with the utmost rapidity, in hopes of finally reaching an enemy who was continually escaping us, as if by enchantment. Without attempting to turn the enemy's position, Murat had thrown the cavalry of

Montbrun against his left; but Davoust, being weak in infantry, had no desire for a general engagement against an entire army. The disagreement of my generals thus prevented the attack. The movement of Montbrun, however, had alarmed the Russian generals, who were fearful of being assailed on their left and driven back on the Dnieper; which certainly would have been the case, had they remained in position. Barclay, therefore, renounced his perilous plan, and abandoned Dorogobuje just as I was coming up to give him battle.

The viceroy followed in the direction of St. Petersburg as far as Doukhowschina, then returned into line, leaving one division at Sourage, where General Wintzingerode with a flying corps, was threatening our communication with Witepsk.

When I reached the head-quarters of Murat I found that the enemy had disappeared from the banks of the Lougea, and discord reigning in our camp. Murat complained that Davoust had failed to engage his infantry, and the marshal replied that false representations had been made to me. I gave Murat the direct command of Campan's division which had previously been refused him. As it was supposed that the enemy would make a stand on the Osma, we followed in the pursuit; he evacuated Dorogobuje and reached Wiasma.

We were now so near Moscow that there was no further reason for hesitation. We were still distant eight days' march, it is true, but what was a march of eight days for men who had come from the extremities of Europe? The motives which might have kept us at Witepsk or Smolensko, had disappeared, for we had already passed over half of the distance that separated us from Moscow. To diminish the chances of this advance, I had directed Belluno to advance from the Niemen, so as to replace my army at Smolensko. Augereau was to carry half of his divisions on Königsberg and Warsaw. Belluno's reserve of thirty-two thousand men, established between Roslau and Witepsk, might either act on the wings or reënforce the main army, as circumstances should require.

The Russians, however, continued their retreat on Giatz. At Posen their rear guard made a firm stand against the forces of Murat and Davoust. It must, however, be remembered that the generals did not agree, and that our horses were too weak to oppose the cavalry of the enemy. With no other food than coarse rye straw, they had been compelled to perform the most difficult and harassing duty. Always acting in mass on the great roads, and checked at every stream, wood, bridge or defile, our squadrons, exposed to the fire of the enemy's batteries, were obliged to hold out till the infantry could come to their assistance, when the enemy would retire. Being again pursued by our horse, he would turn upon the heads of columns, till they were disengaged by the infantry. In the pursuit of an enemy, the cavalry is obliged to perform the most incessant and fatiguing duty.

Character of the Country.—But the ordinary difficulties of a pursuit were here greatly augmented by the hostile character of the inhabitants. After leaving Smolensko we saw alarming symptoms that the war was becoming national. The most formidable army can, with difficulty, sustain itself when the whole population of the country resolve to conquer or die. We now saw no more Lithuanians, immovable spectators of the great events which were passing around them. The entire population, composed of real Russians, deserted their homes at our approach. Everywhere on our march, we found the villages deserted or burned; the inhabitants formed into bands to cut off our foraging parties; every thing seemed quiet, but every where our stragglers were cut off or massacred. The city of Wiasma was burned, with its rich magazines; Giatz experienced the same fate; and if any thing was left undestroyed, it was due to our van-guards, who frequently fought the enemy with one hand, while they extinguished the flames of their burning towns with the other.

New Generalissimo of the Russian Army.—At Giatz I learned that the Russian army had changed its chief, and was now preparing to give me battle. Public opinion having attributed the misfortunes of the war to a bad choice of generals, the Emperor Alexander had conferred the supreme command upon General Kutusof, the conqueror of the Turks. The Prussian Pfuhl was accused of being the cause of the first misfortunes of the campaign, and even Barclay was reproached with his foreign origin, and his numerous retreats rendered him an object of suspicion to the pure Muscovites. All seemed agreed that the conqueror of Roudschouck and the negotiator of Bucharest was capable of rescuing them from peril : in their opinion, none but a Russian could now save the country. The new generalissimo thought, that to preserve his reputation in the army and with the people it would be necessary to give us battle before we could reach Moscow, and he determined to make a stand in the strong position which he occupied near Borodino in front of Mojaisk, where he had been joined by ten thousand of the newly organized militia of Moscow.

Preparations for Battle.—The two armies arrived opposite each other the fifth of September. The enemy had constructed a redoubt in front of his left, near the village of Schwardino, to defend the access to the most exposed part of his position. As it was important to carry this advanced post before assailing the main position, I directed it to be attacked by the division of Campans, who carried it in the most brilliant manner. The next day was employed in reconnoitering the enemy's line, and in examining the ground on which we were to operate. On both sides preparations were making for a decisive battle. The Russians mingled with their military preparations the ceremonies of the Greek Church, and invoked divine assistance to save their country. We collected our scattered forces, concentrated our masses, and prepared our arms and parks of artillery. Our numerical forces were nearly equal, being about one hundred and twenty-five or one hundred thirty thousand on each side. We had about fifteen thousand veterans against an equal number of Cossacks and militia, but they, on the other hand, fought in defense of a city and in a fortified position, and on ground with which they were better acquainted than our forces. Three flèches covered their left towards Semenofskoe, a large bastioned redoubt was traced near the centre on the height between that village and Borodino; while several redans covered the right towards the river Moscowa; they had not yet had time to palisade these works.

The battle took place on the seventh. I have fought many battles in my life, but I have never seen one as terrible as this. It was an extraordinary contest in several respects :— from the nature of the enterprise which it was to terminate, from the greatness of the interests which were involved, and from the singular circumstances which marked the shock of such immense masses, in so narrow a space.

Position of the Russians.— The enemy's position as I reconnoitred it, was as follows : Barclay with three corps of infantry and one of cavalry, formed the right from the great bastioned redoubt to the Moscowa; it was separated into two parts by the ravine of Gorki. Bagration, with the seventh and eighth corps, formed the left from the great redoubt to the coppice-wood between Semenofskoe and Oustiza. This position was defective. The fault was attributed to General Benningsen who was then acting as chief of staff. He had directed his attention too much to the right, which I had no interest or desire to attack. The left, on the contrary, was not so well placed, although covered by three flèches; between them and the old road to Moscow, was an interval of five hundred toises secured only by some chasseurs.

Plan of Attack.—If things had remained in this condition, it was not difficult to anticipate the result. But in the evening the Russian generals moved the entire corps of Touczkof to prolong the left to Oustiza, on the old road to Moscow; we, however, saw only its advanced posts. My dispositions were soon arranged. I resolved to gain the old road to Moscow by my extreme right under Poniatowski, to force the enemy's left with Davoust and Ney, and thus throw their centre and right into the Moscowa, while the viceroy held in check that portion of their line. It was nearly the same disposition of our masses as that made at Friedland, except that in that battle the river was in the enemy's rear, while at Borodino the Russians had in their rear a favorable ground for retreat, the obstacle being on their extreme right.

Unfortunately all my plan could not be executed as I desired; and the enemy made a timely modification in his dispositions. I also changed my intention respecting the destination of the viceroy, to whom I gave a more active part, directing him to attack the centre of the enemy, and at the same time to cover with his left the great road from Giatz to Moscow. For this purpose I reënforced him with two divisions of Davoust's corps. But this marshal wished me to leave him his whole five divisions, and to charge him with a decisive movement by the old road and the coppice-wood; thus turning the position of the Russians before attacking their flèches, and beginning the battle by establishing himself perpendicularly on their extremity. The idea was excellent; but it was to be feared that the Russians might take the alarm at seeing themselves thus threatened, and again disappear on the road to Mojaisk, which would have indefinitely postponed the decisive battle which we so much desired. I, therefore, preferred to attack their line in echelons by the right; this did not promise so easy a success, but it was less likely to cause a postponement of the battle. The corps of Poniatowski was sufficient to manœuvre so as to turn the enemy's left, and secure our superiority in that direction. Having formed my plan, I disposed my masses so as not to attract too much the enemy's attention. Each one received his special instructions. The artillery was to prepare its fire for an early hour, and the hundred pieces of Davoust, Ney, and the guard, were directed to advance at the break of day so as to destroy with their shells and balls the works which were to be attacked by my right.

On the morning of the seventh, I waited with anxiety to learn what the enemy had done during the night. At five o'clock, Ney informed me that the entire army of the Russians were still in position, and the French Achilles, burning with impatience, asked permission to begin the attack. All now flew to arms, and each one took his allotted part in the great contest which was now to decide the fate of Europe. Our batteries advanced into line so as to be within reach of those of the enemy. Campans, who had given so fine a prelude to the battle, by taking the redoubt of Schevardino, was now to begin the battle by carrying the flèche which formed the extreme right of the Russians; he was to creep along the coppice-wood, while Dessaix seconded his operation by marching through the woods. Friant's division was to remain in reserve. As soon as Davoust became master of the redoubt, Ney was to advance in echelons on Semenofskoe; his divisions, having suffered much at Valoutina, now numbered scarcely fifteen thousand combatants; ten thousand Westphalians were to reënforce Ney's corps and form his second line. The Young and Old Guards formed the third and fourth lines. Murat divided his cavalry. Montbrun's corps was opposite the enemy's centre and at the left of Ney ; Nansouty and Latour-Maubourg placed themselves so as to follow the movement of our right; while Grouchy was to assist the viceroy. The latter, reënforced by the divisions of Morand and Gerard from Davoust's corps, was to attack the village of Borodino on the great road to Moscow, and on the left bank of the Kolocza ; the division of Delzons was to establish itself there, while the three others were to cross the Kolocza on three bridges constructed for that purpose in the morning, and attack the grand redoubt of the centre.

The first disposition was the cause of the undecisive turn of the battle. It was necessary to throw Davoust with four of his divisions into the gap between the redoubt of the left and the woods of Oustiza, to follow up his movement by Murat with his cavalry, and support him by Ney and the Westphalians directed on Semenofskoe, while the Young Guard marched in echelons at the centre of the two attacks, and Poniatowski, connected with Davoust, turned the right of Touczkof in the woods of Oustiza. In this way we would have broken and turned the enemy's left with an irresistible mass, and forced a change of front parallel to the great road to Moscow, with the river Moscowa in the enemy's rear. There were in this gap only four feeble regiments of chasseurs ambushed in the coppice-wood, so that the success of the operation was scarcely doubtful.

Battle of Borodino, or of the Moscowa.—At six o'clock the signal of attack is given. The artillery directs its thunders upon the flèches. Davoust rushes forward with his two divisions. The brigade of Plausonne on Eugene's left, which was merely to occupy Borodino and remain in observation, carried away by an ill-directed zeal, goes beyond the village and debouches against the entire corps of Doctorof, who drives it back with loss. Plausonne falls a victim of the ardor of his battalions, and Delzons at last succeeds in disputing Borodino with the superior forces which the enemy concentrated on that point.

In attacking with the first echelon Woronzof's division of grenadiers in a post covered by intrenchments, Davoust is assailed in flank by the chasseurs just mentioned, and suffers severely ; Campans' division, however, carries the redan of the extreme left with rare courage. This brave general is wounded ; and Davoust himself has his horse killed under him, and receives a severe contusion. Dessaix, who has replaced Campans, is also put *hors-de-combat*. Rapp now takes command of this division, which has three times lost its chief. Nor have the Russians suffered less than the French ; Woronzof is wounded and the work carried. But our success is not of long duration. The enemy, under the protection of his batteries, advances the infantry of his second line (Neweroswki's division), and our troops are compelled to evacuate the work which they had but just carried. Bagration now sees his danger and calls in all haste Konownitzin's division from the corps of Touczkof. A division of cuirassiers and a brigade of the Young Guard come from the reserve to sustain the threatened flank.

But this momentary *contre-temps* is soon repaired ; Ney, arriving in echelons, rushes at the head of Ledru's division on the same redoubt, and enters it on the left at the same time that Campans' troops return by the right. The enemy still holds the third flèche, which Ney and Murat attack with the division of Razout. These troops are on the point of carrying the work when they are charged upon by the Russian cuirassiers. There is a moment of uncertainty ; at length our infantry hold firm, and give the cavalry of Bruyères time to disengage Razout's division which, animated by Murat, rush again upon the intrenchments and carry them.

More than two hours have been consumed in these attacks.

Kutusof, who easily discovered our heavy masses ready to fall upon his left, had time to direct a part of his right to sustain the threatened point. At nine o'clock the corps of Bagawouth sent by Barclay, had already passed the heights of Semenofskoe. One of his divisions marches to Oustiza, and the other throws itself into the coppice-wood.

On our side, Junot had just deployed in rear of Ney, and engaged his first line, when the impetuous marshal throws upon the enemy the right of his own troops. To act still more efficaciously, by turning the position which the Russians disputed with so much obstinacy, the second line of Westphalians receive orders to support the right and penetrate the coppice-wood between Davoust and Poniatowski. If this movement had been executed an hour earlier, it would have been decisive; but now Galitzin's reserve of cavalry had time to dispute with the Westphalians the plain where they were to debouch, and the arrival of Bagawouth's corps enabled Eugene of Wurtemberg's division to drive into the woods the column of the Westphalians. Galitzin's cavalry profited by this opportunity to make a fine charge against our right. It had even got possession of a battery of the reserve, when a brave infantry regiment of Dessaix's division, (the eleventh) debouched from the woods, took these audacious cuirassiers in reverse, and forced them to charge in rear in order to open to themselves a passage by which to escape, thus saving our artillery.

Bagration now felt the necessity of giving the reënforcements drawn from the right time to reach their destination, thinking that the battle depended upon the resistance which he might oppose to us. He threw himself on Ney at the head of a division of grenadiers of the prince of Mecklenburg, sustained by a brigade of guards, and eight regiments of cuirassiers; the remains of the commands of Woronzof and Neweroswki, supported by a division of light cavalry, assisted this effort, by attacking Davoust. The whole line of the enemy renewed the attack ; one of the redoubts was retaken, and Murat himself was forced to take refuge in the division of Razout.

Ney now advances at the head of his reserves ; Friant's division receives orders to support the left of Razout by marching on the village of Semenofskoe ; the lost redoubt is retaken ; Friant crosses the ravine of Semenofskoe, and carries the village. Konownitzin's division, which has just arrived from the extreme left, now checks Friant, and obliges him to return to the height of the redoubts, where Ney is still advancing.

Masters of the flèches, but threatened by the attitude of Bagration, who continues to receive reënforcements from the right, Ney and Davoust prepare to drive him behind the ravine of Semenofskoe ; they are supported by all the disposable artillery, and the viceroy also prepares to assist them by attacking the centre.

Nothing can arrest the impetuosity of Ney ; Bagration, fearing to be pierced, throws himself at the head of his lines, who with the bayonet hope to regain the offensive. A terrible melée ensues ; Bagration is seriously wounded, and also his chief of staff, St. Priest ; the Russian troops, deprived of their chiefs, are on the point of being entirely defeated, when the impassible Konownitzin takes the command, rallies them behind the ravine of Semenofskoe, and, under the protection of a well-placed artillery, succeeds in arresting the advance of our columns.

It is now necessary to render these advantages decisive : Murat throws the corps of Nansouty and Latour-Maubourg beyond the ravine ; the first falls upon the extreme left of Konownitzin, where the regiments of the guards of Ismail and Lithuania, formed into squares, receive him with firmness, and give to the five regiments of Russian cuirassiers time to fall upon our fatigued squadrons, and to drive them back behind the ravine. Latour-Maubourg was equally successful near Semenofskoe, where the infantry of Friant and Ney make a firm stand. The enemy, convinced of the impossibility of retaking these positions, nevertheless remain in heavy masses under the fire of our artillery with an admirable constancy. It was easy to see that these brave men had resolved not to survive the misfortunes of their country.

In the mean time the viceroy, after having been held in suspense by the attack of Delzons' division on Borodino, by their inconsiderate passage of this defile, and by the obstacles presented by the Kolocza, had crossed that river upon four small bridges constructed by the engineers. Eugene hastened to oblique to the right in order to carry the great bastioned redoubt which had been erected between Borodino and Semenofskoe to cover the enemy's centre. Morand's division having debouched first on the plateau, threw the thirtieth regiment on this redoubt, and advanced with a deep column to second the attack. These brave men marched steadily to their object without noticing the terrible fire of the enemy; they penetrated into the redoubt notwithstanding the efforts of the first line of Paskiewitsch; but, being prepared for this event, that officer now advances at the head of his second line, upon the flank of our deep column, and also charges it with his first line faced to the rear. Jermolof seconded this attack with a brigade of the guards.

Exposed at the same time to the artillery of Doctorof, and assailed on the right by Wassiltschikof, Morand is forced to return into the ravine. Bonomi, who is left in the redoubt, is too weak to defend it. He falls pierced with wounds, with a part of the thirtieth regiment which had so bravely taken the place. These two efforts on the left not being properly sustained, and not taking place at the same time, rather tend to encourage the Russians, and to dampen the ardor of our troops. The offensive movement of Jermolof, Paskiewitsch, and Wassiltschikof is near causing the evacuation of Semenofskoe; but this is fortunately arrested by the batteries of the reserve being timely placed in rear of that village.

In the mean time the combat was continued with great success on the old road to Moscow. I had expected that Poniatowski would be able to manœuvre without great difficulty so as to turn the enemy; he, however, encountered considerable difficulties. Favored by the departure of Konownitzin's division, and by the efforts of the Westphalians, he charged the right and carried the little hill which commanded it; Tousczkof with a part of Bagawouth's corps soon retook this important post, and paid for this momentary success with his life.

The vigorous attacks of Ney, and the admirable charges of our cavalry, had now produced the desired effect. Ney and Davoust had solidly established themselves on these intrenched heights which had been occupied by the enemy's left at the beginning of the battle: but apart from these advantages, and the possession of the smoking ruins of Semenofskoe, we had no trophies. It was now eleven o'clock. Ney loudly called for reënforcements to complete his victory. It seemed to him more easy to seek new victories, than to remain exposed to the fire of two hundred cannon which were sending death into his ranks. Perhaps the favorable moment had already passed, for the enemy had not only drawn Bagawouth from the banks of the Moscowa to the extreme left, but had brought up the fresh corps of Ostermann to sustain the centre which had been so broken by the attack of Eugene.

I, however, was about to order a new effort to be made, with the assistance of two divisions of the guard, and three of Eugene's divisions, when a tumultuous cry on the road of Borodino indicated that a grand attack was being made against the viceroy. I, therefore, suspended the departure of my guard, and rejoiced that I had done so when I found that Eugene had just repassed to the left of the Kolocza with the Italian guard. As this movement threatened our line of retreat, I resolved to wait till I could ascertain more definitively the state of affairs, and sent Claparede's division to a position where they might be able to act as occasion should require. I soon learned, however, that it was a mere skirmish of cavalry made by Ouvarof's corps, and some of Platof's Cossacks on Ornano's brigade, and the division of Delzons, which received the enemy in squares, and rendered ineffectual their ill-directed efforts. Nevertheless, this incident kept us more than an hour in suspense, and enabled the enemy in the interval to rectify his position, so that it in reality contributed not a little to the ill-success of the battle.

As soon as I was assured of what was passing, everything was disposed for renewing an attack upon the great battery of the centre, at the same time that my right debouched in advance of Semenofskoe. The Russians perceive from the dispositions of the viceroy, Murat, and Ney the storm which is gathering, and relieve the broken corps of Rajefski by that of Ostermann, which enters into the first line, with its left in the direction of Semenofskoe, and its right resting on the great road. My generals mistake this manœuvre for an offensive operation; Murat and Sorbier concentrate on these columns an enormous mass of artillery which causes great havoc in their ranks: but they remain firm and immovable under this terrible fire. Their whole artillery responds to ours; Doctorof, Barclay, and Jermolof direct their fire upon the divisions of the viceroy, which shows the same firm attitude. The fire is general from Borodino to Semenofskoe, and even to the woods. Eight hundred pieces of cannon are uttering their thunders within the space of half a league, and scattering death in all directions. Never was there a spectacle at the same time so imposing and so terrible. All the actors in this grand drama proclaim it, with one accord, *the battle of the giants!*

At the moment when every thing is ready for a general attack, Montbrun, whose corps was placed directly opposite the enemy's centre, is killed by a cannon ball; I order Caulaincourt* to fly to his place and charge the great redoubt, which the viceroy is about to attack with the divisions of Morand, Gerard and Broussier, reënforced by the legion of Vistula. It is now two o'clock. The enemy has had time to complete the movement of Count Ostermann whom Milordowitsch has brought from the right wing, and who is sustained by the second and third corps of cavalry; the shock is terrible.

Caulaincourt, notwithstanding the difficulties encountered, executes his commission with great courage. After having driven off a part of the enemy's infantry, he rushes on the redoubt in spite of the battalions which surround it, and penetrates to the interior with the fifth cuirassiers. But he is killed, and his brave men exposed to the fire of Ostermann's infantry, and the old Russian guard in rear of the work, and threatened by Korf and Pahlen's cavalry, are forced to reform under the protection of the infantry. But a few moments after, the columns of the viceroy again assailed the twice conquered redoubt, now occupied by Lichatschef's infantry (of Doctorof's corps), and captured the place for the third time, taking Lichatschef prisoner. He was about to throw Grouchy's corps forward upon the bat-

* This was Count Augustus Caulaincourt, brother of the Duke of Vicenza. He was the first to surmount the parapet of the redoubt. At that moment a musket ball struck him dead. He had scarcely left the side of the emperor with orders to charge the redoubt, when intelligence of his death was brought to head-quarters, where his brother, the duke, was talking with Napoleon. The scene was most affecting, young Caulaincourt being greatly beloved by all.

talions of Doctorof, when the *élite* of the enemy's cavalry advanced against ours and held them in check long enough to allow Korf and Pahlen's corps to return from Caulaincourt to their assistance, and thus caused Grouchy to rejoin his infantry.

It was now three o'clock. We were at last masters of the great redoubt of the centre and of the flêches of the left ; nevertheless, the Russians formed again behind the two ravines of Goristskoe and Semenofskoe, and continued an obstinate resistance. Wearied with the carnage, both parties limited themselves to a cannonade without renewing the attack.

During these murderous shocks the Poles were not idle. Encouraged by the success of Ney and Davoust, Poniatowski had again attacked the little hill behind Ouslitza ; seeing himself also threatened by the Westphalians, Bagawouth, who now commanded at this point, deemed it prudent to abandon the place and form into line with the remains of Bagration's corps, near the source of the rivulet of Semenofskoe. The battle now degenerated into a cannonade which continued till dark. Convinced that the Russians would retire during the night and allow me to advance upon Moscow without risking another battle, I preferred to abide by this indecisive victory, rather than to attempt a new attack which might, in our present situation, lead to disastrous results. Nor was I mistaken in this opinion ; for Kutusof retired before day and took the road to Moscow in two columns by Mojaisk and the old road.

Remarks on this Battle.—Such were the principal events of this great battle, upon which so much has been written, and upon which critics are so ill agreed. The truth is, my plan was wisely conceived, but not well executed. There are some battles where success depends upon the first shock ; in others the opportune moment for striking the decisive blow does not occur till near the close of the day; this depends upon the respective positions of the contending parties. Thus, at Waterloo, the decisive moment for Wellington was at the approach of Blucher; at Marengo the decisive moment for me was the return of Dessaix from Rivalta; and for the opposite parties in these two battles it was early in the day. If we apply this general principle to the battle of Borodino, it is not difficult to judge of it understandingly. We ought to have struck the decisive blow in the first attack, without allowing Bagawouth and Ostermann time to reënforce the threatened point.

It has been shown in our recital, that we carried the great redoubt of the centre and the flèches of the left, after a reënforcement of forty thousand men and four hundred pieces of cannon had been carried upon the decisive point. This fact is sufficient in itself to prove that the success would have been more complete, if, in the morning, we had thrown Ney and the Westphalians on the flèches and the road to Moscow, his right being connected with Poniatowski. We carried these positions when the thing was more difficult and less decisive. The viceroy, weakened by the departure of one of Davoust's divisions, might have formed into line to keep the enemy in check and cannonade his centre so as to effect a diversion, without making an offensive movement, as that would have been useless after our success on the left.

In reply to the reproach which has sometimes been made against me for not having sent to Ney the Young Guard at eleven o'clock, it may be said that although it would have been better to have done so, nevertheless, under the circumstances, my refusal can not justly be regarded as a fault; for at that time the enemy still exhibited a firm attitude, and all our battles with the Russians had been long, obstinate, and bloody; I thought they had more fresh troops coming from their right, and was ignorant that their guards were all engaged; it would have been improper in me to have engaged my final reserve before they did theirs. It is not at a distance of eight hundred leagues from the base of operations that one can venture upon such a manœuvre. It was for the want of a good reserve that Charles XII. was forced to fly alone into Turkey after the battle of Pultowa. After having reconnoitred the decisive point, I was about to throw upon it Mortier with the Young Guard, when the great noise attending the combat of cavalry on my left, caused me to suspend the execution of an attack which would undoubtedly have decided the victory. In judging of this battle from what actually occurred in the two armies, rather than from what was known to me at the time, it may be said that there was an evident fault in attacking the redoubt of the centre at ten o'clock, with the single division of Morand. If the viceroy had then assailed it, as he did at two o'clock, with all his forces united, and I had at the same moment thrown the Young Guard to the support of Ney on Semenofskoe, the victory would have been certain and complete by eleven o'clock in the morning. As, for the reasons already given, this opportunity was allowed to pass, the next favorable moment was at three o'clock, after the taking of the great central redoubt. At that time the troops of Bagration were almost destroyed, and those of Doctorof greatly broken in the contest with the viceroy and Grouchy, so that Ostermann's corps and two regiments of the guard were the only ones which had not severely suffered.

Bagawouth, and the remains of Touczkof, were scarcely able to oppose the Westphalians and Poniatowski. If I had presented my guards to the right of Semenofskoe between the village and the source of the brook, the Russians would certainly have been beaten and forced to fight in retreat. But I was ignorant of the state of things in the enemy's army; my own troops were dislodged; my cavalry had severely suffered; and I supposed the enemy's reserve still untouched; whereas all were engaged except the militia of Moscow. All this was known after the battle, and it is very easy to find fault after the thing has taken place, and all the circumstances are known.

It is in this way that critics have reproached Frederick with not having destroyed the army of Soltikof at Kunersdorf, a battle which very much resembles that of Borodino. Surprised on the left by the king of Prussia, the Russians held so firm in the ravine of Kuhgrund that the right wing and Laudon had time to come up and gain the victory. I had, over Frederick, the advantage of a strong reserve and a numerical superiority, and, therefore, I gained the battle, while that great king suffered a total defeat.

Always ready to do homage to truth, I confess that there is not to be found in this battle the same vigor that marked our victories at Austerlitz, Friedland, Abensburg, Rivoli, and Jena. Writers who did not understand the reasons of my circumspection, have attributed it to a malady with which I was several times attacked. If it is true that I was suffering from illness, I nevertheless had all my faculties and knew very well what I had to do. My plan was a simple one—to turn the left of the Russians, and all my orders were directed to that object; and it certainly required no great exertion of mind to tell the viceroy when to attack, and Mortier when to assist Ney.

My great circumspection in this battle was very natural, and caused by the peculiar circumstances of our situation. On the one side was an army which had marched eight hundred leagues, suffering every privation, composed of twenty different nations, and exposed to all the unfavorable chances of a reverse; on the other side, an army, homogeneous, disciplined, animated by religious enthusiasm, and resolved to conquer or die ; showing in their long and difficult retreat proofs of their devotion and of the excellent spirit which animated them. All the battles which I had fought with it, for the last ten years, had been strongly disputed ; and could we expect a weaker effort in their own territory and almost under the walls of that city to which they attached the destinies of their empire ? If we found here the same Russians as at Eylau and Heilsberg, but more deeply interested than there, and more than ever resolved on victory ; what was to become of my army in case of the slightest reverse ? Such were the motives which here influenced my mind, which compelled me to avoid every hazardous manœuvre ; and which diminished the vigor of my operations. A victory, however incomplete, would lead me to Moscow ; it was there that I hoped to reap the results of the war. As soon as we were masters of the enemy's positions on the left, I was certhat the enemy would retreat during the night ; why then should I willingly expose myself to the consequences of the defeat of Pultowa ?

This memorable and bloody battle which we had so ardently desired, was far from accomplishing my object. I had hoped to fight it in Lithuania, and to make it decisive ; but I had found it two hundred leagues in the interior, and gained no other trophies than a field covered with the dead and wounded.

The losses on both sides had amounted to eighty thousand men *hors-de-combat ;* from twelve to fifteen thousand wounded Russians regained Moscow, where the most part became a prey to the flames. The wounded French were also carried there ; and almost all perished in the hospitals or during the retreat. The generals wounded on the side of the French were Nansouty, Grouchy, Latour-Maubourg, Rapp, Campans, Friant, Bonamy, Morand, Lahoussaye ; and of the Russians, Galitzin, Charles of Mechlenburg,

Gortschakof, Woronzof, St. Priest, Kretof, Bachmetof, Yermolof and Likaeshef.

Shades of the brave men who fell on this memorable day, posterity will erect for you immortal monuments! Montbrun, Caulaincourt, Plansonne, Romenof, Bonamy, Marion, Compere, Huart; more fortunate than your associates, you have fallen when your glory was at its apogee, and when your country was mistress of half of Europe! Less favored by fortune, the Russian generals Bagration, Kaisarof, Touczkof, fell carrying with them the grief of seeing their country invaded and threatened with impending ruin! But their regrets were of short duration; for the empire of the Czars soon emerged from this contest with glory.*

Napoleon enters Moscow.—On the retreat of the enemy from Borodino, he was pursued by my advanced guard on the road to Moscow. A warm engagement near Mojaisk made me think it possible that we might have another battle before we reached Moscow; the enemy, in fact, had some

---

* In speaking of the battle of Borodino, Napoleon said, at St. Helena: "The Russian soldiers are brave, and their whole army was assembled at the Moskowa. They reckoned one hundred and seventy thousand men, including those in Moscow. Kutusof had an excellent position, and occupied it to the best advantage.

"Every thing was in his favor—superiority of infantry, of cavalry, and of artillery, a first rate position, and a great number of redoubts—and yet he was beaten.

"Ye intrepid heroes, Murat, Ney, Poniatowski, to you belong the glory. What noble and brilliant actions will history have to record! She will tell how our intrepid cuirassiers forced the redoubts, and sabered the cannoneers at their pieces.

"She will recount the heroic devotion of Montbrun and of Caulaincourt who expired in the midst of their glory. She will tell what was done by our cannoneers, exposed upon the open plain, against batteries more numerous and covered by good parapets; and she will make mention also of those brave foot soldiers, who, at the most critical moment, instead of requiring encouragement from their general, exclaimed, 'Have no fear; your soldiers have all sworn to conquer to-day, and they will conquer?'

"What parallels to such glorious deeds can future ages produce? Or will falsehood and calumny prevail?"

intention of making a stand at Fili in advance of their capital, but changed their minds, and General Melorodowitsch merely went through the forms of a negotiation. I entered the capital on the fourteenth of September.

Built, like Rome, on seven hills, Moscow presents a most picturesque appearance. It is necessary to have seen this great city, half Oriental and half European, with its two hundred churches and its thousand steeples of different colors, to form any idea of our feelings on first discovering it from the heights of Fili. I had placed great hopes on the occupation of this city whose nobility had been represented to me as dissatisfied with their government, and disposed to join our party. I hoped to incite this nobility against the throne, or, if they were still hostile, to create a democratic interest against the oligarchy. In this I was doubly deceived, for both the middle class and the nobility, were still more exasperated against me than against their own court, and rallied to the support of the throne. From the representation which I had received, I expected, on reaching Moscow, to meet some deputation from a city so influential in the interior of the empire, and was proportionately astonished when I learned that my advanced guard had found the place almost entirely deserted, and that even the municipal authorities had disappeared.

I entered the city with great pomp, but amid an ominous silence. Alighting at the Kremlin, the antique palace of the Czars, so celebrated for its historical associations, and so extraordinary for its architecture, half Oriental and half Sclavonic, I felt no less emotions on seeing the throne of Peter the Great than in visiting, in 1806, the cabinet of Frederick at Potsdam. The delightful view from the fine balcony of this palace added to these emotions; but my attention was called from the reflections to which these scenes naturally gave rise, to the pressing cares of our present situation.

My first care was the maintenance of order by assigning quarters to the several *corps-d'armée*, where they might establish themselves and supply their most pressing wants. Commandants were appointed for each of these quarters. Order has always been maintained in all the capitals which we have conquered, so long as there remained any municipal authorities or inhabitants to guard their effects. Even at Madrid my entry was marked by no excesses. But here a half-famished soldiery, finding every thing abandoned, regarded Moscow rather as a vast camp deserted by the enemy, and every one felt entitled to appropriate to himself what he pleased. Every precaution was taken to guard the public depôts and great establishments; but there were a thousand private shops which had been stripped by their owners of their most valuable contents and abandoned; and our soldiers, as they could not expect their regular supplies, until we could organize the commissariat, regarded these house and cellars as subject only to their mercy.

The Russians burn the City.—To these scenes of violence succeeded burnings which soon increased in number. I at first attributed it to the imprudence of our soldiers in kindling fires in the middle of the houses, and directed severe punishments to be inflicted. But the ravage of the fire continually increased; and it was soon found that the project had been premeditated by our enemies, and was the result of a resolution at the same time heroic and cruel. On the third day Moscow was an ocean of flame, and the spectacle from the balcony of the Kremlin was worthy of Nero burning Rome. But for me, who could not share the feelings of that monster, it was a sad and sorrowful sight and filled my heart with grief.

My troops were ordered to use their best endeavors to check the flames; but all their efforts were in vain; the engines had been removed by the Governor Rostopschin, who was the principal author of the burning, and the houses, three-quarters of which were of wood, were actually fired by disguised soldiers of the city police. In two days between seven and eight thousand houses became a prey to the flames. The Kremlin, surrounded by high walls, for a time seemed safe, but the burning brands which were flying about in every direction, caused fears for the arsenal and our parks; at length the whirl-winds of smoke and fire rendered a longer sojourn in this place impossible, and it was with the greatest difficulty that I effected my escape from this fiery furnace, and took refuge in the castle of Petrowski.*

---

* Thiers thus describes the burning of Moscow:
"The French army hoped, therefore, to enjoy comfort in Moscow, to obtain, probably, peace by means of its possession, and at least good winter cantonments, in case the war should be prolonged. But on the afternoon they had entered, columns of flames arose from a vast building containing vast quantities of spirits, and just as our soldiers had almost succeeded in mastering the fire in this spot, a violent conflagration suddenly burst forth in a collection of buildings called the Bazaar, situated to the north-east of the Kremlin, and containing the richest magazines, abounding in stores of the exquisite tissues of India and Persia, the rarities of Europe, colonial produce, and precious wines. The troops of the guard immediately hastened up and attempted to subdue the flames, but their energetic efforts were unfortunately unsuccessful, and the immense riches of the establishment fell a prey to the fire, with the exception of some portions which our men were able to snatch from the devouring element. This fresh accident was again attributed to natural causes, and considered as easily explicable in the tumult of an evacuation.

"During the night of the fifteenth of September, however, a sudden change came over the scene; for then, as though every species of misfortune were to fall at the same moment on the ancient Muscovite capital, the equinoctial gales suddenly arose with the extreme violence usual to the season, and in countries where wide spread plains offer no resistance to the storm. This wind, blowing first from the east, carried the fire to the west into the streets comprised between the Iver and Smolensko routes, which were the most beautiful and the richest in all Moscow. Within some hours the fire, spreading with frightful rapidity, and throwing out long arrows of flame, spread to the other westward quarters. And soon rockets were observed in the air, and wretches were seized in the act of spreading the conflagration. Interrogated under threat of instant death they revealed the frightful secret, the order given by Count Rostopschin for the burning of the city of Moscow, as though it had been a simple village on the Moscow route. This information filled the whole army with consternation. Napoleon ordered that military commissions should be formed

This catastrophe entirely changed the face of affairs; but it was not, as some have supposed, a certain cause of my ruin and the salvation of Russia. On the contrary, if I had

in each quarter of the city for the purpose of judging, shooting, and hanging, incendaries taken in the act; and that all the available troops should be employed in extinguishing the flames. Immediate recourse was had to the pumps, but it was found they had been removed; and this latter circumstance would have proved, if indeed any doubt on the matter had remained, the terrible determination with which Moscow had been given to the flames.

"In the mean time, the wind, increasing in violence every moment, rendered the efforts of the whole army ineffectual, and suddenly changing with the abruptness peculiar to equinoctial gales, from the east to the north-west, it carried the torrent of flame into quarters which the hands of the incendiaries had not yet been able to fire. And after having blown during some hours from the north-west, the wind once more changed its direction and blew from the southwest, as though it had a cruel pleasure in spreading ruin and death over the unhappy city, or rather, over our army.

"By this change of the wind to the south-west, the Kremlin was placed in extreme peril.

"More than four hundred ammunition waggons were in the court of the Kremlin, and the arsenal contained some four hundred thousand pounds of powder. There was imminent danger, therefore, that Napoleon with his guard, and the palace of the Czars, might be blown up into the air.

"The officers who surrounded him, and the artillerymen who knew that his death would be their own, thronged about him with entreaties that he would retire from so dangerous a position.

"The peril was most threatening; and even the old artillerymen of the guard, although accustomed to such cannonades as that of Borodino, almost lost their *sang-froid*.

"General Lariboisière at length approached Napoleon, and with the authority he had by virtue of his age and his devotion, entreated that the troops might be permitted to save themselves without having their embarrassment increased by the excitement caused by the presence of their emperor. Several officers, moreover, who had been sent into the adjacent quarters to make inquiries, reported that it was scarcely possible to traverse the burning streets, and that to depart immediately was the only means of escaping from being buried under the ruins of the doomed city.

"Napoleon, therefore, followed by some of his lieutenants, descended from the Kremlin to the quay of the Moskowa, where he found his horses ready for him, and had much difficulty in threading the streets, which, toward the northwest, in which direction he proceeded, were already in flames. The terrified army set out from Moscow; the divisions of Prince Eugene and Marshal Ney, fell back upon the Twenigorod and St. Petersburg roads. Those of Marshal Davoust fell back upon the Smolensko route, and with the exception of the guard, which was left around the Kremlin, to dispute its possession with the flames, our troops drew back in horror from before the fire, which, after flaming

been less tenacious in my projects, I should have regarded so desperate a resolution as a proof that the Russian government and nation would not treat, and as a happy warning to

up to heaven, darted back toward them as though it wished to devour them. The few inhabitants who had remained in Moscow, and had hitherto lain concealed in their dwellings, now fled, carrying away such of their possessions as they valued most highly, uttering lamentable cries of distress, and in many instances, falling victims to the brigands whom Rostopschin had let loose, and who now exulted in the midst of the conflagration, as the Genius of Evil in the midst of Chaos.

"Napoleon took up his quarters at the chateau of Petrowskoie, a league's distance from Moscow on the St. Petersburg route, in the centre of the cantonments of the troops under Prince Eugene, awaiting there the subsidence of the conflagration, which had now reached such a height, that it was beyond human power either to increase or extinguish it.

"As a final misfortune, the wind changed on the following day, from southwest to direct west, and the torrents of flame were carried toward the eastern quarters of the city, the streets Messnitskaia and Bassmanaia, and the Summer-palace. As the conflagration reached its terrible height, frightful crashes were heard every moment; roofs crashing inwards, and stately façades crumbling headlong into the streets, as their supports became consumed in the flames.

"The sky was scarcely visible through the thick cloud of smoke which overshadowed it, and the sun was only apparent as a blood-red globe. For three successive days, the sixteenth, the seventeenth, and the eighteenth of September, this terrific scene continued, and in unabated intensity.

"At length, after having devoured four-fifths of the city, the fire ceased, gradually quenched by the rain, which, as is usually the case, succeeded the violence of the equinoctial gales. As the flames subsided, only the spectre as it were, of what had once been a magnificent city, was visible; and, indeed, the Kremlin, and about a fifth part of the city were alone saved; their preservation being chiefly due to the exertions of the Imperial Guard.

"As the inhabitants of Moscow themselves entered the ruins seeking what property still remained in them undestroyed, it was scarcely possible to prevent our soldiers from acting in the same manner, and accordingly searching among the crumbling edifices, they speedily penetrated to the cellars and found there quantities of provisions still in great part uninjured by the fire, and in an abundance, which was due to the custom prevailing in the country, on account of the length of the winters, of storing up provisions for many months.

"In many of the houses, also, which the fire had injured sufficiently to render their pillage excusable without actually destroying them, were found the most exquisite articles of luxury, furs, and plate, which latter spoil the troops, in their improvidence, preferred to either food or clothing, and superb porcelain, which in their ignorance they despised or idly destroyed.

"It was a lamentable and grotesque spectacle which was now presented, as the crowd of our troops and the inhabitants of the city thronged the smoking embers of the splendid city, laughing at the singular costumes in which they

retreat before winter. In not doing so I committed the greatest error of my whole life. If the Russians had not destroyed their city till the end of October, the effect might have been decisive, but executed about the middle of September, it was calculated to save me and might have become a useless sacrifice. What would have been the result, if, taking warning by this barbarous act, I had the next day taken the road to Kalouga? Although the fire had destroyed two-thirds of our resources, we still had a good deal left; but we were mostly destitute of forage for our animals. We attempted to reorganize the Russian authorities, but the employes failed to perform their duties, and the subaltern agents, instead of rendering us any assistance, required us to furnish them with supplies. Here war could not support war!

Napoleon projects a March on St. Petersburg.—I carefully weighed all the consequences of this great catastrophe; and I saw that peace alone could rescue us from the gulf into which a fatal destiny had plunged us. Four different projects presented themselves to my choice; to pass the win-

---

had robed themselves, bearing in their hands articles of the utmost value, selling them for the most insignificant prices to those capable of appreciating their value, or dashing them to pieces in pure wantonness. And this wild and melancholy scene, in which intoxication was also a great element, for quantities of liquors had been discovered in the cellars, was rendered still more sad by the return of the unfortunate inhabitants who had fled at the moment of the evacuation or the breaking out of the fire, and who now returned, for the most part, to weep over the ruins of their dwellings, or to dispute with an unbridled mob, the fragments still remaining of their possessions. Their only shelter the huts they could construct of the ruins which lay around them, their only beds the cinders of their former dwellings, they had no other food but what they might be able to beg from our troops.

"Thus gradually and mournfully, the population of Moscow returned; and with them, came back, equally in search of their former habitations, and uttering the most dismal croakings, the clouds of crows and ravens whom the flames had driven away. And of this horrible scene, the chiefest horror of all remains to be told; the Russians had left fifteen thousand wounded in Moscow, and incapable of escaping, they had perished, victims of Rostopschin's barbarous patriotism."

ter at Moscow ; to retire to the south on the Wolhynia ; or by Kalouga on Smolensko and Wilna, or finally, to march to the north on St. Petersburg. It was possible that, threatened in his last capital, the Emperor Alexander would treat for peace. If not, we would take Wittgenstein in reverse and force him to fall back on the Ingria, thus enabling Belluno, St. Cyr and Macdonald, to advance on Pskow and form a junction with the main army. After more mature consideration, and after weighing the chances of being attacked in rear by the Russian army and thrown into the marshes of the Ingria, I determined only to make a demonstration on St. Petersburg, and if the emperor would not treat, to retire upon the plateaus of Waldai and Nowogorod on the Dwina by Sebeje. But my generals so strongly opposed this project, as being exceedingly dangerous, that I determined to remain where I was, till I could learn the effect produced by the battle of Borodino and the burning of Moscow on the cabinet of St. Petersburg. The fire having subsided, I returned to the smoking ruins of Moscow on the nineteenth, to wait for news from Kutusof and Alexander.

It would now be difficult to say what would have been the consequences of the adoption of my project of marching on St. Petersburg. If it had been executed immediately, the movement might have conducted us to Nowogorod by the middle of October ; and Belluno and St. Cyr might have effected their junction. But by following in our rear and harassing us with partial combats, Kutusof, after effecting a junction with Wittgenstein and the corps of Riga, and being reënforced by new levies, might have forced us to retreat by Vitepsk on Wilna, and by taking a parallel route he would have rendered our retreat no less disastrous than that by Smolensko.

The only wise course now to be pursued, was to march without delay on Volokolamsk and Toropets, and to take the direct road to Witepsk, or to march immediately against Kutusof, give him battle, destroy the manufactory of arms at Toula, and return by Kalouga and Roslaw on Smolensko. No other operation could save us from ruin.

Upon cool reflection and a full knowledge of the condition of affairs in Russia, I am convinced that a movement to the south was preferable to one on St. Petersburg. The Emperor Alexander had resolved not to treat, so long as an enemy was on the Russian soil; and from the important change which, after the camp of Drissa, he had effected in the personnel of his staff, and the superior military knowledge which was thus introduced into that body, I now have reason to believe that they would have abundantly profited by any movement of ours into so difficult and dangerous a country as that in the direction of St. Petersburg. It is probable, therefore, that the project would have proved exceedingly disastrous, had I persisted in its execution.

Movement of the Russian Army on Taroutina. — But let us leave these discussions, and return to the ashes of Moscow. As has already been said, I again took up my quarters amidst the ruins of that city on the nineteenth. Although the destruction of this capital was calculated to absorb all my attention, I did not entirely lose sight of the Russian army, the rear-guard of which Murat had pursued on the road to Razan. The fatigue which the remainder of my troops had sustained rendered it necessary to give them a little repose. Our situation was becoming complicated. Moscow like all large capitals, was the centre from which twenty different roads diverged like the radii of a circle ; detachments of the enemy's cavalry showed themselves toward Klin on the road to St. Petersburg. Others guarded the roads to Jaroslaw, Wladimir, Podolsk, and Toula. This rendered it difficult to obtain any correct information of the enemy's movements: especially as our own cavalry was greatly broken down, while that of the Russians was much better supplied with forage. Eight entire days passed before I could learn any thing positive. Murat then announced to me that the Russian army had deceived us, and after having followed for a time the road from Razan to the east, it had returned on the Pakra to reach Toula or Kalouga. I immediately dispatched Bessières in that direction. I was preparing to march, on the twenty-eighth of September, by Podolsk to turn the right of the Russians and throw them back upon the Dnieper, when Murat announced that they had again retired. Our troops received a counter order, and I resolved to wait till I could see more clearly into the state of our affairs and the projects of the enemy; fifteen days were thus unfortunately lost.

Kutusof thus gained time to establish himself in the position which he had taken at Taroutina behind the Nara, a point between Toula and Kalouga, on the old road leading to the latter city. He thus covered the fine armories of Toula, and the fertile and populous provinces of the south, and at the same time was near enough to the road to Smolensko to threaten our only line of communication I was impatient to learn the effect of the battle of Borodino and the burning of Moscow, on the Emperor Alexander and the court of St. Petersburg. I still retained some hopes of effecting an arrangement. The circumstances attending these two events were not, in truth, very encouraging; but as the Russian army had suffered such terrible losses, I thought it not improbable that the emperor would be glad to terminate the war upon honorable terms. The Russian army is excellent, but if once broken it would be no easy matter to immediately build it up again.

A conversation which I had with a Russian gentleman, employed in the civil government, induced me to intrust to him a letter to the Emperor Alexander. M. Jacoblef left, on the twenty-fourth of September, with this confidential overture. It required eight days for an answer; but as ten days had already elapsed I determined, on the fourth of October, to send my aid-de-camp, Lauriston, to the headquarters of Kutusof; he was the bearer of a letter for the emperor, in which I proposed to enter into negotiations, and, as a prelude, to form an armistice. The same proposition was sent to Kutusof who replied that he had no power to negotiate, but had forwarded my letter by Prince Volkonski. In the mean time the greater part of my army was cantoned at Moscow and in its environs, while a strong vanguard, under the orders of the King of Naples, was established opposite the Russians near Winkowo.

Embarrassments of Napoleon's Position.—We had already been twenty days at Moscow, and still no propositions for an accommodation; I, however, still flattered myself that we should receive them, although I must now confess that there was little or no ground for such hopes. The fact is, I disliked to look behind me and to submit to the idea of a retreat.

The retreat on Smolensko was difficult; the roads were bad, and we were in want of provisions of which the country was destitute. Nevertheless, it was possible, if undertaken before winter set in, and before the enemy received his reënforcements.

The retreat on Kiew was apparently more advantageous; it led through a rich country where our army could obtain supplies, and would enable us to effect a junction with Schwartzenberg; I might then base myself on Tomosa, Lublin, and Warsaw. But to do this I must rely on Austria; and God only knew whether or not she would then have done what she did, with less security, in 1813, by attacking me at Dresden. Besides, the road by Kiew was then occupied by Tomasof, Tchichagof and Sacken, while our great depôts were at Kowno, Wilna, and Minsk.

I have already spoken of a third alternative,—that of operating at the north on the borders of Twer and Pskow, and thence moving on the road from Nevel to Polotsk, so as to join Belluno and Oudinot. This course would save me the danger of a retreat parallel to the enemy, and of being anticipated at Smolensko, and would take me to the Lower Niemen, where were my depôts of provisions; but this line took me too far towards the Baltic, and, moreover, exposed me to the chances of being anticipated by the enemy at Witepsk or Gloubokoie.

But I could not bear to think of retreating at all. Since the battle of Castiglione, I had but twice retired before the enemy—after Essling and Eylau,—but then it was merely to gather strength for a new advance. At Moscow, however, the circumstances were totally different, and I felt that the least retrograde movement might endanger the very existence of my empire. Although Austria had given me one of her archduchesses in marriage, I knew very well that that bond of connection, although good under ordinary circumstances, would be of no avail in a case like the present. I understood the public spirit of Prussia and Vienna, for I myself had given it birth.

If my army had half melted away during the long days and fine weather of July and August, and during a triumphal march, what would become of it in retreating over the same road in the muds of autumn and the frosts of winter, and during the long nights and tempestuous weather which rendered bivouacs fatal even to the most robust? Where could I repose my suffering troops, and where find a refuge for the sick and stragglers? Where were the horses to transport our provisions and artillery, and to oppose the cavalry of the enemy? This enemy could collect in the country, where we could find nothing, sufficient flour for the supply of men who, even in time of peace, are accustomed to little else ; and his horses, raised in the *steppes* and accustomed to pass half of their lives in bivouac, both in summer and winter, subsist on the bark and branches of trees. The fatigues and privations which killed our horses, were only the ordinary regimen of these wild coursers. What could I do on the Borysthenese, or the Niemen, with a broken army, with my artillery scattered, and my cavalry half dismounted, with a million of enemies on my rear and the whole Russian army before me ?

I should not have hesitated what to do, if my army had been composed entirely of Frenchmen ; but these formed scarcely one-half of my forces. The remainder were Prussians, Austrians, etc., whose attachment to my cause was more than suspected. Many times, in reflecting upon these things, did I regret not having followed the judicious advice of the officer who told me at Berlin, that I would lose my army, if I ever engaged in a great war at the North, without basing myself on Prussia, and without attaching her to our cause by advantageous concessions.

But as it is necessary in such cases to choose the least objectionable of the projects presented, and as the retreat on Kiow offered more favorable chances than any other, I was inclined to adopt it ; but a fatal confidence in my fortune induced me to defer its execution until the return of the courier from St. Petersburg. As any one easily persuades himself into believing what he most desires, I still hoped that the Emperor Alexander would take advantage of the present occasion to enter into negotiations. But I had mistaken his character.

Time passed on ; yet no response came from St. Petersburg. To the inquietude of my situation was added the unfavorable news which I received from Spain and from the wings of my army. Wellington, after his victory of Salamanca, had entered Madrid, and the flames of war had burst forth with more vigor than ever. The army of Moldavia had been directed against Schwartzenberg: Admiral Tchichagof had replaced Tomasof in the general command, and now sought laurels on land which he could not find in the ungrateful service of the sea. Not being able to oppose a force of one hundred and two battalions and one hundred twenty squadrons, in all not less than seventy thousand men, Prince Schwartzenberg had fallen back behind the Bug. Warsaw was again alarmed and Wilna seriously threatened. On the other side, Steingle's corps, returning from Finland, had embarked in Livonia and thus given the enemy a superiority over Macdonald. If Steingle should join Wittgenstein, (whose army had already been reënforced by the cohorts of the militia of St. Petersburg), it would increase his force to seventy-five battalions and thirty-eight squadrons, whereas, with one-half of that number he had maintained a threatening attitude during the whole campaign. To dispel this double storm, Belluno and Baraguay-d'Hilliers were at Smolensko; Duruth's fine division at Warsaw; and I had solicited the Emperor of Austria to send reënforcements to Schwartzenberg, and had asked Prussia to send another division to Macdonald.

In the mean time I was waiting, with apparent calmness, for an answer from St. Petersburg. I affected the intention of passing the winter at Moscow, and even joked with one of my generals about his fears of the cold, asking him "where now is the cold weather from which you have anticipated so many difficulties?" In fact, until the thirteenth of October, we had the finest weather possible; it seemed expressly designed to lull us into a fatal security. But I must confess, now that I look upon things with a vision not distorted by surrounding objects, that the position of the enemy at Taroutina ought to have more fully opened my eyes to the impending danger. This position not only covered the best provinces of the empire and secured to the army numerous reënforcements, but it was actually offensive, threatening our communications. Our victorious position and the calm which reigned around me contributed to the illusion. We were at Moscow, as if at the gates of France ; estafettes succeeded each other daily and the mails arrived with the utmost regularity ; the dispatches of my ministers, and Council of State, were laid before me as usual ; from the Kremlin, I directed the minutest affairs of my empire, and no Frenchman suffered in his interests from an absence which seemed calculated to completely stop the ordinary course of events. It is true that some of the enemy's partisans had appeared on the road to Mojaisk, but strong columns of the cavalry of the guard soon swept them away. The boldest of these partisans, were Davidof, Seslavin, and Fiquener ; the first was a poet, witty and amiable, and an intelligent officer ; the second, active and audacious ; the third, a German by birth, but a true Tartar in character. Seconded by the inhabitants of the country, they attacked our lines of communication and carried away our outposts ; but they were yet too circumspect to approach near our cantonments around Moscow. But they gradually became more bold. Every day our foraging parties lost some of their men in engagements with the armed peasants, militia, or Cossacks, and sometimes even large detachments were captured by the enemy's light cavalry.

www.ingramcontent.com/pod-product-compliance
Lightning Source LLC
Chambersburg PA
CBHW022111290426
44112CB00008B/628